Francis Bacon and the Project of Progress

Francis Bacon
and the Project of Progress

Robert K. Faulkner

Rowman & Littlefield Publishers, Inc.

ROWMAN & LITTLEFIELD PUBLISHERS, INC.

Published in the United States of America
by Rowman & Littlefield Publishers, Inc.
4720 Boston Way, Lanham, Maryland 20706

3 Henrietta Street
London WC2E 8LU, England

British Cataloging in Publication Information Available

Library of Congress Cataloging-in-Publication Data
Faulkner, Robert K.
Francis Bacon and the project of progress / Robert K. Faulkner.
p.   cm.
Includes bibliographical references and index.
1. Bacon, Francis, 1561–1626—Contributions in concept of
progress. 2. Progress. I. Title.
B1199.P76F38   1993   192—dc20   93-14964   CIP

ISBN 0-8476-7857-1 (cloth: alk. paper)
ISBN 0-8476-7858-X (paper: alk. paper)

Printed in the United States of America

⊗ ™ The paper used in this publication meets the minimum requirements of
American National Standard for Information Sciences—Permanence of
Paper for Printed Library Materials, ANSI Z39.48—1984.

There is by this time widespread anxiety and even panic over the dangers of the atomic age; but the public soul-searching and stocktaking rarely, if ever, go to the heart of the matter. We do not ask ourselves what the ultimate ideas behind our civilization are that have brought us into this danger; we do not search for the human face behind the bewildering array of instruments that man has forged; in a word, we do not dare to be philosophical.

William Barrett, *Irrational Man*

Contents

Acknowledgments

For close readings and straight talk as to this whole book, I am very grateful to Robert Gilpin, Harvey C. Mansfield, Jr., and Thomas S. Schrock.

Naomi Rosenberg helped with clear constructions and the right word, and Thomas D'Evelyn, Timothy H. Paterson, Martin S. Staum, and Michael Clarke provided useful suggestions. I owe thanks also to Thomas Hickman, Peter Josephson, and Geoffrey Vaughan, who checked the text or did computer magic, and to Andrew Patch, who checked the footnotes in a preliminary manuscript.

A version of chapter 3 appeared in *Interpretation* (vol. 20, no. 1; Fall 1992) as "The Empire of Progress: Bacon's Improvement Upon Machiavelli." A version of chapter 12 appeared in *Polity* (vol. 21, no. 1; Fall 1988) as "Visions and Powers: Bacon's Two-fold Politics of Progress."

Part I

The Politics of Enlightenment

Chapter 1

A Plan and Its Interpreters

Bacon's Project

Sometimes the importance of a topic is obvious. Need I argue that modernity and its plans for progress have become controversial?

This is the century of totalitarianism, mechanized battle, world wars between countries claiming the cause of the future, and the bomb. It has also become the century of radical environmentalism and postmodernism, not to speak of bleak nihilism. Even in the popular press "progress" appears in quotation marks, shorn of the presumption of legitimacy or goodness: this, in the most modern of countries. The press was once a trumpeter of rational enlightenment; the universities provided the music. Now both are in good part disillusioned. Press and university alike are inclined toward a counterculture that is environmentalist, feminist, and liberated, but above all critical: it would deconstruct the objectivity of science, the mastery of nature, the self-made man, the growth economy, the national-security state.

A more telling sign of the new skepticism is that the class of select thinkers, who were once progenitors of the old credo of progress, now turn away or turn against. The most famous European philosopher of the twentieth century has indicted technological science as *the* danger to man, and he would return to subrational or suprarational intimations, as in prephilosophic Greek poetry or Eastern wisdom. Other thinkers call for a return to classical republicanism, to Socratic philosophy, or perhaps to the creative tension between philosophy and biblical revelation. Now it seems that a thoughtful citizen of a modern country must be prepared to defend the benefits of progress, or at least to reconsider them while being aware of the defects as well as the advantages.

This is a study of the principles of progress in their original vigor and clarity, and it is meant to contribute to efforts at prudent discrimination

3

and philosophic rethinking now underway. In particular, it reconsiders the project for progressive civilization set forth by Sir Francis Bacon (1561–1626). While I shall differ from the recent scholars who depreciate Bacon's originality and historical influence, my focus is not on tracing influences but on grasping the scope of the plan and weighing the merits and premises.

To begin with, I find that Bacon's is an extraordinarily comprehensive plan. The famous writings on experimental science play only the most conspicuous part; reflections on purpose and politics play a definitive part. That Bacon's project of a new science partakes of a new practical aim—to institute the "power of man over the universe"—is common knowledge. But what now seems a commonplace results from a profound rethinking of human purposes in the world. Bacon thinks out why man is above all a "self" and why the self is above all to seek power. He also thinks out what are the most important powers to seek. These prove to be, first, the worldly skills of the self-made man and, second, a state, even a state of civilization, that can supply security for peoples and for humanity at large. Bacon's ultimate ideas prove to be not commonplace but profound, and those who would depreciate Bacon often remain entangled in some aspect of the state of mind that he inaugurated. His clarity proves to be a searing clarity, one that may be indispensable as his heirs reconsider a civilization now beset with self-doubt.

Among his contemporaries, Bacon was best known for vast political ambition. While of a prominent family, he had been left only a negligible fortune and was never favored by Queen Elizabeth I despite incessant pleas, remarkable talents, and many services in Parliament. Under James I, however, Bacon rose spectacularly to become the second or third most powerful personage in the kingdom. He was appointed solicitor-general (1607), attorney-general (1613), and then, in 1618, Lord Chancellor (the chief law officer) for life. Bacon was the king's principal counselor apart from the favorite (the Duke of Buckingham), was elevated to Baron Verulam and then to Viscount St. Albans, and accumulated great houses as well as great debts.

There followed a precipitous fall. In 1621, Bacon was charged with taking bribes and thus corrupting the fount of justice. He confessed. By the justice and jealousy of Parliament, king, and favorite, he was sentenced to imprisonment and to an enormous fine; he was prohibited from holding office, from sitting in Parliament, and from coming within twelve miles of the court. The Duke of Buckingham took the opportunity to appropriate Bacon's London house. While the imprisonment was canceled after a few days, the fine remitted after a few months, and permission eventually granted for him to live in London, Bacon never returned to office or influence. He devoted himself anew and exclusively, for his five remaining years, to the researches and writing that were known already in England and increasingly among European literati. In later times, even in the next "Bacon-faced" generation, as a disgruntled cleric called it, these publications made him famous, especially as father of the movement for a useful and experimental science.

It is not difficult to show that our familiar notions of progress are inherited from a more comprehensive plan, such as Bacon's. Consider some typical ideas of contemporary liberalism and socialism. Certain followers of John Stuart Mill expect that the spread of free expression and of science will provide more and more rationality, happiness, and security for an increasingly civilized mankind. Such liberals have been attacked as softheaded by Marxists, who themselves insist that development is dictated by iron laws of expanding production, and dream that history tends toward a completely rational, free, and social humanity. If one stirs the ground a little around these nineteenth-century growths, one finds them rooted in an outlook more realistic and comprehensive than either: it takes for granted neither historical inevitability nor the likelihood of universal rationality. In this primary version, progress was thought to be an invention of the enlightened founders of the "republic of letters," not the product of a growing popular consciousness. It was a human project, not a gift of History. In short, the later schemes familiar to us take for granted what the men of the enlightenment planned: continuous improvement in the conditions of life, technological advance, economic growth, civil government, humane society, and a class of enlightened intellectuals who would propagate the progressive creed.

Actually, the bones of the story remain vaguely familiar, if only as caricatured by the recent writers who dwell on impersonal historical forces. The founders of the original project included seminal philosopher-scientists (e.g., René Descartes and John Locke), intellectuals who spread the new rationalism (e.g., Voltaire, Daniel Defoe, and Denis Diderot), initiators of scientific societies (e.g., Christiaan Huygens, Robert Boyle, and Benjamin Franklin), and fathers of enlightened political and economic reform (e.g., Robert Walpole, Jean-Baptiste Colbert, and Thomas Jefferson). The project was worldwide, or at least defined the modern or Western world. According to some explicit attributions in the old sources, the father of these founders was Bacon.

Rousseau called Bacon the "greatest, perhaps, of philosophers," who with Descartes and Newton was among the "preceptors of the human race"; Locke had praised the "great Lord Verulam" for imagining how "learning" might be advanced.[1] Such remarks might be multiplied, but they are less revealing than the more popular and well-known tributes, notably those in Thomas Sprat's history of the first distinctively experimental scientific society (England's Royal Society) and in Diderot's *Encyclopédie* (the literary megaphone of the French Enlightenment).

The Royal Society of London for Improving Natural Knowledge was chartered in 1663 and helped inspire a number of such institutions.[2] When Thomas Sprat published his *History* five years later, trumpeting the society's achievements, he acknowledged the "one great man, who had the true Imagination of the whole extent of this Enterprise, as it is now set on foot; and this the Lord Bacon," even if he "could raise a college of Salomon only in a Romance" (the *New Atlantis*).[3] According to Sprat, the society's achievement consists in a new fertilizing of the arts by sciences and rests on a new method of science. The scientists turn "from *Words* to experimental Philosophy," the knowledge thus gained enabling mankind to produce things at will. The "words" they disdain are those of Scholastic disputation, Aristotelian argumentation, and Socratic dialectic, and at one point, Sprat parodies Plato's philosopher-kings with the new possibility: "when either the mechanic laborers shall have philosophical hands, or the philosophers shall have mechanical hands." While Sprat explicitly denies any effects beyond the narrowly technological, he gives examples of some political and moral effects, such as the replacement of widespread idleness with widespread industry. His work occasionally intimates that some vast transformation is in the making. The *History* opens with an epic poem by Abraham Cowley that celebrates only one human being, Bacon, treats him as a new divinity, and describes his project of progress as the embodiment of divine command or perhaps a substitute for the pursuit of divine commands. Bacon is liberator as well as founder, the "Moses" who emancipated philosophy from that "monstrous God" and who took his followers to the "very border" of the "promised land."

Less than one hundred years later, D'Alembert's *Preliminary Discourse* to the *Encyclopédie* expounded these themes more directly and commented upon a certain indirection in exposition that Bacon adopted for himself and fostered in his followers. "Philosophy" has become "the dominant taste of our century," according to D'Alembert, and while much of its "progress" is owing to Descartes, Locke, and Newton, Bacon was "the greatest, the most universal, and the most eloquent of philosophers."[4] Bacon was like light after dark. Before him, "philosophy did not yet exist." Medieval times were "the most profound night"; the Renaissance only restored the mistaken sciences of ancient sects; such promising thinkers as Galileo, Huygens, and Pascal merely "lifted a corner, so to speak, of the veil." It was Bacon's *Advancement of Learning* that originated a reform of the aim and adequacy of all the sciences, including "ethics, politics, and economics." It was Bacon's *New Organon* that set forth the method of experiment, "of which no one was yet aware."

The *Encylopédie*'s full title is *Encyclopédie, ou Dictionnaire raisonée des sciences, des arts, et des metiers, part une société de gens de lettres*. The redefining of all learning, the authorship by a society of intellectuals associated to enlighten a wide public in philosophers' plans, the care lavished on arts and trades, and the rational derivation from a foundation, all recall Bacon's efforts. D'Alembert is actually apologetic. So much is the "principal obligation" for the whole plan to "Bacon's Division of the Sciences" that he feels the need to append a summary of the Baconian division to prove that there are at least "some changes" in the *Encyclopédie*. Nevertheless, D'Alembert chides Bacon for his caution in speaking, since for that reason he failed to press enlightenment as far as he might, and he was not the staunch liberator from Scholasticism that Descartes and Locke became. But D'Alembert eventually excuses Bacon, for the followers too were indirect, and it was from Bacon that they had learned how to avoid the danger of shocking contemporaries: "silently in the shadows they prepared from afar the light which gradually, by imperceptible degrees, would illuminate the world." In effect, D'Alembert eulogizes not least Bacon's immense artfulness in introducing the new under colors and shapes of the old, that is, in using "subdivisions fashionable in his time," even "scholastic principles." Despite "the most rigorous precision" of style, Bacon was "too wise to astonish anyone."[5]

These old suppositions of a vast and revolutionary Baconian conspiracy to enlighten the world, with "imperceptible" boundaries often masked by provisional familiarities, are far from familiar in the twentieth century. They are nevertheless true, if the investigations that follow are sound.

In the remainder of this chapter, I consider various recent assessments of Bacon, concentrating on the depreciation that now prevails, and then turn, in the remainder of Part I, to his rhetorical arts (chapter 2) and to the fundamental innovations (chapter 3). The innovations amount to a much modified Machiavellianism, I argue, modified especially with a view to private security, limited government, economic growth, and progress in conquering nature. Parts II and III proceed to set forth the whole plan, first for the conquest of human nature to enable humanity to contend in an alien world, and then for a man-made state of the world. Part II investigates Bacon's transformation of ethics into the doctrine of the self-made man, while Part III discusses the elaborate new doctrines of the state, the state-builder, the civil state and civil society, and progressive civilization.

The obviously important and political innovations are in Part III, and the reader who wishes to reach quickly much of the meat should turn there first.

To summarize, Bacon sets forth a scientific civilization encompassing apparently independent and yet complementary parts, which are nevertheless to be rigorously governed by a plan for mastery in the name of security. The project involves a transformation of the human world that extends to all experiencing and reasoning, and it can seem total. That is why postmodern disillusionment with modernity can lead to an abyss, the famous nihilism, or belief in nothing, that also seems total. It is also why Bacon's critical beginning, the primary disillusionment with the world that spurs his construction of a man-made world, needs to be confronted and reconsidered. This is a task already begun, and my concluding chapter considers the Baconian premises with a view to contemporary discussions.

Questioning the Importance of the Project

For a century or two the prevailing judgment among scholars and philosophers has disdained Bacon's work and doubted its influence. Only in recent years have a few studies by scholars, philosophers, and environmental activists begun to consider the Baconian outlook as seriously as did, say, Jonathan Swift in Book 3 of *Gulliver's Travels*.

Two contentions chiefly account for the lingering depreciation of Bacon's work: it is said to be unimportant scientifically, and it is said to be derivative philosophically. According to these criticisms, Bacon's reform of method prescribes mere fact gathering and is, in any event, irrelevant in the development of sophisticated mathematical science; his broad views are not much more than reformulations of the Christian tradition or perhaps of Greek philosophy.

Is it true that Bacon's experimentalism is a mechanical data gathering that neglects the role given by modern science to hypotheses, theory building, and mathematics? Chiefly because of such a belief, J. B. Bury's famous study of progress described Bacon as merely a fuzzy-minded precursor of the true idea of progress: he neglected the importance of the "ideal or speculative" to even a useful science.[6] The criticism had been spelled out, perhaps first spelled out, by the philosopher Hegel. While Bacon was a new beginning—like a Socrates in bringing "philosophy down to the world"—his work simply betrays a worldly preoccupation with the worldly, is merely "empirical," and lacks attention to the "universal."[7]

It is enough here to make the obvious reply: Bacon subordinates sense-experience to method, while actually holding natural "sense" as the "greatest hindrance" to reliable knowing ($N\,O$ I, 50).[8] Bacon's method is not empirical, but experimental—"to the immediate and proper perception of the sense I do not give great weight"[9]—and he thought the distinction to be decisive. His chief reform is not, as is often supposed, a return to induction, but what he himself calls the "greatest change," the invention of a new "form of induction." His is not just experiencing but planned experiencing, and it shows something of the radical significance of Baconian planning: "the whole way from the very first perception of the senses must be laid out upon a sure plan." The implications of this plan reach to the aim of the scientist, "to command nature in action," and to the kind of knowledge that he seeks, "laws." These are laws of "action" or "operation" ($N\,O$ II, 2) that relate causes to effects, and they especially relate moving or dynamic causes—the "passions or desires" of matter, or the "latent processes" in nature—to potentially useful effects. The starting point of Baconian method, in short, is less in human perception than in human will. For if "a man wanted to generate and superinduce any nature upon a given body," he would want a law, that is, a "direction" which is "*certain, free, and disposing or leading to action*" ($N\,O$ II, 4). While the method of experiment is complicated and controversial, it is no simple empiricism.[10]

Nor does Bacon neglect mathematics and, in particular, a new role for mathematics in science. On this topic, a profound misunderstanding has prevailed. Bacon failed to mathematize physics in the mode of a Galileo, indeed, but not because he failed to entertain the possiblity. He considered it, and he explicitly rejected it in light of his concern for knowledge of real benefit.[11] He doubted the usefulness of inquiry as to the merely geometrical or mathematical relation between bodies, such as sun and earth, and sought instead the real causes of changes that can serve "the advantage and convenience of man."[12] But alternatively, and precisely to serve such a science, he thought out both a new role for mathematics and a new mathematics to fill the role. This is a point still overlooked. Bacon redefined mathematics to be an instrument of his new instrumental science and reshaped it accordingly. "Inquiries of nature" are to "begin with physics and end with mathematics" ($N\,O$ II, 8), Bacon avers, and, in *De Augmentis*, he ushers away "pure" mathematics in favor of a "mixed" mathematics that is useful for calculating motions of "solids" or the relation of motions to effects.[13]

The *New Organon* expressly summarizes the relation of mathematics so understood to the new physics. Laws of action are to be formulated as correlations or equations, correlating quantities of velocity and matter, say, with the desired effect. By comparing such quantities mathematically, one can measure how much is needed for what effect.[14] As nature is "further disclosed," moreover, the new physics will lead to "more kinds" of mathematics (*N O* II, 8). These are extraordinary and unappreciated Baconian proposals, which suggest an unexpected possibility. They might have helped cause what Bacon is often thought to neglect, the analytic geometry, calculus, and other new forms of mathematics that soon sprang up among modern philosopher-scientists. There could be a connection at the root. According to David Lachterman's recent study of geometry, all distinctively modern mathematics reflects Descartes's redefinition of a geometrical "construction" to be a solution of a problem, rather than a proof of a theorem (as Euclid had held), and the Cartesian recasting of geometry for the sake of problem solving takes its bearings from "the desire to master and possess nature."[15] If this is true, if indeed the "modern transformation of geometry from a contemplative to an operative science" is definitive, the crucial steps might have been the Baconian transformation of the aim of knowing and the corresponding turn he gave to mathematics. But one does not have to see so far to conclude that Bacon is not forgetful of new possibilities in mathematics.

In our time, the biologist Loren Eiseley has confronted the "appalling underestimation" of Bacon by scientists and reminded us, also, that the issues at stake involve more than modern science or mathematics as such.[16] Despite the fact that some formative early scientists regarded Bacon as a founder among founders,[17] contemporary physical scientists find Bacon merely "a stimulating popularizer of new doctrines but not a true discoverer," according to Eiseley. They miss the fact that it was Bacon who "set us consciously on the road of modern science." These contemporary scientists tend to be "technicians," and they fail to recognize how their outlook and work is shaped by Bacon's "vision of the very education of which they are the present-day beneficiaries."[18] But Eiseley proceeds from questions of influence to the more serious question of wisdom. The influence of Bacon's science extends to the whole way of life of vast populations, and it may be an evil influence. Eiseley's account is shadowed by a sense of doom. "Today the 'great machine' Bacon so well visualized, rolls on uncontrolled and infinitely devastating, shaking the lives of people in the remote jungles of the Congo as it torments equally the hearts of civilized men."

It is this supposition of a vast revolutionary project that has seemed especially incredible to the historically oriented writers who, for more than two centuries, have focused more on Bacon's background than the wisdom or foolishness of his proposals. Such writers usually acknowledge some immense transformation in modern times, and to modern civilization, but they attribute it to an impersonal historical development. They have been influenced by the historically conscious philosophers and philosophes. Turgot, Condorcet, and Hume, Marx, Hegel, and Heidegger have all thought themselves part of revolutionary changes. But all doubted the decisiveness of the plans of man. There is no doubt an affinity between the supposition that modern science develops inevitably, independent of any methodical redirection to human power, and the supposition that a modern civilization seeking power over nature develops inevitably. Hence, histories of science dwell typically on mechanics and Descartes's mathematization, and they call Bacon but a popularizer.

But that objection, if thought through, itself slights a fundamental innovation in the relation of science to public life. Could Galileo's mechanics ever be popular? To be popular, a science must appeal to common and powerful desires, and Bacon's writings show how to do it. He supplies a method to guarantee potentially useful knowledge, a utilitarian ethic that directs to what is most obviously useful (health, for example), and a political plan to guide the science and deliver the utilities. His most comprehensive writing is the *New Atlantis*, which presents the first modern or future-oriented utopia, that is, the first to rely crucially on products from methodical research, and the first to organize science and society to satisfy desires for health, subsistence, security, and compassionate care. The people of Bensalem are satisfied, and the scientists of Salomon's House are popular because they are the agents of satisfaction. Shades of Ben Franklin, and his rise to prominence and to worldwide reputation by projects such as streetlights and the stove and by scientific inquiries into electricity.

The writers who deny that the modern vision was planned tend to find its cause in the continuing influence of Christianity and ancient philosophy. This marks a change from the first historically oriented accounts, such as David Hume's appendix to his history of the Stuarts (1754) and the later works, by French philosophes, with titles such as *Universal History, Successive Advances of the Human Mind*, and *A Historical Picture of the Human Mind*. The early accounts seemed to suppose a natural or inevitable expansion of mutually useful enlightenment—a "natural progress of civilization," as Turgot put it—which was less a product of new philosophy and more of the softening and rationalization of customs effected by commerce. Whatever the precise view of the causes, such authors were very certain that the result was an enlightened rationality that surpassed the benighted Greeks and was in deadly war with dark superstition. Perhaps these early accounts were but quasi-historicist, for Turgot supposed that it was Bacon who "traced out for posterity the road it must follow," and Condorcet attributed to Bacon the "true method" of studying nature and of using "observation, experience and calculation."[19]

It was Hegel, *the* philosopher of history, who argued that modernity originated in an historical development out of Christianity and that the Baconian plan (or any plan) was fundamentally unimportant—this despite noting Bacon's practical bent and presenting him, in *Lectures on the History of Philosophy*, as perhaps the first modern philosopher. According to Hegel, there had been developing since Luther an "inward spirit" that "recognized" only the spirit of the self as true, "in contradistinction to works," and Bacon, although making the first "statement" of this modern philosophy, did not invent it. While the older accounts of developing civilization—Turgot's, say, or Condorcet's—had exhibited enlightenment at war with religion, Hegel's dialectical account of the development of spirit encompasses biblical religion as it transforms it. He calls Bacon's outlook empirical, interprets Bacon's utilitarian concern for "fruits" as but residual superstition or alchemy, understands Bacon's philosophic significance as chiefly "critical" (of the medieval worldview that had directed man outside of his own consciousness), and, not least, portrays the primacy of the arts of self-preservation in the *Essays* as but the "common sense" to be expected from a man-of-the-world turned philosopher. Bacon's work "is governed by conceptions of the history of civilization," as J. B. Bury's variant on Hegelianism put it, and did not itself govern the future by a visionary conception of civilization.[20]

The influence of Hegelian historicizing has been profound, and it extends to the very way that Bacon's works now appear to us. James Spedding, the lead editor of the authoritative nineteenth-century edition, insisted that Bacon's writings could not have followed from any "ideal plan." He adopted a chronological order, thus overruling Bacon's crucial and visible literary instruction, in the very "Plan of the Work," for a six-part distribution of the important writings.[21] Spedding also relegated the moral and civil writings, which contain the big schemes for reform, to the volumes "literary" rather than to those serious or "scientific," thus overruling Bacon's express direction, which Spedding quoted, to insert "my moral and political writings" between part one (the works summing up the sciences heretofore), and part two (the plan for a reformed science). This is editing that obscures the immense help that Bacon's advertisements of order provide.[22]

Perhaps the lack of interest by Marx in Baconianism is most glaring among the historically oriented thinkers, if only because Marx, too, was preoccupied with Baconian topics, the means of production and the economic transformation of the world. He did call Bacon "the real progenitor of English materialism," and he allowed that Bacon and Descartes "anticipated an alteration in the form of production, and the practical subjugation of nature by man." But the references are few and far between, and the "anticipations," like all innovations, are treated by Marx as "a result" of an "altered mode of thought." Like his master Hegel, Marx dwells on Bacon's empiricism. In flat contradiction to Bacon, he assures us that Bacon held the senses to be "infallible," and he takes the new science for granted as if Bacon's method is only a "rational method of investigation."[23] Oddly enough, Marx remarks less than Hegel on the *Essays'* provocative little plans for a modern economy of entrepreneurs, investors, a frugal and acquisitive middle class, and limited but regulatory government.[24]

Lord Macaulay's once famous eulogy of Baconian philosophy (1837) shows how even a statesmanlike judgment free of doctrinairism can be blurred by an historicizing conservatism. Macaulay waxes rhapsodic about Bacon as promoter of a benevolent science—"leader of the human race in its career of improvement"—even after indicting Bacon's conduct—"a servile advocate that he might be a corrupt judge."[25] Plato might natter about raising us above "vulgar wants"; Bacon, humane and realistic, would supply them.[26] That appraisal has moral implications, and Macaulay had sharpened the issue: "To make men perfect was no part of Bacon's plan; his humble aim was to make imperfect men comfortable." Bacon's "foundations" might lie low, but they are solid and not "subject to change." To Macaulay, as to Hegel, this occupation with common needs is merely "common sense," despite his acknowledgment of other commentators who hold that Bacon overrated "those sciences which minister to the physical well-being of man and underrated moral philosophy."[27]

Is Bacon's attention to the solid or comfortable, in preference to the good or perfect, in fact common sense, or does it represent an abstraction from a not uncommon respect for the fair and good? There looms a connection between the ambition and avarice that Macaulay decries in Bacon's conduct and the ends of the Baconian science that he praises. Macaulay acknowledges that the *Essays* are not "strict" as to "political morality." But what of morality simply?[28] Macaulay reassures us that the wise Bacon would know that "well-being" depends on regulation of the mind, and that "no bodily comforts" can make happy a person consumed by licentious appetite, envy, hatred, or fear. But neither of these assurances, strictly read, requires morality as such, a respect for decency or duty for its own sake, and neither, even if merely requiring a decent hedonism, is compatible with Bacon's hard-nosed essays on corresponding subjects. Macaulay, in effect, prettifies Bacon's real argument with a veneer of common sense, just as he prettifies Bacon's recommendation that we methodically exploit nature: Aristotle would have prescribed the same, we are told, if only his priorities had been humane. Macauley blurs the new priorities because of his complacent presumption that the new is basically the old, because it originates in the "reform of religion," and basically guaranteed by history, because it is the product of "intellect's career of truth and liberty."

The human or moral problem in Bacon's work could not disappear in such evasive complacencies, and now, in this late twentieth century, it dominates every significant discussion of Bacon. Hans Blumenberg's *The Legitimacy of the Modern Age* is an instructive example for our purposes. Blumenberg may suppose the existence of a historical process, and may suppose theology to be the cause of the project of progress, but he acknowledges and even insists that the core of modernity and of Bacon's thought is a radical "self-assertion."[29] That is Baconianism's strength, according to Blumenberg, not its weakness, and the problem of Bacon's teaching is not its liberation of the self from morality but its failure to fully liberate: it subordinates the self to old restrictions under the guise of a new project.

Blumenberg's is a complicated historical explanation of modernity. Self-assertion is in dialectical development toward a fully free assertion, but has been hindered by the residue of Christianity. While a Hegelian "secularization" has occurred, it has been superficial and merely hides "the harm done by Christianity to the modern." Blumenberg is particularly sharp in showing difficulties in Karl Lowith's version of the old Hegelian equation of the modern with the Christian.[30] How could the idea of a sudden and unpredictable last judgment cause the idea of a forward movement throughout history that gives "stability and certainty" to human life? How could fear, the predominant passion involved in the image of a last judgment, be simply transformed into hope for the future? How indeed can the very "idea of progress" arise? Blumenberg brings out the essential difficulty in the Hegelian account: how could the Christ on whom man is dependent account for modernity's assertion of the self's independence?

But Blumenberg shares Lowith's attack on Baconian progressive planning, although he attacks it as only an anachronistic shadow on the self's liberation. He would permit "Modernity without guilt." That is modernity without moralism, and thus Blumenberg would surpass the old Enlightenment philosophers, who "at their stage" were too "indulgent toward remnants of the middle ages." Blumenberg blames Bacon particularly. While "reoccupying" with new answers the old and inherited questions, especially the question of how to be saved, Bacon limited inquiry by a methodical and secure "holding to the chosen direction," espoused an ascetic domination over nature as a paradoxical precondition for happiness, and replaced the "natural symmetry of necessities and goods" with calculated regulation by a dominating "state."

Blumenberg has succeeded in reaching the three great elements in Bacon's thought, it seems to me, and self, state, and the project of progress are the three topics of my own interpretation. But can one adequately explain those elements by Blumenberg's dialectical explanation of the early modern mind? To begin with, why should an exaggerated reaction to Christian otherworldliness produce Bacon's security-oriented homogenization? It might have led to a Renaissance-like encouragement of worldly glory, nobility, poetry, and philosophy, or to Machiavelli's worldly republicanism and tyrannical unscrupulousness. Bacon's actual reaction tends to the profoundly Machiavellian, as Nietzsche, who could praise the capacity for monstrous and criminal immorality in Lord Bacon, intuited in his own way.[31] Blumenberg misses this, and, treating the Baconian state as a domination that represses the self, he neglects Bacon's treatment of both political state and the state of science as tools of the tyrannically assertive self.[32]

Actually, Blumenberg assumes a key premise that Bacon explains and defends: that human beings are selves, that is, "persons" in the contemporary sense: autonomous and assertive individuals free of natural or divine ends and restraints. He also assumes a key premise that Bacon attacks: that a self's assertion is to be limited by the equal liberation due to other selves. In short, Bacon's thought is more consistently self-assertive than Blumenberg's, and it exhibits more radically the consequences of an attempt at full liberation of the self, among them the overthrow of equal rights and probably of justice altogether.

The most influential of contemporary historical interpretations explains the project of progress more by the philosophic tradition than by the religious, and the most powerful of these by far is that of Martin Heidegger. Here our question is like Sherlock Holmes': why did the dog *not* bark? Why did Martin Heidegger, who considered technology the "extreme danger" to the very being of humanity, not confront Bacon's famous case for a technological science? Heidegger surely believed that modern times pose a fundamental danger to man, and that the danger lies in the very calculative outlook that distorts soul and world so that everything is managed and limited to the manageable; everything is "an energy source for modern technology and industry," and we are but human resources.[33] According to Heidegger, moreover, it was not science that caused this worldview; for modern science itself follows from a "revolution in leading concepts . . . which developed in the seventeenth century first and only in Europe." And the revolution in thought that the Encyclopedists eulogized Heidegger deplores. Like Nietzsche (and followers such as Blumenberg), he understands the new rationalism as basically antiphilosophic or antithinking. Unlike Nietzsche (and Kant and Hegel), he concentrates upon its willfully utilitarian focus. Science serves security, and it intentionally confines inquiry to the causes that secure nature for us, that order it by our command and industry.

Why then does not Heidegger focus on Bacon's imposition on all inquiry of a reliable method for useful knowledge? According to Heidegger, philosophy itself, not modern scientific philosophy, accounts for our thoughtlessness; not Bacon or Descartes but the whole philosophic tradition since Socrates is at fault. It was the Socratic effort to clarify and define that cut off human beings from a mysterious ground of all being. Socrates' supposition of definite goods and forms appropriated thinking for our security; Socrates' political philosophy closed off "openness to the mystery."

An aim of this study is to question the plausibility of Heidegger's influential diagnosis. Might the seventeenth-century turn be crucial, not derivative? While a study of Bacon's revolution in scientific concepts cannot settle the matter, it can show the serious reasoning behind Bacon's very different interpretations of both the modern revolution and the tradition that he confronted.

Bacon himself thematically attacks the Socratic openness to opinions (as if they might involve intuitions or divinations), and the Socratic openness to the difficulties in opinions (which leads to the dialectical effort to refute and correct). According to Bacon, such an inquiry can have no end, and it is thus "the bane of business" ("Of Seeming Wise," *Essays*, 26). To keep the human outlook down to business, Bacon introduces critical knowing, which attacks an orientation by words and opinions, and he then insists on only "legitimate induction," which directs the mind toward powers of nature and powers over nature. In short, the technological reasoning that Heidegger suspects may be found in the Baconian science that he slights. One may go further. Might Baconian critique underlie a crucial part of Heidegger's critical stance? Heidegger seems to presume that human ends are but willed purposes and even that all definite notions are but willfully defined for human security. Do we know that? Bacon devises and defends such an account of ends and notions. Might such a critique of natural consciousness be an important cause of the alienation of modern man that Heidegger deplores, the alienation from being in the world?[34]

Questioning the Project

Supposing that Bacon's thinking is perhaps fundamental in understanding the modern project, and not to be reduced to some time or tradition, what does it actually say, and how good and true are its teachings? We turn to some recent works that offer a comprehensive account or a comprehensive evaluation.

The most widely known of recent specialists on Bacon, Paolo Rossi, deserves credit for reviving among historical scholars an awareness of Bacon's slipperiness and of his problematic Machiavellianism.[35] Rossi showed how Bacon had decisively revised traditional doctrines, including those as to the arts, literature, logic, and rhetoric, and as to magic and science as well. While the Baconian moral teachings may appear in classical fables that sport Aristotelian and Christian doctrines, it is "realistic Machiavellian policy" that predominates. Rossi even discerned a vast "plan of cultural and social reform." Yet, in the end, he withdraws from confrontation and the attempt at coherent clarity: somehow Bacon remained Christian and Aristotelian "except where moralistic theories are concerned." Such an exception tends to ignore the centrality of morality for Christians and Aristotelians, and it certainly ignores the possibility that Bacon's amoralism or immoralism had pervasive consequences for his understanding of politics and religion. Rossi suggests without argument that "pragmatism" or "personal events" controlled Bacon's choice among incompatible doctrines.

It is precisely the sweeping salience of Baconian immoralism within modern civilization, at least in its exploitative stance toward nature, that enrages contemporary environmentalists. Morality returns with a vengeance, and Bacon is the object of vengeance precisely because, as Caroline Marchant puts it, he is responsible for the "total program" of domination of nature for human benefit.[36] This domination is political as well, and Marchant rightly raises the question as to who in "humanity" most benefits from the relief of man's estate. According to her, the benefit is, in fact, class benefit, for middle-class entrepreneurs and men, and the price paid is principally by women as well as by the nurturing mother of us all, nature. The effect really decried by Marchant is domination over women; Marchant like Blumenberg celebrates emancipation, but she goes on to celebrate egalitarianism with a feminist bent. But she, too, neglects the obligation owed by the liberation movements to the enlightened philosophers, such as Bacon, who liberated the self from the soul and in general from natural limits and hierarchies.[37]

While the biologist Loren Eiseley certainly insisted on Bacon's genius and influence, he like the environmentalists questions whether "the 'great machine' Bacon so well visualized" is not "infinitely devastating" for modernizing and modern peoples alike.[38] Yet Eiseley takes seriously the promise of scientific progress, and he raises doubts less about the environment and social justice than about the quality and aims of human life. The account is poignant. The modern crisis extends from the bomb and genetic manipulations to novel techniques of tyranny and a "scientific communication" that dulls and degrades whole peoples, and the cause, according to Eiseley, goes to the root. Science's gift of "power, torn from nature," may be the death of humanity. Yet Eiseley hesitates, and his final word is an ambivalent defense of an ambivalent Bacon, for he faces up to the Baconian humanitarianism that aims to relieve human suffering. Bacon cannot be responsible for "the direst features of the modern age," because humane ends guided his science's aspiration for "power over the universe." Still, the whole "orientation to power must be changed," and Eiseley draws a grim picture of contemporary science as "an iron creed," a machine for production that neglects "happiness and ethical living." The modern biologist Eiseley recurs to "great nature essayists," whom he holds more observant in the decisive respect than their quantitative and analytic counterparts. A work such as Thoreau's *The Maine Woods* contains an appropriate "awe" absent from reductionist analysis, an awareness of nature as it exists prior to human manipulation. Eiseley's defense of Bacon's humanity trails off in doubts about the direction of Bacon's science. Can a science oriented to power be reoriented to contemplation, or a humanitarianism oriented to bodily needs be "a revivified humanism which sets the value of man?"

Michael Oakeshott, the English political theorist, held that Bacon's work cannot be saved from its inherent defects, because Baconian "rationalism" is decisively Machiavellian and dangerous at its core. The core is unlike all ancient and scholastic teachings, for it is a theory of knowledge that would "purge opinions" to concentrate the mind on technical knowing of skills and arts.[39] It was Machiavelli who first concentrated the whole mind on useful knowledge alone, according to Oakeshott; Bacon only formulated the method. The new outlook makes the individual into the sovereign judge, liberates technical skill from cultivated practical judgment, and displaces aristocratic moral dispositions. It leads to a politics of ideology, administration, and training. It also leads to its own dissolution, for the corrosive epistemology dissolves the good habits, broad-gauged abilities for governing, and inherited customs, which any society needs. Yet this vigorous and anxious examination turns hesitant, and Oakeshott's appraisals become blurred in deference to a historical process. The origin of modern rationalism was certainly not in a Baconian "philosophical theory of knowledge," for there are no "origins," and thus Bacon's thought was only the moment when a historical tendency showed itself unmistakably. The rationalistic Bacon is called semireligious; the doctrines of state and knowledge are inherited or responses to "circumstances." Also, Oakeshott's concentration upon "rationalism" neglects somewhat the emphasis on fear, anger, and revenge at the core of Bacon's thought, slights the corrosiveness inherent in the Baconian doctrines of the self and of industrialism, and understates the radicalness of what Bacon intended by his future-oriented vision of improvement.

The most comprehensive attempt in our century to enter into the full scope of Bacon's rethinking is probably Howard White's, and it paved the road that I, as well as a number of other scholars, have taken. White, like Eiseley, is struck by the modern dilemma: unless "guided by wisdom," the power bestowed by science is "a monster of unknown dimensions and unlimited terror." Total war may be the obvious menace, but there are also brainwashers, hidden persuaders, and a flood of distracting inventions unbridled by real needs.[40] Also like Eiseley, White thinks Bacon's responsibility for the new science is clear, and he too is ambivalent as to whether Bacon's thought bounds the unbounded. But White is more philosophic and more pessimistic, although not simply pessimistic. Bacon's dangerous innovations involve the basics of moral and social life, not merely natural science.

The Baconian revolution is fundamentally a variation on Machiavelli's revolution, as Oakeshott thought, but it is a real revolution in political philosophy, according to White, not an evolution of a historical process.[41] White was led to enter seriously into the plans and the reasoning of Bacon's most important civil, moral, and historical works. I follow a roughly similar procedure. This does not necessarily lead to identical conclusions. White thought that Bacon modified Machiavellianism by additions genuinely moral and philosophic, and he described Bacon's practical politics as a rather conventional mixture of Elizabethan monarchy with Elizabethan Anglicanism. About such points I have doubts, which can await the appropriate discussions.

The chapters that follow confront various Baconian writings as they expound different parts of his project. I comment at length on the *History of the Reign of King Henry VII* while explaining the role of a state-builder, on the *Treatise on Universal Justice* while explaining the promise of legal security in a Baconian civil state, on the *Advertisement Touching An Holy War* while discussing his war for enlightenment against Christianity, and on the *New Atlantis* while treating future-oriented utopianism. I turn more regularly to *New Organon, Advancement of Learning,* and *De Augmentis,* which clarify Bacon's thematic recasting of all the arts and sciences. Still, my study focuses on the *Essays or Counsels, Civil or Moral,* in a number of chapters and as to many topics.

While the project of progress obviously involves the management of nature, it involves most of all the management of human nature. The *Essays* contains Bacon's comprehensive pictures of progressive morals, politics, and theology, at least in their more practical aspects. The work's rhetorical technique is especially instructive. Each essay is intended to move its audience from traditional or familiar views to enlightened new views, and the reader who keeps eyes open during the journey can grasp the singularity of the new destination and what has been left behind.

Notes

1. J.-J. Rousseau, *Discourse on the Arts and Sciences,* in *The First and Second Discourses,* ed. and tr. Roger D. Masters (New York: St. Martins, 1964), 63; John Locke, *Of the Conduct of the Understanding,* in *The Works of John Locke* (London: C. and J. Rivington, etc., 1824), II, 324–25.
2. In France, Louis XIV followed the counsel of his enlightened minister Colbert and chartered the Paris Academy of Sciences in 1666; the academy was heavily subsidized, according to Hiram Caton, and far more active in promoting research and inventions than its English counterpart [Hiram Caton, *The Politics of Progress; The Origins and Development of the Commercial Republic, 1600–1835* (Gainesville: University of Florida Press, 1988), 187–203, esp. 189]. A shaping spirit was Christiaan Huygens, the Dutch mathematician, astronomer, physicist, and student of mechanics; Huygens was for fifteen years the French Academy's most distinguished scientist and a member of the Royal Society since the year of its founding. He has been quoted as saying at the Academy's beginning: "the principal occupation of this Assembly and the most useful must be, in my opinion, to work in natural history somewhat in the manner suggested by Verulam . . ." [In Roger Hahn, *The Anatomy of a Scientific Institution, The Paris Academy of the Science, 1666–1803* (Berkeley: University of California Press, 1971), 11, 25, 15]. Some scholars have found Bacon's imprint on all new-style scientific societies that arose throughout Europe. [See Martha Bronfenbrenner, *The Role of Scientific Societies in the Seventeenth Century* (Hamden and London: Archon Books, 1963), 43–44;

Thomas Fowler, *Bacon's Novum Organum* (Oxford: Clarendon Press, 1889), 116].

3. *History of the Royal Society*, ed. Jackson I. Cope and Harold Whitmore Jones (Saint Louis, Mo.: Washington University Studies, 1958), 56, 35, 15, 52, 55–70, 323–25, 342. Although Charles Webster tried to show that Puritanism accounted for the Royal Society, he acknowledges that "Bacon's writings came to have almost canonical authority" by the time of the chartering [*The Great Instauration* (London: Duckworth, 1975), 96, 486, 505–11, 514]. The influence of Puritanism has been investigated and denied by, among others, Marjorie Purver in *The Royal Society, Concept and Creation* (Cambridge, Mass.: M.I.T. Press, 1967), and Caton in *Politics of Progress*, 174–87. In 1671, three years after the *History* appeared and forty-five years after Bacon's death, Henry Stubbe repeatedly denounced "this Bacon-faced generation" and "these Baconian philosophers." Stubbe was the most virulent early opponent of the English experimental movement. He professed to discern in Bacon's writings a swollen ambition to overcome dismissal as Lord Chancellor by gaining "a Chancellorship in Literature." Bacon would revenge "himself on his country by diffusing Heresies in Philosophy," and creating such a "desire of Novelty" as amounts to "a contempt for the Ancient Ecclesiastical & Civil Jurisdiction, and the Old Government as well as Governors of the Realm" (Quoted by Fowler, "Introduction," *Bacon's Novum Organum*, 137–38).

4. Jean Le Rond D'Alembert, *Preliminary Discourse to the Encyclopedia of Diderot*, tr. Richard N. Schwab (Indianapolis: Library of Liberal Arts, 1963), 74, 85, 75, 76, 14–16ff., 159–60. Compare Benjamin Franklin's "This is the Age of Experiments," probably written in 1788 [*The Autobiography and Other Writings*, ed. Kenneth Silverman (New York: Penguin Books, 1987), 185]. Franklin's proposal of 1743 for the first American scientific society is Baconian: the subjects of investigation are to be "all philosophical experiments that let light into the nature of things, tend to increase the power of man over matter, and multiply the conveniences or pleasures of life" ["A Proposal for Promoting Useful Knowledge among the British Plantations of America," in *Franklin's Writings*, ed. Jared Sparks (Boston: Hilliard, Gray & Co., 1836–40), VI, 16].

5. D'Alembert, *Preliminary Discourse*, 76, 74–77, 91.

6. *The Idea of Progress* (New York: Dover Publications, 1955), 36, 50–63.

7. *Lectures on the History of Philosophy*, ed. and tr. E. S. Haldane and Frances S. Simson (London and New York: Routledge and Kegan Paul, 1963), III, 170, 174–75, 180–81.

8. *New Organon*, Book I, Aphorism 50, as translated in *The Works of Francis Bacon, Baron of Verulam, Viscount St. Albans, and Lord High Chancellor of England*, ed. James Spedding, Robert Leslie Ellis, and Dennis Denon Heath (Boston: Brown and Taggard, 1861), VIII, 82. I shall refer also to the English edition in fourteen volumes (London: Longman & Co., 1861) IV, 58, and use the following form: *Works* VIII, 82; IV, 58.

9. "The Plan of the Work" (a translation of the "Distributio" to the *Great*

Instauration), in *Works* VIII, 44; IV, 26. Other quotations in the paragraph are from the "Preface" and "Plan" (VIII, 32, 41, 42, 48, 49, 53; IV, 18, 24, 25, 29, 30, 32), except where noted.

10. The controversies over Baconian science are discussed at greater length in chapter 12 of this volume.

11. Graham Rees, "Mathematics and Francis Bacon's Natural Philosophy," *Revue Internationale de Philosophie* 40 (1980), 401–19.

12. *De Augmentis Scientarum* III, vi, in *Works* VIII, 518; IV, 370.

13. For "quantity (which is the subject of mathematics), when applied to matter, is as it were the dose of nature." *De Augmentis* III, vi, in *Works* VIII, 517–20; IV, 369–71.

14. For example, Bacon would have the scientist measure not absolute but "relative" time, especially "motions and actions in comparison" for "use and application" (*N O* II, 46).

15. *The Ethics of Geometry, The Genealogy of Modernity* (New York and London: Routledge, 1989), 8, 18, 23.

16. *Francis Bacon and the Modern Dilemma* (Freeport, N.Y.: Books for Libraries Press, 1970), 34.

17. Robert Boyle, the founder of modern methodical and experimental chemistry, called Bacon "the architect of natural history" [Quoted by J. R. Partington, *A History of Chemistry* (London and New York: Macmillan St. Martin's Press, 1961, repr. 1969), II, 394]. Boyle's new chemistry disdained alchemy and the ancient doctrine of the four elements in favor of a science of the composition of substances, a Baconian-style science; according to Partington, Boyle "designed many of his experiments as a continuation of the *Sylva Sylvarum*" (Bacon's natural history or experimental findings as to natural processes). He thought that properties of bodies are explicable in terms of the size and motion of particles, not necessarily of individual atoms. This is Baconian; Partington thinks the resemblance "can hardly be accidental" (II, 394). Boyle's contemporary, the chemist and physicist Robert Hook, spoke of "the incomparable Verulam," who had regulated the intellect by a "Method or Engine, which shall be as a guide to regulate its Actions, so as that it shall not be able to act amiss" (II, 392).

18. *Francis Bacon and the Modern Dilemma*, 46–47, 34–35, 42–43, 70. Eiseley's contention is based upon examples from biology. *Novum Organum* suggests that much in nature proceeds by "almost imperceptible progress" and thus laid "the theoretical groundwork which underlies the whole domain of biology from evolution and genetics to embryology"; Bacon described "minute experiments which were later carried out by others," very possibly under his influence. Also, Bacon questioned explicitly, on the basis of contrary examples, the doctrine of the impossibility of "transmutation of species," a skepticism that had much to do with the subsequent two centuries' researches on earth strata, fossils, and animal and plant distributions—the findings that preceded Darwin's generalizations.

19. Ann Robert Jacques Turgot, in *Turgot on Progress, Sociology, and Economics*, ed. Ronald L. Meek (Cambridge: Cambridge University Press, 1973), 58, 88,

94, 101. Antoine-Nicolas de Condorcet, *Sketch for a Historical Picture of the Progress of the Human Mind* (New York: The Noonday Press, 1955), 121, 124. Hume ranked Bacon below Galileo, who disdained neither geometry nor Copernicus and advanced along the road of "true philosophy" as well as pointing it out ["Appendix to the Reign of James I," in *The History of England from the Invasion of Julius Caesar to the Abdication of James the Second, 1688* (Boston: Phillips, Sampson, and Company, 1850), IV, 525].

20. *Hegel's Lectures on the History of Philosophy,* tr. E. S. Haldane (London: Routledge and Kegan Paul, 1963), III, 185, 172–73, 159, 175. J. B. Bury, *The Idea of Progress,* (50–63; compare Fred Polac, *The Image of the Future,* tr. and abr. Elise Boulding (San Francisco and Washington: Jossey Bass/Elsevier, 1973), 92–93.

21. "History and Plan of this Edition," in *Works* I, v, xvii–xix; I, iii, xi–xiii. See also "The Plan of the Work," in *The Great Instauration,* translated in *Works* VIII, 53; IV, 32. Bacon actually prepared his civil and moral writings for the second volume of his writings, according to W. Aldis Wright [*Bacon's Essays and Colours of Good and Evil* (Freeport, N.Y.: Books for Libraries Press, 1972), xvii–xviii].

22. There are signs that literary order corresponds to substantive order. The first part, the summary of the sciences, concludes in both the English and Latin editions by discussing civil science. Civil science is called "secret," and the discussions of government are truncated and enigmatic. The topic is spelled out in works such as the *Essays, Civil and Moral, New Atlantis,* and *Reign of Henry VII*—the sort of works Bacon wished inserted at this point. The second part in Bacon's distribution is the *New Organon,* which sets forth the new method and its fruit: "the real business and fortunes of the human race and all power of operation." The civil works, and most obviously the *New Atlantis,* suggest that ordinary statecraft should provide a platform for an extraordinary scientific establishment. They seem to belong both after the first part and before the second.

23. Quoted from *The Holy Family* of Marx and Engels by Friedrich Engels, *Socialism Utopian and Scientific,* in Marx and Engels, *Selected Works in Two Volumes* (Moscow: Foreign Languages Publishing House, 1958), II, 97, 96.

24. A rather Marxist scholar, Benjamin Farrington, has developed refreshingly both Bacon's "blueprint for a revolution in production" and the orientation by utility. Yet he too ignores the economic essays and the blueprint for an entrepreneurial organization of the means of production, holds Bacon "the voice of his age," and equivocates as to whether Bacon was moved by his own plan or by Christian theology [*Philosopher of Industrial Society,* 4, 5, 19, 29, 46–54, 70, 74, 97, 146, 150, and Farrington, "On Misunderstanding the Philosophy of Francis Bacon," *Science, Medicine, and History; Essays in Honor of Charles Singer,* vol. 1 (Oxford: Oxford University Press, 1953), 443].

25. Thomas Babington Macaulay, "Lord Bacon," *Edinburgh Review,* July, 1837, as reprinted in *Critical, Historical, and Miscellaneous Essays and Poems* (Boston: Estes & Lauriat, 1880), II, 170. Other references in the text are from 226, 229, 232, 216, 220, 221, 234.

26. Or, as Anthony Quinton recently put a similar appraisal: Bacon rejects the "contemplative" and "aristocratic" way of ancient philosophers, accustomed to "a slave-holding society," in favor of useful inquiries that will benefit all [*Francis Bacon* (New York: Hill and Wang, 1980), 56–57].

27. Toward the end of the nineteenth century, a knot of English writers challenged precisely Bacon's priorities as amoral, indeed as systematically base and tyrannical rather than commonsensical or humane. Edwin Abbott's biography of Bacon, for example, indicted a self-seeking Machiavellianism in Bacon's conduct and moral science alike. "Bacon as a moralist and a politician appears to me to have attempted to command the world by obeying the world" ["The Latest Theory about Bacon," *Contemporary Review*, 28 (June 1876), 142.] This and other sharp appraisals were submerged, nevertheless, not least by Spedding and his like-minded fellow editor, Thomas Fowler. Fowler expressed himself uncertain whether Bacon's conduct and moral theory differ from the real conduct of people everywhere, was certain that Bacon makes morality to depend on theology, and assured us that we should not expect consistency from Bacon "at this stage in the history of ethical thought" [*Bacon's Novum Organum* (Oxford: Clarendon Press, 1889), xi–xx; 20–21]. Fowler does allude to "Of Truth" (*Essays*, 1) and "Of Wisdom for a Man's Self" (23) to show that Bacon generally favors "a generous and open line of conduct." These essays recommend something very different (see chapters 4 and 5 of this volume).

28. After a similar assessment of Bacon's moral teaching, Quinton finds a Machiavellianism that he then describes as "unillusioned" (*Francis Bacon*, 13). Does Quinton mean to say (in his own name or for Bacon) that morality is an illusion?

29. *The Legitimacy of the Modern Age* (Cambridge and London: MIT Press, 1983), tr. Robert M. Wallace (Frankfurt: Suhrkamp Verlag: 1966, 1973, 1974, 1976). References in the text are to pp. 28ff, 83ff, 105, 115, 119, 379–81, 389, 405.

30. Lowith had focused on the future-oriented belief in a better world, traced it to an evolution of the Christian's faith in a last judgment and salvation, and indicted both the faith and its evolution. Moved by the catastrophe for Germany of the Second World War, Lowith thought the supposition of rational history belied by the wars, the weapons, the tyrants, and the banality of progressive civilization. He would recur to the premodern and pre-Christian ancient philosophers and their deference to natural cycles [*Meaning in History* (Chicago: University of Chicago Press, 1949); for briefer accounts, with replies to critics: "The Quest for the Meaning of History" and "The Fate of Progress," in *Nature, History, and Existentialism*, ed. Arnold Levison (Evanston, Ill.: Northwestern University Press, 1966), 131–61]. The thesis has been taken up by some who feared the dissolution of the modern faith and would therefore resurrect belief in "the sacred and the mythological" [Robert Nisbet, *History of the Idea of Progress* (New York: Basic Books, 1980), 355].

31. See chapter 3, and Nietzsche's *Will to Power*, tr. Walter Kaufman (New

York: Vintage Books, 1968), sec. 249 ("Of Power," 55) and 848; *Beyond Good and Evil*, tr. Kaufman (New York: Vintage Books, 1966), sec. 252; *Ecce Homo*, "Why I am so Clever," sec. 4, in *On the Genealogy of Morals and Ecce Homo*, tr. Kaufman (New York: Vintage Books, 1967), 246.

32. See chapter 6.

33. *The Question Concerning Technology and Other Essays*, tr. William Lovitt (New York: Harper & Row, 1977), 33 (para. 101). Other references in the text are from pp. 14–16; "Memorial Address," in *Discourse on Thinking* (New York: Harper & Row, 1966), 50, 55.

34. A recent scholarly study by Hiram Caton, more historical than Historical, almost returns to the pre-Hegelian estimate of Bacon's innovations. In *The Politics of Progress, The Origins and Development of the Commercial Republic, 1600–1835* (Gainesville: University of Florida Press, 1988), Caton writes not of the history of the idea of progress, but of the politics of progress, and his massive study agrees with the *Encyclopédie*: Bacon was founder; Descartes, but "one of Bacon's most important recruits." The plan was for both a new science and a new faith. A "polytechnic rationality" would produce new inventions and arts, and this promise, mixing humane relief of common suffering with rewards for the ambitious few, would be the root of a faith that could displace otherworldly faiths. The spread and expansion of this secular faith made Christian Europe become modern Europe, and the ways this was done is Caton's topic. The propagators had to mix visible conformity with conspiratorial revolution. There were circles of enlightenment: the first circles of philosopher-scientists, discussion groups, and journals; the societies for useful science and for application to industry of the new discoveries and inventions; the intellectuals and the media who communicate or mediate the new mores; and the new enlightened institutions of society, politics, the economy, and science. Caton seems mistaken in denying that Bacon could hit upon a " 'bourgeois' embodiment of his project" such as the commercial republic (49, cf. 48, 125, 234–35), in calling Bacon a thorough monarchist and tracing the enlightened monarchies to the medieval tradition of antipapal "Ghibelline" kings (9, 121), and in holding that Descartes originated the focus on the individual or self (83–84). See Paul Rahe, *Republics Ancient and Modern* (Chapel Hill and London: University of North Carolina Press, 1992), 249–541.

35. *Francis Bacon, From Magic to Science* (Chicago: University of Chicago Press, 1968), 92; cf. 82–116, from which the subsequent references are drawn.

36. *The Death of Nature: Women, Ecology, and the Scientific Revolution* (New York: Harper & Row, 1980), xv–xx, 164–90.

37. Karl Mannheim once observed that Bacon's purge of the human understanding, his "critique of the Idols," was the precondition of modern ideologies and of all modern utopianism [*Ideology and Utopia*, tr. Louis Wirth and Edward Shils (New York and London: Harcourt, Brace, Jovanovich, n.d.), 61–62].

38. *Francis Bacon and the Modern Dilemma*, 6, 34, 84, 24, 70, 77, 81, 83, 88.

39. *Rationalism in Politics and Other Essays* (New York: Basic Books, 1962), 13ff, cf. 1–36; *On Human Conduct* (Oxford: Clarendon Press, 1975), 287–91.

40. *Peace among the Willows* (The Hague: Martinus Nijhoff, 1968), 258. Subsequent quotations are from 42, 218, 221, 31.

41. In this, White follows the suggestions of Leo Strauss. See Strauss, *Natural Right and History* (Chicago: University of Chicago Press, 1952), 8; *Spinoza's Critique of Religion*, tr. E. M. Sinclair (New York: Schocken Books, 1965), "Preface to the English Edition," 29–31; *Philosophy and Law*, tr. Fred Baumann (Philadelphia, New York, Jerusalem: The Jewish Publications Society, 1987), 11–18.

Chapter 2

The Art of Enlightenment

The Disorderly Order of the *Essays*

This is a chapter on literary form that originated with questions of political substance and that ends by sketching the substantive ordering of Baconian enlightenment. Literary forms in Bacon's sense prove to be the formulas for communicating vast plans.

I had begun by seeking to clarify the priorities that might account for Bacon's schemes, and the *Essays or Counsels, Civil and Moral* seemed a place to look. There are accounts of truth, goodness, and beauty, to take the obvious examples, as well as marriage, love, empire, ambition, and the true greatness of kingdoms and estates. And even if the *Essays* might be thought silent on science and technology (it is reserved on these topics, but not silent), the work could show the implications of the scientific outlook for other parts of private and public life. But discovering the general teachings of the *Essays*, or even the message of each essay, proved no easy matter. The effort led to a consideration of the difficulties posed by Bacon's peculiar ways of setting forth his thoughts.

I began by looking for the lesson of each essay, thinking to review my collection of conclusions for signs of a general order. This proved to be a daunting task, given the welter of topics, the surfeit of quotations, a plethora of lists, and the visibly contradictory positions—all scattered through fifty-eight separate essays. In the first sections of this chapter, I open up the problem, which proves to be a tantalizing mixture of obscurity and lucidity, and I repair for help first to scholars of Bacon's literary arts and then to Bacon's own thematic discussions of poetry and rhetoric. These resources, especially the Baconian revampings of the poetic and rhetorical arts into an art of effectual communication, help disclose the secret underlying the *Essays'* form.

I conclude that the literary disorder has rhetorical purposes, that is, that disordered arguments are ordered to a political purpose. In *De Augmentis* and *Advancement of Learning*, Bacon explicitly recommends forms of enigmatic and unmethodical writing. As particular and compact, such techniques have power to convey and provoke; as compressed, ambiguous, and scattered, they are politic in disguising a strange whole. In the *Essays* itself, the only essay to treat thematically of argument is "Of Discourse" (32), and it explicitly recommends a disorderly receptivity to others' views, which enables one to provoke, guide, and lead. "The honorablest part of talk is to give the occasion; and again to moderate and pass to somewhat else; for then a man leads the dance."[1] I shall contend that Bacon, dancing with the opinions dear to others, manages to turn traditional opinions into enlightened opinions and to do this while disguising the transformation. His is a revolution more insinuated than imposed. The form of the *Essays* proves to be guided by a formula for political or rather civilizational revolution.

It must be admitted that proving such a thesis is hard, and it is no wonder that no scholar of whom I have heard, even among those who have asserted the existence of an order in the *Essays* or have believed that "every move in a discourse is planned," has described a coherent plan. Most signs point to incoherence. The title of the work suggests plurality, not unity, and Bacon does not supply a unifying preface. There is only a dedication to the Duke of Buckingham, which, while predicting that "the work" in its Latin version will endure as long as books do, tends to speak of the *Essays* in the plural and suggests no plan or intent. It is disorder that seems to dominate. In a typical series of non sequiturs, the first essay, "Of Truth," is followed by "Of Death" and then "Of Unity of Religion." Essays on similar topics are often widely separated. "Of Friendship" (27) is twenty-one essays away from "Of Followers and Friends" (48), and "Of Wisdom for a Man's Self" (23) is separated from "Of Seeming Wise" (26) by discussions of innovations and dispatch. Moreover, each essay is by itself often very hard to make out. The first, "Of Truth," comes across as a parody of fulsome learning larded with quotations and allusions, while the last, "Of Vicissitude of Things," is a succession of clipped, enigmatic, and separate observations.

But there are also tantalizing signs of order that prevent one from resting with an impression of disorder, and, more tantalizing still, increasing signs as one penetrates into the reasoning. Some essays are grouped by topic or at least by title. There are at least eight pairs and one quartet that seem related in place and topic, to say nothing of those related in topic but not in place.[2] Also, upwards of a dozen essays are quite plain and straightforward in argument,[3] and a few are famously lucid in articulating an original point of view.[4] Finally, I came to discern in even the complicated essays a certain direction of movement amidst the deployment of doctrines, quotations, lists, and the like. The key lay in an effort to grasp and follow the argument. The appearance of inconsistencies and contradictions diminished when I went beyond an initial impression of some familiar doctrine, say, of faith, morals, or philosophy, and examined the meaning actually presented by Bacon's precise formulation. It diminished further as I saw this meaning qualified by connected clauses, reformulations, and subsequent reservations. The more convoluted an essay and the more controversial the topic, the more it appeared that Bacon's elaborate dances with opinions were intended to draw the reader in a discernible direction. I found, in short, that the reasoning of even the essays that seem most disjointed spins a coherent thread and that these threads are coherently arranged to serve discoverable purposes.

To show such minute movements of argument is labor-intensive, for author and reader alike, and any such complete recounting would distract from the larger point of the enterprise. Readers will have to be content with summaries of many essays, together with close commentaries on the most important that are relevant to the topic at hand. This chapter surveying the literary artfulness of the *Essays*, for example, examines closely only the four essays on the arts of using speech.[5] Such a mixture of general survey with selected scrutiny will yield a provocative big picture, but it is, perforce, a preliminary sketch. Only in later and substantive chapters do I examine important substantive essays and thus supplement the quick and preliminary epitomes with which the reader must make do here.

The big picture, I shall contend, is this: there is a developing argument among the essays similar to that within each. The *Essays* as a whole, like each essay, moves from undermining to establishing. It moves from corrosion of the most authoritative received pieties at its beginning ("Of Truth" 1, "Of Death" 2, "Of Unity in Religion" 3), to production of a new-model, progressive nation-state in its middle ("Of the True Greatness of Kingdoms and Estates" 29), to intimations of a new-model progressive civilization at its end ("Of Vicissitude of Things" 58). Each essay stands by itself as a separate counsel fitted to move those peculiarly susceptible to its appeal, and is also part of a whole plan that attempts comprehensive revolution. Together they are a paradigm of enlightenment. They are perhaps the classic example of the art behind the light, as D'Alembert said marvelously in his preface to the *Encyclopédie*, "which gradually, by imperceptible degrees, would illuminate the world."

In this literary combination of critique and construction, I see four chief stages, which seem to correspond to the chief divisions in the political work to be done.

1. In the first stage, essays 1–19 chiefly commit sedition on morality, religion, the political hierarchy of estates, and the Lord. Insofar as these early essays advance positive innovations, such as the priority of economic development, they borrow a surface from traditional views.

2. Essays 20–29, the second stage, tutor especially those under cover but nevertheless rising in the new politics. Counsellors who seem to advance the businesses of kingdoms and estates can promote their own place in an expanding and republican nation-state.

3. The third stage, essays 30–46, shows what's in the new project for rising individuals and becomes more open in unveiling the corresponding possibilities of a self-regulating society based on mutual utility. Bacon recasts moral attitudes into personal incentives, channeled to attract planters of economic colonies, entrepreneurs, investors, and financiers.

4. The fourth and final stage, essays 47–58, shows how the superior prince creates an incentive system for superior followers, who are moved more by ambition than by acquisitiveness and who, in turn, will raise him to a superior state of reverence.

While struggling towards the views just sketched, I consulted the recent scholarship on the *Essays*, which has turned increasingly toward discussions of literary form. Earlier in this century, scholars had focused on Bacon's moral philosophy, and in particular on the problematic relation between his "philanthropia" and his Machiavellianism or utilitarianism.[6] It became difficult to deny Bacon's Machiavellianism, and Rexmond C. Cochrane went so far as to argue that the *Essays* spells out the Machiavellian "architecture of fortune" outlined in *Advancement* and *De Augmentis*. The *Essays* is to human affairs what *New Organon* is to nature; both show the method of enlarging the dominion of man by increasing his knowledge, and the *Essays* is "the principal operative part of Bacon's speculations on moral and civil knowledge."[7] More recent scholars have not followed up on such substantive suggestions, partly because of Bacon's literary equivocations. In a study of the *Essays'* style, for example, Stanley Fish noted that the work contains some "spirit of the moralist" in addition to "the boldly analytic or coldly intellectual,"[8] and observed that the typical essay begins with "received generalities," sets out various contrary views, and results in "healthy perplexity." But Fish concludes from his study of form that there is no substance. The essays "advocate nothing," and "the attempt comes to nothing." This conclusion goes beyond the evidence, even of literary form, since some of the most important essays, to repeat, are straightforward and didactic. Also, the work proclaims itself *Counsels, Civil and Moral,* not skeptical meditations, and however Bacon might adopt occasionally the old word "meditations," he attacked the thing. He indicts even Socratic dialectic for its inconclusiveness (essay 26 calls it "the bane of business"), and in *De Augmentis,* Bacon advises that "confutations" be avoided in the "transmission of knowledge" except to "remove strong preoccupations and prejudgments." The point is transmission of a message, and the twistings and turnings of rebuttal are only to remove obstacles to getting the message across. The function of rhetoric, according to Bacon, is to move men: "to apply Reason to Imagination for the better moving of the will."[9]

Some recent commentators have pointed out and clarified Bacon's preoccupation with effective communication. The literary scholar Brian Vickers, for example, gave a startling formulation: Bacon's "whole life's work is geared to persuade and dissuade the world."[10] And Lisa Jardine, in a helpful book, has said that the "extraordinary" thing about Bacon's "method of discourse" is its subordination to a systematic art of transmitting one's own devisings. The whole topic is treated under "wisdom of transmission," which is the art of "producing and expressing to others those things which have been invented, judged, and laid up in the memory."[11] In such an art there are a variety of techniques, and Bacon can be seen going to great lengths in using them: he twists authorities, plays on familiar-sounding notions, quotes misleadingly, makes "opportunistic" use of myths to "communicate precepts in persuasive form," and takes care to manipulate the ear's proclivities for pleasant sounds. But beneath it all is arrangement and calculation, "every move" in a discourse, according to Jardine, being "planned so as to insinuate the desired conclusion into the mind of the audience." Vickers provided a nice expression of an underlying ordering that shows itself only in the movement of considerations: "The structure leads you on clearly through an argument and from one topic to another but without drawing attention to its presence."[12] The order is then hard to know; it may even be intentionally concealed. Another commentator has said that Bacon's rhetoric is a "ready disguise for secret purposes," and that the reader needs a "science of decipherment."[13] This is understandable if Bacon is "presenting to a popular audience," as Jardine rightly thought, "the abstruse and unorthodox conclusions of his own social and ethical theories."

Literary and Rhetorical Methods: Essays as Agitation by "Dispersed Directions"

While Bacon's own discussions of "transmission by discourse" do not focus on the essay as such, they recommend sharp little writings and precisely because they are fit both to move men and to conceal a superior man's intent. Both *Advancement* and *De Augmentis* call such writings superior to methodical composition, to "magistral" texts, while also insisting that the "architecture" of a work or the whole "argument of a book" should be governed by method.[14] Order should govern, but an order, like the order of the *Essays*, expressed in discrete and pungent parts.

Little discourses force the reader to question, and they thus stimulate him to consider for himself. They are "probative" and "initiative." Correctly formed, they provoke the reader about "the roots" of learning and thus foster continual progress by rousing widespread effort. They can invite "men's talents and thoughts alike to criticism and invention," as Bacon puts it in a duality that resonates still. But they can also disguise. Being "enigmatical" or "acroamatic," rather than "disclosed" or "exoteric," they keep "vulgar capacities" from the "secrets of knowledges" and reserve them for "wits of such sharpness as can pierce the veil." An enigmatic essay can provoke the sharp to radical rethinking without irritating the dull.

The special type of brief writing that Bacon proposes is the aphorism. *De Augmentis* and *Advancement* discuss not essays but aphorisms, and it is these that are superior to the "solemn and formal" arts that pass for "methods." The seminal Baconian work on method, *New Organon*, is itself "a Summary digested into Aphorisms," and it gives a definition: "short and scattered sentences, not linked together by an artificial method" (I, 86). Aphorisms may be clipped and singular, but they are also lean and pithy, which is why they test the sharpness of both writer and reader, according to the *Advancement* (which gives no definition). While omitting "illustration, example, and discourse of connection or application," they can go to the "pith and heart" of the sciences. They contain only "some good quantity of observation."

One must go beyond these rather formal remarks, for the key to the Baconian aphorism is a matter of substance: the content of what Bacon means by "observation." The observation at the heart of an aphorism is not a mere look or contemplation, but a formula for action. Consider the third aphorism of *New Organon*: "Human Knowledge and human power meet in one; for where the cause is not known the effect cannot be produced. Nature to be commanded must be obeyed; and that which in contemplation is as the cause is in operation as the rule." Contemplation there may be, but it is for the sake of command, and this aphorism is a command, to those who wish to know and to those who seek power, to cooperate in concentrating on the formulas for power. While methodical accounts are more fit to win belief and satisfaction, the account of aphorisms in *Advancement* continues, they are "less fit to point to action." Aphorisms are formulas for producing human movement. Discrete, and corresponding to dispersed particulars, they are suitable for "dispersed directions."[15]

In *De Augmentis,* Bacon ends an extended discussion of the modes of powerful speech by adding a prescription for sugar-coating: a command to action must be combined with a gloss of the familiar, in order that novelties be accepted more easily. This does not mean that one should argue with others—engage in "confutations"—where one need not. Bacon uses a military simile and issues a politic warning. To proceed by "questions with determinations," rather than positively by "assertions and their proofs," is to proceed like an army that besieges "every little fort or field." Socrates wandered with his questioning; even the assertive Aristotle was not determined enough. Governance by method means not organized curiosity but a strategic plan of attack, and if "the sum of the enterprise" be pursued, smaller things will fall of themselves. But it is also true that method must vary with matter, policy is "the most immersed" in matter, and the advancement of policy must vary with the preconceptions of the audience. Introduce "knowledge which is new, and foreign from opinion received," with "similitudes and comparisons."[16] Wise order is rarely that of a frontal attack. Govern speech by policy, but govern also with a view to the obstacles in the way.

This mixture of prescriptions illuminates Bacon's procedure in the *Essays.* The essays are certainly rather short counsels to action, they are diverse in accord with Bacon's many policies, and they visibly accommodate the preconceptions of their audience. Almost every essay proceeds by positive formulations that sound traditional but are not, formulations that sound like "received generalities" but are merely similar. The initial similitudes are further revamped by reformulation, and they end up suppressed or transformed into formulas not at all traditional. Illustration and example often follow to make the new lesson more memorable, and the connective reformulations and reasoning carry the reader along a definite if unobtrusive march. Method somehow governs, albeit the disordered method suitable for popular persuasion. The plan of each and of the whole adjusts to preconceptions, as to the priority of family, truth, faith, or whatever, while managing to bring forth Bacon's innovative directions: "He that has Wife and Children, hath given Hostage to Fortune"—a maxim that became famous despite the rarely quoted sting, "for they are Impediments to great enterprises, either of Virtue, or Mischief" ("Of Marriage and Single Life" 8).

Why does Bacon say little about the essay, as such, in his thematic discussions of literary method? Perhaps the essay is only a fattened aphorism, fattened by the need to confront gradually the contrary opinions of a heterogeneous audience. Neither *De Augmentis* nor *Advancement* discusses the essay explicitly, and the term "essay" does not even occur in the *Essays* in its final, 1625, form.[17] In the dedication to the 1625 edition, however, Bacon does explain helpfully why previous versions had been his most popular works. They "come home, to men's business, and bosoms." The secret is their service of the desires and occupations that move men. Like aphorisms, they are directions to action along the roads that men desire to travel. A discarded dedication for the 1597 edition calls the essays "dispersed meditations" and defines an essay in terms that remind of an aphorism: "certaine brief notes, sett downe rather significantly, than curiously, which I have called Essaies."[18] A clearer remark in the *New Organon* sheds light on what Bacon considers significant; it equates an essay with an "attempt" or "trial" (II, 20). The equation is still supported dimly by English usage, and more clearly in French, and it points, I believe, to the fundamental purport. Each essay is an attempt to replace a familiar or traditional opinion with an alternative rooted in "real" interests and affairs. Each is a trial that ends with a verdict as to what to think and do. Each may be compared to a critical experiment, which tries key hypotheses until it finds the formula for production of the desired effect. The Latin version of the *Essays*, which Bacon planned and probably supervised, enjoyed the title of *Sermones fideles, sive interiora rerum*. Under a traditional cover of sermons, *Essays* contains a dispersed creed that directs to man-made progress.

The discussion of literary methods in *De Augmentis* and *Advancement* is followed by that of rhetoric, and literary inventions prove to be devices in service to a larger art of managing men by appealing to their wish for future satisfactions. Bacon may use the old name of rhetoric, but he introduces a new thing. His is a comprehensive art of communication that persuades less by arguments and more by images addressed to common passions; it is an art of managing by incentives.

We should not be surprised to see this extraordinary discussion proceed by similitudes. Bacon calls rhetoric the illustration of tradition (or of transmission), and "a science excellent, and excellently well laboured" by such worthies as Aristotle, Cicero, and Demosthenes. But he then proceeds to dig up "the roots." One will miss Bacon's radical innovation if one misses his attack on the fundamental limits, moral and philosophic, taken seriously in Aristotle's classic art of rhetoric.

Aristotle had called praise and blame a starting point of moral reasoning;[19] Bacon treats Aristotle's remarks as merely a rhetorical technique.

He himself equates praise of good with desire to sell one's wares; Aristotle had missed the real use of praising and blaming. In the Baconian "illustration" of tradition, one manages tradition to insinuate one's own transmission. The difference between praising and blaming, Bacon explains patiently, is finally not in the quality, the "significance," but in the use for different audiences, "the impression." The meaning of even moral language is its effect, which is its forcefulness for getting what one wants. Aristotle's preoccupation with forms of character and conduct had distracted him from the forces involved in moving men. "For many forms are equal in signification which are differing in impression; as the difference is great in the piercing of that which is sharp and that which is flat, though the strength of the percussion is the same." For example, "This is evil for you" is less potent than "Your enemies will be glad of this."[20] If the serious orator or writer will begin to consider honesty and truth, say, as but counters for manipulating, he will have more powers at his disposal. He can stoop to conquer without being held back by scruples as to stooping.

Karl Wallace's study of Bacon's art of rhetoric helps to clarify the direction we have noted. Bacon concentrates on a comprehensive "public discourse," according to Wallace, and slights what Aristotle called forensic and epeidectic rhetoric (speeches of the law courts and of display). Bacon also links persuasion with inventive imagination (rather than reasoning) and conceives of rhetoric, in Wallace's apt phrase, as "insinuating reason."[21] One could go further. For Bacon drops the very topics, justice and nobility, that had guided the Aristotelian accounts of forensic and epeidectic rhetoric, and he transforms deliberative rhetoric, the third of Aristotle's kinds, by removing the deliberative core and the orientation by public policy and the common good. That is, Bacon both expands rhetoric toward a comprehensive public discourse and removes its Aristotelian ends and limits: the concern for reasoning, the public or common good, and the just and the noble.

The Baconian alternative to traditional rhetoric is an art for managing mind by appealing to the most powerful images. It is best seen in the essay "Of Discourse" (32), which we consider in the next section, and in the Latin *De Augmentis,* which expands upon *Advancement* by adding to the account of rhetoric two long and difficult lists of aphorisms.

These two Latin lists are Baconian in substance and style, beginning with the critical and turning to the constructive, and appearing as a succession of bland-sounding but singular assertions. I shall argue, in short, that the first list dissuades orators from relying on appeals to what is good; the second, from reliance on appeals to truth. The first urges instead that one set forth the image of a benevolent provider; the second, that the provider promise especially long-term satisfaction of the most powerful desires.

The eleven sophisms in the first list chiefly assert respectable opinions as to the importance of goodness; the last sophism is curiously abstract and suggests that plurality of parts without order is a superior way of proceeding. Disorder is certainly present here; the list is punctuated with disorderly remarks as to the priority of passions, excesses, malice, fortune— and finally of "a powerful and faithful friend." We are told that such sophisms and replies are of "no small importance" as parts of "Primary Philosophy, of Politics, and of Rhetoric." It is hard to grasp the order of parts and the significance of the whole. I can only assert here my conclusion: the succession leads toward a general lesson that the person who takes goodness seriously is beset with illusions, which hide from him or her the real passions and prejudices of human beings. To be effectual, a rhetorician should disdain morality and piety and rely on images that favor willful provision and a human provider. If I am correct, Bacon develops a formula for moving men by the appeal of compassionate social movements, a formula that might produce, for example, images of humane research scientists like those in the *New Atlantis.*

There are forty-seven topics or commonplaces of argument in the second list, and these extend the purview of rhetorical syllogisms not only to "judicial oratory" and "deliberative argument" but also to "demonstrative" argument. The art of rhetoric seems to become part of the all-encompassing art that Vickers and Jardine have brought to light, the art of dominating mankind by a tradition or transmission of enlightened images and ideas. If I read Bacon's proceedings aright, he provides here a formula for an intellectual movement, a formula that would produce the idea of a comprehensive useful science.

Effective rhetoric is especially management by image making, and Bacon takes special care to investigate the most powerful image. It is the image of future satisfaction. "After that force of eloquence and persuasion hath made things future and remote appear as present, then upon the revolt of the imagination reason prevaileth." This formula from *De Augmentis* would account for Bacon's famous image of Bensalem, the future-oriented society of *New Atlantis,* which promises ever-increasing satisfaction of needs and desires. But it is for us as well as others; it applies to "negotiation within ourselves" as well as to "negotiation with others." While we need not bind ourselves by ethics, by some hierarchical rule over passion through reason or virtue, we do need to subordinate ourselves to an enlightened confederation. "Eloquence of persuasions" can "win the imagination from the affections' part, and contract a confederacy between the reason and imagination against them."[22] Such is the comprehensive art of management that controls every mature Baconian work, including the *Essays*. The economic essays promise increase of fortune, the central political essay, "Of the True Greatness of Kingdoms and Estates" (29), promises to rising staffers and politicians a nation-state itself rising in power and security, and "Of Anger" (57) shows how a man angry at his fate can achieve patience by making his "self believe, that the opportunity of his revenge is not yet come, but that he foresees a time for it."

Such an art of managing discourse for one's own purposes must be secretive, and many Baconian passages suggest that one introduce the new under cover of the familiar, bar "vulgar capacities," and single out "selected auditors." Most modern scholars are skeptical of such talk, but the skepticism requires a marked averting of the eyes. The leading case is of Spedding the editor, who made a collection of the Baconian remarks on secrecy and then sought to explain them away. According to Spedding, Bacon was only showing how a teaching fit for all might be introduced more easily or (a more dangerous concession) might be aimed at those who would practice it most usefully to all.[23] Spedding had to presume that Bacon was spreading only his new "system" of experimental knowing and that secrecy was foreign to Baconian "proceedings, purposes, and aspirations," and he had to launder the texts.

But Bacon was reforming more than natural science, and the odor of a subversive, immoral, and anti-religious plan has persisted and among his closest followers. Nor is the question merely of novelty. Bacon had to manage his followers. He had to conceal from peoples of the future how much ambition underlay the humane demeanor of the leaders of reform, to reserve for the ambitious his teaching on managing peoples, and to hide from leaders the extent of their future subordination to institutions that serve peoples. Besides, as preeminent leader, Bacon kept his own counsel for his own purposes. Spedding was an innocent, and he remained silent about the more ominous Baconian statements. All governments are "obscure and invisible"; the science of government is "secret and retired" both as hard to know and as "not fit to utter." A very dark Baconian statement appears far from the thematic discussions of morals and politics and in a chapter on physics and metaphysics. "In civil actions," the passage suggests, "he is far the greater and deeper politician that can make other men the instruments of his ends and desires and yet never acquaint them with his purpose (so as they shall do what he wills and yet not know that they are doing it), than he that imparts his meaning

to those he employs." Is Bacon such a greater and deeper politician? In
New Organon he calls himself a pioneer "following no man, nor communicating his counsels to any mortal."[24] A reader need not be surprised
that it is hard to make out the underlying order beneath the enigmatic
and dispersed directions of the *Essays*.

Of Discourse: Communication as Insinuating Domination

The one essay of the *Essays* that is actually on discourse, "Of Discourse" (32), is a quick little succession of counsels as to persuasion and,
in particular, as to special methods of powerful prose and its disguises.
The key disguises here suggested are blandness and apparent disorder.
The overarching lesson in literary power is now familiar and a lesson in
management: lead by pleasing.

This difficult composition exemplifies Baconian writing at its most enigmatic. It begins without an outline, ends without a conclusion, and provides no names to identify the views rejected or followed. A succession of
declarative sentences is broken only by a Latin maxim, a saying by one "I
knew," and a story of two nobles "I knew." But the repetitive drone of
sentences and references intimates an order to those who grasp and question the assertions. An attack on "some," in the first two sentences, is
followed by fourteen assertions of the parts or modes of discourse, during
which occurs another attack on "some." A reader may sense a certain
lesson: how speech can at once please and lead. If he attends to that dim
impression, and weighs each step by which it is produced, he will see
Bacon transforming the function of speech. Speech is but clever communication, and communication is the velvet glove over the fist of will.
Words are weapons, however attractive, however civil.

In "Of Discourse," as in the corresponding sections of *Advancement*
and *De Augmentis*, the chief target is the supposition that the art of public persuasion is somehow or ultimately subordinate to philosophy and
ethics, that is, to truth and what is good. We find another assault on Aristotle, albeit a muffled one. Bacon begins by attacking "some" who by
discourse seek commendation of their ability to hold all arguments, rather
than of their judgment in discerning the truth. Who could that be? The
allusion would apply to authors of traditional treatises on "topics" of argument and modes of argument (such as Aristotle's *Topics* and analyses
of the syllogism).

Still, one wonders whether the description fits. Aristotle's collections were not indiscriminate; they were meant to furnish premises for arguments seeking truth or at least for arguments enabling the wise to deal with the unwise. What of the priority that the philosophic tradition gave to truth and wisdom? Bacon rephrases, apparently with a view to such a likely objection: the old view of discourse fails to indicate "what should be thought." While the old view collected opinions, that is, it did not adequately determine the flow of opinion. After flashing an orientation by truth before the reader's eyes, Bacon has tacitly dismissed it. He had prepared us earlier, by slyly attributing the motive of "commendation" or glory to the traditional students of discourse, their praise of truth or wisdom being treated as hypocritical. Yet Aristotle's *Rhetoric* had collected opinions for practical purposes. It collected commonplaces of argument not just for knowing, but for defending good people (including lovers of knowing), and it arranged them to arm the orators who were defending justice, the common good, and nobler activities and pleasures. Bacon's next step seems to address just such an objection: "some have certain common places and themes wherein they are good, and want variety; which kind of poverty is for the most part tedious and when it is once perceived, ridiculous." These indirections may intimate that an orientation by the good is too narrow, lacks effective appeal, and lacks merit as well. Perhaps this preliminary conclusion sums up or relies on the lessons of previous essays. They had dismissed aspirations for truth, godliness, goodness, and nobility as, in reality, calculated instruments to get glory or avoid death (essays 1, 13, 14, 16, 17).

The ensuing assertions set forth a discourse freed from the traditional presuppositions. The first we have noted before, and it sets the direction: "The honorablest part of talk is to give the occasion; and again to moderate and pass to somewhat else; for then a man leads the dance." The measure of talk is honor, the aim is to lead, and the way is to organize by occasions the movements of others. The previous essay had suggested that each is for himself; men "will have their own ends, and be truer to themselves" ("Of Suspicion" 31). A later essay confirms that the function of "logic" as well as "rhetoric" is to make a man able to contend ("Of Studies" 50). "Of Discourse" shows comprehensively how to contend by speech. The chief technique: to lead by pleasing. Of the thirteen directions that follow, the first six deal more with pleasing, the last six, more with leading, and the central ones, with ways to reduce rivals and to hide "your" knowledge. Together, the fourteen are a little encyclopedia of arts for civil management of communication.

To avoid paining by boredom, Bacon begins, one should intermingle different modes of speech; for example, mix arguments with tales ("I knew a nobleman . . .''). He warns at greater length against ridiculing things "privileged," such as religion, matters of state, great persons, important business, and any cases deserving pity. Here he attacks "some" who "dart" out remarks that are "piquant, and to the quick." The connotations remind one of the caution in essay 15: "Princes" who deal with tender matters in ticklish times should beware of "short speeches, which flie abroad like darts, and are thought to be shot out of their secret intentions." Does Bacon tacitly correct Machiavelli, whose *Prince* and *Discourses* characteristically mix shocking tales with shocking prescriptions? Bacon's equivalents, *The Reign of Henry VII* and the *Essays*, are by comparison bland, tedious, and secretive. How then can he get noticed?

Bacon proceeds: one can interest some audiences by questioning them in order to learn. This might remind one of Socrates, but the spirit of the questioning proves not to be Socratic. Ask of their skills (so as to please), be not troublesome, and give others their turns to speak. What, however, of the talkers who would "reign and take up" all the time? "Let him find means to take them off, and to bring others on; as musicians used to do with those that dance too long galliards." Perhaps one may interpret this central counsel thus: while one may attract the notice of followers by allowing their interests a place in one's discourse, one is to escort amicably from the dance the bossy talkers, even such as an Aristotle, Machiavelli, or Socrates. The key to overcoming the big arguers by speech is hidden management, not explicit or philosophic confutation. When Bacon attacks Socratic dialectic, in "Of Seeming Wise" (26), he does not mention Socrates or dialectic. "Of Discourse" mentions neither Aristotle's *Rhetoric* nor Machiavelli's *Discourses*.

Accordingly, the eighth counsel (and the first of the second half) advises hiding sometimes what you are thought to know. Thus "you" may obtain credit another time for knowledge you lack. Knowledge is for the raising of the self. Note that Bacon turns from the third person to address "you," a word used five times in this sentence of twenty-five words. The key lesson in managing others is that each is for himself. You are for you, and I for me. An implication: neither of us is for the truth or the good. The next counsel addresses speech of a man's self: speak seldom, but in words well chosen. In the example Bacon gives himself credit for a quotation scorning the mention of self ("I know one. . ."). A like counsel follows: a way to praise self is to praise virtue "if it be such a virtue whereunto" oneself pretends. One praises the good only as useful to the self and the self as the source of things useful to others.

The last four counsels sum up the new art of managing argument. "Discretion of speech is more than eloquence," because "you" must grasp what will make "you" attractive or agreeable. The key art is not of argument but of management, an art of advancement that involves channeling yourself as well as others. To "speak agreeably to him with whom we deal, is more than to speak in good words or in good order." The art of managing should control one's speaking, and the old techniques of rhetoric are encompassed in a technique of control. Bacon counsels a comprehensiveness of technique that will also control one's rivals by taking account of their positions: one must present both a good, settled speech and a good reply or second speech. The final counsel indicates Bacon's mix of direction with indirection. One's persuasion must be neither too indirect, which is "wearisome," nor too "blunt," which would ignore the "circumstances."

Suppose we shake off our weary impatience at Bacon's indirection, apply his advice, and look at the literary circumstances of this statement. The essay that precedes closed with an example of bluntness hiding in blandness: "suspicion" about eternal things "did give a passport to faith; but it ought rather to kindle it to discharge itself" ("Of Suspicion" 31). The essays that follow, "Of Plantations," "Of Riches," and "Of Prophecies," show directly how to gain riches abroad and at home and very indirectly how to replace prophecies of eternal life with a prediction of a growing state (an "Atlanticus," which reminds one of Bacon's literary vision of a progressive, scientific civilization). Thus the ingenuity of enlightened discourse: Bacon mixes bluntness and indirection to communicate his own pleasing revolution with attention to circumstances, not least his Christian circumstances. He can thus discharge the old faith and insinuate a new.

The First Stage: Sedition by Concealed Boldness

If literary art communicates with a view to circumstance, then different methods are appropriate for different circumstances. The *Essays* contains a variety of essays on procedure, especially on procedure as to speech, and I shall argue that they are so chosen as to mark different stages in the work of overturning a world. The first essay on proceeding by speech is "Of Simulation and Dissimulation" (6); it shows how words can be used to hide the self's business. The last is "Of Praise" (53); it shows how to speak about others in a way that favors oneself. The different tenor of these two, the first on concealment and the second on ostentation, corresponds to a progress of the whole argument from attack on old orders to assertion of new. So I shall argue in the remainder of this chapter, which treats in turn the four stages. "Of Simulation and Dissimulation" (6) and "Of Boldness" (12) are the essays on procedure that mark the first and most indirect stage.

"Of Simulation and Dissimulation" seems only reluctantly to grant the need for a little dissimulation to protect the self's secrecy; it withholds approval of "false profession." Yet there is a big qualification: "except it be in great and rare matters." Bacon has Christian Spain recommend simulation as policy: tell a lie about oneself to find a truth about others. The question of when to veil oneself is simply a question of weighing advantages and disadvantages. Bacon weighs. The advantages of lying are knowledge of others, evasion of opposition, and opportunity to retreat; the great disadvantage is that lies deprive one of the "most principal instruments" of action, "trust and belief." The remedy is not integrity, however. It is clever choice of appearances, and Bacon finally provides a famous formula: "The best composition and temperature is to have openness in fame and opinion; secrecy in habit; dissimulation in seasonable use; and a power to feign, if there be no remedy." In short, Bacon recommends an apparent openness which is but part of a policy of contrived disguises. One is always in disguise and the image selected must differ for different followers and enemies.

"Of Simulation" mostly discusses hiding from enemies, and only intimates the appearance one should adopt for advancement. The intimations, if followed up, clarify both the art of putting on appearances and the crucial positive appearance. In the second paragraph, a disjunction between "policy or wisdom" is replaced by a twice-stated disjunction between "arts or policy," which is replaced by the phrase "arts of state and arts of life." Wondering about Bacon's ambiguities, one comes to a startlingly clear formula. Wisdom is equated with policy, and policy comprises arts of state and life.

The art of appearing in state requires a politic discretion in appearances: "that penetration of judgment as he can discern what things are to be laid open, and what to be secreted, and what to be shewed at half lights, and to whom and when (which indeed are arts of state and arts of life, as Tacitus well calleth them)." The equation of wisdom with image making thus appears obscurely (it appears openly in essays 52–54), and one can pierce the fog only by following Bacon in reasoning by similitudes. Some will be soothed by the authority of Tacitus, but editors have not been able to locate this formulation in his works.[25] Some will be soothed by the talk of dissimulation and not of lies, or by the avowal that dissimulation is faint policy (which weighs lies as policy and not also as right or wrong).

Others will not notice that Bacon condemns the habit of lying only to praise the management of lying, or that he praises openness and "a name" of veracity only so far as they are politic.

Bacon finally uses quasi-biblical language to draw a blasphemous conclusion: he explains the appearance of faithfulness as politic and this in the highest instances. The most clever men, thinking "the case indeed required dissimulation, if then they used, it came to pass that the former opinion spread abroad of their good faith and clearness of dealing made them almost invisible." The indirection conceals the bluntness, that is, the inclusion of biblical revelation among the most clever acts, the purpose of which is the "hiding and veiling of a man's self." Such secrecy is politic, because thus one obtains others' confidence and learns of their preoccupations, their "mysteries." The important mysteries are the wishes by which men can be managed. And secrecy is moral as well as politic, for thus one comes more to "reverence." These extraordinary steps are silent about the inherent claims of candor and the truth, and they teach that morality is really the calculated appearance that brings a state of reverence. The veils to be sought are images that make one revered, and they are not bestowed by grace but produced by a simulation.

Such a policy helps explain the simple form of these *Essays* as well as the complications on which we have dwelled. The essays are counsels and of a kind that manages to encompass all within the civil and moral. The most clever appearance is that of counsellor, because he benefits from "the greatest trust between man and man. For in other confidences men commit the parts of life; their lands, their goods, their children, their credit, some particular affair; but to such as they make their counsellors, they commit the whole" ("Of Counsel" 20).

These considerations help explain the tenor of the *Essays'* first stage, especially the surface of essays 1–5. The first three essays conceal critique under an appearance of traditional ways: ways to life everlasting through seeking truth, acting according to eternal moral precepts, or reaching heaven ("Of Truth" 1, "Of Death" 2, and "Of Unity in Religion" 3). In "Of Revenge" (4) and "Of Adversity" (5), the human situation emerges as a state of aloneness in adversity that provokes the passions of fear and revenge. Bacon presents what in Hobbes's version is the state of nature. This account prepares the individualistic recasting, in essays 7–11, of parenthood, marriage, envy, love, and office. One sees a concealed vengefulness directed at the prevailing doctrines of duties and desires, and it is further explained by the indictment of alleged saviors in "Of Boldness" (12).

"Of Boldness" begins by praising bold action, ends by subordinating it to wary counsel, and in between shows warily how to attack mounte-banks—the example is "Mahomet's miracle"—with bold speech. The boldest of bold fellows seem to be prophets whose visions uphold doc-trines of society and conduct. Bacon allows that "great cures" properly tested by "experiments" and not lacking "the grounds of science" may endure. His own daring project may work. Yet the animus here is directed to critique and not promise; he would put down the Mahomets of the world. "Of Boldness" is followed by seven wary but bold assaults. "Of Goodness and Goodness of Nature" (13) converts charity into a human-itarian image that can prove useful, and successive essays attempt similar worldly transformations upon nobility (14), the hierarchical state of king and estates ("Of Seditions and Troubles" 15), religion ("Of Atheism" and "Of Superstition" 16 and 17), education ("Of Travel" 18), and kingly aims and advisers ("Of Empire" 19).

The Second Stage: Getting the Able Down to Business

The second stage of the *Essays* is governed more by Bacon's counsels of business, although it is still covers itself with the traditions on which he wars. It begins by promoting consultants in statecraft and concludes with a new-model state: a ruthless, expanding, yet cautious republican nation-state. This stage contains an unusual proportion of cautionary es-says on proceeding, notably "Of Delays" (21) and "Of Dispatch" (25). These show how to counsel innovations in ways that appear to serve, how to secrete one's plan, and how to advance one's business.

"Of Counsel" (20), at the start of the second stage, proposes that kings be advised by councils, committees, and outside witnesses. "Of Empire" (19) had been insidious, provoking kings to suspicion of traditional coun-selors, such as wives, nobles, and churchmen. Bacon would circumscribe traditional kingship with new sorts of staffers and advisers.

The next five essays (21–25) are on ways of proceeding and not least on ways a counselor can promote his own agenda. They move from ad-vancing secretively to advancing efficiently. The series, like each of the five, starts cautiously. "Of Delays" (21) begins by warning against haste, as does "Of Dispatch" (25), and those between begin by cautioning against what they eventually advocate. The illuminating "Of Delays" is perhaps the most misnamed of the essays. While delay is an instrument for mastering fortune, it must be used with discretion. "There is surely no greater wisdom than well to time the beginnings and onsets of things." The revised counsel is that sluggishness harms as much as precipitateness. Bacon thus corrects the timid counsels he had foisted on traditional kings while writing of sedition and empire (15, 19). He finally counsels good timing, especially watchful beginnings and quick execution, and he equates counsel with secretive innovation and spices the point with aphorism. "For the helmet of Pluto which maketh the politic man go invisible, is secrecy in the counsel and celerity in the execution." Bacon adds an analogy even more arresting: a bullet is quicker than the eye.

"Of Cunning" (22) explains how to insert one's business without revealing one's self. While it implies distaste for "sinister or crooked" tricks, and concludes that small deceits are mean, the essay really distinguishes not the generous from the mean but the "real" from the "small." Those able to debate and consider "the real part of business," or "matters," differ from those expert in the "small wares" of managing "men's humors." The essay nevertheless elaborates the small wares, eighteen ways to prepare minds for a counselor's matters and especially the minds of traditional rulers. All but one of the examples are monarchs; most are English; one, a Roman emperor; another, an Old Testament king. One sees examples of Bacon's cunning in preparing minds: he presents Jesuits as models of cunning, Nehemiah's concern for holy Jerusalem as fraud, and he calls a street name "Paul's" rather than St. Paul's (a trick also practiced in *History of the Reign of King Henry VII*).

Of the eighteen techniques, most advise ways of speaking, and two or three, ways of moving a thing, crossing a business, or conveying an impression. Use the eye, for example, so that a secret heart may appear with a transparent countenance; when seeking an object, distract the listener with other discourse, or move the object while the listener is busy, or appear uneager, or pretend others wished it, or "borrow the name of the world," or "insinuate" lessons through a stock of tales and stories. One example is specially relevant: "It is strange how long some men will lie in wait to speak somewhat they desire to say," Bacon muses, "and how far about they will fetch; and how many other matters they will beat over, to come near it." So the *Essays'* twisting course seems to beat about and lie in wait, before letting out its occasional bold declaration. "Of Cunning" finally tells how to spot such cunning: "a sudden, bold, and unexpected question doth many times surprise a man, and lay him open." To open the *Essays*, perhaps, one must ask forthrightly what are essays, or counsels civil and moral, or cunning, or the author's real aim.

"Of Wisdom for a Man's Self" (23) is a delay that turns to account a preconception against selfishness. While appearing to attack selfishness, the essay eventually authorizes it on a grand scale: selfishness is "more tolerable in a sovereign prince." Bacon first concerns himself with what small cunning neglects, the "public fortune." The cunning man eschews being a prince or a "master" or the furthering of a "master's great and important affairs." He errs or at least is not serviceable. Great projects require respect for the public, and Bacon attacks those wise only for their own gain. Yet early ambiguities lead to a radical revision: respect for the gains of masters and criticism of selfishness only in servants and in citizens of republics and states. Wisdom for the self is only in "many branches" depraved, "many times" unfortunate. This revised homily leaves open the possibility of wise selfishness in other branches and other times.

"Of Innovations" (24) explains this method of indirect assertion through qualification of a respectable generality. "Men in their innovations" should innovate "greatly, but quietly, and by degrees scarce to be perceived." The essay begins by treating new inventions as products of time and ends with a doubt of novelty, which is rebutted by authority, which is in turn manipulated into a novel blasphemy. The gist of the conclusion: only innovations effected by "wisdom and counsel" turn out well, since "time of course alter(s) things to the worse." Under a guise of respecting providence, Bacon ignores it or implies its malice, and opens us to a faith in manmade innovations.

After this quiet instruction to rely only on oneself, Bacon teaches the attitude needed in such an exposed situation: efficient attention to business. While "Of Dispatch" (25) cautions against foolish haste, it commends assiduousness. "Advancement of the business" is the end; "keeping close to the matter, and not taking of it too much at once," the means. "Time is the measure of business" and should not be wasted. Bacon brushes off old ways favoring leisure or devotion; they are of "small dispatch." He seems to allude to the old ways of Spartans (praised by ancient political writers) and Christian Spaniards (praised by theological writers).

The essay turns to efficiency in the writing business, and especially to the efficiency of what might appear disorder. It moves from how to listen to how to write, and from allowing an informant his turn to ordering one's business and speech. Bacon commends repetition to drill men in "the state of the question," and short speeches for efficient effect. Prefaces are vital. The remarks on prefaces illuminate Bacon's beating about in the writing business, which may well be true dispatch. Prefaces may seem a waste of time, but one must beware of "being too material when there is any impediment or obstruction in men's wills: for pre-occupation of mind ever requires preface of speech."

In light of this, one is tempted to see the next two essays as prefaces directed to those influenced by the ancient philosophers. They take on, in turn, wisdom and friendship, two impediments to preoccupation with one's own business. "Of Seeming Wise" (26) is a short but unrelenting attack on Socratic wisdom. It is the most negative of the fifty-eight essays. Is Plato the most dangerous and fundamental enemy? Although Bacon's reasoning brims with allusions that will intrigue and fob off the learned, he manages traditional examples so as to rebut traditional views, even of the Socratics who themselves questioned tradition.

"Of Friendship" (27) is long and complicated, and it does to Aristotle's tributes to friendship and political association what "Of Seeming Wise" does to Socrates' pursuit of wisdom by dialectic. The attack is on the famous teaching that politics is rooted in friendship, that is, that man, unless a beast below humanity or a philosopher above it, is naturally political. Under cover of traditional formulations, Bacon proceeds to turn friendship first into mutual service and then into service by follower to leader or master. The eulogy to masters stands out. Four harsh Roman emperors are called the "wisest and most politic" of princes. Still, masters need followers (a point positively asserted in "Of Ambition" 36), because the art of life requires friends to keep one in state. Being in a state of memory or glory is the immortality that the self can conquer, and if a man "have not a friend, he may quit the stage."

After these prefatory skirmishes against philosophic doctrines that subordinate the self, Bacon proceeds to show how to obtain a state that advances oneself. "Of Expense" (28) shows how to manage frugality to get rich; "Of the True Greatness of Kingdoms and Estates" (29) shows how to manage a country into a growing nation-state. "Above all things," Bacon concluded in "Of Dispatch" (25), "order, and distribution, and singling out of parts, is the life of dispatch." What appears to be disorder in the *Essays* is the careful juxtaposition of parries and blows, veiled sedition and veiled constructions.

The Third Stage: New Men and New Orders

In essays 30–46, Bacon becomes more open in his constructions. This stage addresses more directly the new self-made men and sets forth new systems of mutual utility. The first twenty-nine essays had addressed men as traditionally ordered, as nobility, fathers, counselors, friends, kingdoms and estates. The new order had been largely couched in traditional terms. The surface argument in "Of Great Place" (11) and "Of Wisdom for a Man's Self" (23) directs one to a public duty, and the underlying counsel concerns the public persona of a rising man. "Of Goodness and Goodness of Nature" (13) and "Of Friendship" (27) had merely indicated the priority of mastery and of the self's endurance.

"Of Regiment of Health" (30), the first essay of the second half, is also the first essay whose title and text are about an unambiguously private good. It and the last essay of the first half, "Of the True Greatness of Kingdoms and Estates" (29), alone have titles connoting government. Perhaps the first half of the *Essays* deals more with traditional types of government, the second with unambiguously private interests (such as health, acquisition, and making one's fortune) and with new social systems that can govern by channeling private interests. The third stage mingles lessons in acquiring security, wealth, and power, in rejecting traditional aspirations, and in mastering our nature and fortune by utilitarian customs and opportunistic negotiations.

This section's two procedural essays first teach how to raise suspicions, such that faith may "discharge itself" ("Of Suspicions" 31), and then how to regulate "what should be thought," by insinuating substitutions for the old beliefs ("Of Discourse" 32). For example, "it is the sinfullest thing in the world to forsake or destitute," not the Savior or His Church, but "a plantation once in forwardness" ("Of Plantations" 33).

"Of Regiment of Health" (30) replaces health in the traditional sense, a fit body apt for activity, with the bodily ability to preserve oneself. It weighs all activities and feelings, from "wonder and admiration" to exercise, with a view to "endur(ing)" or "long lasting." In essay 29, Bacon had distracted statesmen from Christian politics by directing to worldly greatness; essay 30 distracts humanity from Christ's saving and the pagans' fitness by directing to bodily enduring. Essay 29 shows an obvious part of the art of state, essay 30, of the art of life. The one medical authority Bacon cites, Celsus, was known chiefly as an attacker of Christianity, and Bacon misquotes him to appear as also an opponent of the traditional art of medicine. Celsus had prescribed exercise, training the body to retain youthful fitness, and little reliance on doctoring. Bacon prescribes apprehension about symptoms, choosing activities so as to endure the weaknesses of age, a "benign" tolerance as to eating, sleeping, and exercise, and "physic." Health is not a natural good to be cultivated, but a state of pleasurable power obtained by easy regimen and reliance on experts. The essay closes by commending doctors. But it also says that "age will not be defied." However doctored, the body can obtain only a limited enduring.

Other essays in this part set forth other private aims, especially wealth and power. "Of Riches" (34) removes any scruples about making money, after a becoming simulation at its start, and suggests effectual ways such as monopolies and investment in new techniques. "Being the first in an Invention, or in a Priviledge, doth cause sometimes a wonderful overgrowth in Riches." Bacon also speaks of investing in plantations abroad (33), of the handling of ambitious men (36), and of houses and gardens (45 and 46). These essays seem to show how to motivate the leaders of the new order of "civility and elegancy," especially lesser leaders who can be pastured on wealth, country houses, and subordinate places, and how to channel off similarly the leaders of the old regime who had once sought fortresses and splendor.

A number of essays indict various traditional goods, including the promises of prophecies, the promises of the Christian drama, noble triumphs, and beauty. The treatment of triumphs shows Bacon's special skill in escorting unwanted partners from his dance. Essay 29 ("True Greatness") had praised "triumphs" as the rewards of victorious generals, but essay 37 mentions triumphs in title but not in text ("Of Masques and Triumphs"), and the last mentions are in "Of Building" (45), which merely recommends a room for "feasts and triumphs." In short, celebrations of great military deeds disappear into a private and defenseless pile. Conspicuous consumption can soak up heroic ambition as well as riches. "Of Prophecies" (35) consolidates Bacon's liberation of acquisitiveness and ambition from supernatural limits. While appearing to discredit some prophecy, the essay indirectly discredits all and hints at a politic substitute, a faith in predictable progress that improves on Plato's "Atlanticus." "Of Ambition" (36) indicates the social role-players that are to replace the old nobles: ambitious men rather "stirring in business, than great in dependencies."

The indictment of masques and triumphs follows, a preface for poets and patrons who incline to venerate a divine playwright or dramatically good men and women. Masques are reduced to "toys" that entertain a prince, and there remain mere intimations of the ceremonies thereby deflated. It is poor taste, Bacon says, to bring on "angels" or "devils" (although "beasts" are tolerable). In *New Organon*, Bacon had called the traditional teachings of theology and philosophy but idols of the mind, plays staged for their ambitious authors. "Of Masques and Triumphs," I think, revamps ordinary drama to fit pedestrian tastes; his maxims of masque making prescribe appeals to luxury and variety. Is not this mixed appeal a secret of Bensalemite society in the *New Atlantis*? In this Baconian drama of conversion to faith in progress, the general run of Christian Europeans is bedazzled by luxurious food of novel taste, luxurious clothes of novel colors and textures, and a plethora of technological novelties. We glimpse the calculated charms of consumer society.

In the three essays that follow, Bacon seems to address those moved less by tales and more by thought: these essays rethink the relative importance of nature, custom, and fortune (38, 39, 40). The next four essays revamp objects customarily thought natural or unnatural into instruments for mastering fortune (41, 42, 43, 44).

"Of Ambition" (36) had set forth an art of managing others' ambitions, while leaving obscure the object of ambition and especially of the masterful man who manages the ambitious for his ends. Essays 38–40 clarify this object, which might be called the mastery of fortune for the sake of enduring. They intimate the primacy of natural forces and the power, nevertheless, of artificial systems for channeling such forces. "Of Nature" (38) teaches that nature is but a private and hidden force, a blind passion that can be taught mastery by a "vocation." A vocation proves to be a skill in advancing oneself; it is a realistic improvement on moral and spiritual virtue. Which vocation is to be preferred? Without explicitly answering, Bacon implies that it is that of a master.

At least, he turns to show how one can determine or manage many vocations by managing custom ("Of Custom" 39). The key means of mastering men, it seems, is by determining the customs of "society." At first Bacon dwells on the management of religious customs. The way to overcome the "reign or tyranny" of such custom, as well as of religious vocations, is through family and society in general. "Certainly the great multiplication of virtues upon human nature resteth upon societies well ordained and disciplined." Bacon hints that a well-ordained society is one for mutual use, that is, for business. Perhaps such customs underlie the quite remarkable discipline of the *New Atlantis*, in which (if the ceremonial parade be indicative), there are "companies of the city," but no nobility or military associations and only a whiff of religion.

"Of Fortune" (40) is to the superior man what "Of the True Greatness of Kingdoms and Estates" (29) is to public affairs: a realistic redefinition and a formula for production. Virtue is ability, the "faculties and customs" that enable a man to improve his fortune. Attention to business is only the beginning. A man should be able to adjust to the times, to concentrate his thoughts on himself (not too much on country or master), to concentrate on advancement, to be reputed able while ascribing success to fortune, to hide his policy. These small virtues—Bacon revises his disdain for the arts of cunning—are the secrets of a "slide and easiness" in mastering fortune.

Essays 41–44 complete this part of what can be called by Nietzsche's name: a "transvaluation of values." In particular, they show how to win followers by providing what they must want. "Of Usury" (41) is the most candid of all the essays and puts on open stage the economic art whereby private gain can be managed to provide public benefit. It openly disdains Christian and classical disparagements of taking interest, and introduces the custom of managing interest rates so as both to further trade and industry and to ease credit for consumers. "Of Youth and Age" (42) shows how to compound what might seem natural promise and decline with a view to their use in progressive society. Imaginative inventions and new projects can win and use the young; sober counsel and judicious management, the old. "Of Beauty" and "Of Deformity" (43 and 44) provide a formula for another social compound. Bacon weighs the bloom of youth (and the prime of life) only as to its contribution to making one's way. After toying with the traditional view that beauty lies more in form and soul than in body and motion, Bacon dismisses it and defines beauty finally as "decent motion," which proves to be no more than a gloss (often distracting) on the ability to rise. According to "Of Deformity" (44), belief in one's deformity is more useful than belief in one's beauty, for it better spurs rising, at least in "a great wit."

The Fourth Stage: Image Making and the Father of Enlightenment

The *Essays* concludes with a series of lessons in praising the leader, and "Of Praise" (53) is the characteristic procedural essay of this stage. While "Of Discourse" (32) had shown how to determine what men should think, "Of Praise" shows how to make men think well of oneself. The essay is one of a quartet in the middle of this stage. The first five essays (47–51) show how to win cunning followers, the quartet (52–55) teaches "arts of ostentation" for leaders ("Of Vainglory" 54), and the final three show how the superior leader subordinates himself to the laws, policy, and civilization that will uphold his self in the long run.

Bacon comes to the essentials in managing followers: one manages them to one's own advantage. All dealing with others is negotiating, and in negotiating, "all practice is to discover or to work" ("Of Negotiating" 47). It follows that friendship is merely mutual dealing among individuals whose "fortunes may comprehend the one the other," and that he whose plan encompasses others has them as followers ("Of Followers and Friends" 48). Managing means especially the ability to slip from follower to follower; one rises above some, such as the wealthy, not least by dropping their "suits" or interests in favor of others more useful ("Of Suitors" 49). This lesson illuminates the orotund effusions that concluded the prior stage, "Of Building" (45) and "Of Gardens" (46). The "royal" scale of the building Bacon commends reminds us that building can be a "toy" for a restless king ("Of Empire" 19), and thus conspicuous consumption can smother even those followers who aspire to "state and magnificence" (46).

"Of Studies" (50) only appears to break the series on negotiation, followers, suitors, and factions, for studies turn out to be an aid in the planning needed to win followers. Studies aid "ability" in business, especially in "general counsels, plots, and marshalling of affairs." The importance of learning is conspiracy, not truth, but in conspiracies, especially great conspiracies, studies are needed. Studies are cunning writ large. By ordering "things, which are general," out of "a trueness to a man's self," a man can rise above the factions that helped him rise ("Of Faction" 51). In essay 58, Bacon calls the triumph of a new state of learning *his* toy.

The four essays on ostentation begin by reinterpreting ceremonies into effectual images for oneself. They end by considering which images are most effectual, the greatest being "founders of states and commonwealths" ("Of Honor and Reputation" 55). The first of the four, "Of Ceremonies and Respects" (52), hints at its blasphemy; there is an absence of respect for religious ceremonies such as the Christian sacraments. The hints are the backdrop for a novel lesson, the need to produce "good forms." The essay sets forth without scruple the doctrine of lying merely intimated in "Of Simulation and Dissimulation" (6). The problem: how to obtain "praise and commendation" by impressing others. The counsel: convey effectual compliments, "keep state" with acquaintances, be familiar among inferiors where "reverence" is likely, keep one's eye on one's business, and vary one's appearance accordingly.

"Of Praise" (53) shows that one's business is to get a name for oneself by demeaning others, such as the religious, and by advancing one's own vocation, such as civil business. The essay begins with Aristotle-like praise of virtue and then detours to lessons in praising oneself by attracting the many and the few. Ordinary people must be "served" with "shows." This explains Bacon's show of humanitarianism (13) and the "aspect" of pity and "shew" of the ceremonial that varnishes the scientist in *New Atlantis.* People of "quality and judgment" are needed to provide a good name, which is like a precious ointment. The biblical simile may remind the reader that Bacon is not praising Him from whom all blessings flow. "Of Praise" (53) advises management of false praises by flattery. The cunning flatterer follows "the arch-flatterer," which is not the devil but "a man's self."

Bacon slights the words of the Bible that show the way to Christ and appeals to what is the root of sin for the Christian. So the cunning of the essays. They "come home to men's business and bosoms," Bacon's dedication told the Duke of Buckingham, and finally to the very self of each. Still, praise can manipulate as well as flatter, and can indeed manipulate by flattering. "Some praises come of good wishes and respects, which is a form due in civility to kings and great persons, *laudando praecipere* (to teach in praising); when by telling men what they are, they represent to them what they should be." This explains much of the blandness in these essays, which are a type of false praise. The Latin and the biblical allusions remind one especially of Bacon's irreligious representations of religious imagery.

"Of Praise" closes with the culminating lesson, which is how to praise oneself. Rarely praise the self directly; praise instead one's "office and profession," and thus will come "grace" and "magnanimity." Bacon hints at his transformation of Christian Aristotelianism, which had subordinated self to God and to greatness of soul. Whereupon he attacks as boasters the "Cardinals of Rome" and their "high speculations," which belittled "civil business," and St. Paul who magnified his mission. Bacon shows how to blame grace and religious pride while raising one's self under cover of promoting civil business. To blame is to raise envies, which are slanders to reduce others; "Of Envy" (9) had concluded with a comparison to "Of Praise." Bacon's slandering of high prophecy magnifies his civil vocation, while his praise of civil business slanders his rivals' devotion to otherworldly business.

While "Of Praise" condemns especially those who raise a god above human effort, "Of Vain-Glory" (54) concentrates on the secular historians and philosophers who subordinate human glory to truth or morality. The essay mostly cites ancient pagans. Although it seems to attack pursuit of glory, it actually attacks those who use glory ineffectually. Then it develops the real uses. Glory-seekers are useful for trumpeting opinions and thus for involving enemies or factions in mutual strife. A man "that negotiates between two princes" may draw both into a war against a third, as Bacon draws traditional kings and learned Aristotelians into a war against the church. When a man raises his credit with both by "pretending greater interest than he hath in either," he produces a political miracle; "somewhat is produced out of nothing: for lies are sufficient to breed opinion, and opinion brings on substance." Bacon provokes a war by the learned on the ancient philosophers, who talked of truth but felt glory.

"They that write books on the worthlessness of glory," he says in Latin, "take care to put their names on the title page." And after that nasty slander: "Socrates, Aristotle, Galen, were men full of ostentation."

Whatever their hypocrisy, the ancient philosophers also missed the real use of glory. "Certainly vainglory helpeth to perpetuate a man's memory; and virtue was never so beholding to human nature, as it received his due at the second hand." Immortality is only by the intercession of glory; image making, not philosophy, is the art of preparing to die. Bacon proceeds to defend the "art of setting forth to advantage" all that one does. Modesty itself when properly governed is but one of the "arts of ostentation," and effectual modesty consists in praising oneself by praising vocations like one's art and the "perfection" of selves like oneself.

"Of Honor and Reputation" (55) discusses which likenesses to choose. To be a master of names so that one can live on after death, one must seek the reputation of a master of men, a Caesar. This very difficult essay replaces a worthy opinion, that honor is properly the mirror of virtue, with a realistic lesson, that one can conquer a life in the opinions of others. The lesson has three parts: that which wins honor, the degrees of honor, and degrees of honor in subjects.

What wins most honor is an innovation that satisfies every faction in part, outdistances all competitors, and wins discreet followers. The secret of glory is a superior and politic benefaction to humanity. Among the degrees of claimants to this "sovereign honor," Bacon ranks first the founders of "states and commonwealths" (Bacon's civil translation of the Latin that he also supplies, *conditores imperiorum*). Second are the lawgivers; third, liberators or saviors from civil war or servitude to strangers or tyrants; fourth, expanders or defenders of territories (*imperii* in the Latin equivalent); and, fifth, just rulers. The scope of the founders of states or empires appears from the examples: Romulus, Cyrus, Caesar, Ottoman, and Ismael. All are emperors or founders of empires, one or more was regarded as divine, at least two founded cults as well as empires—and not one founded a commonwealth in the sense of a free government. A commonwealth seems merely a prince's state, the shadow cast among his followers.

This famous passage differs from its still more famous counterpart in the *New Organon* (I, 129),[26] where it is the authors of "famous discoveries" who deserve "divine honors." Those who do "good service in the state," such as founders, legislators, liberators, and the like, deserve merely "heroic" honor. The difference is real. I suggest that it is due not to variations in Bacon's outlook, but to different functions of the two works in his plan. Because the *Essays* recruits civil leaders, it veils higher glories, although it intimates in this and other essays what is missing. Glory comes from "that which hath not been attempted before," not least from innovations that do what no civil state or empire can: "content every faction or combination of people" (55). *New Organon* develops the point at which *Essays* points. Discoveries "may extend to the whole race of man"; they may confer benefits without "causing harm or sorrow to any." To see the image that accords with the formula, one need only look to *New Atlantis.* Bacon produced a humane vision of a welfare state that can encompass Jews, Persians, and the other sects excluded by its otherworldly rival. By such, the praise of humanity and humanitarians may be won.

Yet section 129 of *New Organon* remains enigmatic. Probably this is for a cause also visible in *New Atlantis:* the image of beneficence to come requires the concealment of dangers that will also come. In section 129, the assertion of complete beneficence is belied by an example used, gunpowder (*pulvaris tormentarii* in the graphic Latin), and, more important, Bacon equates the growth of inventions with imperial and religious domination. "No empire, no sect, no star" has exerted "greater power and influence" than inventions such as the compass, printing press, and gunpowder, which have changed "the face and state of things throughout the world." Indeed, he who might invent "the power and dominion of the human race over the universe," through a method "by which all things else shall be discovered," would most deserve imperial fame. This culminating promise of empire turns on the power and the method that is promised in Bacon's *Great Instauration:* the great institution of the power of man over the universe by the invention of the art of invention. In section 129, Bacon hints that such fame will supplant the "face" of divinity that men have hitherto bestowed on the gods above them. It moves from calling inventions "imitations of God's works" to calling man "a god to man."

The last essays of the last stage prescribe a reformed judiciary (an important follower in the transition to a civil state), explain why even a leader who would dominate like god must be civil, and outline the sect that might overcome time. "Of Judicature" (56) shows how judges, in performing their business, can contribute to great innovations of which they are almost unaware. The secret is Bacon's formula for their business. Judges are to be lions under the throne, in a famous phrase, and unobtrusively can help devour the old order and introduce the new. Bacon leads judges away from traditional equity and from laws that favor church and estates; they are led to interpret law according to "business of state" and "true policy." "Of Anger" (57) only apparently interrupts. It explains why the self's desire for revenge against oblivion must be channeled into policy. Do not, like the bee, put one's "life in the sting." Subordinate revenge to a policy of ostentation. "Of Vicissitude of Things" (58), which I discuss in the next chapter, shadows forth the most artful and indirect ostentation. A sect that mixes a science of production with civil supports can triumph over worldly rivals and even over the fate visited on a man by an indifferent nature.

The form of the *Essays* is a formula for managing men by discourse toward such a future.

Notes

1. I quote the modern spelling and capitalization, as in the edition of Clark Sutherland Northup, *The Essays of Francis Bacon* (Boston: Houghton Mifflin, 1936). I rely also on the text established by Michael Kiernan, ed., *Essays or Counsels, Civill and Morall* (Cambridge, Mass.: Harvard University Press, 1985), and upon notes from various editions, not least Northup's and Kiernan's.

2. The quartet: "Of Ceremonies and Respects" (52), "Of Praise" (53), "Of Vainglory" (54), and "Of Honor and Reputation" (55). The pairs: "Of Parents and Children" (7) and "Of Marriage and Single Life" (8); "Of Goodness and Goodness of Nature" (13) and "Of Nobility" (14); "Of Atheism" (16) and "Of Superstition" (17); "Of Plantations" (33) and "Of Riches" (34); "Of Nature in Men" (38) and "Of Custom and Education" (39); "Of Beauty" (43) and "Of Deformity" (44); "Of Building" (45) and "Of Gardens" (46); "Of Followers and Friends" (48) and "Of Suitors" (49).

3. Numbers 11, 18, 19, 23, 28, 29, 33, 34, 41, 45, 46, 58.

4. "Of the True Greatness of Kingdoms and Estates" (29), "Of Plantations" (33), and "Of Usury" (41)

5. "Of Discourse" (32), "Of Simulation and Dissimulation" (6), "Of Praise" (53), "Of Honour and Reputation" (55).

6. Michael Macmillan called Bacon the "Father of English Moral Philosophy," whose attention to "philanthropia" and utility anticipated later teachings of altruism and utilitarianism. ["Bacon's Moral Teaching," *International Journal of Ethics* 17 (October, 1906), 66, 68–70.] But Macmillan never explained how philanthropia is consistent with individual utility, and he expressly set aside "the many passages" in the *Essays* in which Bacon "betrays a tendency to Machiavellianism and to pursuit of selfish ends by base means." Jacob Zeitlin subsequently explained the selfish and moral sides historically, as different stages in the *Essays'* development. The 1597 edition is politic; the expanded 1615 edition is moral; the final and much expanded 1625 edition, politic again. But there is a mixture in the new material in each of these editions, as Zeitlin admitted, and a mixture also within the particular essays he designates as selfish or moral. ["The Development

of Bacon's Essays—with Special Reference to the Question of Montaigne's Influence upon Them," *Journal of English and Germanic Philology* 27 (1928), 503, 505–14, esp. 508, 513–14.] Ronald S. Crane, another historical scholar, made the promising suggestion that the *Essays* carries out the moral and civil program expounded in the *Advancement of Learning*. Yet Crane abstracted from the actual effects Bacon sought; making a common error, he presumed the Baconian program to be essentially "research." ["The Relation of Bacon's Essays to His Program for the Advancement of Learning," *The Schelling Anniversary Papers* (New York, n.d.), reprinted in Brian Vickers, ed., *Essential Articles for the Study of Francis Bacon* (Hamden, U.K.: Archon Books, 1968), 272–92].

7. "Francis Bacon and the Architecture of Fortune," *Studies in the Renaissance* 5 (1958), 176–95]. Cochrance deserves the credit for striking gold, although he did not bring it up. He did not spell out this operative part, the arts of advancement, which is what the meandering course of the *Essays* presents.

8. "Georgics of the Mind: The Experience of Bacon's *Essays*," *Critical Quarterly* 13 (1971), 4546.

9. *Advancement of Learning* II, xviii, 2, ed. Wright; *Works*, VI, 297; III, 409. *De Dignitate et Augmentis Scientarum* VI, 3, tr. James Spedding, in *Works* IX, 131; IV, 455.

10. *Francis Bacon and Renaissance Prose* (Cambridge: Cambridge University Press, 1968), 15.

11. *De Augmentis* VI, in *Works* IX, 121, 108; IV, 448, 438–39. Jardine, *Francis Bacon: Discovery and the Art of Discourse* (Cambridge: Cambridge University Press, 1974), 169; see 226, 173, for the subsequent references.

12. *Francis Bacon and Renaissance Prose*, 56.

13. John Briggs, *Francis Bacon and the Rhetoric of Nature* (Cambridge, Mass.: Harvard University Press, 1989), xi.

14. *De Augmentis* VI, in *Works* IX, 127–28; IV, 452–53. *Advancement of Learning* II, xvii, 12, ed. Wright; *Works* VI, 294; III, 407.

15. *Advancement* II, xvii, 2, 7, ed. Wright; *Works* VI, 289, 290–29; III, 403, 405; *De Augmentis* VI, 2, in *Works* IX, 125; IV, 45.

16. *De Augmentis* VI, 2, in *Works* IX, 126–27; IV, 452.

17. *A Concordance to the Essays of Francis Bacon*, ed. David W. Davies and Elizabeth S. Wrigley (Detroit: Gale Research Co., 1973).

18. The dedication was to Prince Henry, who died before the work was published. Reprinted in Wright, ed., *Bacon's Essays and Colours of Good and Evil*, xii.

19. *Nicomachean Ethics*, 1103a 3–11.

20. *Advancement* II, xviii, 6, ed. Wright; *Works* VI, 301–2; III, 412.

21. *Francis Bacon on Communication and Rhetoric* (Chapel Hill: University of North Carolina Press, 1943), 214–16 and ch. 12.

22. *De Augmentis* VI, iii, in *Works* IX, 131–33; IV, 455–57. See chapter 4 of this volume and J. Weinberger, *Science, Faith, and Politics: Francis Bacon and the Utopian Roots of the Modern Age* (Ithaca, N.Y.: Cornell University Press, 1985), 267.

23. "Preface to the *Novum Organum*," Note B, *Works* I, 182–89; I, 107–13.

24. Sources in the order quoted: *Advancement* II, xxiii, 47, ed. Wright; *Works* VI, 387–88; III, 473–74; *De Augmentis* III, iv, in *Works* VIII, 511; IV, 364; *Novum Organum* I, cxiii (my translation).

25. See *Essays*, ed. Kiernan, 190.

26. *Works* VIII, 113; *Works* IV, 79–80.

Chapter 3

Improvements on Machiavelli: Empire Humane, Civil, and Visionary

Machiavelli and the *Essays*

It is an old question whether the complicated Baconian innovations somehow originate in Machiavelli's simpler project. Recent students of Bacon's political writings are inclined to say yes. That answer leads to a new question. How could scientific method and a humane utopianism rest on a teaching so apparently incompatible? That problem guides this discussion. I examine with care Bacon's four explicit treatments of Machiavelli's doctrines in *Essays or Counsels, Civil and Moral* and conclude that Bacon builds on Machiavellian fundamentals, but attempts an improved edifice. While the previous chapter supplied a survey of Bacon's plan, this chapter clarifies the purpose and premises.

Whatever others have supposed of Machiavelli's originality and influence,[1] there is no doubt that Bacon himself believed the great Florentine's thought a turning point and one to which he was indebted. He said so. "We are much beholden to Machiavel and others that write what men do, and not what they ought to do."[2] This much-quoted formulation was no aside, no trifle, and no exception. It occurs in the midst of Bacon's comprehensive revamping of moral science in the *Advancement of Learning*. It encapsulates the Machiavellian turn to efficacy and success and the rejection of an orientation by morality or the good; "For it is so far from how one lives to how one should live that he who lets go of what is done for what should be done learns his ruin rather than his preservation" (*The Prince*, chapter 15).[3] And it is but one of many like remarks. In *Advancement* alone, Bacon refers ten times to Machiavelli by name, almost always favorably, and this pattern of explicit references is unprecedented. According to Richard Kennington, no other seventeenth-century philosopher published under his own name and during his lifetime so much as *one* mention of the much-decried Machiavelli.[4] Bacon consistently treats Machiavelli as respectable company and fosters—albeit ironically—his influence. The first reference in the *Essays* calls Machiavelli "one of the doctors of Italy" and treats him as an authority on theology.

If Machiavellianism is apparent in Bacon's work, its actual extent and character is not apparent, and controversy has flourished on this very point. Many writers talk of a hard-nosed opportunism informing Baconian moral and civil writings. One scholar contended that Bacon was "more Machiavellian than Machiavelli," for example, and another, that "the whole of Bacon's political writings" exhibit a "preoccupation with vast schemes" that leads to "neglect of rules of morality."[5] But others express doubts, and Bacon's own references give grounds for doubting. In the *Advancement*, Bacon qualified his deference to Machiavelli precisely as to the status of morality: we should attend to what men do, and not what they ought to do, if only because "it is not possible to join the wisdom of the serpent with the innocence of the dove, except men be perfectly acquainted with the nature of evil itself." The modification shows an un-Machiavellian respect for Christian innocence, although the final counsel, that men devote themselves to perfect knowledge of evil ways, gives pause.

Indeed, the general tone of all of Bacon's works differs markedly from anything Machiavelli ever wrote. The works on scientific method have no Machiavellian parallel. Supposing that the methodical works are crucial, James Spedding dismissed airily Edwin Abbot's contentions of amorality, and the example and his biography have often been followed.[6] Also, Bacon's *New Atlantis* advances an imagined land of future health, peace, affluence, and parentlike care, while chapter 15 of *The Prince* had turned away from "imagined principalities and republics." Even if Machiavelli's supposedly historical descriptions might be thought a cover for his prescriptions of new modes and orders, the prescriptions differ from Bacon's. The surface of Bacon's more practical works lacks the immoral ruthlessness for which *The Prince* and *Discourses* are infamous. The *Essays* counsel humanity, appear businesslike and respectable, and are filled with learned quotations from traditional authorities. None of Bacon's works exhibit Machiavelli's trumpeting of the strategy and metaphor of war. Nor do they revel in characteristic Machiavellian themes: a princely decisiveness reminiscent of Cesare Borgia or Julius Caesar, and liberty, *patria*, and popular republicanism reminiscent of the ancient Roman republic.

In short, Bacon defers to Machiavelli in ways that some consider fundamental, and yet differs in ways that others consider fundamental. In this chapter, I try to clarify the disputed relation by considering a sample of Bacon's own appraisals, the *Essays*' four references by name to Machiavelli and his doctrines. This is a narrow sample, and I am aware of the cost. An adequate treatment would have to weigh the express references in other works. Then there are all the tacit allusions. For example, Machiavelli is not mentioned by name in the most obviously Machiavellian essay, "Of the True Greatness of Kingdoms and Estates" (29), which draws many of its examples from the *Discourses*. But we discuss this essay in chapter 10 and touch Bacon's Machiavellianism in many other chapters. Here I take advantage of a limited scope to ponder not only obvious differences of doctrine but also progress of reasoning, selection of detail, and, in general, the more subtle differences and implications.

All four references use the authority of Machiavelli to deal with matters of religion or sects, three times directly. All occur amidst crucial discussions of fundamentals—"Of Goodness and Goodness of Nature" (13), "Of Sedition and Troubles" (15), "Of Custom and Education" (39), and "Of Vicissitude of Things" (58). All take issue with Machiavelli, the last two expressly. But the disputes prove to be over means, although vast means extending to whole civilizations. Like Machiavelli, Bacon is impressed with the imperial glory that attends the head of a conquering sect. The superior man should be the comprehensively calculating political man, not the contemplative philosopher. His aim is the glory that ensures an immortality for himself. But Bacon corrects Machiavelli's calculations about the sect that will glorify. In essay 13, he advises the adoption of a humane cause that retains an aura of Christian charity. In essay 15, he encourages kings to be parental rather than partisan. Economic development, and in general a management of hopes more than fears, is the way to undermine an old order and engender a new. In essay 39, he criticizes Machiavelli's bloody words, suggesting instead revolution through civil customs that afford opportunities, most obviously in business. The last essay (58) links Bacon's vision of scientific progress to a series of growing and businesslike nation-states. Together, the modernizing nations, as we may call them, can spread an imperial sect and overcome the Christianity that Spain upheld in Bacon's time.

Bacon thought that his combination of nation-state with visionary progress appealed more broadly than Machiavelli's mixture of republican empires with dictatorial generals, better hid its founder's ambition, and better imitated the successful Christian vision of an otherworldly provider. Using Machiavelli's reputation for boldness to shield his own innovations, the more cautious Bacon means to enlist Machiavellians among the subordinate parts of his own movement.

The Policy of Humanitarianism

> And one of the doctors of Italy, Nicholas Machiavel, had the confidence to
> put in writing, almost in plain terms, "That the Christian faith had given up
> good men in prey to those that are tyrannical and unjust."
>
> ("Of Goodness and Goodness of Nature" 13)

The *Essays'* first and ironic introduction of Machiavelli as a theological
authority barely glosses—in fact, it accentuates—an indictment of Christianity. The original indictment occurs in Dr. Machiavelli's *Discourses*, II,
2.[7] It is startlingly ruthless. Machiavelli celebrates democratic liberty and
democratic "ferocity" toward nobles and contrasts the freedom of ancient warlike peoples with modern servile peoples. He traces the difference to the "magnificent," "ferocious," and "bloody" sacrifices in pagan
religion, which celebrated worldly glory, as opposed to the delicate equivalents in "our religion," which glorifies humble, abject, and contemplative men. Machiavelli does indicate repeatedly that liberty is but a means
to growth in population and private acquisitions, and that a conquering
republic is a tyrannical ruler. He plans a calculated liberty and a regulated
populace. But these cautions come only after bold praise of bold militancy, a boldness absent from Bacon's account. Bacon's thirteenth essay
does not celebrate peoples, liberty, or pagan ferocity; neither does the
Essays as a whole, except very quietly, as in numbers 15 and 29.

Bacon's is a veiled militancy. He follows his display of Machiavelli's
scandalous indictment by his own respectable-sounding explanation:
"Which he spake, because indeed there was never law or sect or opinion
did so much magnify goodness as the Christian religion doth." Apart
from identifying "the Christian religion" as but a "sect" (he develops this
in essays 16 and 17), Bacon appears to withdraw from Machiavelli's
charge. But the appearance is misleading, and provides another lesson in
Baconian indirectness. He has substituted goodness for charity and identified Christianity with goodness and not Christ. The essay begins with
this sly identification, moves on to say that goodness "answers to" the
theological virtue charity—for those who don't ask questions—and then
says that charity admits of error if not of excess. That big qualification of
the goodness of goodness becomes thematic after Bacon turns "to avoid
the scandal and the danger both." He will avoid the scandal of Machiavelli's way and the danger of Christianity's way by proceeding in his typically indirect way.

Essay 13 exemplifies both Bacon's humanitarianism and his hard-nosed
Machiavellianism and shows how each is revised to support the other. In

his seminal study, Howard White had argued that humanitarianism was a genuinely moral moderation by Bacon of the imperial and acquisitive spirit of Machiavellianism. But essay 13 is the *locus classicus* of Baconian humanitarianism, and there Bacon turns humanitarianism toward self-reliance on one's own acquisitions, and toward a social tool of political acquisitiveness. Actually, White's own investigations led him toward such a conclusion. He came to describe Baconian charity as uncharitable—as "a political weapon" to recruit followers and as "depersonalized charity," the "unwitting charity of the spirit of capitalism."[8]

Essay 13's first description of *philanthropia* abstracts from the distinctively Christian name of charity and from its pious spirit of caring for those sharing a divine soul. There follows a series of restatements that move first to compassion for common bodily needs and then, very delicately, to self-advancement as the means of providing, and then to cautions against regard for people's "faces" or "fancies," for precious gifts, and for equal distribution of things. That is, in benefitting others, think of bodily necessities and self-reliance, and disregard what people appear to wish or say they wish, or their rare needs, or mere inequalities. Bacon proceeds to suggest benefits such as food, or "barley-corn" by which people can provide food for themselves. He then slips in self-regard as a limit upon the whole duty of benefitting of others. The language may be biblical, but the words are blasphemy. Bacon, having revamped the Christian law of charity, replaces the fundamental biblical commandment with a foundation in the self: "For divinity maketh the love of ourselves the pattern; the love of our neighbors but the portraiture." Love of neighbor for God's sake has been replaced by one's own provision for human necessities, and love of God, by love of self. The revolutionary implications of the lord thyself are quickly developed: advancement, not love, is the point. Concentrate on providing for oneself by a "vocation": "for otherwise in feeding the streams one driest the fountain."

It is Machiavellian, this criticism as ineffectual of both Aristotelian liberality and Christian charity and this movement toward the un-Christian charity of Machiavellian humanity.[9] But Bacon's insinuations, quiet restatements, and focus on economic needs and attitudes differ markedly from chapter 17 of *The Prince*. Essay 13 lacks Machiavelli's spectacular theme: men must be governed more by cruelty than by humanity, because more by the motive of fear than that of hope. Bacon relies more indirectly than Machiavelli on fear and more directly on hope, while managing both with a show of humanity.

The show of humanity hides a fearsome passage, which few commentators note and fewer weigh. Great politicians are not good but bad by nature, and their humanity is rooted in malice. "Habit" or "disposition" may take some people toward goodness, but nature seems to tend toward "a natural malignity," and the deeper sort of malignancy is inclined to envy and even to "mischief." In "Of Envy" (9), Bacon had said that great envy tends to slander things established; here, in essay 13, he says that "in other men's calamities," the malignant "are, as it were, in season." A bit of complicated prose then makes the big point. These "dispositions are the very errors of human nature"—so deeply does the error of goodness go—"and yet they are the fittest timber to make great politics of; like to knee timber, that is good for ships, that are ordained to be tossed; but not for building houses, that shall stand firm." Bacon is what Richard Hooker called Machiavelli: a "wise malignant." He advances both humanity and malignity, and both have a place in his politics. While humanity has the conspicuous place, malignity is the determining foundation, for "the inconstancy and fluctuations of human life," as Bacon tells us elsewhere, is "as the navigation of the oceans."[10] Malignity accounts for the leader's humanity.

The profoundly evil teaching that barely breaks the surface of essay 13 had appeared as ominous but muffled notes in earlier essays. "He that hath wife and children hath given hostages to fortune; for they are impediments to great enterprises either of virtue or mischief." This despite the fact that "Of Marriage and Single Life" (8) chiefly lays out various advantages of marriage; "wife and children," for example, "are a kind of discipline to humanity." But the advantages are coolly laid out, as if they might serve for social control and thus perhaps for the controller. The essay also says, "A man shall see the noblest works and foundations have proceeded from childless men." More open statements appear outside of the civil *Essays*. The strongest occurs in the *Advancement of Learning*, and precisely in Bacon's thematic discussion of morality. The principal good is "active good," and it proves to be private domination on the grandest scale. It is a "gigantine state of mind" in men "who would have all men happy to unhappy as they were their friends or enemies, and would give form to the world, according to their own humors." This is the true account of even divine power, the "true theomachy," and for such powers humanity and society alike are but tools. "Neither hath this active good any identity with the good of society, though in some case it hath an incidence into it. For although it do many times bring forth acts of beneficence, yet it is with a respect private to a man's own power, glory, amplification, continuance. . . ." This passage concludes with a foggy qualification on behalf of the "good of society," which "we have determined to be the greater."[11]

Essay 13 concludes with a very foggy paragraph that may show how such a man can use the good of society "with a respect private" for his own power. It actually intimates, I think, how Bacon's own gigantic state of mind "determined" upon his plan for a humane society. The topic is what goodness, in its new sense of regard for others' real needs, "shows" about a man. Bacon mentions various aspects (or exhibitions) of goodness, such as courtesy to strangers and compassion toward the afflictions of others, easy pardon and remission of offenses, gratitude for small benefits, and, a boldly nasty rephrasing of "St. Paul's perfection," a "wish to be an *anathema* from Christ for the salvation of his brethren." There follows a very elliptical conclusion. "If a man be gracious and courteous to strangers, it shows he is a citizen of the world, and that his heart is no island cut off from other lands, but a continent that joins to them. If he be compassionate toward the afflictions of others. . . ." I suspect that thus Bacon alludes to the island society of Bensalem, the scientific utopia in *New Atlantis,* where Strangers' House and Salomon's House afford parentlike compassion to the strangers from Christian Europe. He elsewhere calls his comprehensive advancement of science a "citizen of the world."[12] The founder of Bensalem's scientific establishment, Solamona, had laid down the way of dealing with strangers to progress: "join humanity and policy together." While humanity is conspicuous, policy governs. The scientist-father appears compassionate, but it seems a calculated appearance. At least, he has merely "an aspect as if he pitied men."[13]

Like Machiavelli, Bacon seems impressed by Christ's worldly success. Like Machiavelli, he traces the success to Christ's promise of satisfaction, a promise of immortality. Unlike Machiavelli, Bacon can supply an analogous vision of future satisfaction. Not fear but hope, he writes elsewhere, "is the most useful of all the affections."[14] Herein lies the art of management that is the deepest art of the politics of progress. "Certainly, the politic and artificial nourishing and entertaining of hopes, and carrying men from hopes to hopes, is one of the best antidotes against the poison of discontentments" ("Of Seditions and Troubles" 15). Like some other antidotes, it can serve its turn as a poison.

Sedition by Economic Development

Also, as Machiavel noteth well, when princes, that ought to be common parents, make themselves as a party and lean to a side, it is as a boat that is overthrown by uneven weight on the one side; as was well seen in the time of Henry the Third of France, for first himself entered league for the extirpation of the Protestants; and presently after the same league was turned upon himself.

("Of Seditions and Troubles" 15)

Bacon praises Machiavelli for a statement I cannot find in *The Prince* or *Discourses*, and for a neutrality that misses Machiavelli's conspicuous recommendation of princely decisiveness. This essay (15) suggests that great sedition and great authority can come from a teaching that displays the means of satisfaction or at least of hope. Thus, princes might appear as "shepherds of people" (the essay's first words) or like the Aristotelian prime mover (a metaphor for a prince). That is, one can appropriate for one's own glory the roles of benevolent god and mover of nature. The essay shows Bacon's new civil science: the formula for transforming irreconcilable human divisions of class and sect into a mutually useful division of labor and advancement.

There are analogous Machiavellian passages. One should deal with a disunited city by killing or eliminating the leaders of the parties (*Discourses* III, 27); do not remain neutral in wars among your neighbors but take a side and join the war (*Prince*, 21). Each of these blunt counsels is quietly qualified. One suspects Machiavelli of leading on, perhaps over a brink, a preliminary wave of more established (but less Machiavellian) allies. *Discourses* II, 21 and 25, on the other hand, are closer to Bacon's point. A prince dealing with a disunited free city may hold it as a benefactor by being an arbitrator between parties, especially between plebs and nobles. He avoids uniting them and may favor the weaker so as to weaken both. Yet these discourses recommend a prudent adoption of both sides, if only as expedient and to weaken both, and do not obviously deal with religious sects.

Bacon's "Of Seditions and Troubles," by contrast, sets forth a sect, and a sect suited to reduce the dominant sect or sects. It is from start to finish about seditious slanders and envies, which are eventually shown to be products of human speeches. The sign of tempests in states is libels and licentious discourses (*fraudesque* in the Latin saying that Bacon supplies), or females of sedition, as Bacon calls them. He transforms a Virgilian origin of fame, the rebellion of earth against the gods, into the origin of seditions. Sedition is inevitable, perhaps natural, for it is self-assertion against the domination always over men, including the domination by the gods (for the guise of gods is a form of domination by some men's fame). Tempests in states, are greatest when such domination is challenged, "when things grow to equality," as Bacon puts it, and notably when the most honorable, sacred, or authoritative acts of a state "are taken in ill sense, and traduced." That summarizes the challenges that are attempted prior to essay 15. The earlier essays reduce the established hierarchy toward an equality, and reduce to exploitation and illusion the old order's claims of divinity, nobility, truth, and goodness. In the previous essay ("Of Nobility" 14), Bacon pointed out certain "democracies" that do not need a nobility; "utility is their bond, and not respects."

Essay 15 follows its first diagnosis, of sedition by slander, with a first prescription: relax. When confronting alien teachings, a prince ought to avoid "too much severity" and too much "disputing." Is this a pacifier? If Bacon can encourage royal and episcopal passivity in the face of his attacks upon the supports of royalty and religion, he accomplishes sedition under cover of prevention. In the sequel, he notes both that open discords signal that "reverence of government is lost" and that "reverence is that wherewith princes are girt from God." His very topic had already undermined reverence by a fundamental heresy or sedition; the topic is tempests of state, rather than blasphemies against God or treason against king and estates. But how can kings and estates be made so dumb as to be so passive? Bacon will suggest two ways: blandness of speech to veil sedition and economic development to insinuate it.

It is in this context that Bacon's correction of Machiavelli occurs. Machiavelli had guided rulers to expand by war, and those ambitious for rule to advance by hidden war. The discourse on conspiracies (III, 6) is the longest in the *Discourses*, and it turns quickly from defending princes to encouraging conspiracies against princes, often violent conspiracies. It only briefly urges upon princes a doubtful passivity: let them postpone action until they obtain full knowledge.

Bacon writes euphemistically of "seditions and troubles," not of conspiracies, and his demeanor throughout the essay is of a counsellor preventing troubles, not a rebel stirring them up. His counsel is of unity; a prince should be common parent and avoid being a religious partisan. This counsel, nevertheless, would separate kings from their supports, from aristocracy and church. The rest of the essay follows suit. Bacon lists religion, justice, counsel, and treasure as the four "pillars of government," and then sets forth a general diagnosis and "general preservatives" that in effect restructure the old pillars into supports for a new civil order.

He proceeds to discuss the materials, the causes and motives, and the remedies of sedition. The crucial "matter" is neediness, less of the articulate few than of the many, and "discontentment," vaguely stated as "fears." Bacon does not enter upon the justice or injustice of discontents or even their strength: a "prince, or state," should anticipate dangerous forces and inevitable forces. While Machiavelli puts political men in motion through fear of inevitable war, Bacon fosters a vague insecurity and vague hopes for victories in a war on poverty. He quickly acknowledges a long list of "causes and motives" of sedition, and he acknowledges that a "just cure" must answer to the "particular disease." But he sets forth "general preservatives," that is, a general solution that may not solve particular problems of particular states. When Aristotle had analyzed civil strife in the *Politics*, especially enmity between democrats and oligarchies, he recommended different remedies for different regimes and circumstances. Bacon advances a now-familiar revolution in civilization. General preservatives turn out to be the general institutions of a progressive economy and movement, and these can encompass everywhere both the many and the few. Of nine such preservatives, the first four encourage economic growth and regard for democracy, the fifth prescribes "moderate liberty," and the last four prescribe a politic nourishing of hope, especially in ambitious men.

The first preservatives treat "the material cause of sedition" and consist in organizing an economy to conquer "want and poverty in the estate." Bacon waxes enthusiastic in praise of trade, population growth, and manufactures; he attacks idleness and waste. A political agenda surfaces as he attacks "the multiplying of nobility and other degrees of quality," "an overgrown clergy, for they bring nothing to the stock," and an excess of "scholars." He spells out the premise of this attack upon leisurely or pious activities: great industry produces great gains, for "*materiam superabit opus.*" Work is superior to the material, and, the Baconian conclusion, "enricheth a state more." It is a worthy slogan for the political economists to come, as well as for natural scientists bent on conquering nature, and a slogan antipathetic to the leisured classes. Bacon selects as example a democratic republic recently freed from Christian Spain: the low-countrymen have "the best mines above ground in the world."

The third preservative draws another political conclusion. "Above all things" keep the "treasure and monies" of a state from "few hands." The reason is worthy of an investment-oriented Lord Keynes: "money is like muck, not good except it be spread." Machiavelli himself had so praised republics, because free peoples and liberated acquisitiveness encourage growth in wealth and population. According to Bacon's scheme, however, economic growth can be an object of royal patronage and thus a means to republics. A growing middle class and a corresponding democratization can evolve as if by chance, and, thus, reformers can avoid the risks of war. Bacon rarely mentions democracies or republics and discusses the possibility of warring for liberty only with the greatest reticence (29).

This, despite his clear awareness that the breakup of the old empire, Spanish or Christian, will occasion great wars (58). Why risk the dangers of war when economic development will do much of the transformation of the world? This plan for insinuating sedition is elaborated in later and thematically economic essays, which we discuss in chapter 10. They nourish new parties, such as the self-made men, entrepreneurs, investors, financiers, and the like, who can shoulder aside the old regime, and who will advance themselves and their new order without losing their dependence on the mutual system of exchange and on the middle class.

Preservatives four through nine deal with "removing discontentments" other than poverty. The fourth quietly advances on political grounds the antiaristocratic policy: in strife between "noblesse, and commonalitie," the few are chiefly to blame. This shows "how safe it is" for monarchs to seek "the good will of the common people." The remaining five preservatives are stated quickly and elliptically, perhaps because their bent to overturn, rather than preserve, is otherwise hard to hide. "Moderate liberty" is the central prescription, the fifth, and it modifies Bacon's preliminary elevation of democracy. The moderation comes largely, according to the sixth recommendation, from a management of hope. "And it is a certain signe, of a wise government, and proceeding, when it can hold men's hearts by hopes, when it cannot by satisfaction, and when it can handle things, in such manner, as no evil shall appear so peremptory, but that it hath some outlet of hope."

The last preservatives deal with managing the hope of a prince. Bacon slips from preventing unity of the hopeful beneath an enemy of the state, to avoiding sharp speeches that cut off the hopes of followers for their own dictatorships or places, to a prince's need for a valiant defender. The prose is terse, and the final point shows that Bacon fundamentally follows Machiavelli in understanding his crusade as a war. "Princes" need a "military person" who can repress seditions against "the state" and keep correspondence with "other great men in the state." What does this mean? I suspect that Bacon is that "great person" who will defend new princes and their secular states. He is a shepherd of peoples who can fight: he can aid enlightened kings with speeches like the ensuing essays (16, 17), which take on Christianity under cover of a skirmish with atheism and superstition. Bacon thus keeps enemies of the new order, such as nobles, kings, and followers of ancient philosophy, from uniting beneath the old regime. The theologian of Anglicanism, Richard Hooker, had sought such a Christian Aristotelian England in the 1590s, and Archbishop Laud eventually went a long way, even to his death, in imposing it. Whatever his tactics as general of liberation from the old order, Bacon keeps unity within his progressive sect. He keeps up "correspondence" with leaders of a like state of mind, including great scientists, enlightened kings, and followers of comprehensive chiefs such as Machiavelli.

In "Of Followers and Friends" (48), Bacon presents a crucial saying of Machiavelli as an example of the advice to be taken from friends. Yet Machiavelli's sharp speeches had driven away many whom Bacon's project can satisfy, advance, and keep in hope. Immediately after taking Machiavelli's advice, Bacon concludes that friendship is only between "superior and inferior, whose fortunes may comprehend, the one the other." Bacon means to comprehend Machiavelli's militant crusade within his own engaging project of progress.

Custom as Regulated Opportunity

> And therefore, as Machiavel well noteth (though in an evil-favored instance), there is no trusting to the force of nature nor to the bravery of words, except it be corroborate by custom. His instance is, that for the achieving of a desperate conspiracy, a man should not rest upon the fierceness of any man's nature, or his resolute undertakings; but take such an one as hath had his hands formerly in blood. But Machiavelli knew not of a Friar Clement, nor a Ravillac, nor a Jauregay, nor a Baltazar Gerard; yet his rule holdeth still that nature, nor the engagement of words, are not so forcible as custom.
>
> ("Of Custom and Education" 39)

The third reference to Machiavelli by name is the first to criticize Machiavelli explicitly. It is not a prince's impiety and immorality that Bacon criticizes, but the inefficacy of bloody impiety and immorality. Bloody conspiracies are not said to be evil; they are, however, "desperate." In welcoming assassins as a matter of course, rather than as a desperate measure, Machiavelli had underestimated the power of otherworldly assassins. The four that Bacon names were all Catholic assassins of politic kings. Friar Clement, for example, murdered the politic Henry III of France, the very king Bacon mentioned in essay 15 when he used a similar "noteth well" to criticize a policy of siding with a sect. Nevertheless, Bacon approves Machiavelli's general rule as to the force of custom. Still, Machiavelli erred about the force of devotion, and therefore about the power of custom, a consequence of his error about the force of hope.

In his quick and quiet way, Bacon has involved us in one of the nastiest passages of a writer known for nastiness. Machiavelli calls not exactly for different customs, but for men tried or experienced (*isperimentati*) in bloody deeds. Murdering a revered man, especially a religious man, is difficult; it is hard to be so bad or altogether bad. The context is again the discussion of conspiracies in *Discourses*, III, 6. Since even accustomed killers are often bewildered by the "majesty" and "reverence" of some great target, the job requires men "experienced" in such murders. Machiavelli has more in mind, namely, accustoming men by speech. People may become experienced or accustomed by ruthless words about bloody deeds, but the words must be shrewdly chosen so as not to alarm. Machiavelli's writings, which advise alike republican conspirators and tyrants, will help and harden the variety of followers to come, not least in overcoming an otherworldly empire.

Bacon fears superstition more than does Machiavelli and hopes for more from his special replacement, the prediction of progress. His fear and hope reflect a greater estimate of the power of custom. He seems to describe "nature in men" as but body with passion or force (38, immediately before "Of Custom and Education"); it may be the same as the universal nature described in the Plan for the *Great Instauration* and in the *New Organon*. If so, all that appears distinctly human is wholly invented, including speech or reason. If our deeds are not products of impulse, they are but the effect of custom or of someone's invention. In *Advancement of Learning*, Bacon explicitly offers a larger estimate of custom's power than Aristotle's (II, xxii, 8), and the ambiguous beginning to "Of Custom and Education" implies as much: "Men's thoughts are much according to their inclination; their discourse and speeches according to their learning and infused opinions; but their deeds are after as they have been accustomed."

The problem is how to institute suitable customs, and Bacon's solution is society. It was a problem that Machiavelli had not solved. Bacon follows his criticism of Machiavelli thus: "superstition is now so well advanced, that men of the first blood are as firm as butchers." Five examples of custom's "reign or tyranny" follow, all examples of disdain by the religious for even their own deaths. Bacon reduces religious disputation and zealotry to a discussion of custom. While other essays prescribe what customs are useful, essay 39 indicates chiefly how to make them effective. Start young, and rely on mutual interaction, that is, on what we call "society." Bacon may originate our usage. Effective custom, he tells us, is "custom copulate and conjoined and collegiate," because "there example teacheth, company comforteth, emulation quickeneth, glory raiseth." After perhaps hinting at the secrets of the church (and of the roots of goodness), Bacon dwells on the role of "societies well ordained and disciplined." Governments and commonwealths depend on seeds otherwise planted. What societies Bacon has in mind are left obscure in this essay, except for an implicit dig at the churches: "the most effectual means are now applied to the ends least to be desired."

One suspects that Bacon wishes to replace churches by associations for gain: businesses. In various places, *Essays* commends merchants, manufacturers, and financiers, and certainly the word "business" recurs incessantly. This suspicion is strengthened by *New Atlantis*, in which a Jewish merchant is the most prominent civil figure among the very organized and very disciplined Bensalemites. Discipline may follow more easily if the association is for mutual utility. Nevertheless, the essays on custom (39), making one's fortune (40), and economic science (41) say little about companies or enterprises. What association, then, is based on wary and anxious neediness ("Of Superstition" 17), is rather democratic and has the bond of utility ("Of Nobility" 14), and fosters a self-reliant opportunism? Bacon, I suggest, advances businesses less than a world of business. Businesses can discipline us in a world of business, in what we know as civil society. If this is true, then much of Bacon's reformulation of religion, ethics, economics, and politics is designed to produce what we often take for granted. Much artifice and governance is involved in the production of modern society.

The chief opinion to be infused into social custom is that of self-reliance, that the mold of a man's fortune is in his own hands ("Of Fortune" 40). Self-reliance should be customary; not providence but providing for oneself is the magistrate for the self. Bacon had intimated as much when he transformed "goodness" (13). In essay 40, he elaborates the difference between his self-reliance and any sense of goodness. A number of "virtues, or rather faculties and customs," make men fortunate, and two are crucial: do not be too devoted to country or master, do not place one's thoughts too far outside oneself. Like Machiavelli, Bacon replaces virtue with ability to succeed. Unlike Machiavelli, he encourages customs that do not scandalize, and do not lead toward wars that the politiques are likely to lose. His customs have "a slide and easiness," as "Of Fortune" puts it, and a slide and easiness that can be quite easily regulated. Bacon's teachings come home to men's business as well as their bosoms.

In two essays that follow Bacon explores the systematic connections between individualism and businesslike society. One connection is the art or science of economics, and "Of Usury" (41) shows how the author of such an art can advance himself by showing a society how to advance itself. It begins by rebutting seven religious and moral arguments against lending at interest. The rebuttal is an argument from the "necessities" of borrowing and lending. The account of necessity is in fact an invention, for Bacon proceeds to "invent" the disadvantages and advantages of lending at interest—strictly from the viewpoint of economic progress. Among the disadvantages are the damping of "industries, improvements and new inventions"; among the advantages are the encouragement of "young merchants" and of "industrious and profitable improvements." Before our eyes, yet with a slide and easiness that come from transforming a necessity into a priority, Bacon overturns moral and religious distaste for moneylenders and invents a comprehensive art for directing the customs for civil society.

"Of Youth and Age" (42), which follows, shows how such a society will channel different temperaments through diverse vocations, that is, "compound employments." The young commonly will shine on the inventive side, the older as executives or managers. Some young may be judicious before their time—Bacon's examples are generals and emperors—but he confines himself to supposing that "heat and vivacity in age is an excellent composition for business." While both he and Machiavelli praise young over old, Bacon is more reserved; his economic society is more stodgy, more "of settled business" than of daring military exploits. Accordingly, Bacon favors the young not as combative but as inventive and open to "new projects" and "new things." This openness may be gullibility: "for the moral part" the young are superior, as are the older for "the politic." His example: "your young shall see visions" rather than merely dream. There will be a division of labor between young visionaries and older executives. Perhaps the new project of progress, as portrayed in the visionary half-light of *New Atlantis*, is designed especially to channel the adventurous young. The Europeans in the story left from the far edge of the known world and were prepared to sail for a year over uncharted seas. Conquering nature and the earth may avoid the danger of more bloody conquests.

States and States of Learning

> As for the observation that Machiavel hath, that the jealousy of sects doth much extinguish the memory of things; traducing Gregory the Great that he did what in him lay to extinguish all heathen antiquities; I do not find that those zeals do any great effects, nor last long; as it appeared in the succession of Sabinian, who did revive the former antiquities.
>
> ("Of Vicissitude of Things" 58)

The fourth and last reference to Machiavelli, and the second criticism, occurs in the culminating essay. The criticism distances Bacon from Machiavelli's impiety and name, while tacitly confirming his own more respectable name. There is less here than meets the eye, and yet what there is indicates a real difference. To visionary humanitarianism, a war on poverty, and discipline by socialization, Bacon adds in essay 58 the key to his new movement, a science that promises progress in power.

Bacon appears in the lists of opinion as defender of Pope Gregory the Great against Machiavellian slanders. The defense barely exists when closely viewed, and is, in any event, misleading. He defends Christianity's efficacy for empire, not its truth, and defends it as a sect, again tacitly denying its claim to be the one and Catholic faith. He defends a pope (while not defending the ecclesiastical name), after having heretofore favored the Protestants. He fundamentally defends Christianity's weakness in dealing with its predecessors, and by dignifying one Sabinian (also a pope whom Bacon deprives of the name) for saving things of a former sect. Actually, this pope seems best known for introducing the ringing of bells at canonical hours and for celebration of the eucharist; the Latin *Essays* indicates that his alleged "revival" of antiquities was but the creeping out of things forbidden. Like Machiavelli, Bacon is silent about the Renaissance popes' patronage of Greek and Roman philosophy and art. In effect, Bacon adopts Machiavelli's treatment of Christianity in *Discourses* II, 5, except for adding a fraudulent retraction that itself mirrors Machiavelli's hints about the impotence of the unarmed conqueror. Besides, after a two-paragraph intermission, Bacon asserts what is close to the Machiavellian statement that he has just questioned: "The greatest vicissitude of things amongst men, is the vicissitude of sects and religions. For these orbs rule in men's minds most." What is going on in this little woods of contradiction and half-light?

To begin with, the paragraphs between dubious correction and imitative paraphrase contain a serious correction of Machiavelli. Machiavelli overestimated Christianity's disposition to transform an old sect, and he underestimated its capacity to be transformed into a new sect. Bacon's correction is a new science that can be presented as leading by regular progress to a new heaven on earth. Like Machiavelli's political science, Bacon's natural science is part of a sect to rule the world. The sequel discusses the fundamental science, which is the political science of causing "new sects."

The first of these intervening paragraphs is studded with "I's." It shows how to learn causes of useful effects, rather than alleged causes of an allegedly eternal nature. There are allusions to Plato's supposition of natural cycles and to Aristotle's prime mover. Bacon shows himself observing useful causes and effects and then generalizing about them. In such generalizations will be found the true prime for man, the prime that essay 15 intimated: man can move nature for his benefit. He can predict floods, for example, and control some of their effects. The first advantage of Bacon's correction is a power to influence natural vicissitudes, a power absent from Machiavelli's project.

Yet Bacon grants that human sects, not natural disasters, are the decisive causes of oblivion. But for this purpose, too, his way is an improvement, since the art of prediction affords a tool for manipulating hope, a tool that Machiavelli lacked. Elsewhere, Bacon remarks that kings seek "toys" to provide against an incessant fear that their fame will not endure; he illustrates with arts or feats "of the hand" ("Of Empire" 19). In essay 58, he suggests a "toy" that is an art or feat of the mind. In another work, Bacon shows prominent persons relying on astronomy as "fortune-teller"; he discredits reliance on such "toys."[15] But Bacon's art of prediction and invention can really master fortune, and can thus engage the patronage of both the prominent and the learned.

These two paragraphs are directed to those tempted by the old learning (as are such works as the *Advancement of Learning*, *De Augmentis*, and the *New Organon*). As a growing nation-state attracts the statesman, progress in useful science will attract the studious. Bacon provides an easy channel for those who might otherwise fall for the charms of philosophy or theology.

The big lesson of these two paragraphs is that the advancement of science will bring advancement of the scientist; the quieter lesson is that it will advance the honor of Bacon himself. Serving humanity, the scientist can benefit himself. In Bensalem, the Fathers of Salomon's House obtain extraordinary reverence, and their inventions may earn them not only a liberal and honorable monetary reward, but also a statue, which may be of a degree of richness ranging up to gold.[16] Bacon plans for Nobel prizes. But the scientists do have to serve, that is, to research and to apply their research. They work at the great laboratories; they periodically bestow inventions and "natural divinations of diseases, plagues," and the like. The new science is the scientist's power to serve, and by so empowering the scientists, Bacon can lead.

Bacon took care to put his chief books in the language of the learned; Machiavelli did not, except for chapter titles. Even the English version of the *Essays* is stuffed with Latin quotations; the bar to the unlearned is a toy to the learned. While Bacon helps Machiavelli contribute to the oblivion of the Greek language, he insinuates himself into the power of Latin. In his ironic dedication, he assures the Duke of Buckingham that "the

Latin volume" of the *Essays*, being in "the universal language," may last as long "as books last"—longer than an English kingdom and its dukes.

It is very difficult to compare the remainder of essay 58, on the science of sects, to the corresponding Machiavellian discourse, *Discourses* II, 5.[17] Both are among their authors' most cryptic writings, probably because in both, shocking statements cover more shocking intimations. The fruit of Bacon's meditations, I shall argue, is a sect composed of various civil states, advancing and declining in turn, that harbor separately the progressive and semiautonomous movement devoted to useful science.[18]

Machiavelli's discourse on sect production is, as usual, more nearly direct in title and text. The title: "That changes of sects and languages, together with the accident of floods and plagues, destroy the memories of things" (II, 5). At the start of his argument Machiavelli confronts expressly "the philosophers' " contention as to the eternity of the world. Bacon allows this contention to appear only in quotations from Seneca, Plato, and, a nasty cut, an abstruse astrologer who reads rather like Aristotle. He finally confutes Plato, however, twice and expressly. Contrary to Plato, and like Machiavelli, Bacon maintains that immortality must be made or conquered. For there is nothing relevant to man's immortality that is immortal in nature. "Certain it is, that the matter is in a perpetual flux, and never at a stay."

Like Machiavelli, Bacon touches primarily upon floods as the chief cause of oblivion. He omits from this biblically significant attribution a Machiavellian jibe, that some survivor might conceal the past to get a reputation and name. More interesting, his account rebuts a myth from Plato's *Timaeus* blaming the sun, and an account from the Old Testament blaming fires. Instances of floods in the "West Indies" follow, in a way that alludes to the Americas ("their Andes"), asserts the inhabitants to be "a newer or a younger people," and alludes to the Atlantis that the *Timaeus* describes. Elliptical indeed. Can a coherent message be discerned?

Bacon seems both to be rebutting old myths that have a supernatural tint, myths set forth by his rivals for empire over the mind, Plato and the Bible, and to be indicating a new myth that promotes belief in his project. While he turns to observations, to what might be examined in a particular place and topography, his purpose is to imagine what might newly be accomplished.

There are uncanny parallels with the imaginary *New Atlantis*. A Bensalemite official, dealing with Christian Europeans, tells a broadly similar tale of flood and surviving mountaineers, similar down to "West Indies," equated with "America," which is inhabited by a "young people."[19] This official explicitly calls "poetical and fabulous" the divine or religious features of Plato's Atlantis. The whole drama of the *New Atlantis* rebuts the biblical drama: Christian Europeans are shown converting to faith in a land of progress. The official, an enlightened priest, rejects any implications that "magicians" or "spirits of the air," even "angelical" ones, are responsible for Bensalem's artfulness. The origin of Bensalem lies not in a divinely guided golden age but in an ancient time of great commercial and naval empires. The world to look to is the earthly world of power politics, the world set forth in "Of the True Greatness of Kingdoms and Estates" (29).

The *New Atlantis* indicates, I think, Bacon's strategy for spreading his worldly sect. The Atlantis of the title is America. The text conflates curiously the empire of Atlantis-America with those of Mexico and Peru, and this indicates, I suggest, that a variety of states may exist in one new world. Bacon's ways will be humane to the lands it conquers. This is symbolized by the victory of King Altabin, whose mixture of ingenuity and humanity is not easy to interpret as a feat of real generalship. Like "a wise man and a great warrior," he handled the enemies of Atlantis, "so as to cut off their land-forces from their ships; and entoil both their navy and their camp with a greater power than theirs, both by sea and land." Might this symbolize Bacon's mode of conquering his political-spiritual rival, Christian Spain, whose forces in Europe and America carry the spiritual empire? Could Bacon possibly be alluding to British navies on the seas and expanding British plantations in the New World? Essay 29 urges a naval power; essay 33, industrious plantations. If these reasonings are correct, then Bacon plans a way that Christendom may eventually surrender its real power without a real battle. The appeals of progress might undermine the old spirituality even within its Spanish homeland. In that case, the father of enlightenment could content himself, as did Altabin, "only with their oath that they should no more bear arms against him," dismissing them all in safety. This is a strategy of combined forces, a combination of not only sea with land forces but also of the new civil forces, which the *Essays* summons forth, with the new humane vision, which the *New Atlantis* propounds. Essay 58 comprehends the combination, and it intimates wars involving the Spanish-Christian combination.[20]

Essay 58 concludes with Bacon's greatest policy. The last counsel of the counsels civil and moral prescribes formulas for producing new sects, albeit under cover of formulas for a "stay" to such "revolutions." This is the Machiavellian science of averting oblivion from the most powerful selves, and it is the greatest science. In turn, Bacon discusses three conditions that are appropriate for the rise or founding of new sects, two

necessary properties and then a third, and three manners of "plantations."

The three properties of a successful sect are opposition to existing authority, provision of license to pleasure, and—if "speculative heresies"—
the "help of civil occasions." Bacon's new sect, like Machiavelli's, will
oppose existing authority. Like Machiavelli, Bacon removes the traditional moral restraints or virtues, although for a liberty more moderated
by business than *Mandragola* and *Clizia* portend. Like Machiavelli's sect,
Bacon's is comprehensively planned and not merely antiestablishment and
licentious. Indeed, Bacon's is more attuned to speculation or learning. Yet
such a sect can spread if linked with a civil movement. Works such as the
Essays are to produce the civil movement of expanding nation-states,
modernizing plantations, and so forth.

In essay 58, Bacon has a more comprehensive type of plantation in
mind. Of the three methods of founding, he treats coolly "signs and miracles"; here as always he appears one of the "great atheists," ever handling "holy things, but without feeling" ("Of Atheism" 16). He treats
almost invisibly the second means, "by the eloquence and wisdom of
speech and persuasion." Yet there is deep policy in his recommendation
that new sects and schisms be stopped through reform, fostering agreement, and mildness, and "rather to take off the principal authors by winning and advancing them than to enrage them by violence and bitter-
ness." This preservative would transform a struggle over creed into a plan
of tolerance and of opportunity. It is his general strategy for civil society.

Behind the counsel of moderation, then, is a strategy of war. Virtually
the whole remainder of the essay is about war, and Bacon shows his followers the strategy by which a new civilization can conquer. A little sign:
he substitutes the comprehensive term "war" for his first description of
the third means, "the sword." This war is conducted in good part by
"eloquence and wisdom in speech and persuasion." It will be largely a
war of ideas.

Bacon appears to expect to contrive with words a rise by the northern
powers (perhaps including North America), a rise in wealth, numbers,
and power. Cold weather makes "the bodies hardest, and the courages
warmest"; yet he notes the difference that "discipline" makes. Wars will
follow the fall or rise of a great state and empire (Spain is his last example), and when a state grows to a great overpopulation, it is sure to overflow. The "ancient northern people" did. We recall that Bacon plans
many ways to increase population, and not least by what he mentions
here, growth in "means of life and sustentation." Will modern northern

peoples increase, forcing some to overflow into colonies abroad, or perhaps into the Catholic countries of southern Europe?

Abruptly, Bacon notes that rich states tend to become soft and vulnerable, whereupon he turns to the effect of weapons and technology upon military strength. Does he imply that a civilization devoted to increasing power can with new weapons overcome warlike barbarians? Perhaps. It is hard to say. The argument here grows more strange and abstract. One wonders whether this discussion of artillery, like Machiavelli's in *Discourses* II, 17, is actually about how to spike and redirect the canons and big guns of the church. The sequel intimates the use of a strategy of simulation and dissimulation. Warfare of old was waged more by peoples and now is more by "number rather competent than vast"; it relies on planning, cunning, and skill, rather than force of numbers.

In Bacon's next and last step, he turns from the rise and fall of nations to the rise and fall of learning. Even an enlightened political state will fall as well as rise, especially when "mechanical arts and merchandise" replace the arms of its youth, the learning of its middle age, and the union of the two. Does this mean that the economic cast of Baconian states, the prominence given to merchants, the soft affluence portrayed in Bensalem, are causes of eventual downfall? Bacon shows himself aware that growth will slacken and industrious people soften, when affluence arrives and necessity is considerably overcome. But he turns toward a further type of empire, of "learning." One state of learning can exist in a variety of civil states. In Bensalem, both the ordinary father who is regulated by a governor, and the scientist-father who keeps secrets from state institutions, appear beneath a "cloth of state."[21] There can be a variety of enlightened and progressive nation-states, rising and then declining while all embrace the state of progress.

Yet Bacon indicates in essay 58 that even the sect of enlightenment will be finite. Learning too has an infancy, a youth, a strength of years, an old age. It too may become "dry and exhaust." Probably Bacon alludes to his own science established and progressing, to science developed and applied. The essay had earlier intimated an uncertainty whether "the world should last." Bacon knows of limits to progress, even of his own progress in enduring. At this point, he counsels averting the eyes from such "turning wheels of vicissitude," lest they make us "giddy." Yet he tells us that he himself eschews tales of cycles or other names. He is steadfast in making his empire and himself endure, even while knowing that he cannot do enough. If my argument has been accurate, Bacon's steadfastness produced an effectual plan for our progress.

Notes

1. Zera Fink contended that Machiavelli himself merely advocates the old mixed government set forth by Aristotle, Polybius, and Cicero [*The Classical Republicans* (Evanston, Ill.: Northwestern University Press, 1962), 10–21]. But her argument simply ignores the obvious differences. It neglects the difference between Machiavelli's recommendation of an expanding and rather democratic empire (for security abroad and managing faction within), and the ancient republicans' characteristic preference for a small and at least partially aristocratic city (which Machiavelli condemned from the start, as in *Discourses* I, 2, 5). Machiavelli's imperial republic sets passions of fear, gain, and ambition into managed conflict, whereas the ancient republicans' mixed regime is attuned in part to differences of ethical character. Machiavelli dwells on the importance to republics of ruthless executives and aggressive generalships; Aristotle, Cicero, Polybius, do not. In short, while the ancient political science took the good life seriously even when it was politically impractical (Aristotle's political science pairs the *Politics* with a *Nicomachean Ethics*), Machiavelli questions as ineffectual any serious orientation by morality or philosophy and is a master of the arts of force and fraud (he pairs the republican *Discourses* with *The Prince*).

According to J. G. A. Pocock, Machiavelli and his fellow Florentine intellectuals advanced an Aristotelian account of the "political nature of man" under special Christian circumstances that denied the possibility of secular fulfillment, and the result was a participatory and public-spirited "civic" humanism that is essentially classicism although not a simple classicism [*The Machiavellian Moment* (Princeton: Princeton University Press, 1975); my discussion fixes on pp. vii–x and 156–218]. While Pocock only mentions the core of this refurbished "Hellenic mind"—items such as "balanced government," "dynamic virtue," and "the role of arms and property" in shaping the civic "personality"—he dwells on the epochal achievement of a "Machiavellian moment," which gave to a whole "Atlantic" tradition a civic republicanism that is able to counterbalance individualistic capitalism. But Pocock's attempt at a civic and moral interpretation of *Prince* and *Discourses* is silent as to Machiavelli's crucial critique of "imaginary" republics and principalities and of an orientation by what is thought good instead of what is necessary (*The Prince*, chapter 15), and silent also as to Machiavelli's corresponding legitimation of private acquisitiveness: "it is a very natural and ordinary thing to desire to acquire"; and only if men fail are they to be accused of "error and blame" (chapter 3). Precisely "dynamic" *virtu*, Machiavelli's liberation of ambition and avarice, is incompatible with the Aristotelianism that Pocock attributes to him— the thesis that moral and civic restraints are natural to man. It is compatible with capitalistic versions of individualism. Also, Pocock continually ascribes an "ideal" of active citizen participation to a thinker who advocates a republic that mixes peoples and elites so as to protect opportunities for individual striving. Finally, Pocock is silent about or explains away Machiavelli's advice to princes on how to acquire, destroy, or make use of a republic.

2. *Advancement of Learning* II, xxi, 9, ed. Wright; *Works* VI, 327; III, 430.

3. Tr. Harvey C. Mansfield, Jr. (Chicago and London: University of Chicago Press, 1985), 61.

4. "Bacon's Humanitarian Revision of Machiavelli," unpublished paper, 1983, 2. Spinoza's praise in the unfinished *Political Treatise* (chapter 5, end), to which my attention was called by Daniel Gallagher, was published posthumously.

5. Edwin Abbott, "The Latest Theory about Bacon," *Contemporary Review* 28 (1876), 141–68, and *Francis Bacon, An Account of His Life and Works* (London: Macmillan & Co., 1885), 457–60; N. Orsini, *Bacone e Machiavelli* (Genova: E. degli Orfini, 1936), 9; see also Felix Raab, *The English Face of Machiavelli* (London and Toronto: Routledge & Kegan Paul, University of Toronto Press, 1964), 73–76; Jonathan Marwil, *The Trials of Counsel* (Detroit: Wayne State University Press, 1976); and works previously mentioned: White, *Peace among the Willows*; Rossi, *Francis Bacon*; and Quinton, *Francis Bacon*.

6. *Francis Bacon and His Times* (Boston: Houghton, Mifflin & Co., 1878); cf. "The Latest Theory about Bacon," *Contemporary Review* 27 (1875–76), 653–78, and Abbott's reply, same title and journal, vol. 28, 141–68. Fowler's reply to Abbott contains nothing beyond Spedding's; *Bacon's Novum Organum*, xiii–xviii.

7. Alan Gilbert, ed. and tr., *Machiavelli, The Chief Works and Others* (Durham: Duke University Press, 1965), 3 vol., vol. I. I occasionally translate from *Il Principe e Discorsi*, ed. Sergio Bertelli (Milano: Feltrinelli Editore, 1960).

8. *Peace among the Willows*, 17–39, 42, 197. See also Kennington, "Bacon's Humanitarian Revision of Machiavelli," 7–12; J. Weinberger, *Science, Faith, and Politics, Francis Bacon and the Utopian Roots of the Modern Age* (Ithaca: Cornell University Press: 1985), 17–39.

9. Clifford Orwin, "Machiavelli's UnChristian Charity," *American Political Science Review* 72 (1978), 1217–28.

10. "Promethus; or the State of Man," in *Of the Wisdom of the Ancients*, in *Works* XIII, 154; VI, 752. See chapter 7 in this volume.

11. *Advancement* II, xxi, 1, ed. Wright; *Works* VI, 319; III, 424–25.

12. In a letter to the heir to the throne, 1623, reprinted in James Spedding, ed., *The Letters and the Life of Francis Bacon* (London: Longman, Green, Longman, and Roberts, 1874), VII, 436–37. I owe the reference to Michael Kiernan, ed., *Essayes or Counsels*, 200.

13. In an earlier work that Bacon left unpublished, the point is explicit. A philosopher addressing an international convention of sages shows a face that "had become habituated to the expression of pity. [*Refutation of Philosophies*, tr. Benjamin Farrington, in *The Philosophy of Francis Bacon* (Chicago: University of Chicago Press, 1964), 104]. Paoli Rossi suggests that Bacon never published this pungent little piece because he had yet to master the envelopment of daring plans in the mantle of traditon and the half-light of insinuation (*Francis Bacon, From Magic to Science*, 88–97).

14. *Historiae Vitae et Mortis*, para. 90, in *Works* III (Boston, 1864), 426; in *Works* (London, 1861) II, 172.

15. *History of the Reign of King Henry VII*, in *Works* XI, 319; VI, 213–14.

16. *New Atlantis*, ed. Alfred B. Gough (Oxford: Clarendon Press, 1924), 46–47.

17. I have been helped here as elsewhere by Harvey Mansfield's *Machiavelli's New Modes and Orders* (Ithaca and London: Cornell University Press, 1979).

18. Howard White investigated Bacon's advocacy of an "imperialism of the human mind" that wins by "subversion." He also inferred that Bacon's universal science calls for a "world community" or "world state"; the evidence is Bensalem's humane hospitality and the absence of political coercion, aggressive commerce, and imperialism. Yet White acknowledges that *New Atlantis* hints at a pervasive hidden state, at mercantile power, at new and terrible weapons, and at industrial and scientific espionage to build up Bensalem at the expense of other countries (*Peace among the Willows*, 230–39, 243–50). Is it possible that an imperial state will overcome the world of independent nation-states, as Richard Kennington suggests? "World utopia is imposed by imperial power" ("Bacon's Humanitarian Revision of Machiavelli," 14–26, n. 40). Yet Bacon reduces humanitarianism to a policy for domination and empire, in essay 13, and no one has shown a Baconian writing that prescribes world government or world community.

19. The quotations in this and the next paragraph occur in *New Atlantis*, ed. Gough, 16–25.

20. A reader may well wonder whether such scattered and allusive references to Atlantis amount to a Baconian plan for world empire. To the reasonings in the text, one can add that there there are similar allusions elsewhere, and they too are hard to explain otherwise.

The bizarre "Of Prophecies" (35) contains the only other reference in the *Essays* to Atlantis or at least to Plato's "Atlanticus." It intimates that a philosopher may act the poet ("Seneca the Tragedian") to provide "natural predictions" of disease and floods, which are the "divinations" for which human nature hungers. The phrase reminds of the scientists in Bacon's poetic Bensalem; during their circuits they bestow "natural divinations" of diseases and floods. The end of the essay recurs to Seneca's alleged prophecy, in his *Medea*, of new worlds, which Bacon interprets as a prophecy of the discovery of America. He takes care to dwell on the rational causes of such a prophecy: the fact that land lay beyond the Atlantic might be demonstrated, and "the tradition in Plato's *Timaeus* and *Atlanticus*" (Bacon even misnames the *Critias*, as if to bring out his own scheme). These books of Plato encouraged Seneca to invent a "prediction." Bacon makes Seneca appear to do for Plato what the poet and philosopher Bacon did for himself. He made a *New Atlantis* that predicted new worlds in America, and its clothing of powerful science with a visionary form helped to make the prediction effectual.

"Of Prophecies" indicates the art beneath Bacon's renovation of prophecy. By the end of a catalog of some fourteen foolishnesses, Bacon has discredited heathen oracles, divine prophecies ("in the East," of "Judea," etc.), and ancient predictions, which in hands like Seneca's are no better than prophecy. The account moves from prophecy in Greece and Rome to modern kings and empires and the Spanish Armada (the only subject of two prophecies, the last two), which was "the greatest in strength" of any fleet ever. Catholic Spain remains, the great empire and the great vehicle of Christ's empire, and Bacon's last accounts of prophecy are his predictions of danger from Spanish expansionism.

An allusion of comparable obscurity occurs in the *History of the Reign of King Henry VII*. Bacon singles out as a "memorable accident" John Cabot's discoveries in North America, and he praises the explorer for following other sailors, rather than prior "conjectures," such as "Seneca's prophecies," or Plato's antiquities (*Works* XI, 293–94; VI, 196–97). Could such a likeness to "Of Prophecies" be mere coincidence? The *History* clearly encourages English kings to patronize "the discovery and investing of unknown lands," particularly the lands of North America. While Bacon praises Henry VII for "dexterity" in confronting immediate dangers, he tasks him for lacking "providence to prevent and remove [dangers] afar off." Bacon seems to insinuate his own providence as tacit remedy for a defect noted in Henry but never remedied. The account of Cabot's discoveries occurs expressly out of chronological order and as memorable. It is immediately after the king's defeat of Perkin Warbeck, who was the latest in a line of pretenders whom Bacon presents as magical or supernatural idols. The Baconian substitute would turn affections away from supernatural remedies, and it appears as instrument, not enemy, to the king's unending desire for security of state.

21. *Works* V, 587, 397; III, 148, 156.

Part II

Self, Society, and Domination: Reconsidering Baconian Individualism

For when a man placeth his thoughts without himself, he goeth not his own way.

("Of Fortune" 40)

Chapter 4

The Self-Made Man

Bacon and the Varieties of Individualism

While Francis Bacon is best known as a proponent of modern science, he also formulated a famous version of individualism, the doctrine central to modern politics. It is not easy to articulate the relation between scientific rationalism and the enterprising self. In this Part II, I spell out the essentially Machiavellian relation that was outlined in the previous chapter. A radical individualism is basic, and humane science follows from a rethinking of human ends and needs. The Baconian rethinking discovers a needy self that must make its own provision to the point of making its own world; the rethinking consists of critique and construction. Skepticism about morality, philosophy, and divinity is combined with construction of the arts of the self-made man, that is, the man of ability who can manage himself and others into the power that will preserve him and them. This outlook governs not only Bacon's applications of his new science, but also its end, human power, and the type of knowledge that it seeks, laws of operation or production.

After suggesting the relevance of Bacon's thoughts to contemporary reconsiderations of individualism, I turn in this chapter to expound the essentials. Bacon replaces guidance supposedly above the self, be it divinity or natural inclination, with management of passion and image for the sake of long-term interests. We are to act not for the good but for future satisfaction of our chief passion. Nevertheless, private interest requires public policy and, in particular, a public persona as an image to win followers. Bacon was aware of the singularity of his moral and political theory, and chapter 5 considers his rebuttal of what he regarded as *the* philosophic alternative. He rejects the priority that Socrates gave to wisdom and love and that Aristotle gave to politics and friendship. According to Bacon, the effectual truth of wisdom is policy; of love, gain; of friendship, followers; and of politics, a political-economic nation-state for the mutual business of leaders and followers. The culminating image for a man is the topic of chapter 6, the last of this part. A new-model Caesar is to blend civil supports with promises of humane benefactions.

The proposals just summarized are in many ways more revealing than what is often supposed the *locus classicus* of individualism, the writings of Thomas Hobbes. Hobbes may be blunter and clearer, but these advantages are achieved at the price of doctrinairism. Hobbes excludes goods that men might share, such as friendship, and reduces noble inclinations to bodily forces. Bacon at least takes care to deploy moral and religious scruples, and, if he, too, intimates a foundation in amoral forces, a reader can see the things given up and the reasons for giving them up. Besides, Hobbes is inconsistently soft. He adds a kind of justice, a right to flee death, to the passion that he announces as dominant, the revulsion from death. If this produces a more decent and liberal doctrine, it also introduces an inconsistency, and it obscures somewhat the original and harsh premises. Also, while Hobbes's insistence on equality and bodily preservation is dogmatically narrow, Bacon allows for the glory and the visionary plans that go with superior selves.

Above all, Bacon clarifies the paradox of individualism that Hobbes tends to leave in a dogmatic dark: how private interest can be managed to serve public interest. While Hobbes's blunt insistence on sovereign force is balanced by a blunt insistence on a morality of contracts and inoffensiveness, that is child's play to a Bacon who specializes in refined arts of management. Like Machiavelli, Bacon employs the carrot and the stick; unlike Machiavelli, Bacon specializes in the carrot. This it is that causes him to devise the economic arts, and Bacon's writings, as much as anyone's, help us understand the outlook behind that distinctively modern phenomenon, "the economy." They explore how individual ambition can be channeled into the work ethic, a growing society, a powerful nation-state, a new civilization, and—the great carrot that can tip the balance from fear to hope in managing men—a new science that will spin off a cornucopia of forecasts and inventions.

Few contemporary commentators on economic science attend to its individualistic premises and hence to its philosophic forebears, but there is an occasional indication of Bacon's importance. In a well-known book, Albert O. Hirschman noted the "political arguments for capitalism before its triumph," and argued that a number of seventeenth- and eighteenth-century writers showed how "self-interest" can at once inform passion with reason and provide reason with "direction and force."[1] Hirschman, following Leo Strauss, notes Bacon's responsibility for an effectual moral science, one that manages passions so that they modify and regulate one by another.[2] Still, Hirshman refrains from pursuing the new outlook to its radical premises. He arrays brief quotations to illustrate the tendency of an age, explains Baconian doctrines by Bacon's experience and experimental outlook, and while acknowledging a Machiavellian root, locates the root in Machiavelli's new doctrine of the state. But Bacon's experience was hardly unique, the purport governing his experimentalism has itself to be explained, and the doctrine of the state follows from Machiavelli's new account of "the prince," that is, of individual interests. In general, one has to penetrate to the more moral and political side of political economy. While Hirschman concentrates on economic interests, the Baconian corpus includes discussions of Henry VII, Caesar, science, and empire, as well as of acquisitiveness, work and industry, and the spirit of business. The ultimate self-made man is a conqueror or emperor, according to Bacon, and about more serious business than economic business.

Ours is a time when many moralists are seeking to get beyond the difficulties of individualism and especially of the old economic individualism. But they often run afoul of the old starting point. In such circumstances, Bacon's radical clarity about the bite of individualism may be peculiarly important. I illustrate the point with a recent effort at criticism and advocacy, Steven Lukes's *Individualism*.[3]

The old economic and political individualism had merely furthered private interests, according to Lukes, but a "historically progressive" version, focused directly on autonomy, can promote equal dignity. While Lukes tends to reduce the old to mere epiphenomenon—it reflected the bourgeois society of its day—he also confronts it philosophically. Even by its own measure, he argues, it is insufficiently individualistic. Hobbes's "abstract" individual of fixed appetites and wants was not unequivocally an individual, for example, for Hobbes relied on "definitions, typifications, categories or labels," and these have the effect of delegitimating whole classes of persons. Lukes proposes instead a version that conceives the individual as "the source of (yet to be discovered) intentions and purposes, decisions and choices, as capable of engaging in and valuing certain (yet to be discovered) activities and involvements, and as capable of (yet to be discovered) forms of self-development."[4]

This is a version, as the parentheticals show, that strains to welcome everyone as unique, as only having to be autonomous. Yet the effort, however intensely pushed, fails Lukes's test. For this version also remains defined, and it is definite enough to delegitimate whole classes, such as those who conceive of themselves as citizens, good people, or gang members (rather than autonomous persons); those who follow custom, law, or fashion (rather than their own choices); or those who choose piety, gentlemanly ways, or license (rather than self-development). Lukes sees the problem, and he faces it. He is explicit in rejecting the relativism that dogs "ethical individualism," and he brings himself to insist on rational choice and "a determinate range of characteristic human excellences."[5] This road, however, leads away from individualism. It leads toward some notion of excellence that would make quality, not uniqueness, the test. "Characteristic human excellences" sounds rather Aristotelian. But this direction is feared by Lukes as reactionary, and he would avoid it at all costs.

It is because of a theory of moral evolution that Lukes can assume that the old is reaction and that the new encompasses the morally best of the past. His historical philosophy precludes return, and interprets an advanced individualism as the culmination of progressive moral development. Aristotle and St. Thomas, Reformation, Renaissance, and Enlightenment—all culminate in the moral teaching of Immanuel Kant and his liberal successors.

But can one complacently suppose that historical development has bred progress, when Nietzsche, Heidegger, and the deconstructionists have been controverting precisely that point? If *Individualism* is indicative, liberal individualism is in grave danger, for the book supplies no real reason to believe its optimism as to liberal progress. Its historical account is surely wrong. What Lukes presents as one road is a battlefield of different and contradictory paths, and the path of individualism is not that of "characteristic moral excellences." Petrarch and other humanists may have held that "nothing is admirable but the soul," as Lukes asserts, and also that the soul is to be admired especially for its excellences, but the soul is not the self, and the meaty Aristotelian virtues that Petrarch praises are not self-expression. Aristotle and St. Thomas may be teachers of moral virtue, natural right, the law of nature, divine law, and friendship, but these are not individual rights and autonomy. The obvious origin of individualism, as Lukes himself notes, is not such teachings, but those of Hobbes and his followers Bernard Mandeville and John Locke. If so, Lukes's moral superstructure lacks a moral genealogy, just as it lacks a real morality. The genealogy of the autonomous self is in the epistemological treatises that attack any supposition of conscience or inherent ideas and, not least, the supposition of teleology, of a human inclination to "characteristic excellences."

A variety of individualisms linger on among modern thinkers, some temporarily shiny and up-to-date (doctrines of liberation of the authentic self, of self-expression, and of the inherent dignity of every self), others corroded by time and doubt (doctrines of natural rights and of self-interest). But all such doctrines are more than mere selfishness (for all rely on a theoretical critique of goods above the self), and most turn to an artificial project. They set forth more than our love for ourselves, for pleasures and desirable activities, for those dear to us, like us or connected to us, and for good things. All such individualisms maintain that every good is reducible to a passion decisively private, whether it be fear, self-development, or will to power. They deny the reality of love for things or people good for their own sake, and thus of admirable activities and qualties in which others can genuinely share. They thus deny a common good, as opposed to a collective interest. Such opinions may remind one of the views of bad men. But ordinary nastiness is not a comprehensive criticism of morality and religion, and even less a new foundation that promises political and economic progress. Individualism is not a moral or religious opinion, nor is it an everyday opinion. It is an "ism" produced by modern philosophers to replace moral and religious opinions, common and uncommon.

Opportunistic Individualism

The special formula of Baconian individualism is that of the self-made man. Whatever the minor differences, Bacon's version is fundamentally similar to the famous teachings spread by Ben Franklin's *Autobiography* and *Poor Richard's Almanac*, Daniel Defoe's *Robinson Crusoe*, John Locke's *Two Treatises*, and numberless other works preaching hard work, "a penny saved, a penny earned," keeping's one's eye on the main chance, and like lessons in rising to fame and fortune. The lessons in rising are especially instructions in wariness and in work, that is, in a foresighted fear as to one's general neediness, and in industrious provision for oneself. These are moral instructions in revamping one's attitudes and, in that sense, in making one's self. The positive Baconian teaching is then of radical self-reliance, and, while differing somewhat from moral autonomy and other recent versions of individualism, is similar to the formulations by Bacon's immediate successors.

According to Hobbes, even the intellect or speech that appears to distinguish man is but an invented tool, a product of human effort. Locke's account of labor-value, and of labor as a factor of production, is better known. Labor being the source of prosperity, and even of all things of value except the virtually worthless materials, Locke would have us believe that human industry produces 9/10, or perhaps 99/100, or even 999/ 1,000 of everything valuable.⁶ But Bacon takes a backseat to no one in insisting that man is a god to man, and, in particular, in his counsel that the self itself must be artificially constructed so that a man may conquer a place for himself. In a little "Image" of Julius Caesar, of which we will say more later, Bacon sets forth his model. Caesar, he says, was "a consummate master of simulation and dissimulation, and made up entirely of arts, insomuch that nothing was left in his nature except what art had approved."⁷

An Art of Life

If arts are so important, if the self or "nature" of even a Caesar is to be "made up entirely of arts," as Bacon suggests, what is to guide all the artifice? If the self is to make itself, with a view to what is it to make and be made? The question is serious, for the answer determines what arts are to be sought and what self is to be made. The leading answer to the leading question seems to be self-preservation, or, as Bacon puts it, "endur(ing)" or "long lasting" ("Of Regiment of Health" 30).

In the *Essays*, the term "art" or "arts" first appears in "Of Simulation and Dissimulation" (6), and the complicated argument there centers on arts of life and arts of state and gives primacy to the arts of life.⁸ In turn, Bacon suggests that wisdom is policy and that policy is the art of preserving oneself in state. The crucial distinction is not between good and bad, for to suppose the primacy of good is to miss the hardness of things: there is "rarely any rising but by a commixture of good and evil arts" ("Of Nobility" 14). Yet the art of rising is subordinated to the art of life. It is the essays on studies and health that set forth the primacy of life. While "Of Studies" tells us that our conduct is a studied behavior, to be calculated methodically, it also tells us that there is a wisdom outside studies and methods that is "won by observation" (50). The character of that observation appears in "Of Regiment of Health" (30), which contains the only similar literary construction in the *Essays*. "There is a wisdom in this beyond the rules of physic: a man's own observations."

In speaking of health, Bacon weighs all activities and feelings, even "wonder and admiration," with a view to "endur[ing]" or "long lasting." Health is not fitness, a body apt for its characteristic activity; it is the ability to preserve oneself. The crucial observation, then, is of the self's revulsion from the death that nature finally visits on us. By nature, we are but insecure bodies, and yet we are driven to seek a security beyond what nature provides. This teaching, we will argue, governs the psychological dynamics in "Of Death," "Of Adversity," "Of Revenge," "Of Anger," and in the *Essays* as a whole.

The apparently pedestrian reformulation of health begins the second half of the *Essays*. The first half had ended with an account of "the true greatness of kingdoms and estates," which sets forth the civil advantages of the new civilization. Essay 30 seems to set forth the fundamental advantage, self-preservation, which is the advantage for individuals as individuals.

Thus, Bacon's central teaching is like that for which Hobbes is famous. There are differences, to be sure. Hobbes leaves penury in the background, together with natural or accidental death, and focuses almost entirely on violent death at the hands of man. For Bacon the enemy is not violent death alone, but death of all kinds—death as such. Hobbes sets forth a teaching of natural right and an impersonal sovereign enforcing the peace for human beings regarded as equals. Bacon's teaching is more simply selfish, since it provides above all for one's own, and therefore for his own. Whatever these differences, Bacon and Hobbes alike begin with the primacy of avoiding death, a primacy based upon a basic observation or (as Hobbes calls it) "introspection."

But is this observation primary? It is an observation not merely of fear of death, but of the primacy of this fear as opposed to the other feelings, inclinations, or divinations one might have. Whence the judgment of primacy? Is it by experience of nature—or by a pruned experience of nature? Is observation primary, or a skepticism of other human inclinations, especially those moral and religious? Is nature primary—or critical thinking? The concluding chapter reconsiders this difficulty at the starting point of Bacon's thought.

The Skeptical Critique

Bacon is famous for mixing skepticism about what man has been given with hope for what he can make, and the combination is especially obvious in his writings on method. Almost the first words of the *Great Instauration* insist that the very "primary notions of things which the mind readily and passively imbibes" are mistaken. But precisely the critique of apparent natural limits permits new hopes from a turn to artifice; we are to "try the whole thing anew upon a better plan" and effect a "total reconstruction of science, arts, and all human knowledge."[9] The limits of nature as we see them need not hold us back.

Bacon's discussions of moral and civil knowledge seem to follow the same movement of critique and construction. The *Essays* begins by refuting the natural human understanding as to ends, and then constructs its artificial orientation on what Bacon thinks a more solid foundation. The first essay, "Of Truth," rebuts the illusion of religious and philosophic men that one should live by the Word or truth, and others refute the claims of the good (13), the noble (14 and 47), and the divine (3, 16, 17, 35). The second essay, "Of Death," intimates the origin of such illusions in a revulsion from death and alludes to an "earnest pursuit" for accommodating that drive. Other essays elaborate on our state of adversity ("Of Adversity" 5, "Of Atheism" 16), ways to channel our impulsive reactions ("Of Revenge" 4, "Of Anger" 57), and the sorts of power to seek, those for life and state. Gradually, we see the self's production of its crucial power, which is the mind. The mind is the ability to generalize influence (40, 50, 58), and, thus, while a lion can bite, a man can lay down an enduring law or doctrine. We will begin by considering "Of Truth" and then turn to the other essays that establish the bareness of the human situation.

The first words of the first essay have "jesting Pilate" asking "What is truth?" which might well seem a thrust at Christ's claim to bear witness to the truth (John 18:38). They are followed by a dance of opinions that reduces theological and philosophic truths to vanities—platforms for confidence in one's superiority—and moral truths to civil instruments of vanity. In this first essay, every mention of a Christian opinion is succeeded by an obscure allusion to a famous critic of religion (Lucian, Lucretius). The essay also corrects Lucretius' celebration of wisdom (however materialist and atheist), corrects also a halfhearted defense of honesty by a peculiar reference to the first modern essayist, Montaigne, and then tacitly corrects Montaigne by signaling Bacon's more aggressive ways of attacking honesty and the faith. I shall try to spell out part of this procedure, compressed and circumlocutory as it undoubtedly is.

According to Bacon, truth is more alien to human thought and human nature than even Lucretius had supposed. For people, in fact, prefer not light but flickering candlelight—"vain opinions, flattering hopes, false valuations, imaginations as one would, and the like." Vanity and flattery are the motive, and even "the fathers' " deepest opinions—that is, the Patriarchs' reverence for Jehovah—result from wishful self-flattery.

Just at this point, so risky theologically, Bacon backs off to defend truth, albeit the traditional opinion of philosophers that truth is the "sovereign good" of human nature. He uses, I suspect, the philosophers against the religious. Yet even this defense proves to be but a diversion, for Bacon first makes truth set forth its own defense in its own name—a form of self-flattery?—and then gives the game away with the unphilosophic assertion that "belief of truth," not inquiry or presence of truth, is what is enjoyed. The religious are, in this respect, on a more realistic path. Whereupon Bacon returns to religious matters, to the book of Genesis, which leads us to believe that God created the world for our benefit. He implies that faith in a provider is the real motive underlying an alleged love of truth. He then tacitly corrects the Bible's provision. God merely created light on "matter or chaos," Bacon announces, and divided the light into sense, reason, and spirit. The biblical creator ex nihilo should be turned into a more enlightened provider.

Bacon then reinterprets the role of light into an instrument of one's superiority. "Of Truth" quotes Lucretius, as "poet," to the effect that the pleasure of seeing is in perceiving one's safety *above* others' struggles at sea and on land. It omits two relevant points in the original, Lucretius' eulogy of a serenity protected by the teaching of the wise, and his explicit disavowal of pleasure in others' misfortunes. Bacon corrects the poet-philosopher's supposition of the worth or pleasure of contemplation. Instead, he sharpens Lucretius' references to artificial bulwarks—boats at sea and fortresses on land—and omits Lucretius' disdain for those who struggle "night and day by surpassing effort to rise up to the height of power and gain possession of the world."[10] The philosopher may flatter himself that his wisdom makes him safe, but he too requires the art he disdains, the art of conquering a place for himself. Realistically understood, then, Lucretius was not a philosopher but a poet, not a seeker of wisdom but a maker, and a poet-prophet, a maker of his own "sect." Bacon ends the discussion by correcting Lucretius explicitly: the thinker's outlook should be "with pity, and not with swelling or pride." The philosopher's pride is out of place, since he is needy, and to secure followers for his own sect he must sympathize with the neediness of others.

"Of Truth" closes with a serpentine defense of "winding and crooked" ways, although under the appearance of a condemnation. The last topic is practical truth, not the philosophic and theological variety hitherto analyzed. Dishonesty is odious, Bacon says, and gives a reason: because one is brave to God while fearing men. Does this mean that dishonesty is not odious in itself? Bacon does not pause here to consider this. But he proceeds to insinuate a doubt about the basis of even the scruple he has allowed, for faith in "the judgments of God upon the generations of men" will fade. In "Of Simulation and Dissimulation" (6) Bacon actually defends dishonesty, albeit under the protective names of simulation and dis-

simulation. But how does Bacon know that the faith that supports conscience will fade?

"Of Unity in Religion," the third essay, provides a shocking answer: it
plans the demise of Christianity. Bacon shows how faith in God can be
civilly undermined by putting civil things first.[11] Unity is indeed the focus
in "Of Unity of Religion," but it is social unity. The essay finesses the
question of religious truth and appraises religion according to its fitness
as "the chief band of human society." On such terrain, Bacon can measure religion by its civility and attack it in the guise of making it civil.
"Therefore it is most necessary that the church . . . do damn and send to
hell for ever" the facts and opinions that inspire "actions of murthering
princes, butchery of people, and subversion of states and governments."
The damnation of doctrine can go a long way. For the facts and opinions
in question are the distinctive devotions and views on which the churches
divide, and which divide them from Caesar. This is the fiercest attack in
the *Essays*, and the only use of "hell," and it condemns to hell the heart
of the faiths and anticipates the more direct attacks on religion in "Of
Atheism" (16) and "Of Superstition" (17). Bacon will announce that
"utility" may be "the bond" of certain societies ("Of Nobility" 14), and
it is the bond of the business-oriented society advanced in the *Essays*.

In "Of Death," the second essay, Bacon cautiously brings out the new
foundation for reasoning, which can lead to useful arts and replace the
old philosophic orientation by truth or *honestum*. "Of Death" minimizes
death, but it also indicates quietly that revulsion from death is the real
motion of men. The real remedy, which can help put death out of mind,
is confidence in some project that will keep one's name alive. The authoritative quotations here are from Roman emperors, not from Holy Rome.
They suggest that he who dies with success in sight, knowing such a death
opens the gate for honors and extinguishes envy, feels death less and, in a
way, overcomes it. Death is overcome by the glory that lives on. While
the essay seeks to discourage the preoccupation with death characteristic
of friars and Stoics, the arguments are wan in denying the importance of
death. They tacitly admit it. Bacon calls those who give their lives the
"truest" followers, for example, as if theirs was the supreme sacrifice. The
six emperors all died speaking of life and expecting to be part of Rome in
memory or in action. All were deified.

In the course of intimating that fame or honor is the means of overcoming death, Bacon's dance of opinions never directly confronts the
possibility of an afterlife. But it deflates hopes. After mentioning a "holy
and religious" opinion that death is the consequence of sin and rectified
by another world, the argument quickly conflates it with consideration of

"vanity and of superstition." Bacon also makes a point of introducing Stoics such as Seneca, "a philosopher and natural man," to suggest that death is bad only in its trappings. Actually, the Stoics' famous virtue is used by Bacon as a temporary eminence from which to attack the Christians; that accomplished, he turns against them and their virtue. He exaggerates Seneca's impassivity toward death and suicide, and then substitutes, for eulogy of Stoic virtue, a eulogy of the way passion mates and masters fear of death. Eventually, he shamelessly misquotes the satirist Juvenal as an authority for a criticism of the earnest Stoics and extols instead "business" with "worthy ends and expectations."

"Of Adversity" (5) shows the depth of man's adversity, or the real scarcity that accompanies the human condition. It is in this discussion that Bacon gathers together his assault on the two major premodern schools of apolitical philosophy. The Epicureans had celebrated pleasure (especially pleasure of the mind), and the Stoics had advocated virtue (especially a philosophic austerity). "Of Adversity" takes up these arguments for a philosophic life and rejects both. They are incompatible with man's true situation of adversity, which endangers life itself.

"Adversity doth best discover virtue," or necessity is the mother of invention. Bacon shows how a state of nature worse than Lucretius imagined might provoke a virtue more effective than the Stoics imagined. Lucretius had proposed sober atomism to explain the world and human fears. But he had also granted some efficacy to human arts, such as medicine and politics, and a decisive efficacy to human wisdom. Death, plague, war, and the end of the world may be inevitable, according to *Of the Nature of Things*, but "the truest reasoning" (*ratio verissima*) exhibits the necessity of change in bodies and can reconcile men to the inevitability of their death. Bacon thinks that Lucretius overestimated both the ability of our senses to know atoms and the ability of our bodily nature to abide by reason. He supplies a different remedy: how to conquer our nature by satisfying its impulse. The old atomists were rightly materialists, he says in *New Organon* and elsewhere, but they failed to find a solid starting point for reasoning.[12]

Bacon is much harsher on the Stoics than on the materialist and antireligious Epicureans. He uses Lucretius' doctrine of nature ("Of Death") and magnifies his attack on religion: if Lucretius had to confront the religious wars, he would have been "seven times more Epicure and atheist than he was" ("Of Unity in Religion" 3). But "Of Adversity" openly criticizes the Stoics and by name, probably because the Stoics (like the Christians) are too passive and too intent on virtue.

"Of Adversity" shows how really to perform a political-religious miracle: how to transform Christianity by appropriating its hope for life ever-lasting. One sees a succession of quick strokes. "Certainly if miracles be the command over nature, they appear most in adversity." Bacon thus focuses on ruling nature, not on achieving perfection, and by human ac-tion, not by providential delivery. Then he meditates on Senecan words as if on a sacred text: the goods of prosperity may be wished, but those of adversity are admired. "It is true greatness to have in one the frailty of a man, and the security of a God." Human frailty is the point, but reme-dies in "transcendences" are immediately called the stuff of poets, and the Christian remedy, in particular, is likened to the ancient poets' picture of a Hercules who unbinds Prometheus. Prometheus signified "human nature," and Hercules' journey signified "Christian resolution," which sails in the frail human body through the world. In short, "Of Adversity" reduces Christ's miracle in saving the body to part of a poetic account of transcendence and suggests the serious alternative. Real resolution and real transcendence are human inventions.

"Of Adversity" proceeds to develop *the* secret of resolution, which is the art of the armored heart (to use the Machiavellian idiom). Bacon de-fends "fortitude," the virtue of adversity that can lead out of adversity into prosperity. The argument suggests that Bacon has learned both from the worldly wisdom of the Old Testament and from the worldly success that accompanied the promise of salvation in the New Testament. Both Old and New Testaments, he says, suppose the primacy of adversity—"[T]he pencil of the Holy Ghost hath labored more in describing the afflictions of Job than the felicities of Solomon." While the afflictions of our state by nature are in the background of Bacon's thought, he, like Christ (and unlike the Old Testament and Lucretius), can promise a fu-ture state of security. He will promise not only wealth and power, remi-niscent of God's covenants, but also a future of increasing security, remi-niscent of Christ's promises. Reminding us of the pain of our neediness, Bacon prepares the way for pleasure in our progress. "[I]t is more pleas-ing to have a lively work upon a sad and solemn ground."

Elsewhere in the *Essays*, Bacon thematically undermines the supposi-tions that man should act as if divine, or look up to a god-man, and shows instead how really to promote "the raising of human nature." The chief discussions are in "Of Atheism" (16) and "Of Superstition" (17). While "Of Atheism" appears to attack atheism, it really introduces arguments and doctrines that serve more to induce it. It interweaves fables, Epicu-reans, Plato, Lucian, and other doubters, and deftly identifies "a received religion" with "superstition." Here is an example of Bacon's art. After noting a "custom of profane scoffing in holy matters," which will "by little and little deface the reverence of religion," he proceeds to illustrate a theological argument, that denying God destroys "magnanimity" and "the raising of human nature," with a dog brave under his master's protection. Are we convinced by the equation of risen man with brave dog? Lest we are not, Bacon then speaks of a "force and faith" beyond human nature, and finally of the means to "exalt" human nature above "human frailty." But the force and faith in question turn out to be not divine. The eminently respectable Cicero is quoted to prove that theism enabled the Roman "state" to surpass "all nations and peoples." Not grace or the good Lord, but an expanding state, will prove to be the power that overcomes human frailty.

While "Of Unity in Religion" (3) had omitted an account of true religious principles, and "Of Atheism" (16) implies that there are none, "Of Superstition (17) announces that "no opinion of God at all" is better than an unworthy one and almost announces that for civil purposes every truly religious opinion is unworthy. Bacon provides, in effect, a survey of the advantages of atheism for life. The key advantage is the spur for self-reliance, since, in atheistic times, people feel their neediness and may learn to depend on themselves. While superstition erects "an absolute monarchy in the minds of men . . . , atheism did never perturb states; for it makes men wary of themselves, as looking no further: and we see the times inclined to atheism (as the time of Augustus Caesar) were civil times." The Roman Empire in its pre-Christian beginnings, that is, was a "civil time." To encourage in its own way a new birth of civil times, the essay concludes with six causes of superstition, of which two prove to be beliefs central to Catholicism, two to Protestantism, and two to both.

The Dynamics of Self-Making

The actual art of self-making is an invention, an art of managing the passions. While awareness of one's neediness is a necessary precondition, the precondition is not the thing, and a spur to self-reliance is not the obtaining of it. Artifice is needed, according to Bacon, and the art in question, like all Baconian arts, is a management of the forces at hand. Those forces are more than fear, more even than the fear of death. Anger and revenge prove to be crucial, for the art of saving ourselves is occasioned by fear, but originated by anger at our misery, or even by revenge against those who cause our misery. "Of Revenge" (4) comes after "Of Unity in Religion" and before "Of Adversity," and in it Bacon implies that religion originates in "a kind of wild justice" retaliating at our natu-

ral fate, at death. The discussion anticipates Bacon's proposal for a real
overcoming of death and is linked (if only by mention of anger) with the
suggestion (in "Of Anger" 57) that a man's anger at his natural state
fuels a passion for revenge against all superiors. His satisfaction lies in the
prospect of revenge. "He foresees a time" for revenge, that is, for his own
rise to superiority. Real revenge, then, is far-sighted domination, such a
domination that gives the self a life after death. But this requires the devising of a self that can live on, which is a public image, and the devising
also of the attitude of opportunistic patience that looks to the long run,
which is the private self. The need for rising to a public place is the topic
in "Of Great Place" (11); the devising of attitudes that enable one to
master fortune is the topic in "Of Fortune" (40). This management of
the passions by the devising of remedies, and even the devising of the self
or selves as the supreme remedy, is Bacon's art of self-making.

Bacon's politics begins with a consciousness of ill-use; it might be characterized, with the phrasing of Friedrich Nietzsche, as a politics of resentment. It may be the precise kind that Nietzsche hated, preoccupied as it
is with security. While the peak of Baconian politics is a dominating foun-
der-prophet, his glory and his domination are in the service of his security.
Just as fear can make followers warily inoffensive, so an extraordinary revulsion from death can cause dominating virtue in the Baconian sense.
This leads to a transvaluation of values, so to speak, but a rather un-Nietz-
schean one. Bacon chooses between beauty and deformity, for example,
and favors deformity ("Of Deformity" 44). It is awareness of defect that
provokes a man (at least a "great wit") to industry. The example is Socrates, whom Nietzsche also interpreted as deformed, but by an inherent
plebeian deformation of soul. According to Bacon, the bodily deformity
of Socrates was "a perpetual spur in himself to rescue and deliver himself
from scorn," and this root is the effectual truth about Socrates' pursuit of
truth.

Given these forces at hand, the key to successful management is wit or
ingenuity in the inventing business. Bacon admits a certain freedom in
man for art. There is a possibility of "election touching the frame of his
mind," despite "a necessity in the frame of his body" ("Of Deformity"
44). Accordingly, one can affect the mind, perhaps even frame the mind.
One can thus mix mind with matter, invention with a deterministic physics, and social planning and civilization with an account of nature as forces
and bodies. "The sun of discipline and virtue," as Bacon puts it, can obscure "the stars of natural inclination." Still, the metaphors should not
obscure the fact that the light of Bacon's sun is artificial, or that Bacon
substitutes his doctrine of malleable mind for the desire for knowing that

a Socrates displayed, or that the artificial light subserves the passions. Consider deformity, Bacon says, not as a blight on natural perfection, or as a sign of the sin that disrupted an original perfection, "but as a cause, which seldom faileth of the effect." Our election is rigged by the powers behind the scenes, it seems, and mind seems to have little of its own inclination. It is drenched with desire to endure and with a corresponding anger at anonymity and disdain.

The knowing manager of mind elects to advance the self accordingly. The spur to ambition comes from relative disadvantage, and the spur to a remedy for our natural disadvantages comes from the fact that our relative disadvantage is changeable. While we will all die, some may live on in name and for a longer or shorter period. To remedy natural disadvantage by directing our changeable composition calls for special ability. The secret is "spirit." What is this spirit? The first sentence in "Of Deformity" tells us. "For as nature hath done ill by them, so do they by nature . . . and so they have their revenge of nature." Those who by nature do such ill seem to be those of the "natural malignity" described in essay 13, who "in other men's calamities are, as it were, in season," and who are "the fittest timber to make great politics of." Not ambition for some good, but revenge against their ill condition, is the motion of great politiques. Theirs is a passion for revenge against the death that nature will deal them, and Bacon shows how the passion can be satisfied with a state of revenge.

In the essays on envy (9) and suspicion (31), this motive is further spelled out. While envy has usually suffered from a bad press, Bacon's extended appreciation analyzes it as a useful force. Aristotle had defined envy as a pain aroused by the good fortune of others, and even the *Rhetoric*, which treats envy as a powerful force requiring the orator's preparation, characterizes it as mean and allied with injustice. Bacon omits the *Rhetoric*'s distinction between envy and virtuous emulation, treats envy as "most importunate," and concentrates on ways of managing it to one's advantage. For example, one can use "screens" to remove envy from oneself by delegating controversial tasks to "violent and undertaking natures" (as, say, Ben Franklin does to John Paul Jones in Herman Melville's *Israel Potter*). Or one can rouse it against enemies by "public envy," which causes "discontentment" against "public ministers" and even their whole state (as Bacon does to nobles and priests throughout the *Essays*). Bacon on envy is largely a lesson in slandering the establishment.

Bacon on suspicion is similar, and "Of Suspicion" (31) mentions envy. While Bacon cautions against suspicion, this proves a caution only against those suspicions that prevent "business" from going on "currently and constantly." A fundamental or Machiavellian suspicion is politic, for one should know that men "will have their own ends, and be truer to themselves than to them." Those strong of heart and brain can exploit the selfishness they suspect by leading the public to suspect, for example, that religious men entangle consciences "for their own ends" ("Of Unity in Religion" 3). Suspicions can have "stings," a phrase that is reminiscent of the stinging "darts" of seditious speech ("Of Seditions and Troubles" 15). Managing slanders and suspicions, then, is fundamentally sedition, and by it those of profound malice can tear down what stands in the way of their projects.

While Bacon's analysis of suspicion and envy shows what one must overcome in others, the accounts of revenge and anger show, first, the use of turning to others, and second, the dynamics of overcoming one's own nature in order to make a self that can endure. Bacon begins his discussion of revenge by condemning revenge, for preempting the "office" of law, and he concludes by characterizing persons preoccupied with private revenge as obsessed witches (4). In between, however, he shows that the problem is not the passion for revenge but choosing a foolish vehicle for one's revenge, that is, a private vehicle. Injuries from others are inevitable, he says; people injure for profit, pleasure, or honor, and, as the sixth and central contention maintains, they in fact act by "ill-nature" and "can do no other." Revenge reconsidered loses all ties with justice, wild or not. It is only anger striking out willy-nilly against obstacles to satisfaction. Considered revenge, then, is not moderated passion but studied passion. There are politic paths to vengeance, and the most politic are the public paths. "Public revenges are for the most part fortunate, as that for the death of Caesar; for the death of Pertinax; for the death of Henry the Third of France; and many more." The most fortunate revenges are those best managed and have nothing to do with justice, for they use a ruler's death to obtain one's own rule, as did Augustus with respect to Caesar's death, and Severus with respect to Pertinax's. The public ways are ways to domination, and to dominate one must manipulate others' feelings of injury to serve one's own anger at the fate given by nature. As one would manage others' ambitions, one must manage their resentments.

While the discussion of revenge near the beginning of the *Essays* suggests managing the resentments of others, the discussion of anger near its end concentrates on managing one's own ("Of Anger" 57). There Bacon brushes aside Stoic or Christian hopes of extinguishing anger or turning the other cheek; anger is natural and the remedy is not virtue but management. The remedy for anger at one's present state is an image that will provide for a secure state in the long run: an image of the self leading to future domination. The image of future satisfaction can hold back present passion, by winning for passion an eventual satisfaction, and is the secret for transforming passion into a more rational regard for one's interest.

"Of Anger" may begin with a stance above the passions, but various little reminders of an Aristotelian scorn of baseness lead to Bacon's rather un-Aristotelian conclusion: a man should "seem" above injuries and "give law to himself." But Bacon replaces God's law of righteousness, as well as Aristotle's virtue of gentleness, with a formula for one's own law: one must give a law to one's lawless nature. The formula may remind one of a Kantian categorical moral imperative. But it prescribes not a moral law but a calculated policy: "to make a man's self believe, that the opportunity of his revenge is not yet come, but that he foresees a time for it, and so to still himself in the meantime, and reserve it." We are advised, in particular, to refrain from bitter words, from revealing secrets (as to one's stake in beliefs that are spread), and from interrupting "business." Patience is with a view to a project: to contain anger "from mischief" is to maneuver anger into policy. While we may have some "election" as to the discipline we impose on ourselves, the secret of successfully maneuvering ourselves, of winning the election, is to hold before desire an image of security for the object it already wants. Moved by resentment at obstacles, driven indirectly by fear that its motions will end, the self of great wit will find a way if it can abide the long term.

It is by considering such discussions that one gets some inkling of what Bacon means by the self. The self seems to be precisely the constructed image that can win a state of security. Bacon only indicates this, and by using and abusing biblical meditations on the soul through his usual vehicle in the *Essays* for such purposes, the much-abused Seneca. On Seneca's exhortation "to possess our souls in patience," "Of Anger" imposes its own meditation: "Whosoever is out of patience is out of possession of his soul." It seems that it is one's own patience that keeps one's soul, and that without the one, one lacks the other. The exhortation itself alludes to Luke 21:19, which in context teaches a very different lesson. The scripture commands men *not* to meditate should authorities question their faith in Christ, and it concludes that by enduring in Christ's name "you will gain your lives." Bacon's meditation is the one and only occurrence of "soul" in the *Essays* that is not quoted from authority. It suggests that we keep or lose soul by our own efforts. While Bacon holds elsewhere that the artful man must impose upon himself the abilities that preserve the self ("Of Fortune" 40), in this discussion of anger he shows that the power to govern oneself by checking one's desires is *the* saving ability. He goes on to misquote Virgil: be not a bee who "puts his life (*anima*) in the sting." Patience is part of one's long-term policy, not of the Lord's commands, and one's own patience produces the self that can live on.

But there remains the problem of the self that controls. That is, is the self the power that produces the image that enables one to have patience, or the image? Bacon seems to suggest both, that there is some natural power of "election," or choice, and that the invented image of the future enables man to have "patience," that is, some power of checking and electing. This problematic heart of Bacon's psychology is illuminated by a triad of essays on nature, custom, and fortune (38–40). The message seems to be that nature is but an inhuman force, which coexists in almost all men with custom and "infused opinion," but that some few, who concentrate on themselves and view everything as opportunity for their rising, may master others, and thus fortune, by infusing opinions and thus customs. I remain unsure whether the first ability in the superior man is merely superior force.

Bacon describes nature as a force that is alien to us as human being. "Of Nature in Men" (38) does not speak of human nature, and therefore human choice as we know it does not seem natural. Yet choice is very much the concern of this essay, which is more about control of nature than about nature. While nature repels the application of force, it can be made "less importune" by doctrine and discourse, and most of all by custom. Custom changes and even "subdues" nature. How and to what extent might these give a man a "victory over his nature?" Bacon focuses on the effects of custom and explores methods of victory and, after revealing the power of passions that makes a victory untrustworthy, he explores methods of management. The customs that will work are the customs that satisfy passion. However Bacon may parade notions such as "perfection" or "habit," scents of a virtuous soul inclining to its good, they only serve to mislead the gullible, for nature is force without an inclination to good.

At this point Bacon quotes, without translating, a revealing mention of soul from Ovid; freedom comes from bursting the restraints that gall one's soul.[13] A man reveals his nature, Bacon follows up, not through the goods of which men speak, but "in privateness, for there is no affectation; in passion, for that putteth a man out of his precepts; and in a new case or experiment, for there custom leaveth him." To look for human nature, suppose that things public, moral, and customary are artificial. Nature is not what inclines to the goods of which we speak, but what secretly drives.

Bacon then indicates that the way of mastery is by a useful profession or vocation. Vocations, not moral character or obedience to God's laws, are the way to self-control. "They are happy men whose natures sort with their vocations, otherwise they may say, '*multum incola fuit anima mea*,' when they converse in those things they do not affect" (Psalm 120:6). The phrase quoted by Bacon is part of a cry to the Lord for relief from lying, deceit, and war: "my soul has been in much a stranger." But a religious vocation to converse with the Lord is not what Bacon has in mind. He twists the psalmist's cry to counsel an art that conforms with what we "affect."

The ensuing discussions of custom and fortune indicate the vocations Bacon has in mind, which are those that channel the powerful affections of gain and revenge, and they also acknowledge that only some minds "exceeding rare" can keep themselves free of customary ways. It seems to follow that patience in almost all depends upon vocations devised by exceeding few, perhaps by one. That means that the very existence of a self in almost all people results from the vocations, the society, the devisings, of few or one. In this profound sense, according to Bacon, a man will be a god to man and will be even a creator God. The "raising" of human nature comes not from a divine savior but from "custom" and "infused opinions." While "Of Custom and Education" does not consider expressly how to infuse, or who infuses, it does show Bacon infusing a new opinion as to the means of putting virtues "upon" our nature. "[T]he great multiplication of virtues upon human nature resteth upon societies well ordained and disciplined."

The power of social conditioning may now be an old chestnut, but it is thinking such as Bacon's, as I suggested in chapter 3, that develops the tree from its Machiavellian root. The essay title speaks of education as well as of custom, but Bacon assimilates what "we call education" of mind to an early customing, and, ultimately, to an early conditioning on the model of bodily conditioning. Custom affects especially the young, perhaps because of their greater bodily "pliancy." Moral education by family or church is replaced with conditioning through the mutual dealings of society.

In "Of Fortune" (40), Bacon sets forth the new opinion to be infused and especially the fundamental opinion that is to go into the rare and most open minds. He sets forth the "virtues" that are to raise human nature, and they are of his own devising. It is true that "Of Fortune" begins by mentioning "overt and apparent virtues" that earn praise, before it turns to the "secret hidden virtues" that bring real fortune. The beginning probably alludes to the moral virtues (a sign of which, according to the *Nicomachean Ethics*, is praise). But neither in this essay, nor in the *Essays* as a whole, does Bacon follow Aristotle's lead. Of the eleven moral virtues discussed in the *Ethics*, only one is the topic of an essay, "Of Ambition" (36), and Bacon's treatment of ambition is predictably un-Aristotelian. The *Ethics* had sought to define the proper form of ambition (a mean between unconcern for honor and desire for even petty honors). But the theme in "Of Ambition" is not the appropriate form of the virtue, but useful channels for the force of the passion. Bacon shows how a prince can manage the ambitious and his own ambition.

The secretive "Of Fortune" is not some imitation of traditional ethics, but a cautious Baconian variation on chapter 25 of *The Prince* ("How Much Fortune Can Do in Human Affairs, And in What Mode It May Be Opposed"). Machiavelli's famous discussion had been bold in the extreme. It contrasted fortune with providence, asserted that all men seek glory and wealth and that the good varies according to what succeeds, and paraded in turn Pope Julius to illustrate worldly daring and the conquest of a woman to illustrate the superiority of daring. The next and concluding chapter exhorts to a patriotic war of national liberation. By comparison, the Baconian prose is bland. "Of Fortune" is both less republican and less offensive, and the next essay, "Of Usury," shows how to revolutionize moral attitudes insidiously because economically.

The surface argument in "Of Fortune" instructs in Bacon's special art of blending innovation with an appearance of the customary. The essay indulges in some conspicuous (and ridiculous) name-dropping (Bacon gives one hidden virtue a Spanish name; another, an Italian; a third, a French). But this seems an ironically pedantic cover to distract the reader from Bacon's real boldness. He is replacing the opinion that dominates those Catholic lands, the faith that fortune is really providence and providence provides because Christ saves. Similarly, Bacon also tosses in the authority of ancient poets, historians, and leaders (including Sulla and Caesar), and tops off the concoction with references to an Athenian, to Homer, and to Plutarch's judgment about the Greek leaders. The learned of the Renaissance may miss his revamping of the opinions that dominate ancient learning, especially the Aristotelian opinions about nobility, justice, and philosophy that inform Plutarch's *Lives*. The real Bacon can hide behind the customary authorities he transforms and can inveigle readers into being followers.

The real argument in "Of Fortune" propounds a vaguely Aristotelian moral opinion (that sufficiency of external goods is needed for a good life), retracts it (and drops any mention of the good life), and then accepts and modifies the Machiavellian improvement. While external accidents conduce much to fortune, "chiefly, the mold of a man's fortune is in his own hands." To punctuate the new emphasis, Bacon quotes a favorite Latinism: *faber quisque fortunae suae* (every man is the maker of his own fortune), and then issues a formula that helps explain his own confrontation of Aristotle: the external cause of one man's fortune is often another man's folly. Wisdom may not be the highest good, as the foolish Aristotle had claimed, but a politic wisdom can be a studied weapon for rising above the old authorities.

Not virtue but power is the aim of studies and arts, and the key ability for making one's fortune is an agility in fixing without scruple on the image that advances oneself and depresses the others. The key secret virtue is opportunism on a grand scale: a determined eye for the main chance and especially the main reputation. "Of Fortune" dwells first on the negative side. The language is of moderation, but the bent is of a trimmer: be neither too firm nor too eager. There should not be "stonds nor restiveness in a man's nature; but that the wheels of his mind keep way with the wheels of his fortune." Here Bacon inserts the Spanish *disenboltura* (agility), and a Livian description of the austere Cato, which serve as ironic authorities as he sets aside the fixed principles of faith and morality. Then he proceeds to positive counsel. A number of scarcely discerned virtues, "or rather faculties and customs," light the way to fortune. They may be compared to the Milky Way, which sheds light by the conjunction of many dim stars. What are these shadowy attitudes, so far from both magnanimous splendor and Christian humility? First, concentrate on one's own affairs, avoiding "too much of the honest" and too much devotion to master or country. "For when a man placeth his thoughts without himself, he goeth not his own way." Second, be resolute, driven, in pursuing one's rising. For "the exercised fortune maketh the able man." Confidence and reputation result. Third, adopt a cause which will buoy one aloft beyond envy. "To decline the envy of their own virtues," wise men ascribe their success to "providence and fortune," and the result is that the fortunes of some will have a "slide and easiness."

The last counsel is explained by the examples, which are of Homer the poet and Timoleon, a Greek general and statesman. Timoleon overthrew the tyrants in Syracuse and then founded democracies, among which he lived in perfect security and honor. Bacon indicates, I suspect, the vocation that will "sort with" the rise of the "exceeding rare" mind, a vocation that somehow combines a great poet's appeal and a great liberator's work. One will probably not go too far astray if one thinks of all that is symbolized by the *New Atlantis*. That little story both conveys poetically a drama of human progress, and promises liberation for humanity from sickness, scarcity, and, perhaps, from death itself.

Public Persona as a Delivery of Self

In "Of Great Place" (11), Bacon makes a thematic argument for a public life, and the discussion, while apparently contradicting the secretive opportunism advanced in "Of Fortune" (40), actually complements it. "Of Great Place" insists on a mask of public concern, "Of Fortune," on a radical selfishness that must hide its every move. But the two essays prove to contain the same foundation; the public and private spheres are mutually dependent. The arts of ostentation (as they are called in "Of Vain Glory" 54) are the most important arts of rising, and the best of such ostentations is the image of public service. It was just this facade that roused Nietzsche's special ire at "the moral hypocrisy of those commanding" in the modern representative state, those who lower themselves into "first servants of their people."[14]

Still, "Of Great Place" could seem a eulogy of old-fashioned duty. It commends even in biblical prose a life in which not mere power, but "power to do good, is the true and lawful end of aspiring." "Merit and good works is the end of man's motion," the essay also tells us, and therefore you should exercise authority without delays and without corruption, favoritism, or roughness toward the public. It seems very different from "Of Fortune." "Of Fortune" is short, cold, calculating, and sinister. Among accidents contributing to one's fortune is "death of others"; among attitudes contributing to one's fortune is having "not too much of the honest." Nevertheless, precisely there Bacon writes that in order to rise a man must hide beneath "deliveries of a man's self." The self like all associations must become politicized, its form produced for its effect on others.

"Of Great Place" proves to contain the same dichotomy of motive and appearance, although with a special emphasis on the power needed for a great appearance. There may be a counsel of selfless duty, but it occurs only after Bacon deduces the need for great place from the self's desire "to seek power over others," and just before he deduces virtue in place from a concern for rising. As Bacon reworks phrases recalling Aristotelian greatness of soul, and a Christian king's duty to the great Lord, the theme first and last is that a public life is alien to the self. "It is a strange desire, to seek power and to lose liberty; or to seek power over others and to lose power over a man's self." The role of a public man is a role; he has "the virtue of a player" (to use the words of the next essay, "Of Boldness" 12). Still, Bacon dwells on the need for playing the role despite the troubles, for rising albeit "by a winding stair." Implicitly, he replaces the Christian's self-abnegation before God; implicitly, he criticizes the Aristotelian magnanimity that reserves the self for the honor attending noble actions. "By indignities men come to dignities."

A crucial premise appears: there is no inherent sense of dignity by which people may measure themselves. Even "great persons" but follow custom or fashion, for they "had need to borrow other men's opinions, to think themselves happy; for if they judge by their own feeling, they cannot find it: but if they think with themselves what other men think of them, and that other men would fain be as they are, then they are happy as it were by report; when perhaps they find the contrary within." Men need great place to be happy, because they are happy only by comparison and in report. The argument is in tacit contrast to Aristotle's portrait of the great-souled man, who knows himself and in particular his loftiness or dignity.[15] The great-souled man thinks he deserves great things and in particular great honor, and he disdains small honors and common praise, because they seem small next to the nobility of soul that he has and knows. This mixture of great worth and awareness of worth Aristotle calls the (crown of the virtues.)But Bacon thinks greatness of soul does not exist; there is no soul, and no nobility of soul. There is only a self, and its greatness is of one's making and the product of one's rising. One does not really stoop to conquer, because the distinction between stooping and loftiness is illusory. Yet one does have to conquer a place and a name, and with respect for, or at least management of, the wants and illusions of others.

It is characteristic, then, that the essay's nine injunctions for "discharge of thy place" are advanced in language very reminiscent of biblical commandments, while they actually set forth counsels on serving others to advance oneself. Bacon may advise that one follow the best example, but he next suggests that one examine whether one did the best. Lead, not follow. The two middle injunctions suggest creating one's own precedents, and, in the words of Machiavelli, reducing things "to the first institution." Look to the elemental necessities, which are one's own necessities, not to one's duties to a lord. The helps one needs are to be found in followers, not in providence, and the whole set of injunctions deals with preserving a place for subordinates, except for the concluding counsel for suitors. In later discussions of followers, suitors, and factions, Bacon treats followers as but instruments, suggests without reservation that some "make other men's business a kind of entertainment to bring in their own," and indicates that "the even carriage between two factions proceedeth not always of moderation, but of a trueness to a man's self, with end to make use of both" (38, 39, 41). In effect, "Of Great Place" redefines duty as a tool of self-advancement, and makes one's choice of public duties to follow from a calculation as to what serves one's advancement. The famous formula in full: "All rising to great place is by a winding stair; and if there be factions, it is good to side a man's self whilst he is in the rising, and to balance himself when he is placed."

Notes

1. *The Passions and the Interests* (Princeton, N.J.: Princeton University Press, 1978), 41.
2. *The Passions and the Interests*, 21–23
3. Steven Lukes, *Individualism* (Oxford: Basil Blackwell, 1985).
4. *Individualism*, 146.
5. *Individualism*, 156.
6. *Two Treatises of Government* II, v, 37, 40, 41, 43.
7. *Civil Image of Julius Caesar*, tr. in *Works* XII, 37; VI, 336; reprinted in this volume as Appendix 2.
8. See chapter 2 in this volume.
9. *Proemium*, in *Works* VIII, 17–18; IV, 7–8
10. *Of the Nature of Things*, tr. Cyril Bailey, in Vol. I of *De Rerum Natura* (Oxford: Clarendon Press, 1947), II, 1–13.
11. Bacon's strategy is clear enough. It is called later in the *Essays* a "form due in civility to kings and great persons, *laudando praecipere*, when by telling men what they are, they represent to them what they should be" ("Of Praise" 53). The concluding example in that essay is of praising things civil to the detriment of what "theologues, and friars, and Schoolmen" praise. Bacon takes full advantage of the realm of Caesar, which is the strategic summit (as Machiavelli had pointed out) that Holy Romans and Christians in general have left undefended. (*Discourses on the First Ten Books of Titus Livy*, III, 39. Consider the commentary of Mansfield, *Machiavelli's New Modes and Orders*.)
12. *Works* VIII, 85–86, 509–10; X, 287, 292; XIII, 123; IV, 60, 363–64, V, 419, 422–23; VI, 730.
13. *Remedy for Love*, 293, according to Kiernan, ed., *Essays*.
14. *Beyond Good and Evil*, aph. 199.
15. *Nicomachean Ethics*, 1123b1–25a35.

Chapter 5

The Ancients Corrected:
Wisdom as Policy, Friendship
as Leadership

The Illusion of Wisdom, the Policy of Knowledge

Bacon knows that his construction of the opportunistic self replaces the Platonic and Aristotelian accounts of what is good for the soul. He may vary from Machiavelli in secondary ways, but he differs decisively from the Socratic kind of political philosophy. There are obvious differences with Aristotle, and the profound differences go to the Socratic root that Aristotle shares with Plato. Bacon differs as to what philosophy is and how good it is, and as to whether politics is according to nature or but a useful convention. He rejects the ancient political philosophers' orientation by philosophy and politics, while nevertheless treating public policy, and a theoretical project for knowing nature and human nature, as necessary instruments of the self.

The Greek political philosophers had presupposed, or observed, both a certain natural desire for knowing and some degree of natural sociality in political association and in friendship. Bacon contends against any such suppositions. In essays on wisdom, love, beauty, and studies, Bacon denies, in effect, any such love of wisdom, and in two essays on friendship he contends, in effect, that there is no friendship except for followership. According to Bacon, Socratic dialectic is bewitched by seemings, and especially by the supposition that justice exists, and love of friends is also like being possessed by witches. Both slight the real necessities of life, and what seem natural goods are but illusions that "check with business." The conquest of nature begins at home.

The *Essays* has two essays with titles that refer to wisdom (23 and 26).

111

Each in its way indicts the subordination of the self and its business to goods beyond the self, to justice and wisdom in particular.

Admittedly, that is not the appearance given by these essays, and especially by "Of Wisdom for a Man's Self" (23), which seems to teach a rather traditional lesson favoring the public and disdaining the merely private. Self-love "wastes" society, the public, and governors, we are told; it is a depraved wisdom of animals; it is usually unfortunate. In a word, it is bad.

When one presses to find how bad and why bad, however, the first impressions of the essay begin to fray and a very tough underlying outlook comes to light. For one thing, each indictment of selfishness proves to contain a disconcerting qualification. Duty to society or the public belongs especially or perhaps only to "servants"; "the referring of all to a man's self is more tolerable in a sovereign prince. . . ."; only "in many branches" is selfish wisdom depraved; only "many times" are great lovers of themselves unfortunate. Also, the impressions of altruism or justice—a word never used in the essay—exceed what is said. "Divide with reason between self-love and society"; Bacon leaves the reader to infer where to draw the line. "[B]e so true to thyself, as thou not be false to others; specially to thy king and country"; Bacon leaves the reader to fix the degree to which truth to self is falsity to others. Eventually he provides guidance, and the emanations of biblical formality and parable are succeeded by distinctly unbiblical suggestions. Turning from selfishness (as "right earth") is reasonable—only if one can depend on a heavenly Lord. But Bacon then says that self-love is reasonable in a sovereign prince, which would imply that the earthly prince need not fear a heavenly prince. Beneath bland but distinctive reformulations of biblical teachings, Bacon replaces deference to divinity by deference to a sovereign and finally to one's own sovereignty. Continuing to prescribe a certain duty, he leads a submissive reader to replace simple duties of charity and piety by qualified duties to society and civil authority.

This argument does for justice what Bacon had already done for goodness in essay 13, which was also aimed principally at submissive readers and had reinterpreted Christian goodness first into humanity, then into self-reliance, and finally into an instrument of the political founder. While the language of both essays is rather pious and moral, "Of Wisdom for a Man's Self" reinterprets in a direction civil rather than humane. It transforms duty into civil duty, while intimating that duty belongs only to the weaker, to servants of princes and subordinates of states. Even this essay intimates that civil politics is a tool of the strong. The argument moves from talk of king and country, and citizen and subject, toward talk of master and servant, and this despite Bacon's inclusion among servants of rather important officials ("officers, treasurers, ambassadors, generals"); then the talk turns to the ways subordinates may profit by appearing to serve. In effect, all this talk authorizes inferiors to think of their interests as superior under cover of thinking for the public, which they now learn is only a state imposed by a superior. In a civil way, Bacon here tries to convert servants of a king and the Lord into ambitious staffers of enlightened states and princes, while only presupposing the radical and exploitative selfishness legitimated elsewhere.

If it is now clear why wisdom for the self is only "in many branches" depraved, it may remain unclear why Bacon even calls it depraved. Such a moral-sounding formulation, I suspect, is the initial waystation on the road from old Christian belief to enlightened belief, from a belief that selfishness is sinful, to a belief that unenlightened selfishness is useless.

Bacon is determined to eradicate moral as well as pious scruples. While the concluding argument at first says that wisdom for the self is the wisdom of animals, by argument's end one might well think that the animals have it right. Three sentences recount three examples of self-regarding animals: the rat leaves a falling home; the fox takes over a home by evicting the badger who built it; the crocodile cries while he devours. The author draws no conclusion. But the reader, especially if he or she now suspects that a wise selfishness is tolerable in superiors, might wonder whether man might learn from these lessons, not least from the fox who wrests his home from others' labor. Three times "wisdom" is attributed to the animals (Bacon begins by speaking of the "wise" ant). We are made to question what wisdom is, and whether it rises to a dignity above animal instincts (as seems evident and was alleged by Christian theology and ancient philosophy). Does one err in presuming a divinity above or an intellect within, which is heaven or happiness to know and sin or depravity to ignore?[1] Yes, according to Bacon. There may be a real problem with self-love, but it is a problem of shortsightedness, not of immorality or irreligion. "[T]hat which is specially to be noted" is that "lovers of themselves without a rival" are many times pinioned by the "inconstancy of fortune." This is a difficulty with a remedy, as Machiavelli would say, and Bacon, like Machiavelli, specializes in remedies for the vicissitudes of fortune. The next essay, "Of Innovations," indicates how a self might hide and nonetheless innovate. With that in mind, one might note that "Of Wisdom for a Man's Self" itself hides while innovating. It hides Bacon's liberation of selfishness. There is no essay on justice in all of *Essays or Counsels, Civil and Moral,* and Bacon's complicated revampings here hide the substitution of civil duty and enlightened self-interest for the authority of law and justice, human and divine.

What Bacon slides by in essay 23, which is for lesser followers, he confronts in "Of Seeming Wise" (26) and "Of Friendship" (27), which are for innovative leaders. In turn, they attack the Socratic activity of philosophizing and Aristotle's famous assertions that man is naturally political and inclined to friendship.

"Of Seeming Wise" (26) begins with an opinion, a "seeming," that contrasts two seemings with true wisdom, and this seems a sardonic reference to the Socratics, whose search for wisdom begins by attending to the surface or appearances of things. The argument is a series of attacks on "formalists" especially and thus, I believe, on the authors of the theory of forms or ideas. The formalists undertake various "shifts" that make "*superficies* to seem body that hath depth and bulk," but we must dismiss the looks we see in favor of the "body" that Bacon knows. We see that critique of traditional philosophy may depend upon Bacon's materialistic suppositions, a point considered in chapter 12.

Some formalists hide their teaching in obscurity, others only give out signs, while some, "speaking a great word," then "go on, and take by admittance that which they cannot make good." I suspect that Bacon here indicts the Socratics for arriving by supposition at the starting points of inquiry, as the *Nicomachean Ethics*, for example, begins by proposing that every art "seems to aim at some good." Bacon next attacks those who "would have their ignorance seem judgement," who are also those preoccupied with distinctions. As authorities, Bacon quotes Gellius (perhaps a stand-in for ancient teachers of rhetoric), and "Plato in his *Protagoras*," who "bringeth in Prodicus in scorn" with a speech stuffed with distinctions. But he proceeds to use the *Protagoras* inquiry, into a sophist's artifices, to condemn Socratic inquiry as an unreliable artifice.

In the *Protagoras*, Prodicus' woolly speechifying is but one effort to mediate a great contest between Socrates and Protagoras, who was the prince of sophists at the time and the first in Athens to promise openly to teach education and virtue and to make inquiry pay. Socrates leads Protagoras both to maintain that his lessons suffice for teaching the art of ruling and to admit that lessons other than in true knowledge may be overpowered by pleasure; he then shows that Protagoras cannot define true knowledge. But Bacon discredits Socrates' distinctions, including the distinction of truth from sophistry, and in general Socrates' dialectic, which would show the difficulties in common distinctions in an effort to arrive at a pruned and more truthful definition. "Generally, such men in all deliberations find ease to be the negative side, and affect a credit to object and foretell difficulties; for when propositions are denied, there is an end of them; but if they be allowed, it requireth a new work, which false point of wisdom is the bane of business." Bacon will show how inquiry directed to real business will yield an education that can really pay.

Bacon is especially concerned to discredit inquiry for its own sake, that is, from love of knowing. Plato's *Protagoras* is a festival of wisdom, gay and erotic, with a parade of leading sophists who claim wisdom and a crowd of young followers who want it. Socrates appears first as an admirer of the youthfully handsome (*kalon*) Alcibiades, and his struggle to win Alcibiades to his side in argument matches Alcibiades' desire for the young scions of Athens. Plato playfully characterizes the battle as titanic, and it seems a civilized version of the old struggles among Homeric heroes. It is a philosophic version. Socrates, the Platonic Achilles, eventually emerges victorious in argument over Protagoras, who reluctantly enters the Socratic arena of dialectic. Protagoras, mostly desiring applause and fees, prefers long speeches and fables. At the core of the drama is the difficulty of teaching virtue if one does not desire most to know what it is. But Bacon denies the dignity and even the reality of love, beauty, and charm, and especially of the love of knowing.

Bacon would discipline love, for if love "check once with business, it troubleth men's fortunes, and maketh men that they can no ways be true to their own ends" ("Of Love" 10). *Eros* may be the stuff of poets, and lead us to what seems high, true, and delightful, but Bacon discourages the poets' depiction of life as a festival or drama, treats love as "wanton," and never mentions love of truth, good, or beauty. Love of wisdom is probably the principal target in the essay on love. Bacon trickily manages an indictment: "It is a poor saying of Epicurus, *satis magnum alter alteri theatrum sumus* (Each is to another a theatre large enough)." Poor, comments Bacon in weighing this kind of drama, because man, made for "contemplation of heaven and all noble objects," should not kneel before objects of the eye. Even the courteous editor Clark Sutherland Northup called this "a curious perversion of the original." In the original, Seneca wrote that Epicurus, when writing to "one of his companions in study," said that he intended the writing "not for the crowd but for you; for we are theatre enough for each other."[2] While emanating a scent of philosophic concern for higher things, Bacon disdains philosophy and philosophic friends.

The real spur to knowing is not the good we love but the evil we fear; when Bacon for this reason rates deformity above beauty (for it "is an advantage to rising"), the example is Socrates ("Of Deformity" 44). In "Of Beauty" (43), Bacon first defines beauty as "strangeness" in proportion and touches its relation to virtue, but these, again, are but disarming scents of the familiar. For the virtue proves to be Machiavellian *virtu*, the proclivity for empire of such as Sulla, Augustus, and Tiberius, and beauty is redefined as "decent and gracious motion" and then "decent motion." Considering the examples, and considering also Bacon's reduction of goodness to a tool of ambition (13), a decent motion might be not more than an image that covers one's rising and one's place having risen. In "Of Vain Glory" (54), Bacon links Socrates to Aristotle and Galen as "men full of ostentation." The real aim of the philosophers was a dictatorship of opinions to get glory.

Bacon's own essay on knowing is in "Of Studies" (50), and it is a far cry from the playful *Protagoras*. Hippocrates had awakened Socrates at an ungodly hour with news of Protagoras' arrival in town, and shortly the two were off to listen and dispute. Bacon's best all-encompassing beginning in "Of Studies" reminds of that—studies "serve for delight, for ornament and for ability"—but the first two are soon put by, and the last becomes a matter of "use," indeed, of grim conspiracy. "For expert men can execute, and perhaps judge of particulars, one by one; but the general counsels, and the plots and marshalling of affairs, come best from those that are learned." The most useful men are those most useful to themselves, and they are not just expert in particular arts but in counsel in general, that is, in plots about human affairs in general.

The subordination of wisdom to advancement of the self is thematic in the *Essays*, especially in its critique of truth at the start and its replacement of the priority of wisdom with arts of self and state. The old word "wisdom" proves to be but a seeming. Socratic dialectic is not "divine madness." It is only madness, however bewitching. The wise are the politic, and the truly politic are the comprehensively politic, they who are coolly immune to the witchery of the goods, beauties, and truths that men claim to divine. Wisdom for the self begins with criticism of natural consciousness and culminates in the construction of an artful consciousness. The *Essays* applies to human nature the twin poles of Bacon's science of nature: skepticism and method, and thus the politics of progress can create a world for human use. But is the godlike power bestowed by Bacon, the self-conscious Prometheus, worth the cost? Apart from the bomb and other such powers, is it worth alienation from the human world we naturally know, and most poignantly from the good things which the most promising love?

Friendship as Negotiation with Followers

"But little do men perceive what solitude is, and how far it extendeth" ("Of Friendship" 27). The tenor of that sentence is as up-to-date as the last twentieth-century novel exploring a self alone in a whiteout of nothingness. Nor is the similarity of old and new merely of words or accident. Bacon contributed to the modernist worldview, which has culminated in existentialism and postmodernism. The *Essays* in particular beats repeatedly at a theme: the self's illusions as to a natural happiness that may be shared are but illusion; the self's desires for things beyond it are but vanity; the self is a bare self and bare not least of friendship. Still, according to Bacon, the self's very vulnerability goads it to progressive provision and especially to aid from others. Just this insistence on a calculating provision for progress is what the existentialists indict, for human authenticity requires, they say, that our aloneness be faced and lived by. "Existence precedes essence." But there is a prior premise to be faced and questioned: the supposition that the self is bare of an inclination to goods and, in particular, to friends.

According to Bacon, friendship is another misleading cloud or witchery, another illusion that leads human beings away from being true to themselves. Two essays thematically reduce friendship and friends to alliance and followers, and the connection between the two is obvious despite the fact that they are some twenty essays apart ("Of Friendship" 27, "Of Followers and Friends" 48). The pair begins by attacking a premise of the Aristotelian doctrine that men are naturally political, the supposition that they share thoughts and aspiration, and concludes by replacing, with a Machiavellian maxim that friends are really followers, the Aristotelian doctrine that friendship is among equals. "Of Friendship" cautions princes against friendship, and then more boldly leads the prince to followers who can perpetuate his desires by following them. "So that a man hath, as it were, two lives in his desire." "Of Followers and Friends" calculates the followers most useful to the self, which are those whom Bacon elsewhere describes as "of mean condition, but industrious and active,"[3] and is emphatic in its Machiavellian solution as to even the greatest colleagues: "There is little friendship in the world, and least of all between equals, which was wont to be magnified. That that is, is between superior and inferior, whose fortunes may comprehend the one the other."

Perhaps the greatest eulogy of friendship is in books 8 and 9 of the *Nicomachean Ethics*, and it is independent of the *Politics'* account of politics. Fellow citizens share a lesser form of friendship, according to Aristotle, and only the most thoughtful human beings share the fullest form. Bacon's "Of Friendship" takes as its target the Aristotelian account. He denies that men divine something above their desires, and he denies, accordingly, both a natural tendency toward community or friendship and a natural superiority of a best form of friendship.

Perhaps the most famous of all Aristotelian doctrines maintains that man is naturally political. The person who remains outside the city as self-sufficient or incapable of association is either a god or a beast. But Bacon repeatedly suggests that humans by nature may indeed be beastlike ("Of Atheism" 16 and "Of Wisdom for a Man's Self" 23). Aristotle had suggested that it is speech that marks the particular sociality of man. Speech serves to reveal "the advantageous and the harmful, and hence also the just and unjust"; man alone has "a perception of good and bad and just and unjust," and it is "partnership in these things" that makes a household and city. The authoritative distinctiveness of speech is not only the basis of man 's natural politicality, but also of a friendship that rises above politics. For those who are most moved by speech are those who consider their thoughts and those of others. The rationality that underlies political association culminates in the conversations of the most thoughtful.

But Bacon in many places denies the authoritative status of the insights of speech (since "primary notions" are but mistaken abstractions from the facts). He denies as well that there is a peak of sociality to which politics points, a philosophic friendship that seems higher and more divine than the doltish compromises of politics. Earlier in the *Essays* he had disposed of the supposition that a godlike wise man might be decisively self-sufficient ("Of Truth" 1, "Of Love" 10, and "Of Seeming Wise" 26); any man needs aid in protecting himself. "Of Friendship" attacks principally the effect that the supposition of divinings has upon a leader's search for aid. It distracts him from his aloneness, and it misleads him into searching for divine help. The essay attacks especially the supposition that man partakes of divine friendships by "divine conversations." While Bacon deals not in high visions, but in real effects, or in visions only as they can have real effects, his argument here suggests that the real effect of a belief in the divine within us is various pretenders to a higher conversation with the Lord. "Of Friendship" itself juxtaposes heathen pretenders with their holy equivalents as if to suggest doubts about the divine conversations of "holy fathers."

Having disposed of divinations, "Of Friendship" turns to the solitude that men little perceive. Aristotle had said that cities arise for the sake of life but exist for the sake of a good life; a good common life requires a small city with a regime in which good men can rule well.[4] Bacon treats such thoughts as illusions. From its start, essay 27 talks of "society," not of polity or regime, avoiding the term "city" and even describing Babylon as a "great town." A fundamental solitude accompanies crowds, faces, talk, and towns.

Nevertheless, friends warily understood are *the* aid to the lonely self. While "Of Friendship" says that friends serve one's affections, judgment, and action, these traditional-sounding names veil discussions first of followers and then of the true self. The true self appears here as a mixture of natural force and invented image, the image needed to obtain followers and even new countries of followers. The essay discusses first the "use" of friendship, and the first use, venting the affections, might remind one of the obvious pleasures of companionship. The resemblance, however, only introduces the usual Baconian slide from the familiar to the new. Bacon speaks not of pleasure, but of "ease and discharge" of "heart" or "passions," words that convey relief from the pain of pressing forces, and the examples of passion, while curiously varied, bear out the point: "griefs, joys, fears, hopes, suspicions, counsels," and whatever else oppresses the heart. Even "counsels" are included among these forces or passions, and this strange equation is quickly developed. Diseases of the mind are quickly equated with those of the body, and remedies for bodily ailments with recipes for the "health" of the mind. Bacon had put out signs earlier, as when he explained envy as an "ejaculation or irradiation," a "stroke or percussion," a "blow" of the eye ("Of Envy" 9). But "Of Friendship" is almost expansive in unveiling a materialistic account of mind or soul. It explains the way friendship doubles joy and halves grief: "But yet without praying in aid of alchemists, there is a manifest image of this in the ordinary course of nature. For in bodies, union strengtheneth and cherisheth any natural action; and on the other side weakeneth and dulleth any violent impression, and even so of minds."

Still, the great Baconian teaching as to friendship is less of its nature than of its art. The art of friendship is the art of managing those close to one, and this, like all the Baconian formulas for managing forces to maximum use, begins with critical thinking. Princes need to learn how friends can strengthen natural action, not betray it, and the first lesson is in seeing that friendship itself is an illusion and a dangerous one. "[G]reat kings and monarchs" go astray because they befriend many times "at the hazard of their own safety and greatness." Nor are only "modern" princes concerned with "grace or conversation" (Bacon hints, perhaps, at the role in his day of chaplains, poets, the learned, prayers, and confession). "The wisest and most politic" rulers in other times have erred by faith, and Bacon illustrates with five successful and ruthless Romans and two similarly ruthless moderns. Even such empire-builders have been bewitched by the illusion of friendship with men or gods. They did not know how to be altogether alone.

This is an extraordinary discussion, and it should cure anyone who still believes that the Baconian enlightenment, however humanitarian, is at its root humanitarian. In this list of the most wise and politic rulers, four of the five Romans were emperors, and these four were famous for destroying the republic and in particular the patrician class; all five of the Romans were notably self-centered. Caesar overthrew what remained of the republic, Augustus settled imperial authority, Tiberius made it despotic by destroying the independent aristocrats who remained, and Severus destroyed anew a revived senate. While Lucius Sulla indeed defended the republic, or at least the senate and patrician order, Tacitus, at least, had seen a tyrant beneath the pretense: "L. Sulla, cruelest of the nobles, turned liberty conquered by arms into tyranny."[5] But Bacon judges these five to have enjoyed a "felicity" that was "as great as ever happened to mortal men," and he even twists a story to make Sulla seem inadequately preoccupied with his sovereignty and future greatness. Later in the *Essays*, Bacon singles out Severus as the ablest, almost, of the Roman emperors— Severus, who was ruthlessly and even spectacularly cruel. In conquering his way to the diadem, Severus threw the heads of his rivals over ramparts defended by their partisans, held and then killed the children of one of them, and upon victory killed more than sixty of the most honorable senators. He openly defended severity and cruelty and ruled by terror, albeit a calculated and not an impulsive terror.[6]

There is a thematic discussion of the dangers of friendship in the *Civil Image of Julius Caesar*, which holds explicitly that happiness comes from dominating like an emperor and as one radically alone. Caesar, says Bacon, undoubtedly had "greatness of mind . . . in a very high degree; yet such as aspired more after personal aggrandizement (*quae magis amplitudines propriam*) than merit towards the public. For he referred everything to himself, and was himself the true and perfect center of all his own actions: which was the cause of his singular and almost perpetual felicity. For he allowed neither country, nor religion, nor services, nor kindred, nor friendships to be any hindrance or bridle to his purposes."[7] Yet Caesar was not sufficiently alone. According to Bacon, he was not sufficiently wary as to all other human beings. A liberation from family, gods, goods, and friends is the product of critique and art, not of the actual Caesar. The *Civil Image* concludes that Caesar erred decisively in forgiving his enemy Brutus, and "Of Friendship" concludes that all these emperors threw themselves away upon friends, as if by a religious faith in magical aids. Caesar was enchanted by Decimus Brutus (who led him to the senate and death), as by a "witch," and Tiberius Caesar evidently believed in religious consecrations of friendship. Even Augustus and Severus, who were more calculating, were insufficiently artful. While they used friends to "overlive" them, they used agents and heirs forced upon them, instead of the men most useful to themselves. There seems to be a different problem in the rulers of Bacon's time, a reliance not on men without but on a god-man above. "Of Friendship" examines the cases of Charles the Bold (last Duke of Burgundy, 1467–77), and Louis XI (who took Burgundy for France, 1461–83), and finds excessive solitude. They communicated their secrets to no one and were hence "cannibals of their own hearts." While venting of the heart is a "civil shrift or confession," these princes lacked a realistic venting that might lead to a real life after death. This came from looking to an illusory friend or to no one. Louis XI, ruthless and deceitful as he was in unifying France and breaking the nobility, confessed to priests and was infinitely superstitious during his last fearful years, and he thus ate his heart in fear while attending to holy mysteries and lacking hope in his own devices. Charles retreated to a melancholic austerity after he lost the battle for Burgundy.[8] Natural friendship, in short, combines blind passion with misleading illusions.

"Of Friendship" sets forth the artful way, which invents real remedies and exposes illusory ones. First Bacon proceeds to expose the mysteries, by referring the force of friendship to the force of natural bodies, and then he invents an artificial light, to manage friends for real benefits to oneself. A friend can provide "dry light," which both teaches bodily limits and provides formulas for a life beyond the body's death. This formula is of course Bacon's formula, and a suspicious mind might wonder whether Bacon suggests here that he can be the friend of every tyrannical ambition. There follow two teachings, less and more common. A less "vulgar" teaching turns back responsibility to "you": whetting our thoughts on others helps to develop our wits and to determine how to use others more extensively. A more vulgar teaching suggests how counsel by friends may help us, while hiding, perhaps, how counsel serves the counsellor. I spell out these steps.

First Bacon talks to "you," to the abler who will follow the quick Baconian sketch of the art of thinking that follows the quick reduction of passion to bodily force. You learn that the art of thinking, and perhaps speech itself, is more an invention than a natural gift. One must "break up" thoughts, which otherwise "lie lost as in packs," and turn them into speech. Bacon misquotes words to imply that Themistocles distinguished thoughts from speech, and there is a puzzling brevity that hides the radical innovation. Bacon has suggested that thoughts are not in speech, but precede speech, and thus that words (and speech) are not coeval with human thought, but added, indeed invented. Bacon talks around the Aristotelian understanding of speech, which had distinguished reasoning from intellect and supposed that the words and opinions with which reasonable people reason are loose approximations of insights divined by intellect. Instead, he portrays a man using his "wits and understanding" to break up, then to toss, then to "marshall" thoughts, and finally to turn them into words. So "a man learneth of himself" and "whetteth his wits." He learns of the natural forces that move him, and he sharpens his artificial forces, which are *his* wits, as instruments.

In this essay, Bacon clarifies the relation between our nature and the artful self. What is primary are natural forces that yield our observation of what we want. Bacon makes us conscious of necessity within and without; in managing the motions of things without, including other human beings, the self carries on its primary desire to endure. But precisely because the "understanding" is drenched with "affections," as well as "customs," counsel is valuable. While "there is no such flatterer as is a man's self," and a man may have "high and fond imaginations" to "think himself all in all," he will have to face up to the necessities that Bacon poses. He may suppose that one eye sees as well as two, or a gamester as well as a looker-on, or a man in anger as well as one who has calmed himself, or that a rifle can be fired from an arm as well as from a rest. But he will therefore fail in his seeing and fighting. Bacon counsels observation, calm, and a support amidst our motions, if only to aim our weapons well. A wary friend can help us take a stand against the passions that hurry us along. The crucial friends seem to be doctors and counsellors (as to "business"). Bacon speaks first of a physician of "your body"—he tacitly rejects curates and philosophers who promise cure of the soul—and then turns to him who in treating of "business" is familiar with one's "estate." Bacon may be our great friend in this as in others parts of the relief of man's estate.

In the concluding reasonings of "Of Friendship," he shows the connection of friendship with body, business, and estate. Since the body will go, it is your business to acquire an estate that will preserve your name in state. The argument begins by considering a man's necessities, the things that a man "cannot do himself," and turns to attack Plutarch's Aristotelian maxim that "a friend is another himself." Bacon attacks the opinion that a friend might be desirable for his own sake. The *Nicomachean Ethics* had found the best friendships rooted in self-concern, but in self-love, not in self-interest, and in love of self understood as a virtuous soul's love of good things. Seeing in a friend the things that one loves, is like seeing them in a second self and thus having them oneself.[9] Bacon contradicts, for a self is concerned with itself, not its good. A friend "is far more than himself," because men die desiring to finish a work, and by a friend a man has "two lives in his desires." A body is confined to place, whereas friends like seeds may cause growths that allege a man's merits. Friends seem to be bodies on which may be grafted new powers to expand, keep, and resurrect oneself. Perhaps the aim of action is most bluntly stated at the start of the second book of the *New Organon*: "On a given body to generate and superinduce a new nature, or new natures, is the work and aim of Human Power."[10] If so, *the* work and aim of human power is to superinduce on followers a work that will keep alive one's name. To put the point in civil terms, the core of civil science is negotiation, according to *Advancement of Learning*, and negotiation is for followers.[11]

How to treat followers is the theme of the second essay on friendship, "Of Followers and Friends" (48). It comes after "Of Negotiating," which describes dealing for followers, and precedes "Of Suitors," which describes how in dealing to take advantage of the wants of others. These essays are difficult and enigmatic, perhaps because they explore how to exploit by seeming to aid, and they neither quote nor rely on any other man, which perhaps indicates Bacon's own originality and superiority.

From its start, "Of Negotiating" speaks of instruments for dealing and presumes that all dealing is a quest for instruments. One should seek emissaries who are plain, who "affect" the plan, and who are "fit" for it. The problem even with those "in appetite" is their "conditions" of agreement, especially if they seek some satisfaction prior to their performance. To the difficulty in dealing with those who look for equal satisfaction Bacon does not offer a solution, but talks first of possible solutions and then of general ways to manage others—without necessarily providing them real satisfactions. As to possible solutions: perhaps the nature of the deal requires the other's performance, or the other can be persuaded that he will be needed for something else, or one can be counted the more honest. Whatever these suggestions may imply, the essay closes with unequivocal instruction in how to "work any man." You can lead him by his "nature and fashions" (with fashion now substituted for custom or opinion), persuade him by his ends, awe him if he is weak, or "govern" him through "those that have interest in him." Governing is the effect on some through others with an interest in them. But how do you get that "some" to follow you, especially since Bacon does not indicate that they take an interest in you? Bacon seems to answer as he concludes this general account of management. After noting the special difficulty of moving the cunning, he gives a final prescription that might get some to follow you while hardly interested in you. You can prepare a long-term plan and "ripen it by degrees." I suspect that all this indirection indicates the strategy behind Bacon's immense and future-oriented project.

"Of Followers and Friends" seems to investigate the instruments required for such a plan and to conclude that a combination of the ordinary and the active are to be preferred to the oligarchic or aristocratic. The essay begins by favoring "ordinary" people over the costly, factious, and glorious. After some reservations (Bacon mixes criticism of the gossipy and nosy, with commendation of their use as spies), Bacon proceeds to recommend unequivocally being followed by "estates of men," and then adds that it is "most honorable" to be followed because one is thought to advance "virtue and desert." This scent of gentlemen and aristocrats arises only to be dispelled. "And yet, where there are no eminent odds in sufficiency, it is better to take with the more passable, than with the more able." So much for the dignity of virtue, which Bacon tacitly equates with ability. That deflation accomplished, he revises his deflation of the able, albeit in language that retains the scent of virtue: "in base times" side with the "active." The stirring, the energetic, the busy, the mobile—these are the class to seek. In short, Bacon sets forth here the ultimate reasons why his civil writings patronize the mixture of ordinariness and energy that is the modern middle class.

"Of Followers and Friends" concludes by considering by whom one should be "governed (as we call it)." Why does an essay on followers consider one's governors? Perhaps there can be governors who are friends, that is, followers of one's plans, and for that reason have an interest in one's plans for their own ends, that is, for their own rising. Bacon, that is, has plans that will obtain power because they serve those who want to rise to power.

This passage is weighing, I suspect, which governors of states or states of mind he would have follow him. Bacon introduces it with the advice that one "not make too much of any man at the first," and this fits the *Essays*; the work refrains from deference to superiors, at least after the malicious letter of dedication. The discussion slides off to consider who should be sought as advisors, but the succession of assertions is hard to put together. While you should not choose one favorite, nor choose a crowd or democracy of advisers, to take advice from a "few friends" is "ever honorable," and, as if from a friend, Bacon sets forth a maxim: "for lookers-on many times see more than gamesters, and the vale best discovereth the hill." Scholars have not found the origin of this precise maxim, a favorite of Bacon, although Clark Sutherland Northup points to the dedication to *The Prince*. The second half of the maxim indeed resembles the second half of Machiavelli's maxim: one must be on high to know the low and down low to know the high. Yet the whole seems Bacon's, and it announces, perhaps, that governors should look for a certain adviser, a "looker-on" whose counsels encompass the real forces of action and can guide the game of life. Bacon's edge in human affairs, even over Machiavelli, is the promise of prediction. While he closes the essay by confuting Aristotle's suggestion that friendship must be of equals, he quietly incorporates Machiavelli, with his tough-minded maxims and followers, within his own more civil movement. He manages Machiavelli into being a follower, and he will govern others through the interest that Machiavelli had in them and Machiavellianism has for them.

In the third of this trio on high-level management, "Of Suitors" (49), Bacon shows his more legal and public way of servicing private claims and wants. He adopts the legal rubric of lawsuits and begins and ends with the suggestion that a multiplication of private suits hurts the "public good" and "public proceedings." Yet the theme of the essay is not legal, and certainly not fairness in decisions (as by just corrections of damage or injury). "Of Suitors" shows instead how leaders can use private needs or wants, not least of the cunning, even to making "other men's business a kind of entertainment to bring in their own." Good matters may be brought by bad minds who are, Bacon explains patiently, not corrupt but crafty minds. The essay is a lesson in craftiness when dealing with suits, especially crafty suits. Someone might take up suits for his or her own purposes, it notes, or take them up only to make use of the suitor's hopes, or for an occasion or to cross a rival. Followers who have served their turn may be left to fall. I have suggested before that Bacon plans luxurious but defenseless houses and gardens, in part, to ease the princely and triumphant in their fall. These Bacon has befriended for his own purposes, and they will serve in Bacon's plans for a time, but in the long run, they will be eased by modernization from real rule and power.

Justice in suits, then, is not the point, although it may be managed to favor the followers one would like to get. While there is "some sort of right" in every suit, the sequel takes up not the justice of the suit, but the use of the suit to the governor of the suitors, and it follows up with suggestions for handling the parties if "affection" makes one lean to the "wrong side" in justice or equity. For example, one might by one's "countenance" manage to "compound the matter," and thus put a face of justice on a desire that one can satisfy under cover of a civic compound. Such helpful counsels, a political science of advancing the self through images that appear to satisfy other selves, might show the benefit of a "friend of trust and judgement" in handling suits (which is the next counsel). Soon the argument turns to "suits of favor"—should a man of deep judgment treat all requests as appeals to his interest or favor?—and moves beyond cases at law, and from deciding suits to raising them. These lessons in rousing demands, and not just legal demands, become very clipped and enigmatic. Bacon seems to be considering whose wants and appetites a great revolutionary like himself should favor. Know what is at stake; decide upon secrecy or upon an openness that may encourage like suits; consider, principally, "timing of the suit." We are reminded of the counsel that closes "Of Negotiation": ripen gradually a future-oriented plan. "Of Suitors" continues: in asking or dispensing favor, choose the fittest instrument, certain for the purpose, not the greatest in general. An example: Bacon elsewhere recommends that one foster a rising economy by favoring industrious entrepreneurs and active investors, not the rich or the noble. The pleasure of friends must be replaced by patronage of the followers that will carry one's work. Finally, Bacon warns that one must have a "good cause" in applying to "a great person," else one loses reputation. So Bacon with his cause of progress and power can both attract old princes and rouse new classes, thus to win new friends in the future who will not know him, who will not know even when they are let down by him, but who will follow and help even when they do not know.

Notes

1. *Essays* uses "depravity" three other times, each in a religious context. In the fifty-eight essays, the term "sin" occurs but twice: in the second essay, as part of a preliminary opinion called "holy and religious" and in the next-to-last essay, in an opinion attributed to an oracle.

2. Quoted by Northup, ed., *The Essays of Francis Bacon*, 189–90.

3. "Imago Civilis Julii Caesaris," in *Works* XII, 40; VI, 345. The original and translation of the brief "Images" of Julius and Augustus are reprinted in this volume as appendixes 1–4.

4. *Politics*, 1253a, 1–18.

5. Cornelius Tacitus, *Histories*, II, 38. This reference was provided by James Leake.

6. J. S. Reid, "Lucius Septimus Severus," in *Encyclopaedia Britannica*, 11th ed., 1911, vol. 24.

7. As translated in *Works* XII, 35–36; VI, 341.

8. James T. Shotwell, "Louis XI," in *Encylopaedia Britannica*, 11th ed., 1911, vol. 17; Kiernan, ed., *The Essayes or Counsels, Civill and Morall*, 229.

9. 1168a28–69b2.

10. II i, in *Works* VIII, 167; IV, 119.

11. Of the fifty sections into which W. A. Wright has divided the account of civil science in *Advancement*, forty-three treat of negotiation (II, xxiii, 4–46; in *Works* VI, 350–87; III, 447–73).

Chapter 6

The Emperor over Time

Baconian individualism culminates in a leader who seeks to be one alone by rising above human neediness, and who proceeds above others, and even above oblivion, by providing for others in their neediness. The good, the true, and the beautiful may be merely witcheries, in Bacon's opinion, and yet there is immense grandeur in the plan for a prince with a public cause that can conquer the minds of future generations. But Bacon's point is not the grandeur, but the generality and durability. Bacon's is a studied grandeur, or rather a calculated domination; it follows from conspiratorial studies of "general counsels" and "plots," as "Of Studies" (50) puts it. The prince's aim is security of life, radically understood, and what immortality a man finds, he must conquer for himself. The best images for conquering time are those of the great rulers who are also humane benefactors, for the humane benefactor has the more general appeal. King Solamona, the founder of the scientific establishment in Bensalem, wins a glory separate and superior to that of the nation's defender, Altabin the general-king.

I spell out these two sides of the supreme Baconian prince by considering, first, Bacon's little "civil images" of the two greatest Caesars[1] and, second, his reworking in *The Wisdom of the Ancients* of the legend of Prometheus, the mythic inventor of the arts. If one were to place these epitomes in Bacon's big picture, they would be among his comprehensive arts of life and state, and they would illustrate the peak of the art of appearing in state. This is the art of ostentation set forth in *Essays*, 52–55. There Bacon commends, in turn, production of reputation by an impression on others, a civil reputation by which one might put down prophecy, the sort of reputation that obtains perpetual glory for oneself, and, finally, the reputation of a master of men who is also a lawgiver and a liberator or savior. While essay 55 ranks "founders of states and commonwealths" first in degree of "sovereign honor," Bacon's work on scientific method asserts that "the introduction of famous discoveries" holds "by far the first place among human actions."[2] Bacon overcomes this duality, I suggested in chapter 2, when he discovers the possibility of a civilization that wins an empire over men's minds, that is, when he discovers the "arts and sciences" that "establish and extend the power and dominion of the human race itself over the universe." His is a comprehensive art of governing that combines the arts of Caesar with those of scientific benefactor. Bacon will enjoy not only the founder's place, first in honor according to essay 55, but also the "lawgiver's" second place and the "savior's" third. He is a lawgiver and thus a "*perpetui principes,*" such as Lycurgus or Solon (who republicanized the ancient oligarchy of Athens). He is also one of the "*liberatores* or *salvatores*" who "compound" civil wars or "deliver their countries from servitude of strangers or tyrants," such as Augustus Caesar or Henry VII of England.

It is surely significant that Bacon's works abound with praises of Julius and Augustus Caesar, and that he praises most Augustus, the founder-emperor, and mixes his praise of Augustus with his expositions of the new science. It is true that the little civil image of Augustus is but a brief supplement to that of Julius, but it is also true that it suggests how Augustus' civil arts improved on Julius' more natural impulse (*impetu*). Bacon shows how, for the sake of enduring glory, the passion for glory must be mastered by art. And why do many of the highest praises of Augustus occur in the writings on science? Perhaps Augustus is a model for the mastery of nature in the crucial respect. In "Sphinx, or Science," chapter 28 of *Wisdom of the Ancients,* Bacon remarks that Augustus "certainly excelled in the art of politics if ever man did," and in a chapter on mastering fortune from the same work, he says that "I" count Augustus "the most fortunate of any man" ("Nemesis, or the Vicissitudes of Things" 22).[3]

There is an art of empire at the core of Bacon's science of nature, and while the "Civil Images" show how Machiavellian arts of mastering human nature improve on even the arts of the Caesars, the "Prometheus" exhibits not only such improvements but also Bacon's chief improvement on the Machiavellian arts. The subtitle of "Prometheus" is "The State of Man." In recasting the traditional myth, Bacon shows how he is founding a tradition that liberates and saves. It will liberate mankind from divinity, notably from the faith that had enabled priests to conquer Augustus' state, and it will save mankind from a barren nature.

Lessons of the Caesars

The *Civil Image of Julius Caesar* asserts with forceful prose what the *Essays* tends to advance much more indirectly. Perhaps that is why Bacon did not publish it. Caesar's climb to power as one alone illustrates fortune exercised (Bacon is silent about good luck in family and wealth). The one bit of fortune Bacon mentions is Caesar's great mind, which is identified, after a glancing reference to "intellect," with a mix of great desire (*impetu*) and great decisiveness. Caesar's "self" was the "true and perfect center of all his own actions," and this single-mindedness caused his "singular and almost perpetual felicity." He almost always sought "real power" and was a master of the arts of winning men; he was "made up entirely of arts." Still, there was a big cunning that enabled him to forgo little ones: "It was in the business of war that his ability was most conspicuous." Managing all things by himself, especially "men's minds," he achieved the rule that Bacon (and Plutarch, too) says he always sought.

Bacon analyzes Caesar's rise. He first broke the senate by becoming popular, then defeated the leaders (Pompey and Crassus) with whom he had allied. He obtained his own army and territory (in Gaul) and triumphed easily, and in a manner that sheds light on Altabin's victory over Atlantis: Caesar "won the battle almost before it began" by distributing various "private benefits." In war he was cautious, letting others fight when possible, and friendship was an instrument, not an impediment. His "interest and main business" governed his pleasures; else Caesar was "not particular in his lusts." This is Bacon's bland assessment of the voracious appetites at which Cicero had sneered: "He was every woman's man, and every man's woman."[4] Among these remarks and others (every word needs commentary), Bacon inserts reservations and concludes decisively. Caesar was insufficiently ruthless and insufficiently calculating, especially in being too forgiving (Bacon probably refers to his pardon of Marcus Brutus after the defeat of Pompey's cause at Pharsalia). Whether out of "virtue or art," this gentleness cost Caesar his life and empire. Caesar, one might say, did not know how to be altogether bad. The lesson is consistent with remarks on Julius in other Baconian works, including the *Essays*. Not only did Julius choose as an heir Decimus Brutus, who persuaded him to go to his death in the senate ("Of Friendship" 27), he was too frank in declaring both his ambition to be dictator ("Of Sedition and Troubles" 15) and his ability to control the favor of the gods.[5]

The "Civil Image" is precise about the root of Caesar's defects: he too directly glorified himself, and he neglected his fate after death. Despite his hunger for fame, Julius confined his thoughts to his times and did not attend adequately to "perpetuity." He did not establish a "state of affairs," or pretend to reestablish the commonwealth, or found a building or "institution," or subordinate power to reputation. "By natural impulse, therefore, not through some discipline of mores, he sought supreme power" (*itaque veluti naturali impetu, non morata aliqua disciplina ductus, rerum potiri volebat*). He was too much moved by unbounded impulse (*impetu infinito*), according to the "Image" of Augustus. While Julius selected good means to his ends, he had not his ends (*fines*) themselves arranged "in good order." Insofar as he sought glory, he sought it by glorious names, such as "king," that had no long-term general appeal: he aimed at "things beyond the reach of mortality." He wanted the title of king despite the people's hatred of that name, and, as to learning, he was impressed with the omens of astrology and wrote only about practical business.

By contrast, the sober Augustus (Bacon adopts his great name) arranged his ends "mindful of his mortal condition" and marshalled his desires so that he might turn himself and his inheritance into a name that could dominate. Even without his uncle's *impetu*, Augustus' more reposed nature better managed itself to power, to esteem and merit, to enjoyment, and finally to memory. Art is superior to nature in the decisive case. Augustus sought the first place and worked to make himself esteemed in it, luxuriating only then, and even then he provided for transmitting to "the next ages the impression of the image and the effects of the virtue of his government." Still, one has to note that Augustus does not rectify all the defects of Julius. His image and effects in Rome were effaced by Jesus, he too failed to pretend to a republic, and he did not write. Bacon will improve upon his model by a civil teaching and a humane science. Also, it was Julius and his *impetu* who overthrew the republic and founded the empire of the Caesars. When Bacon provides in the *Essays* his "true Marshalling of the degrees of sovereign honor," he gives "Caesar" the central place in the first rank of *conditores imperiorum*, which he translates as "founders of states and commonwealths" and which also includes the legendary Romulus and founders of great religio-political empires, such as "Ottoman" and "Ismael." "Augustus" is placed in the third rank, of "liberators" and "saviors."

These Baconian portraits are preoccupied with imperial success, and the point is highlighted when one compares them with other accounts, such as that of Julius by Plutarch and that of both Caesars in Shakespeare's *Julius Caesar*.

Plutarch had painted a nobler Julius, with a "natural inclination for great deeds," not merely for domination, with ambition for "new glory," not merely for power. While Plutarch, too, notes a certain lack of foresight, he praises Caesar for generous clemency in civil war; despite the necessities of the time, he criticizes him for occasioning the calamities of civil war and staging a triumph over the sons of Pompey, "sons of the bravest of Romans." Plutarch dwells on Caesar's remarkable qualities (mostly for good, but for evil, too), and on Rome's public good, and this infuses his account with the drama of grand events and of the rise and fall of noble men. While reading Bacon's version, one forgets the finale of the friendship with Brutus: "Et tu, Brute?"

In Shakespeare's portraits, magnanimity governs, and Julius' ambition for a godlike self-sufficiency governs most. "What touches us ourself shall be last served" (III, i, 8). Admittedly, this is brittle. At home and out of the public eye, Shakespeare's Caesar evinces some apprehension and superstition; in the senate he professes himself as the North Star and Olympus, and this just before he is stabbed. The claims to greatness, though, seem less dissimulation than an extreme manifestation of Caesar's magnanimous desire for self-sufficiency. It is Roman grandeur of soul that Caesar exalts to imperial proportions, and perhaps beyond any man's deserving. But this is tragic exaggeration on a grand scale, rather than a failure of calculation on a huge scale. Caesar is genuinely greater in soul than the patricians Brutus and Cassius, and it is his spirit that the playwright makes preside over their tragic end. Caesar conducts himself as a god, seeks apotheosis as a god through martyrdom, and avenges himself as a spirit after death.[6] It is understandable that Suetonius begins his *Twelve Caesars* with the words "Julius Caesar, the Divine." Actually, Shakespeare portrays Brutus and Cassius as also aspiring in their politics to something divine. But it is Caesar's victory, his winning the honor befitting a god, that exhibits on an imperial scale such an ambition and its difficulties. Bacon substitutes for magnanimity, thus understood, calculated purposes useful for an empire over the future. This is surely a part of what in the late twentieth century is called the "disenchantment of the world," the part that removes nobility from the peaks of the political world.

Shakespeare reserves his grim colors for Octavian Caesar. In *Antony and Cleopatra*, we see the future Augustus in the midst of his conquering, and while he is great in conquering the world, one is tempted to think him less appealing in many ways than the visibly flawed Antony. Octavian is politically knowing and preternaturally forceful, voracious for news of his enemies, swift in disposing his forces, and dominated by passion for "my state" and the great prize. Adept at rising by friendships and alliances and then at dissolving them, he eliminates young Pompey, then Lepidus, then Antony. He channels former adherents of Antony into the front lines, and his own lieutenants fight his battles. He promises gentleness to Cleopatra if she will submit herself as a trophy in his Roman triumph, and he threatens to kill her children if she refuses. "Let determined things to destiny hold unbewailed their way," he tells his sister Octavia after she leaves the incompatible Antony, with whom Octavian had knowingly allied her for his own purposes. He swears by "the elements," not by the gods above.

It is true that Octavian sheds tears at Antony's death, but that, according to Mecenas, is because he sees himself in the "spacious mirror" provided by Antony and his fate. It is also true that Shakespeare portrays Octavian's determined craft and force as austerely great and also as necessary. Monarchy is the only good alternative in face of the "strong necessities" accompanying the breakdown of the republic. But Shakespeare keeps in mind the better and best even while acknowledging the greatness and the necessities; he shows the price of a great dictator. Although Octavian exhorts his troops a final time with the promise of "universal peace," his own Thyreus arraigns him while warning Cleopatra, "Put yourself under his shroud, the universal landlord." The universal empire will be death to freedom. It is a comprehensive dictatorship, which will cater to the rough army that elevated Octavian and will be the prop of any emperor. To govern will require ruthless force and fraud above and servility below, and old Romans of the old republican virtues will find no place. Enobarbus kills himself; Octavia is rejected by the pleasure-loving Antony; Antony's aging manliness is betrayed by Cleopatra and his love of pleasure; he and his faithful Eros die by their own hands. We see a corrupt Antony drawn to the soft relaxation of the East and drawn especially to Cleopatra, who surrounds herself with women and eunuchs, never has to govern, and longs for saving gods to send infinite blessings.

Shakespeare makes us think that something splendid departs the world with Antony, despite his part in the fall of old Rome. Antony is in the title, and his death is as memorable as Octavian's victory. Whatever Antony's vices—his brain is softened by hopes and passions, and he loses to Cleopatra command of himself, his forces, and his fate—he retains some nobility of action even in the soft residue of his virtues. At his end, he will "not basely die, not cowardly put off my helmet to my countrymen"; he will be a "Roman by a Roman valiantly vanquished." While he shows himself a soldier and not a general, he fights heroically. By his dreadful and soft indulgence, he drives away Enobarbus and dallies with Cleopatra, and yet his generosity and magnanimity inspire these opposites to follow him to the death, indeed to suicide. Even his love of pleasure is on the magnificent scale of a Cleopatra. If Octavian may be mean in his virtues, Antony is splendid in his vices. "His delights were dolphin-like," remarks Cleopatra, certainly an authority on the subject, "that showed his back above the element he lived in." Octavian navigates calculatingly among the elements. Although Augustus succeeds, and there is sober greatness in him, Shakespeare suggests what Tacitus narrates, that the universal landlords will have to be cruel and drab. How can Bacon defend his omission of the other dimension, of the virtue, nobility, and divinity sought by admirable men?

Lessons of the Inventor-God

The Baconian answer is summarized in the extraordinary "Of Prometheus." The real state of man is of scarcity, it is nature's fault, and the niggardliness of nature is especially of human nature. So niggardly is human nature that it lacks intellect, and so far are we from intuitions of the good, true, and beautiful, that they are but misleading illusions. Not admiration and gratitude, but accusation and industry, should govern our demeanor toward nature and human nature. The good that men get, even their purposes, they make for themselves. In his essay "Of Adversity" (5), Bacon said that Prometheus represents human nature. The chapter on Prometheus in *Of the Wisdom of the Ancients* shows both our natural state of adversity and how to use arts to better it. It is bolder than "Of Adversity" about the bodily composition of human nature, about improving on human nature, and about liberation from a lord and from natural necessity. Also, it is quite explicit about the truly saving counsel: choose long-term security over short-term pleasure. "Of Prometheus" elaborates "matters intellectual," including "religion" and "morals," as well as matters natural.

In general, *Of the Wisdom of the Ancients* rather obviously advances Baconian wisdom under cover of ancient wisdom. After a series of inadequate arguments, the Preface simply "gives up" the contention that the work merely presents old wisdom from old fables. It eventually equates pagan fables with "parables," an equation that raises blasphemous possibilities, and then asserts that they originated in primitive times, when the natural human understanding was "impatient of all subtleties that did not address themselves to the sense." Ancient fables or parables prove to be unlikely harbors for wisdom of any sort. But Bacon brings forward another use: "parables" are a "method of teaching, whereby inventions that are new and abstruse and remote from vulgar opinions may find an easier passage to the understanding." The Preface gets right to work, correcting fables pagan as well as Christian and transforming, in particular, fables of the pagan gods into civil and moral inventions of a Baconian stamp. Disenchantment must begin early, because our natural genius misleads from the start. At first Bacon says that the fable of Prometheus, in particular, carries "many true and grave speculations both on the surface and underneath." Finally, he calls it "common and hacknied" and recounts the views "which I conceive to be shadowed out."

In discussing matters intellectual, "Prometheus" begins with a show of gratitude to providence for our intellect, but the argument zigzags away, first replacing "mind and intellect" with "mind and reason." To derive mind from "principles brutal and irrational would be harsh and incredible," Bacon reassures us, and it follows "almost necessarily" that our foresight derives from the greater foresight in the sky. But such a formulation means that it does not necessarily follow, and what is harsh and incredible might nevertheless be true. Bacon proceeds to gives us reasons to think it true. He asserts man to be the center of the world; there are no "final causes" beyond him (for example, some higher truth, nature, or law). Toying with tradition, Bacon then introduces a harsh novelty. Man is a "microcosm," because in "man's business" he can use all things and because he is most mixed of particles. So much for reflecting the order of things in his intellect, and for a divine spark. The reason for man's "wonderful powers and faculties" is bodily complexity. He is "most composite," and "the powers of simple bodies, though they be certain and rapid, yet being less refracted, broken up, and counteracted by mixture, they are few; but abundance and excellence of power resides in mixture and composition." We see why the *Essays* speaks of "soul" only once in Bacon's voice, replaces it with an image of invented satisfaction, and mentions intellect never.

The discrete steps of "Prometheus" have to be connected to be grasped, and this is especially true of the most radical step, a certain indication that intellect is really arts, artificial arts produced by the heat of the passions combined with an awareness of human exposedness. "[I]n the first stage" of existence, man was not only "naked and defenseless" but also unable to help himself. Then came the invention of fire, and Bacon covers this replacement of providence with a little Aristotelian smoke: "if the soul be the form of forms and the hand be the instrument of instruments," fire may rightly be called "the help of helps and the means of means." But Aristotle had called intellect (*nous*), not soul, the form of forms. Providence is ignored, and intellect is replaced by soul. Soul is the next to go. Bacon had left hypothetical his account of soul, and elsewhere, while he uses the term "form," he manages it for rhetoric's sake and expressly denies the existence of intellectual forms in the Aristotelian sense. "Matter rather than forms," he says in a thematic formulation, "should be the object of our attention, its configurations and changes of configuration, and simple action, and law of action or motion; for forms are figments of the human mind, unless you will call those laws of actions forms."[7] The form of forms is really the formula of formulas, and that is the artifical art for producing all other arts.

"Prometheus" shows the application of forms in this sense to human nature and to the production of science itself. It shows, that is, the formula or law of action for producing the arts that benefit man. The key is fire, for "through it most operations are effected, through it the arts mechanical and the sciences themselves are furthered." Fire is traced, in turn, to "violent percussions" of bodies, whereby matter is moved and prepared to receive "the heat" of "the sun." If this applies to the very start of invention, the impetus of the self and of invention is heat, that is, bodily motion.

In the *Essays*, Bacon had remarked that ambition originates in "heat and viviacity," and that great ambition is from "natures that have much heat and great and violent desires and perturbations" ("Of Envy" 9, "Of Youth and Age" 42). These hotter and bolder natures lead to "visions," for love and envy, in particular, "will frame themselves readily" into "imaginations and suggestions" (4, 27, 25, 42, 46). "Prometheus" suggests accordingly that passion is the impetus that gives birth to invention, and that the crucial passion, as we concluded in chapter 4, is anger, anger at our natural state. It is "the accusation and arraignment by men" of "their own nature and of art," and even of "nature and the arts" in general, that causes invention. Only by anger at nature and our gods, even "accusation of Prometheus, our maker and master," will we be "stimulated perpetually to fresh industry and new discoveries." Not the old gods, and not merely a blind force, but a new critical thinking, is the secret behind the arts.

The remainder of "matters intellectual" reveals the art of arts, which is the key discovery induced by natural passion otherwise unsatisfied. Bacon begins with critical skepticism, rejecting the complacent Peripatetics in favor of some skeptical ancient materialists, and then he replaces the ancient physicists altogether by his own innovation, a critical atomism that subjects nature to "law and method" for man's use. "Prometheus" provides an invaluable thumbnail sketch of the premises, which are dispersed in the works on method, and it thus provides a superior indication of Bacon's intention and plan.

The account diminishes the Peripatetics, as "but a portion, and no large portion either, of the Greek philosophy," and attacks especially their awe or respect for the surface of nature; they show an "overflow of congratulation and thanksgiving." He resurrects instead the complainings of

Empedocles ("madly"), and of Democritus (soberly), that "all things are hidden away from us, that we know nothing, that we discern nothing, that truth is drowned in deep wells, that the true and the false are strangely jointed and twisted together."

Actually, Bacon's is a new skepticism, for the pre-Socratic philosophers were skeptical, but not that skeptical. A fragment from Democritus declares that "we know nothing in reality, for truth lies in an abyss" (fr. 117),[8] but none of the other 309 fragments are so skeptical, and Democritus seems to mean that our perceptions come through the senses, which miss what is real. But he and the others thought they knew what was real: the four elements of fire, air, earth, and water, according to Empedocles; indivisible particles ("a-toma," not to be cut), according to Democritus and Lucretius. These parts are known by true reasoning, which analyzes what is given by sense perception. Had Democritus wandered into the seventeenth century, Bacon's indictment of senses as well as mind, in favor of controlled experiencing, might have provoked his old warning: "Miserable Mind, you get your evidence from us, and do you try to overthrow us? The overthrow will be your downfall" (fr. 125). He would not have been far off.

The point is that these pre-Socratics supposed that knowledge is possible through the *ratio* of fundamental bodies, however this varies from sense-perception itself, and that they also thought that the knowing of such fundamentals was in itself the most serious human activity. That is, they also supposed themselves knowledgable about the goods of the human world. They thought they knew, in particular, that knowledge and intelligent friendship are good for the soul, and that a life of avarice, envy, and anxious striving is bad. "Medicine heals diseases of the body," according to Democritus, but it is "wisdom" that "frees the soul from passions" (fr. 31). He also says that "imperturbable wisdom is worth everything" and that "the friendship of one intelligent man is better than that of all the unintelligent," while "men who shun death pursue it" and "the envious man torments himself like an enemy" (fr. 216, 98, 203, 88).[9]

Bacon, however, thought that the doctrines of the pre-Socratics were contradictory, that is, that their materialism was contradicted by their rationalism. He points out that Democritus, for example, supposed the existence naturally of "words," some "well ordered."[10] But while Bacon did not exactly follow the pre-Socratics in any of their positive doctrines, he does not therefore, in "Prometheus" or elsewhere, accept an unequivocal skepticism. In "Prometheus" itself, Bacon acknowledges "truth" and quietly dismisses the most radical of ancient skeptics, the New Academy of Carneades, who doubted the reliability of senses and intellect alike. Instead, in a Promethean revelation, he announces an art more solid than the natural awareness that the old atomists presupposed (and that Carneades questioned). The new way is an indictment that will try nature in our courts and for our purposes: "let all men know that the preferring of complaints against nature and the arts" overcomes want by bringing alms and bounties. It is a "gift" that is earned, that men receive as "reward of their accusation." At first, Bacon describes the gift as "the unfading flower of youth"; the *New Atlantis*, with its "fountain of youth," had paraded the same hope. Then "Prometheus" turns more sober. It promises "methods and medicine for the retardation of age and the prolongation of life," the twofold remedy actually promised in *New Atlantis*. Bacon does not expect that medicine will conquer death in the foreseeable future (it had not been conquered in the Bensalem we are shown, although the new science had been established 1,900 years before), although he will raise a banner of hope.

However important are inventions for progress, there has to be some uninvented awareness, if only an awareness of what we are after on the march. The conclusion of "Prometheus" clarifies the wisdom won by "observation," but also shows a certain dependence on studies. Bacon's teaching comes from "meditation upon the inconstancy and fluctuations of human life, which is as the navigation of the oceans." Our life is as a frail vessel that must navigate what we know to be the dangerous and trackless sea. The meditation in "Prometheus" is not on the methods of obtaining power over nature, the topic of the so-called logical works, but on something more important: on what is the most important power to be sought. The crucial transformation of nature proves to be the transformation of human nature to cause the effect most desired by the self, endurance or at least prolongation. The final section in "Prometheus" discusses "morals and the conditions of human life," and shows the reasoning behind such essays as "Of Health" (30) and "Of Death" (2). It explains how our natural composition may be suitably reformed, to what mixture, according to what foresight. The decisive lesson: human motion must be redirected from morality, or human quality, to security, or the conditions of life.

The conquest of the natural moral consciousness is the most important conquest of nature and the key to the civil and moral science that is itself the peak of Baconian science.

"Prometheus" surrounds the new wisdom with sharp criticisms of two old pretenders, religion and the Platonic tradition in philosophy. First, we are fed a suggestion that what some animals (including a serpent) do naturally, men can achieve by art. So much for the difference in dignity between man and animals. But man needs especially an art to enforce pursuit of the arts, for laborious experimentation can easily be forsaken for the "old things." This guardian art is critical thinking of the Baconian kind, that is, critique of natural consciousness with a view to its failure at useful knowledge. "Prometheus" turns on religious devotions with a vengeance, first interpreting rites as merely arts and then as useless arts that are only instruments of designing men. Critical thinking is especially critique of worship, which is "immediately seized on and polluted by hypocrisy" and allows man's heat or zeal to escape as merely smoke. Translation: religion distracts human energy from productive work, and the conquest of the natural consciousness requires, not least, a war against religion. Bacon particularly ridicules here the belief that God would prescribe various ceremonies; a day of rest to honor Himself, for example, is another case of "hypocrisy." Religion is an excuse for most men's indolence and indulgence and a vehicle for some master's glory.

Having set forth a formula for liberating humanity from the traditional and lazy way to be saved, Bacon propounds a new and industrious way. Critique of what we have supposedly been given is followed by his formula for what we must provide for ourselves, a formula quoted from Seneca (and repeated in "Of Adversity" 5): "it is true greatness to have in one the frailty of man and the security of God." Bacon sets forth the new way in the guise of old traditions, as if Pandora's box in releasing sensual pleasure endangered men. The danger, as one might expect, turns out to be other than sin or baseness. "Repentance" is mentioned as a remedy— but as a remedy "too late"; evidently no savior redeems the lack of human providence. The dangers are not to souls but to minds, bodies, and fortunes, and they are dangers to "kingdoms also and commonwealths" because of wars and tyrannies.

Nevertheless, Bacon suddenly turns solicitous of pleasure. He paints "prettily and elegantly" a parody of the fable about Hercules at a crossroads, where he must decide between lives of virtue and vice. In Bacon's version, Hercules' choice is not a dramatic choice between good and evil, for the moral issue so dwelled upon by ancient philosophers is not the real issue. Bacon's fable prettifies a cost-benefit analysis. The choice is between anxious foresight and indulgent pleasure, according to Bacon, and these are "two conditions" to be mixed, not "pictures or models" to be admired or condemned. The argument proceeds to the proportions in the compound. Hindsight or the way of present pleasure is the way of Epimetheus, and it allows men to "indulge their genius" while sweetening their "minds" with hopes and dreams. Thus is confirmed what "Of Fortune" (40) made us suspect: "genius" differs from mind (which invents solutions) and seems no more than a particular composition of bodily passions. The way of the rational and industrious is the way of Prometheus, and it removes dangers and miseries, but at a painful price. The foresighted "stint themselves" and "cross their genius."

Thus, we have Lord Bacon's version of the Promethean torment: anxiety keeps the rational and industrious from indulging in pleasure, and pleasure keeps the indulgent from providing for their security. For this, too, Bacon has a remedy, one that encompasses the advantages of both compositions. First obtain power to surpass natural frailty, and then mix indulgence without moral limit with patience without unlimited hope. Bacon is trenchant: "Neither is it possible for any one to attain this double blessing, except by the help of Hercules; that is, fortitude and constancy of mind, which being prepared for all events and equal to any fortune, foresees without fear, enjoys without fastidiousness, and bears without impatience."

The sequel removes any connotation of philosophic steadfastness. What sounded like patience and constancy proves to be what is familiar to us from "Of Fortune" (40): the confidence that accompanies a foolproof plan. One needs "meditation," but it is meditation "upon the inconstancy and fluctuations of human life, which is as the navigation of the oceans." Meditation is not contemplation, but planning, that is, planning the course to safety across the restless wastes that nature leaves to men. Turning to guard his new way, now from those tempted by the old contemplation, Bacon uses quotations from Virgil and Seneca to revamp the Socratic way of acknowledging natural necessity. Virgil had suggested that knowledge saves, or that knowledge of necessary causes can reconcile thoughtful people to the thought of death. But Bacon can produce more for "the consolation and encouragement of men's minds." Virgil (and Socrates) missed the primacy of the self, for which the Socratic philosophers could not provide, Christianity promised to provide, and Bacon can provide. Despite the "narrowness and frailty" of men, they should not mistrust their capacities for "fortitude and constancy," the "true nature" of which is the "security of God." Constancy of mind resides in security of self, which comes only by a human plan for a certain immortality.

In the brief concluding sections of "Prometheus," we see Bacon alternately as liberator, founder, and liberator. He appears as liberator from theology and ancient political philosophy, founder of the new rites of a competitive but progressive scientific movement, and liberator again, this time from the Christian Lord Himself. They show, if I am correct, Bacon's plan for his own godlike fame as founder-liberator.

These sections begin by confronting the charge against Prometheus that Bacon has hitherto evaded. Did not Prometheus ravish Minerva? Does not the ambition to conquer nature violate natural awe and the nature at which we wonder? It would seem that Bacon must confront the ancient philosophers, but his reply is not a confrontation but another evasion. He simply insists on separating human wisdom from divine wisdom, wisdom based on "oracles of sense," from those based on "oracles of faith," and he separates studies of human things from what men (as he quotes Seneca) "divine" or grasp by intellect. In effect, he treats philosophy in the traditional sense, with its starting point in opinions, as a mere faith. Presuming the old philosophy to be but a faith with its own dictators and disciples, he turns against the philosophers the antireligious crusade he means to arouse.

"Prometheus" concludes with a strange discussion of races with torches in honor of Prometheus, and this plans, I believe, the scientific crusade that Bacon means to arouse. While the discussion is hard to interpret, it seems to be chiefly about the effective organization of disciples. The key to a real scientific movement is effective incentives, and they must be more reliable than the love of wisdom by which the ancient philosophers, Socratic and pre-Socratic alike, professed to be moved. Progress in the arts and sciences will come not from the "strongest and swiftest runners" (they may put out the light), but from a "succession." While Bacon plans races "in honor of Prometheus, that is, of human nature," behind this return from theology to humanity is hidden Baconian art, that is, the arts of stoking the heats of human nature with fuel stronger than the ancients provided. Let "competition, emulation, and good fortune be brought to aid." Bacon plans the rivalry, prizes, and advancements that mark the professionalism and careers of modern scientists. In its primitive meaning, "career" meant racecourse (the French equivalent can still mean this), and Baconian professionalism, the so-called "expertise," serves the opportunistic racers that he plans. He plans especially for liberating the energies of many to advance themselves in a system of opportunities: let each rouse himself or herself and not stake "the whole venture upon the spirits and brains of a few persons." This is close to the culmination of Baconian science, at least on the supply side. One Baconian discovery about motion is the dynamics of a scientific establishment, the formula for putting into action the scientific movement.

In the *Essays*, it becomes clear that morality is humanitarianism realistically construed, and that realistic humanitarianism mixes a show of provision for humanity's needs with primary provision for one's own ("Of Goodness and Goodness of Nature" 13). The Baconian culmination, if the argument of this chapter has been correct, is a method of conquering nature for human benefit that provides for Bacon's conquest of mankind. The scientific movement will bring a reverence for Bacon like unto that which devotees of the Gospel brought to the Lord. It is hard not to be reminded of Friedrich Nietzsche's strange formulation for his superman—Caesar, with the soul of Christ—when thinking of Bacon's more complicated and calculated version: Caesar, showing the compassion of Christ and mixing the civil arts of Augustus with the saving arts of Prometheus.

Notes

1. *Works* XII, 27–44; VI, 335–47, reprinted in the appendixes to this volume.
2. *New Organon*, I, 129, in *Works* VIII, 14; IV, 113.
3. *Works* XIII, 162, 134; VI, 757, 738.
4. Quoted by C. Tranquillus Suetonius, "Julius Caesar," *The Twelve Caesars*, tr. A. Thomson and T. Forester (London: G. Bell & Sons, Ltd., 1914), lii.
5. *De Augmentis* VIII, in *Works* IX, 268–69; V, 58.
6. David Lowenthal, "Shakespeare's Caesar's Plan," *Interpretation* 10:2/3, 1982.
7. *N O* I, 51, in *Works* VIII, 83; IV, 58.
8. Quoted from Kathleen Freeman, ed. and tr., *Ancilla to the Pre-Socratic Philosophers* (Cambridge, Mass.: Harvard University Press, 1957), 104.
9. Quoted from Freeman, 99–111.
10. *Descriptio Globi Intellectualis,* in *Works* X, 419; V, 514.

Part III

The State of Progress

Chapter 7

Bacon and the Modern State

Bacon's admirers praise his extraordinary prescience, and Loren Eiseley goes so far as to call him "the man who saw through time." Yet the Baconian art of prediction was second to an art of production. Bacon foresaw what he could produce. The new method of science would provide for the "real business and fortunes of the human race, and all power of operation."[1] The science of innovations would produce immense innovations, the most important of which was to be a new state of progressive civilization.

The first section of this chapter outlines the complicated Baconian teaching as to the state, and the second compares it with some more recent and familiar diagnoses of modern government. My comparisons are pointed, for I am confronting a point of view, still powerful, which denies the formative influence on the modern state of plans such as Bacon's. To put the chief point of the chapter in a nutshell, I contend that Bacon's doctrine of the state is worlds apart from the Elizabethan monarchism with which it is often identified. The new world for humanity is to begin with a hard-nosed political world. Bacon plans a nation-state of the type we call modern, one given over to economic and industrial growth and presided over by a republican but effectual government, quite administrative and juridical. A world of such growth-oriented nations will be the "great powers," but will harbor the science with a humane face that Bacon also proposes.

In the later chapters, I shall argue that each major political writing is shaped to play its part in producing the new orders. The *History of the Reign of King Henry VII* shows enlightened despots how to establish a state. The *Essays*, the little *Treatise on Universal Justice*, and like works show how rising men can transform an established state into civil society and civil government, the elements, that is, of the civil state. The *New Atlantis* shows how progressive intellectuals, and their allies among the mercantile class, can introduce into the civil state a visionary project for ameliorating human suffering.

The Enigmatic Outlines

Most commentators on Bacon's diverse writings concentrate upon the promise of experimental science, and, for this or other reasons, few discuss whether comprehensive ideas on purpose and authority might tie together the Baconian corpus. Yet the turn to useful knowledge involves a radical dependence on human purpose and hence on the establishment of enlightened purposes. The argument underlying Bacon's separate accounts of the various sciences, in *Advancement of Learning* and *De Augmentis*, snakes steadily toward the moral and civil sciences that define what is useful.

However important one might think the Baconian principles of government, there is a real problem in discerning them. Few are advertised. The sketches in *Advancement* and *De Augmentis* are slight and enigmatic, as we have remarked before, and a similar lacuna appears in *New Atlantis*. The fable of Bensalem culminates in an account of an immense laboratory, says little of government, and breaks off (according to a preface by Bacon's chaplain) before adding "a frame of Laws, or of the best state or mould of a commonwealth." There are certainly some explicit proposals, but the few that do appear in various writings often seem slight, partial, and inconsistent one with another. To reconcile a visionary *New Atlantis*, which says little of civil government, with a sober *Essays*, which says little of the vision of scientific progress, is hard. To reconcile a certain republicanism in the *Essays*, with an incipient monarchism in *New Atlantis* and the *Essays*, and with a model of energetic monarchy in *Reign of King Henry VII*—is at least as hard. And then there is the barrier posed by concealment. Bacon openly warns us of the importance of secrecy in politics. In *Advancement* and *De Augmentis*, Bacon divides civil science into three parts, spends the bulk of his discussion upon negotiation (the second), and is slight and elliptical on government (the third). *Advancement* may have fifty paragraphs on civil science, but only four discuss government, and three of these insist on secretiveness or silence. One phrase is ominous: "We see all governments are obscure and invisible."[2]

Although such a phrase is ominous, it is not conclusive. The obscure may become clear, the invisible be inferred from its effects. The words actually say as much, since they say that an underlying trait of governments can be seen. Also, Bacon's phrase indicates what is necessary to "all" governments, and what is necessary is not random but knowable. Governments can be known, it seems, although to know them is hard because governments find it necessary to be secretive. We are entitled to suspect that Bacon intends his obscurity about government to be the half-light that fits the subject. Such obscurity also may fit Bacon's own political ends, and thus his governing of the argument about government; obscurity is dispelled as fits his purpose. In short, I hope to show that Bacon dispels enough of the obscurity in his two sketches of civil science to indicate his fundamental plan, and that if we take them in conjunction with two appendices on empire and justice that Bacon adds in *De Augmentis*, they show how diverse proposals are decisively interconnected, albeit in ways hard to figure out.

The sketches of civil science in *Advancement* and *De Augmentis* are largely alike, and they share a defining distinction: both tacitly distinguish state from government. Each introduces the topic of civil science by considering "governments" or "states," closes by a reserved and elliptical treatment of government, and intersperses a very long discussion of the art of getting on, "the architecture of fortune." The form of the discussion, I suggest, is a sign of its content. The new account of private aims is itself part of a new state of mind, a state separable from government. "States" are "great engines" whereby a man might "better drive" people in a flock or flocks, and coercive government is only one of the machines for channeling human energy.[3]

The two summaries of civil science first manage Christian language and Cato's authority to move the reader toward a state of mind unconcerned with either salvation or virtue, and then divide civil science into three parts: wisdom as to conversation or behavior, negotiation, and government. These correspond, we are told, to the three "summary actions" of society: comfort, use, and protection. The formula summarizes Bacon's reformulation of the purposes of politics. Indeed, the first two divisions, conversation and negotiation, summarize the new doctrines of individual and society that we discussed in Part II. Wisdom of conversation concerns putting on a proper "countenance," and the image to adopt depends on what will serve to make one's way. How men may make their way is treated under negotiation, which *De Augmentis* describes as a "new and unwonted art" to "improve their own fortune and assail the fortunes of others."[4] Bacon acknowledges that this art of private causes, like that of ostentation, was one that most ancient authors disdained. He nevertheless locates a great precedent. His discussion is in the form of a commentary on "those aphorisms" of "Solomon the king." Bacon takes as guides to self-advancement the inspired proverbs of a king who looked up to the

Lord, and he eventually identifies his sayings with "parable" as well as aphorism and fable.[5] But Bacon uses the old state of otherworldly religion to cover a state of opinion oriented to worldly gain and glory. Bacon's version of this Machiavellian project dwells on managing gain, a fact to which he explicitly (but quietly) alludes here. Traditional states of mind are to be replaced with an "art of Empire or Civil Government, which includes economics."[6] Allusions of this sort are one way of combining talk with secrecy.

The science of government is part of Bacon's new state of mind. While insisting in *Advancement* and *De Augmentis* that government is secret and hidden, he uses as illustration God's government of man and the soul's of the body. The discussions are very engimatic indeed, and they make one wonder whether these governments are hard to know because they do not exist. The discussion turns toward real government. The real state involves knowledge of the real motives of peoples and a corresponding knowledge of human governments and laws. Despite the secrecy Bacon has counseled, he goes on in both *Advancement* and *De Augmentis* to indicate the fundamentals of government and law, and the Latin version goes on in its appendices to elaborate two complementary applications: a growing nation-state and a new legalism that patronizes individual security and private acquisitions.

The fundamental Baconian political outlook appears here chiefly by negations. Avoid the mistake of the philosophers, whose "discourses are as the stars, which give little light because they are so high," and avoid the mistake of the lawyers, who write what is received law in the state where they live. The twin negations confront the twin recommendations in the most famous political science of the philosophers, Aristotle's. Aspire in theory to the best regime, of the kind that the *Politics* recommends in Books 3, 7, and 8, but vary practice to make the best of recalcitrant circumstances and authorities, as the *Politics* varies its recommendations in Books 4, 5, and 6. Bacon adopts Machiavelli's criticisms of the duality of traditional political philosophy. The ancients' way is useless because it aims too high, respects conventional forms, and for both reasons misses the effectual means of successful reform. He tacitly endorses Machiavelli's promise: a plan can be both general and effectual when it is an instrument of the solid desires that necessarily move men.

Yet there is a Baconian step that makes one wonder whether he does not break with Machiavellianism. In *Advancement* he recommends an inquiry into "certain foundations of justice" and their applications, and the second appendix to *De Augmentis*'s discussion of civil science presents such a treatise on "universal justice" and the "foundations of equity."

Bacon seems to take law and justice seriously, whereas Machiavelli conspicuously did not. Yet the difference is more subtle than it appears. Bacon's topical outline for such a treatise, in *Advancement*, is dominated by the Machiavellian spirit of political efficacy. It begins with concern not for justice but for certainty in application, and it proceeds to suggest that laws "touching private right of meum and tuum" may influence the "public state" and be "apt and easy" to be executed.[7] This formulation comes near to the suggestion that a reinterpreted private law is a politic and secretive way to move "estates" toward a new and stable "state," which is the thought that guides Bacon's famous essay "Of Judicature" (56). I will contend, in chapter 11, that this thought also guides the appendix on justice and equity. A legalism that promises security for life and property is another ingeniously civil means to an imperial order.

In general, the Latin *De Augmentis* is less secretive about the tough side of Baconian politics than is the *Advancement*. That is, it is explicit about the orientation by empire. What *Advancement* calls civil science, *De Augmentis* calls "the Art of Empire or Civil Government," and when *De Augmentis* defends breaking silence, it excepts "the secrets of empire." It even defines the arts of government as those whereby empire is preserved, made happy and prosperous, and extended. Unlike the more civil and English version, in short, *De Augmentis* virtually announces the imperialism of Baconian politics, and if titles are announcements, it makes the announcement. *De Augmentis* calls the second appended essay "Doctrine concerning the Extension of the Bounds of Empire," whereas the *Essays or Counsels, Civil and Moral*, gives to virtually the same essay a traditional title: "Of the True Greatness of Kingdoms and Estates" (29). There is also a significant alternative title in *De Augmentis*: "the Statesman in Armor."[8] Not only is politics about empire, empire is about private ambition. We can probably go further. If the state is decisively the statesman's armor, it is also and fundamentally the founder's army.

We will turn in the next chapter to the state-builder and the state-builder's work. But first we consider a few alternative accounts of the cause of the modern state.

Modern State and Modern Thought

Some recent writers hold that the state is not even a particularly modern type of governing; others, that the state while distinctively modern is not the product of a comprehensive plan; others, that the liberal state does not originate in the comprehensive planning that underlies the authoritarian European state.

The most common of these opinions holds the state to be a political phenomenon of all times and places, not a modern type of rule. Contemporary translators, for example, routinely use "state" to render the Greek *politeia* and the Latin *civitas*. But the old terms lack the modern distinction of government from people or state from society, and they do not connote an institutional, sovereign domination, which is separable from society and its classes and character. This objection is not new. Decades ago, H. C. Dowdall said that when Otto Gierke, the German historian of law and society, "discusses the medieval theory of church and state, he uses a word which is not used in that sense by the writers to whom he refers."[9] Nor is the question merely of words. Behind the loose usage lurks loose thought, a characteristic blurring of difference by an alleged historical synthesis. Despite the admittedly distinctive constitutionalism, efficacy, and humane ideals of the modern state, it is often described as simply an evolution from older political forms. A recent history of political thought is typical. "The modern concept of the state" is to be located in Lutheran, Thomistic, and Renaissance movements.[10]

Ernst Cassirer's *The Myth of the State* is a revealing example of the equation of old and new.[11] While Cassirer's book was occasioned by the rise of fascist totalitarianism, it treats totalitarianism as a contemporary example of an age-old phenomenon: the intrusion of irrational myth into rationally guided politics. It was Plato, according to Cassirer, who had proposed the first "rational theory of the state," in opposition to poets, sophists, and the pious, and fascism is just another irrational eruption against reason.[12] But Cassirer's own portrayals of fascism seem to belie the equation. While fascism may or may not be like old irrationalisms in being about heroes and heroic races, as Cassirer asserts, he shows that its irrational creeds had a strikingly rational origin. They were invented and propagated by intellectuals (or philosophers, if one adopts Cassirer's usage for Thomas Carlyle and Arthur Gobineau). The upper reaches of Nazidom were full of propagandists who were imposing political-racial creeds, and who prided themselves accordingly on their psychological arts. They invented rites and ceremonies and calculatedly manipulated words for emotional impact alone . The Nazi myth, if it was that, seems less some popular eruption of passion than a voluntary turn by intellectuals, following philosophers such as Nietzsche, toward the cave and away from enlightened rationalism.

One probably cannot understand the radical movements that have tried the twentieth century without confronting the nineteenth- and twentieth-century philosophic revolts from modern rationalism. These have been revolts not least from "reason of state" in its instrumental and calculating sense, and this was as true of the unheroic Marxian totalitarianism that Cassirer neglects as of the semi-Nietzschean variant that he discusses. Marx attacked the state as "the executive committee of the bourgeoisie" and as "nothing but," in Lenin's words, a cold tool for exploitation, and Nietzsche, too, indicted the cold, cold state, although as the tool of democratic man's insecurity. Yet both, on far left and far right, retained in their own way a key feature of modern state doctrine going all the way back to Machiavelli: the proposition that all rule is domination. This idea abstracts from the obvious distinctions between good rule or bad, between governing for the common good and tyranny, and it is perhaps not surprising that the alternatives proposed by Marx and Nietzsche were extreme: either no rule or rule without limit. Marx defended unlimited domination by a ruthless vanguard of humanity, during a temporary transition, and then "human emancipation" from all rule of man over man. Since even the realm of freedom had to be administered, Marx and Lenin both floundered into suppositions of an automatic social machine. The resolute Lenin showed what a Marxist state would have to become in the real world, that is, as the working class and the world failed to become what dialectical history was supposed to provide. Lenin seemed never to doubt that history would eventually provide, but he had to inflate the political side of the creed. That side had been ill-defined by Marx because supposedly transitory and inevitable, and unlimited for the transition because the socialist future was the end that justified all means. Lenin was emphatic: the dictatorship of the proletariat was simply force without law or morality. Because it was the tool of a party that embodied the scientific truth about the proletariat and its enemies, it had the duty "to combat spontaneity," as Lenin put it, and not least to combat "the spontaneous development of the working class movement" that was merely producing trade union consciousness.[13] Is there a better example of the mix of theory and ruthlessness that infected twentieth-century statecraft?

Nietzsche is a worthy rival, and this despite his contempt for modern theories. In his thought, domination remained and was to be spiritualized or ennobled. Yet it remained with a vengeance, so to speak. There was an animus against any moral limits, especially humane limits, and also against any political restraints. Nietzsche's remedy was permanent domination by a spiritual aristocracy, a resolute class moved by a will to power somehow at once noble and beyond good and evil in any ordinary sense.

In short, an explanation of fascism or communism by age-old irrationalism misses the roots in philosophies of irrationalism, that is, the influence of newly brutal rationalisms. Cassirer misses especially the extremity of the philosophic animus against modern liberal rationalism and its penchant for compromise, self-interest, calculation, free markets, representative government, and middle-class civilization.

While there are certainly many scholars who acknowledge the distinctiveness of the modern state, most of these find its root in historical circumstances and not in any Enlightenment plans. They may admit the existence of particular modern states, but they deny any plan for *the* modern state. Such writers can certainly appreciate the variety of modernizing tendencies, such as Henry VIII's centralized monarchy, Richelieu's raising of bureaucracy and monarchy over nobles and church, Frederick the Great's renovation of Prussia, the rise of the American republic, and Walpole's renovations in Great Britain. There have existed, even apart from the Marxists and the fascists, enlightened despotisms, liberal republics, social democracies, welfare states, and so forth. All this is true. Still, can one assert that such states are distinctively modern while denying to them a distinctive modernization and modernity? What of the important similarities of policy and aspiration among the seminal modern countries? They turned toward a government efficient and sovereign (subject to neither pope, duke, nor law of God), toward systematic accumulation of wealth and power (and away from otherworldly crusades or traditional class rule), toward technical and scientific development (not piety, pleasure, or leisure), and toward mobilizing and providing for their society (no longer conceived as citizens or subjects in traditional senses).[14] Some such modernization has transformed a vast diversity of countries, from the American colonies, to princely states in Germany, to orthodox Mother Russia, to small republics in Italy, to Singapore and the warrior monarchy of Japan.

Even writers who have some awareness of the connection between modern state and modern theories often trace the causes to particular historical events. Dowdall, for example, shows that neither Greeks, Romans, nor Christians used the term "state" in the modern sense, that of an institution of domination. The Latin term *status* was typical of similar terms in various European languages at the time of the Renaissance. Its root meaning was of a stable rank within a whole, that is, of dignity, privilege, and duty within an order. The "estates of the realm" was an English version. A kingly state was the rank or holdings of the monarch; the estates, the rank or holdings of the classes of nobles, ecclesiastics, and commoners.[15] According to Dowdall, it is Machiavelli's *Prince* that contains the first consistent usage of "state" as an independent, substantive noun meaning a dominating power, and Machiavelli's usage in turn influenced the later doctrines of sovereignty and government advanced by Hobbes, Raleigh, Bodin, and Locke. The traditional connotations of a portion of a community, and of a part superior in dignity and duty as well as wealth and power, disappear. One might add that the very first chapter of *The Prince* makes a point of defining *stato* simply and coolly as a domination having *imperio* over men. Still, even Dowdall places the fundamental cause not in Machiavelli's thought, but in his times. The old imperial order imposed by Rome was breaking down; the holy church could not impose worldly order; "the need for a sovereign stato was felt by all."[16] Such a supposition, that "the quest for sovereignty" characterized a general, early modern crisis, out of which developed the "modern state idea," is now trite.[17] The prominence of Machiavelli's doctrines is noted, but they are traced to time and place; he absorbed his concept of the prince from "the Italian tyrant and his stato." While Dowdall says nothing of the obvious reasoning in *The Prince* that supports Machiavelli's choice of words, he avows "the subconscious operation of a logic which is more reliable than obvious."

But is this derivation of invisible logic from existing tyrants so reliable? To begin with, it misses the republican half of Machiavelli's remedy. The *Discourses* advocates republics and of an ununusual type, an unstable, warlike, popular republic constantly in growth and motion. Nor does Dowdall's historicism account for the unusual type of prince Machiavelli advocates, who is to found republics and to overturn not only the empires of existing princes, but also their scruples and theology. Ordinary tyrants do not know how to be *tutto* evil or good, especially altogether evil.[18] Besides, was there ever in actuality a universally felt need for a sovereign state? Dowdall never proves that it existed. Could he? Italy was divided into cities and principalities we now call petty. These were in turn divided between partisans of pope and worldly claimants to rule, and into infinite smaller divisions. Where is the universal subconscious? Nor does Dowdall show that the Italian tyrants spoke of *stati*, or that they so stood out as to imprint themselves on Machiavelli's brain above pope, empire, foreign invaders, the Lord, and free republics. Nor does he explain why a solution bred for Italy should spread so quickly, as he shows it did, to circles in France, England, and Germany as well as Italy, nor why a solution must exclude reformed and politic ecclesiastical polities, such as Richard Hooker proposed, and Aristotelian secular solutions, such as Marsilius of Padua and many Renaissance statesmen proposed. In short, Dowdall omits what Machiavelli's reasoning provides: an account of why Europe should reform its arrangements to a politics of states. At the end of his argument, Dowdall mysteriously equates the state with "the absolute."

Some Hegelian philosophy underlies the supposition that history and not planning developed the modern state.

J. H. Hexter, in a more compelling denial of Machiavelli's influence, has argued that Machiavelli's *stato* is predatory, not impersonal, and hence "radically at variance with the modern conception of the state."[19] Virtually all the 115 usages of *stato* in *The Prince* differ not only from the medieval *status*, according to Hexter, but also from the modern notion of an institution or body politic. The notion appears as someone's state of domination, a tool for the ruler to exploit the ruled. Machiavelli gives *stato* an "exploitative tonality," which is out of place in an independent and impartial government.

Still, even if Machiavelli's is not exactly the representative and institutional state that we know, it may be that his doctrine is fundamental to it. This is the contention of Harvey Mansfield, Jr., who contends that there is a decisive family resemblance between Machiavelli's innovations and the later state doctrine.[20] Mansfield grants that Machiavelli's *stato* is someone's and for his purposes, as Hexter said, and he even goes further: it is personal like Aristotle's *politeia* or regime, or like the pre-Machiavellian meaning of *status*. It reflects the claims of rulers and differs from universal, impartial, or representative government. It is not impersonal, as some have characterized Machiavelli's contribution, nor the civic republic that others dwell on. Nevertheless, Machiavelli provides the basics. The basic innovation is the recasting of rule into acquisition, which thus prepares Hobbes's invention of the impersonal sovereign, a state that "might acquire for all and facilitate the acquisitions of all impartially." This acquisitive, personal state has many of the familiar features, for it promotes change and growth rather than stable classes and character, promotes indirect control by management and by conspiracy rather than visible ruling and forming, and shows a certain impartiality because it is neutral between claims of parties and between princes and republics: it shows the way for each to acquire. The secret of Machiavellian management is a promise of satisfaction to all, that is, to both the glory-seeking few and the security-seeking majority.

One can add a bit to Mansfield's diagnosis. Machiavelli's *stato* seems especially personal, even more so than regime and *status*, because it is the instrument of the particular persona, the self or ego. It is unlike the Aristotelian regime, which manifests the character of those in power, and unlike the medieval estates, which abide by a God-given ranking. Accordingly, rule by *stato* is domination, not shaping or regimenting. It is a power to imprint oneself, rather than authority to do good things or an office attended with duties. Paradoxically, the personal *stato*, in Machiavelli's sense, proves to be peculiarly instrumental and cold. It is only an instrument of the self, not a manifestation of character and belief, and only a system of controlling others, not a way to benefit or guide them. Warmth and spontaneity are missing, the feelings that come from helping the good and sharing, liking, and admiring, and from hindering the bad and harming, hating, and disdaining. To that extent, Machiavellian structures for management prefigure the independent existence, as well as the objective necessity and universality that Hobbes would later attribute to the state. And from such an angle, Bacon's vision of humane progress is a warming and beautifying of Machiavellian instrumentalism and institutionalism. Still, Bacon no more than Machiavelli took the step Mansfield attributes to Hobbes: the establishment of a doctrine of universal rights, and of an impartial state, upon a foundation of individual selfaggrandizement.

There is an extensive study of the modern state that reconsiders seriously its Machiavellian foundations, and that is Friedrich Meinecke's *Machiavellism, The Doctrine of Raison D'État and Its Place in Modern History*.[21] Meinecke was a German historian whose previous works had advised the statesman to resolve conflicts of moral duty with a view to the "ego of the state," which he identified with the *salus populi*.[22] *Machiavellism* marked a rethinking. It was provoked by the German "catastrophe" of World War I, just as Cassirer's *Myth of the State* was written in response to National Socialism and World War II. According to Meinecke, the nineteenth-century European balance of power had been destroyed by three long-developing causes, namely, militarism, popular nationalism, and capitalism. All modern European nations had universal military service and a professional military vocation; all exhibited "mass passions"; and each was filled "like a sponge" with men, wealth, large-scale industry, and technical methods of war—products of "a monstrous and unheard-of degree of material accomplishment."[23] Unlike Cassirer, Meinecke found the underlying cause in the European tradition of the state. That had spawned "the Great Power guided on rational lines (which together with rational wholesale manufacture is the most striking product of modern Europeanism)."

Although it was Meinecke's reservation about a Hegelian glorification of the state that made him question Machiavelli's first steps, it was a latent Hegelianism, I believe, that rendered Meinecke's diagnosis finally inconclusive. Machiavelli had originated the power-state that disdained scruple and set itself upon increase and empire, according to Meinecke, and in face of this "monism" there arose, dialectically, "natural law" limits on the state, that is, the Lockean and Kantian doctrines of natural rights and moral law. Hegel sought to overcome this unbridged duality between amoral state and universal morality by incorporating a higher morality into the state, but this also put the state above ordinary morality. The struggles of states to advance world history, according to section 345 of the *Philosophy of Right*, are above the merely partial considerations of "justice and virtue, wrongdoing, power and vice." While Meinecke did not think that Hegel originated the tradition of *raison d'état*, and while Hegel infused it with idealism and spirituality, his historicism tended to "excuse and idealize power politics by the doctrine that it accorded with morality." It contributed in its own way to young Germany's disaster. Hegel and his followers made Machiavelli and his followers respectable to the founders of the German nation. Excusing Machiavellianism before the throne of the world spirit, Hegel "legitimated a bastard." He cast a palliating light over the "primitive, bestial and nocturnal aspect of raison d'état." The "cunning of reason" was to make blood and iron bring progress and justice, but the First World War made such a philosophy of history unbelievable. This first terrible twentieth-century European disaster destroyed most the state that thought itself most advanced, according to Meinecke, and the world is more obscure, its progress less certain, than it seemed to "the generations that believed in the triumph of reason in history."[24]

Meinecke was clearer as to diagnosis than remedy. He proposed to restore "moderation" to politics by a new dualism, a doctrine beyond Machiavelli's power-politics monism, which he identifies with natural appetite, and Hegel's ethical-state monism, which identifies mind with the actual state. Yet he thought that this restoration cannot involve a return to the traditional non-Machiavellian teachings. Christian morality is insufficiently political, entering too little into the needs of the state, and the ancients' philosophies are obsolete, their "absolute morality" and "best state" having been surpassed by what Hegel analyzed, the dialectical development of nature and mind through the modern idea of the state. Nor can one turn to the English tradition of natural rights and civil society, since it views the state only "from underneath," from individual self-interest and not from general morality. In the face of all this, Meinecke's proposal is finally Kantian. He would restore moderation by restoring awareness of the "antinomy" between moral law and state power.[25] While the state may be spiritual and necessary, it always bears the flaw of self-interest, and one must both destroy the false sanctification of state power and restore some autonomy for the mind's moral laws. States should recognize their mutual right to life in a family of nations, Meinecke concludes vaguely, and should not cover their ambitions by the Hegelian excuse that struggle alone raises mind above nature. *Machiavellism* barely sketches these abstract and neo-Kantian suggestions, and they fail to address a number of dangers that Meinecke himself identified. One might recognize others' rights to life, as Hobbes did, while goading a state to pile up arms, people, and wealth, as Hobbes also did. Meinecke abstracts from the unbridled quest for power at the core of the modern state, a quest that underlies such disparate versions as Machiavelli's imperial nationalism, Bacon's plans for industry and invention, and Locke's invention of a natural right to the fruits of one's own industry. More radically put, limiting morality to the recognition of equal rights to life and liberty puts a premium on pursuing the means to such rights—and the great nation-state, together with useful science, is the greatest of means. "[T]hat prince," remarks Locke, in the midst of the most influential defense of private acquisition ever written, "who shall be so wise and god-like as by established laws of liberty to secure protection and encouragement to the honest industry of mankind, against the oppression of power and narrowness of party, will quickly be too hard for his neighbours."[26] In short, while reconsidering the relation of morality and the state, Meinecke reconsiders neither rights nor the state, the two elements of his dualism. Nor does his proposal address another danger, which he barely identifies and which he as well as Cassirer had later to face: the turn from liberalism's equal rights and popular security to a philosophic glorification of will and violence. In espousing a version of the state limited by Hegel's historical dialectic, and idealized by Kant's generalization of rights into universal law, Meinecke presupposes some of the Machiavellianism that he proposed to reconsider.

I conclude this sampling of accounts with a suggestion, once influential and still heard, that the state is a continental institution irrelevant to the liberal democracies of English-speaking lands. English legal and political theorists have shown little enthusiasm for the term "state,"[27] as if the word reminds one of Frederick the Great, Hegel, and Otto von Bismarck, with Kaiser Wilhelm II as a preliminary conclusion and Hitler as a horrific consummation. It reminds, in short, of an efficient, organized, and dictatorial Germany that somehow turned grotesquely tyrannical. Whatever the elements of truth in such a reaction, it overlooks the importance for the liberal democracies of sovereignty in government, a national and organized economy, a professional army, an efficient executive, and a scientific and progressive state of mind. Substitute "government" and "civilization" for various senses of "state," and much meaning is kept while the unfamiliarity disappears.

A half-century ago Sir Ernest Barker put elegantly the case on the other side: the "state has generally been discredited in England," and the implications are not merely semantic.[28] While a minimal English state exists, devoted chiefly to law and order, this is not a state sovereign over its subjects. The jurist John Austin and the philosopher Hobbes may have championed sovereignty, but Barker denies their influence and blames their deviations on foreigners, especially that papacy and that Frenchman Bodin. But Barker seems mistaken on the point. The doctrine of sovereignty was not papist but antipapist, indeed anticlerical. Hobbes and Bodin were *politiques*. Besides, few now would agree that Hobbes failed to influence English law and such influential liberals as Locke and Bentham. According to an authority on cabinet government and the English constitution, it was "academic lawyers" who introduced the doctrine of sovereignty into English institutions,[29] and the first and principal academic lawyer in England was Sir William Blackstone, whose definitions of law and state are noticeably Hobbist. Law is a rule of civil conduct "prescribed by the supreme power in a state," Blackstone wrote, and a state is "a collective body composed of a multitude of individuals, united for their safety and convenience and intending to act together as one man."[30] Nor does Barker account for the tradition of parliamentary sovereignty, or for the strong executive lodged first in crown and then in cabinet. Admittedly, these lines have been blurred with the democratization of Britain (as Geoffrey Marshall has shown). Doctrines of nation and public now modify those of state and sovereign.

Against such contentions, Barker argued that British government is divided and not overarching and also that British law and custom admit claims from outside of government that limit government, claims on behalf of nonconforming religion, aristocratic power, and natural rights. Even if such features marked Britain of the 1930s as neither Hobbist nor Hegelian, one might reply, they are certainly compatible with a liberal state. Also, Barker slights the rise of industry, the middle class, and secularization, which together helped undermine the old regime, and he slights the corresponding decline of aristocracy toward a minor ornament or irritant, monarchy to hardly more, and the churches to husks of their former strength. While Barker treats British religious toleration as if it fostered a spiritual land, liberal spiritualism put (and puts) toleration before true faith. It tends to tolerate only sects that patronize, in the words of John Locke's *Letter Concerning Toleration*, "those moral rules which are necessary to the preservation of civil society," that is, that give priority to "the security of each man's private possessions, for the peace, riches, and public commodities of the whole people; and, as much as possible, for the increase of their inward strength against foreign invasions."[31]

What has replaced the old political and religious regime are the institutions of parliament, party, cabinet, and administration, and these are agents less of gentry and the devout than of labor, the middling productive classes, professional and entrepreneurial elites, and the liberal press. Barker makes much of the "interpenetration" of parliament by society, but such an arrangement differs little from the counsels of Bacon and Locke, not to speak here of Machiavelli and Montesquieu, who sought to strengthen the public motion with private passions and correspondingly to introduce private interests into institutional channels. Nor is it true that the British executive was only a "bundle of officials" individually responsible to judges, as Barker contended. A rule of law solicitous of procedures and individual rights might go hand in hand with the elevation of one overarching government effective at protecting rights. Tocqueville feared such a development in modern democracies, and Blackstone, the great eulogist of a common law reinterpreted in accord with natural rights, urged a reinterpreted and sovereign parliament. Besides, Barker surely understated the discretionary powers of cabinet, parliament, and the civil service, powers of a sort that British courts will protect. Even if Britain prior to World War II were largely concerned with law and order, the night-watchman state embodied final authority with respect to defense, civil peace, and protection of capital. In short, whatever the attractions of Barker's pluralism, it presupposes the overarching state of mind that he denies, and, in particular, the sovereignty of the liberal state and the domination of the idea of progress.

Notes

1. "Plan" of the *Great Instauration*, in *Works* VIII, 52; IV, 32.

2. *Advancement of Learning* II, xxiii, 47, ed. Wright; *Works* VI, 388; III, 474.

3. *Advancement* II, xxiii, 1, 37, ed. Wright; *Works* VI 347–48; III, 445. See the close commentary on this chapter by J. Weinberger in *Science, Faith, and Politics* (Ithaca and London: Cornell University Press, 1985), 302–21. Weinberger shows that Bacon's accounts of negotiation and government are Machiavellian, and that they guide and limit his project for conquering nature by science. He supposes that the project and the Machiavellianism are compelled by the "charitable" culture of Bacon's time, and that Bacon is basically moved by the "realistic utopianism" of the later ancients.

4. *De Augmentis* VIII, in *Works* IX, 291; V, 74.

5. *Advancement*, II, xxiii, 8, ed. Wright; *Works* VI, 359; III, 453.

6. *De Augmentis* VIII, 3, in *Works* IX, 297; V, 78.

7. *Advancement*, II, xxiii, 49, ed. Wright; *Works* VI, 389; III, 475.

8. VIII iii, i, in *Works* IX, 297–99, 233; V, 78–79, 32.

9. "The Word 'State'," *The Law Quarterly Review* 153 (Jan. 1923), 98–125.

10. Quentin Skinner, *The Foundations of Modern Political Thought*. Vol. II: *The Age of Reformation* (London and New York: Cambridge University Press, 1978), x–xi. Skinner's failure at assimilation is demonstrated by Nathan Tarcov, "Review Article, Political Thought in Early Modern Europe, II: *The Age of Reformation*," *Journal of Modern History* 54, no. 1 (March 1982), 56–63.

11. Garden City, N.Y.: Doubleday Anchor Edition, 1955 (original edition, 1946).

12. *Myth of the State*, 72, 89–94.

13. Quoted by Leszek Kolakowski, to whose discussion I am indebted, in *The Golden Age*, vol. 2 of *Main Currents of Marxism, Its Origins, Growth, and Dissolution* (Oxford: Oxford University Press, 1981), 387; see also 373–412.

14. See Heinz Lubasz, "Introduction," *The Development of the Modern State* (New York: Macmillan, 1964), 1–13, esp. 2–3.

15. "The Word 'State'," 98–125. See J. H. Hexter, "The Predatory Vision: Niccolo Machiavelli. Il Principe and lo stato," chapter 3 of *The Vision of Politics on the Eve of the Reformation* (New York: Basic Books, 1973), 154–55.

16. "The Word 'State'," 112.

17. J. H. Shennan, *The Origins of the Modern European State, 1450–1725* (London: Hutchinson University Library, 1974), 113.

18. *Discourses* I, 27.

19. "The Predatory Vision," 171.

20. "On the Impersonality of the Modern State: A Comment on Machiavelli's Use of Stato," *American Political Science Review* 77, no. 4 (Dec. 1983), 849–57.

21. A translation by Douglas Scott (London: Routledge & Kegan Paul, 1957) of *Der Idee der Staatsraeson in der neueren Geschichte* (Munich and Berlin: R. Oldenbourg, 1924).

22. See Richard W. Sterling, *Ethics in a World of Power, The Political Ideas of Friedrich Meinecke* (Princeton, N.J.: Princeton University Press, 1958), 230 ff.

23. *Machiavellism*, 418–23, 430, 20.

24. *Machiavellism*, 424, 368.

25. *Machiavellism*, 432, 431, 428.

26. *Two Treatises of Government* II, v, 42.

27. Geoffrey Marshall, *Constitutional Theory* (Oxford: Clarendon Press, 1971), 14.

28. "The Discredited State," *Church, State, and Study* (London: Methuen & Co., Ltd., 1930), 151, 162, 163.

29. Sir Ivor Jennings, quoted by Marshall, *Constitutional Theory*, 35.

30. *Commentaries on the Laws of England*, 16th ed., bk. I, 46; quoted by Marshall, 16.

31. *A Letter Concerning Toleration*, ed. Mario Montuori (The Hague: Martinus Nijhoff, 1963), 83, 89.

Chapter 8

Henry VII, the State-Builder

History as Enlightenment by Civil Memory

The *History of the Reign of King Henry VII* is an account of the first of the Tudor kingships (1485–1509) and a work of no mean scope. While evidently composed in but four months, the first months after Bacon was freed from prison, it occupies more than 220 pages in Spedding's *Works* and was for centuries, if Spedding's comments are to be believed, the authoritive account of Henry VII. According to recent historical scholars, however, the *History* is not dispassionate history, and the work is far more problematic than had been thought. The evidence they submit is persuasive. Wilhelm Busch found that Bacon ignored and improved upon chronicles and documents that must have been at hand; he evidently invented speeches, anecdotes, and even notable incidents in foreign and domestic policy.[1]

While the acknowledgement of such radical distortions is now common, their cause has not been adequately explained. This chapter contends that the inaccuracies fall into a pattern, and the pattern serves a political purpose, a purpose visible in the obvious tenor of the *History* as well as in its subtle eccentricities. Under the guise of history, Bacon manages an influential royal tradition to advance a model of a state-builder, one portion of his formula for producing an enlightened state of progress. While the work is not accurate history, it is ingenious politics.

That *History* provides a Machiavellian model, and not a just portrait, is in itself an old observation. It was already the "very prevalent" impression in the nineteenth century to the regret of editor Spedding, who excused the many distortions as but little carelessnesses. Bacon's Henry VII, Sir James Macintosh had written, was "too much of the ideal conception of a wary, watchful, unbending ruler, who considers men and affairs merely as they affect him and his kingdom."[2] A recent variation is by Jonathan

Marvil, who amplifies Busch's bland conclusion that Bacon was indifferent "as regards simple historical truth."³ According to Marvil, the *History* differs from earlier accounts of Henry VII in the very priorities systematically imputed to the king. Bacon dwells on Henry's manipulation of popular approval and of titles of kingship, on parliaments and laws (topics that make up 15 percent of Bacon's narrative and hardly appear in the chroniclers), on trade and usury, and on dominating his rivals at home and abroad. Since Henry exhibits Bacon's "policies and principles," and especially his Machiavellian deduction of policy from utility, he is Bacon's "model of kingcraft" as well as a mentor to please and instruct James I.⁴

This conclusion carries much truth, and yet it cannot be the whole truth. If Henry VII is a model, why does Bacon conspicuously impute to him an oppressive avarice? According to C. H. Williams, the *History* "fixed for all time the main outlines of the first Tudor monarch," and the image of a "petty, mean-spirited skinflint," while false, occasioned "not a little of the contempt" that subsequent generations felt for Henry.⁵ If the model is in particular that of a dominating Machiavellian prince, why does Bacon exaggerate the importance of Henry's parliaments and laws? Bacon distinguishes his history from that of even the "best writers on history" by its attention to "good laws."⁶

Henry VII seems indeed to be a model, but a model for a limited function. The Baconian account, I suggest, exhibits a state-builder whose achievement is necessary but preliminary and who therefore must be eased offstage when his work is done. Such an intent explains why the *History* both sets forth Henry as a model of state-building by blood, iron, and fraud, and provokes as a subordinate theme the civil institutions and attitudes that will oppose future Henrys when no longer needed.

But contemporary historians tend to reject out of hand the possibility that Bacon's Henry VII might be a calculated part of a calculated plan. According to Marvil, for example, Bacon's historical contriving had to be "quite unwitting"; he could not imagine that "he was creating a fiction."⁷ Marvil gives no reasons for this opinion, and it would not be an easy task to provide adequate reasons. Bacon was superconscious of methodical attention to fact, and superconscious as well of political fiction, having with his *New Atlantis* perhaps invented modern science fiction in order to image forth a project of future progress. On the other hand, Marvil's own skepticism is intrinsically incoherent. While he calls Bacon's Henry "a mixture of error, contrivance, and projection," he suggests that Bacon is "as much persuaded by him as generations of readers have been."⁸ Apart from the problem that contriving is artful, and to that extent Bacon's manipulations must be acknowledged to be intentional, it is a fact that not all readers have been persuaded. According to the argument, then, Bacon need have been no more persuaded than is a Macintosh or a Marvil. They are not persuaded. Bacon was famously self-involved, preoccupied especially with his own projects, much closer to his own times, and a disciple of the calculating Machiavelli. Is it reasonable to believe that he was less conscious of his errors and contrivings than were Macintosh, Busch, or Marvil?

There are some signs on the surface of the *History*, allusive and equivocal as it is, that suggest self-conscious distorting and shaping. According to the historians, the most massive distortion is the prominence of law and legislature, and Bacon calls singular attention to himself, using "I" six times in one paragraph, precisely while praising his concentration on laws as superior to "the best writers on history" (147; 97). Also, the *History* ends and begins with formulations that are strange enough on their face to make one wonder just how accurate Bacon intended to be. It concludes with a hope that Henry "dwells more richly" in Bacon's monument than he did alive, and it begins with a dedication to Prince Charles that intimates a revamping of kingship even while promising "one of these ancient pieces" to supplement the "living pattern" of Charles's father (James I, the patron who elevated Bacon and let him fall). The dedication commends study of Henry VII for his "rough" times (43; 25). This classification of lives, into those of easy and rough times, is from the extraordinary chapter 6 of *The Prince*, complete with an explicit preference for princes who establish their state on foundations all their own despite the roughness of the task. Elsewhere, and after quoting Machiavelli as an authority on goodness, Bacon had legitimated precisely the great exploiters who are able to found states in the rough times of adversity: "the fittest timber to make great politics of; like to knee timber, that is good for ships, that are ordained to be tossed" (*Essays*, 13). One might infer from this slippery keynote that Bacon is managing the *History* to separate Prince Charles, and other influential readers, from the paternal image of Christian monarchy, albeit by an ancient image that covers the innovation. If these observations and inferences are sound (and they correspond to the modified Machiavellianism the text sets forth), what appears flattery is actually sedition. In essay 55, Bacon ranks Henry VII below lawgivers, which also implies that the *History's* repeated praise of Henry as lawgiver is a knowing inflation.

These observations and suggestions as to the *History* may seem farfetched, and they can only serve as a preliminary rebuttal and a preliminary indication of Bacon's intent. But it is important to know that they are confirmed, and indeed illuminated, by Bacon's own prescriptions for the writing of history. To these I briefly turn.

The *Advancement of Learning* (as well as the *De Augmentis*) contains an extensive discussion of historical science, and this proves to be startlingly political, even propagandistic.[9] If one keeps putting two and two together, one can discern in *Advancement* a plan for the writing of all histories, that is, not only civil history, but also literary and natural history, and ecclesiastical and world history. The plan is semiexplicit, the scope, breathtaking, and the intent, I shall argue, is to construct an enlightened memory that will help to build an enlightened future. The first topic in *Advancement*'s discussion is civil history, and the account recommends a biography of Henry VII.

Bacon divides civil histories into those of times, lives, and actions and commends first those of lives and particular actions. History of lives goes beyond "magnitude of actions" and "public faces" to the smaller and inward causes. Biography, that is, is of more "profit and use," for it reveals the real forces.[10] History of actions is truer than history of times because manageable, and thus the argument may be "within the notice and instructions of the writer." Thus, a history of a life may be governed by the historian's concern with the action accomplished. Nevertheless, Bacon proceeds to speak of times (as if such a history can also be governed by the historian's concern). An English historian of times should focus upon actions from the uniting of the Roses (under Henry VII) to the uniting of the kingdoms (under James I), and should attend especially to monarchs' actions, beginning with the "mixed adeption of a crown by arms and title" by Henry, "one of the most sufficient kings of all the number."[11] Precisely Henry's adoption or adaptation of the crown governs Bacon's history of Henry: by ambition, arms, and title, Henry turned a kingship into his state, a state that could be the foundation of a unified Britain.

Advancement then suggests that "some good pen" can raise "worthy personages" from oblivion or ill fame to memory, as if Bacon would exhibit not only the fame that may accompany the power of founders, but especially the "notice and instructions" that give power to historians. A "fit" writer may provide even "a complete history of times," he now allows, which would be a world history that may control or affect, one supposes, what actions and what people will become memorable.[12] For such purposes a writer or writer prince may use various modes, such as annals (the example is Tacitus who recorded Roman emperors of the Julian line from Tiberius to Nero) and journals (the examples are a king known from the Bible and the world conqueror Alexander who had his journalists).

At this important juncture, Bacon turns aside to consider "a form of writing" that some "grave and wise men" have selected: "a scattered history of those actions which they have thought worthy of memory, with politic discourse and observation thereof."[13] This reminds one of the novel technique Machiavelli used in *The Prince* and *Discourses*; Bacon rejects it, as fit for "books of policy" rather than "books of history." The "true office of history" is to represent "the events themselves together with the counsels," although Bacon immediately allows that such a mixture is "irregular" and not subject to definition. The twisting path first asserts the historian's power and power of choice and then reminds of the uncertain constraints of history. The movement prefigures Bacon's choices, in limiting his *History* to the powerful memory of Henry, and in nevertheless mixing in his own counsels by singling out "notable particularities" and inventing speeches and memorable incidents.

But the account of civil history in *Advancement* does not end where one might expect, for it proceeds on to "cosmography," the exploration and mapping of the globe *plus ultra* and *imitabile fulmen*: beyond the old ultimates and in imitation of the thunderbolt.[14] This seems a very strange movement. It is less strange when the reader sees it end in a familiar destination: new discoveries may plant a further expectation of the "proficience and augmentation of all sciences," and, Bacon adds, such progress would realize the prophet Daniel's hope. Bacon shows, I suggest, how political historians are to insert into old traditions the core of a new history of times, that is, an account, such as *The Advancement and Proficience of Learning* and the *De Augmentis* proffer, of the progress of useful knowledge. Civil historians are thus instructed to write with a view to the world-historical progress of human science, as if that answered human hope, not with a view to divine revelation and a hope for a messiah. The *History* makes a point of commending Henry's alleged patronage of John Cabot's enterprises of discovery and invention—and of deprecating churchmen and Henry's piety.

In short, the *Advancement* provides a formula for making civil history into enlightened propaganda, which is control of civil memory for the sake of progress in politics and learning. Baconian civil history is enlightened history, if not quite the Whig history that came to dominate under the influence of Locke's liberalism, and Bacon extends the same sort of revising to literary, natural, and even ecclesiastical history. The crucial revision is in the very historical form: these "knowledges" are understood historically, that is, as produced human movements. They are sects to be produced and managed. Their proper study is not philosophic, an attempt to weigh the truth in various examples and to discover the truth, but is instead historical in Bacon's sense, the attempt to discover how they were produced and how to produce them. Literary history hitherto lacks accounts of "knowledges and their sects"; natural history should emphasize the subjection of nature by human art.[15] While enlightened history should reduce to sectarian creeds the previous miscellany of creeds, opinions, and sciences, it should also foster a new sect of enlightened science. The treatment of ecclesiastical history is illustrative. Bacon only touches it, and just prior to the consideration of poetry, and the discussion seems designed to raise awkward questions about accounts of church, prophecy, and providence.[16] Enlightened ecclesiastical history is to be biblical criticism. Bacon shows historians how to undermine revelation as well as how to popularize progress.

We turn now to a close examination of the *History* itself, for the remarks thus far have been merely preparatory. What follows is a variation on Howard White's admirable examination of thirty years ago, an account that has not been assimilated by many historical scholars. White saw that Bacon's *Henry VII* advances a Machiavellian model, and, in search of Bacon's intention, he ignored as inconclusive the variations from historical practice and concentrated wisely on the variations from Machiavelli. He concluded that *Henry VII* is how the *"Prince* would have been written by a cautious man."[17] Henry seems more concerned than his Machiavellian counterpart with legitimacy and with law, and more flexible in interchanging cruelty and kindness as well as law and caprice. He relies on reverence, in addition to the love and fear that Machiavelli prescribed, and he displays none of the spectacular wickedness for which *The Prince* is famous. White attributes Bacon's focus on a historical figure to the provisional status of Baconian civic knowledge, which is in "progressive creation" as science advances, and to Britain's Baconian role as carrier of modernization. He also notes Henry's economic preoccupations; they show Bacon's blending of public and private spheres, which Machiavelli had separated, as well as his introduction of mercantilist arrangements favorable to the new technological science. Still, something more should be said about the defects Bacon paints in Henry, about why a model is portrayed as defective, and about the place of the *History* in Bacon's broad plan. Also, White's description of Henry's "classical sense of practical wisdom" seems at odds with the king's incessant and Machiavellian calculating.

Marks of Statecraft

There is a theme obvious throughout the *History*, even if not exhaustive of its teaching, and that is Henry VII's consolidation of his own state.

The name of king is only a start, for Henry rises throughout his reign. He is continually destroying domestic rivals and neutralizing the foreign powers that he cannot dominate, such as France, Spain, and Scotland. Henry establishes power and reverence beyond the perquisites of English kingship, and Bacon finds it good; the new establishment brings "temporal felicity," "worldly bliss," and, finally, "felicity" itself (353; 97). A less obvious theme is the establishment of "good laws" for an enduring and expanding "commonwealth," and Bacon eventually develops the contradiction between good laws and Henry's incessant extension of his domination. The least obvious but most pervasive theme is the replacement of church, nobles, and traditional monarchy by the modes and orders of state building. The modes commended are the arts of making one's fortune; the orders are the institutions of one's empire. Virtue and nobility go uncommended, except as nobles should be cleverly channeled into instruments of the new order, and churchmen commonly appear as civil instruments or foolish hypocrites, with religion a facade for policy. At *History*'s end, Bacon calls the king religious and notes some religious works, but adds a potentially blasphemous qualification whose potential the work had developed: Henry could "see clear (for those times) through superstition" (355; 238). Henry is never praised for raising churchmen or blamed for slighting piety or the nobles. While the king does not preside over the feudal estates, he seeks his own estate or state by satisfying the persons he needs. As "retribution" for "treasure" he "remunerated his people" with good commonwealth laws (140–41; 92). Henry promotes security through his courts, economic growth by laws favoring commerce and manufactures, and an adequate soldiery through growth of an independent middle class. All this is for Henry's own state. While Bacon calls Henry's mind "wise" and "high," Henry is not portrayed as looking up to wisdom, divinity, or nobility of deed or soul. Henry looks to his self. He "revered himself, and would reign indeed" (358; 240), he sought to be "governed by none" (358; 240); he would be one alone like a Machiavellian prince.

We can see, in Henry, Bacon's version of Machiavellian statecraft, which is continual acquisition in a more cautious mode. While *History* does not say, as does book III of *The Prince*, that "to desire to acquire is truly a very natural and ordinary thing," it shows the more bland and economic Baconian version. Once Henry's state was consolidated, "nature," freed from the strictures of fortune, "began to take place" in him and to extort benevolences, exactions, penalties, and seizures (324ff.; 217ff.). This avarice, Bacon takes care to interpolate, was not for its own sake; it complemented Henry's ambition. Henry sought to leave his son "such a kingdom and such a mass of treasure, as he might choose his greatness where he would" (336; 225).

While moved powerfully to rise, Henry was especially distinguished by his uncommon arts of rising, what Bacon calls the "wonted and tried arts" of making his fortune (303; 202–3). Henry was wary like the perpetual warrior, just as Bacon advises in "Of Suspicion" (*Essays*, 31); "there was not a more suspicious man than Henry." Yet he mixed external daring and provision with his inner wariness, and was thus an exemplar of the Baconian equivalent of courage, "stout without and apprehensive within" (243; 162). Supposing nothing given without his taking, and success his only measure, he sought incessantly to extricate and to provide. His blandly daring arts made the king "a partner with fortune, as nobody could tell what actions the one and what the other owned" (301; 201).

Bacon dwells on how Henry mixed "safe courses" with his resolution (350, cf. 346–53; 235, cf. 231–37). Seeking the means most certain to succeed, he measured forces with extreme care, as in certain revealing negotiations concerning a match between Henry's son and the daughter of Ferdinand of Spain: the "two Princes, being Princes of great policy and profound judgment, stood a great time looking one upon another's fortunes, how they would go" (317; 312). If the balance of forces were doubtful, Henry preferred not to play, and to gain what he could by threatening to play. He did "but traffic" with war on Charles VIII and a newly consolidated France, thus to "make his return in money" (181; 119), and the profits were double: "upon his subjects for the war, and upon his enemies for the peace, like a good merchant that maketh his gain both upon the commodities exported and imported back again" (182; 120). Subjects and enemies are alike material from which the shrewd manager will profit. The dishonor of retreat, Henry shifted to allies, whose unreliability he predicted and then was able to blame. In general, Henry preferred to gain by ways short of war. Negotiation, Bacon's specialty, was the way most preferred, and the culminating policy was the negotiation of the judicious marriages that linked Henry to Scotland and Spain. Bacon especially praises a counsellor, Bishop John Fox, who transformed the Scottish king's irritation at insult into a match that led to union and English expansion. Even in the heat of war, Henry provided for cool negotiators: his "heralds were the great ordnance" (68; 43).

When Henry was superior in force, he could be calculatingly intimidating, as he was in extracting concessions from Charles of Castille, who had been forced by a storm into an English port. Bacon presents another conversation between kings, here of an inequality of power that was temporarily overwhelming. We see Baconian policy. Under a velvet cover of royal hospitality, Henry holds Charles prisoner until he agrees to return a prominent English rebel hiding in Castille. It is a civil menacing, which is a menacing considerate of Charles's saving of face, that is, of state (344–46; 230–32). While Henry continuously warred to gain, he preferred to war in the mantle of peace. Bacon expressly commends the image of mediator and peacemaker (355–56; 238–89), but beneath the image is management for advantage (113; 73–74). At one point, Bacon remarks that "airs of peace" interrupted Henry's preparations for war; bits of intelligence, that is, told that his forces were declining (194–95; 128–29). Although the image of peacemaker may be useful, that of warmaker may serve as well; the point is to use the image that advances one's policy while concealing one's intent.

Henry is peculiarly praised for his artfulness in concealing himself while knowing his enemies. While other princes and states stood as "in the light toward him," he was as "in the dark towards them" (359; 241). The secret was a "semblance of mutual communication." Mutual communication is fraudulent—a mere semblance—and in its appearance of honesty or aid, it disguises real communication, which is acquisitive. *History* is alive with the king's spies and counterspies, with conspiracies for and against Henry, with his mines and countermines for knowledge. Henry had a gift for winning and buying the allegiance of foreign emissaries, a special art of acquiring knowledge that Bacon praises repeatedly and at length (213, 340ff., 359–60; 141, 228ff., 241–42).

Whatever the Henrician arts of safe courses, negotiation, intimidation, and communication, it often came to war, and when there must be fighting, let the effort be unstinting. Henry obtained intelligence of his enemies, hindered them with dissensions, planned ingenious campaigns, assembled overwhelming force, struck quickly and in person. We see Bacon's version of the spirit of efficient execution. In a campaign against a popular uprising in Cornwall, which is described at length, Henry mustered complete victory "with that providence and surety as should leave little to venture or fortune" (269; 179).

The King and His Rivals

The state-builder's arts are chiefly for domestic consumption. Bacon's Henry is more restrained about foreign empire than is Machiavelli's prince, and this is probably because Bacon is more daring in his plans for economic growth and technological progress. For such an insinuating imperialism, the first necessity is national unity and effectual governance, and Henry's arts are the means to the peace and order that progressive society requires. The *History of King Henry VII* shows how to establish a state of peace.

Henry rid himself of legitimate rivals to the throne with steady resolution and in the process intimidated his other subjects. He immediately imprisoned Edward, Earl of Warwick, the last direct heir of the old house of Plantagenet, and eventually beheaded him for involvement in Perkin Warbeck's schemes; Bacon hints that Henry encouraged the involvement. The dowager duchess of York was cloistered in a nunnery where she languished and died, her wealth forfeited to the king, although Henry no doubt foresaw that the act would arouse "great obloquy," since the reasons were "dark and unknown" and Henry's pretensions "strange" (80, 77; 41, 49). It was worth it to be rid of the Yorkist matriarch. Henry also executed the powerful Lord Chamberlain, Sir William Stanley, for saying that the Yorkist title was stronger than the Lancastrian on which Henry relied, and for linking himself with Warbeck; this, although Stanley had saved Henry's life at Bosworth field, achieved high station, and been powerful, rich, and deserving. Henry suspected his ambition and wanted his riches. The beheading of Stanley struck "great terror" into "servants and subjects" alike, for he had only affirmed what everyone had opined as to the superiority of the Yorkist claim. No man knew who was friend or who was spy, every man feared for life and property, and the population turned sullen and resentful. Henry the king seemed Henry the tyrant, an impression we consider later.

It is true, but odd, that Bacon attends much more to conspiracies by pretend heirs than to those by legitimate heirs, and by following the accounts, we learn of other and more profound rivals to Henry's state of sovereignty. Lambert Symnell pretended to be Edward Plantagenet (escaped from the Tower); despite slim credentials he won to his cause the duchess of Burgundy and all of Ireland. Perkin Warbeck pretended to be Richard Duke of York, the second son of Edward IV, one of two princely heirs allegedly murdered by Richard III; he won to his cause the kings of France and Scotland. Does Bacon believe that pretend names and pretend connections by blood, these "engines and products of invention," are as valid as any titles to legitimacy and as real as any political phenomena? The *History* concentrates on Warbeck, whose conspiracy was one of the "longest plays" of its kind, one of the "strangest examples of a personation" (304, 199; 203, 142). Warbeck stands for more than he was. He is described as a sprite, idol, or phantasm (199, 213; 132, 141) and his reappearances as miraculous, like a "resurrection" from "death to life" (210; 139). The *History* considers the rise of pretenders that mix divine and royal claims and uses a pretender to royal authority to cast doubt on pretensions to divine authority.

Bacon sets forth at length Henry's politic policy for bringing such airy phenomena to earth, and the exhibition involves first a Baconian public enlightenment as to the human causes of the apparently miraculous. These "phantasms" were invented as instruments of ambitious and malicious nobles, Bacon tells us, and he expounds the intricate coaching, the wondrous genius of Warbeck, the patronage provided by Henry's rivals, and the easy sway over the gullible. He also expounds Henry's more earthy responses, which combined his own frauds with superior force; he mixed mines and countermines with arrests and battles. While Henry publicly displayed the real Edward and spread a tale of the princes' murder, he was especially successful in inserting spies into his rivals' camp, for thus he learned of Warbeck's circle in Burgundy and could win back crucial devotees. He proceeded to threaten the pretender's refuges abroad, arrested and executed the confederates, such as Stanley, that he could reach, and overwhelmed Warbeck's invasions.

The lesson conveyed above all is that phantoms when caught should be kept and not killed, for thus their pretensions can be exposed and ridiculed. Symnell was kept as a falconer, and Warbeck was enticed from sanctuary with a promise of life and then paraded as a figure of fun (292; 195). A continual spectacle is "a kind of remedy against the like inchantments of people in time to come" (91; 59). In short, Henry's way denies the opportunity of martyrdom and thus the opportunity to establish a state of sacredness; it permits the deflation that death prevents. Once made ridiculous, a pretender may be killed with impunity, as Henry killed Warbeck for having compromised the last Yorkist heir. In the *History*, Bacon seems to follow his own politic counsel. He gives the phantom Warbeck the only defense of the old English regime that appears in the book. There are seven set speeches quoted (counting Warbeck's proclamation to the English), and only Warbeck and Morton, who as "Chancellor" seems to enunciate Baconian policy, have more than one. Warbeck's alone are more or less drawn from actual records; his words alone are kept alive or resurrected, but only in order to be deflated. Warbeck's defense of the old regime is called a "tale," and his proclamation, a "perfume" to justify his invasion of England.

Warbeck's speech (248–57; 165–71) was addressed to a king, the king of Scotland, and it presented the issue between him and Henry as a "righteous quarrel." Henry is called a particularly mean and ignoble tyrant. He is but Henry Tudor, a tyrant to the royal Plantagenets, and his domination extends not "just to us" but to an oppression worse than that of Richard III, who at least loved the honor of the realm and the contentment of his nobles and people. In a passage not in the original proclamation (252–53, n. 2; 168, n. 2), Bacon's Warbeck charges that Henry has sold out confederates, accumulated monies by feigned wars and dishonorable peace, put aside nobles and relied on mean "caitiffs and villains," broke the prerogatives of "our mother the church" in the name of heathenish policy, and indulged in murders, treasons, and extortions. Warbeck would recur to "our noble progenitors kings of England" and govern the people arranged in "all degrees and estates," and he would rely, in particular, on God's grace and the help of the great lords. Bacon makes Warbeck's exposition familiar and contemptible—and can then dismiss it. Yet he permits followers to see what must be destroyed for the new state of things.

Laws and Legislature

Henry's arts won by laws as well as by arms and policy, and this art, of which Bacon is so proud, is distinctive. In chapter 12 of *The Prince*, for example, Machiavelli had deprecated laws in favor of arms; since "where there are good arms there needs must be good laws, I shall omit the reasoning on laws and speak of arms." Even this passage acknowledges the importance of good laws, however, and Machiavelli adds much about laws in the republican *Discourses on Livy*. Bacon is both more cautious as to republicanism and more sanguine as to control by fixed institutions. Although he forbears an ostensibly republican work, he quietly outlines in *Essays* republican modes and orders and reinterprets in *History* the monarchy crucial for his project, England's, as itself the producer of "good commonwealths laws" (141; 92). The account of laws makes his history better than any before, because laws can govern those to come: the historian becomes himself a lawgiver because he can "inform the judgement of kings and counselors and persons of estate" (147–48; 97).

Bacon's Henry VII, however, proves Janus-like as to law. While Henry governed with Parliament and courts, and fostered good laws and justice civil as well as criminal, he appears a great hawk by *History*'s end, absolute with Parliament and master of extortions. Both impressions, as I have remarked before, seem to be intended. The reader will favor Henry's work and institutions, while thinking also that such monarchical power is to be feared and should be checked.

As the *History* recounts the limitations that law and parliament put upon Henry's reign, it systematically exaggerates the truth. To begin with, Bacon singles out only certain Parliaments. The second and third Parliaments were sources of laws "good and wholesome," "good and politic," and of "good commonwealths laws." He is quiet about other Parliaments, notably ignoring the first, which established Henry and his party, and the last, which enforced Henry's reach and exactions. More to the point, Bacon inserts his own limitations and policies into the descriptions of parliamentary action. The laws of the second Parliament, for example, are said to follow the "Lord Chancellor's admonition" (130; 85), and thus the ex-Lord Chancellor Bacon laconically defers to a speech by Lord Chancellor Morton, the very first speech quoted in the *History*. But is it a speech quoted or a speech invented? Editors such as Spedding express doubts, for there is no evidence, apart from Bacon's report, that such a speech was ever given (116, n. 1; 75–76, n. 1). Be that as it may, the content and even the language are reminiscent of Baconian counsels elsewhere.

One should first note that this same Lord Chancellor, John Morton, figures prominently in Sir Thomas More's *Utopia*,[18] and that the picture drawn by Bacon is very different indeed. In More's account, the "Cardinal" appears a peak of Christian and Aristotelian statesmanship amidst monarchic and oligarchic oppression of the humble. This cardinal was "as respected for his wisdom and virtue as for his authority," and he especially sought out counsellors of "spirit and presence of mind," who would speak freely. He attended sympathetically to Raphael Hythloday, More's Platonic-Christian traveler, even when Hythloday, talking during the reign of Morton's patron Henry VIII, attacked tyrannical exactions, wars, enclosures, miserable poverty, and capital punishment for theft. Bacon's Morton is also wise, but his wisdom seems less the product of virtue and justice than of ingenious policy of state. This chancellor is able to set forth a system of laws that can appeal to an oppressive king and nobility, and that will nevertheless be as effectual at undermining the old monarchy as at establishing his own position.

Bacon's Morton advises three domestic policies—repress force in court, country, and country house; encourage trade, manufactures, and the arts; and allow the king his revenues—and the *History* proceeds to interpret the second Parliament's laws accordingly, not without signs of strain and distortion. Bacon describes a first law as parliamentary confirmation of jurisdiction in certain cases of the Court of Star Chamber, but he barely touches the actual law and turns instead to describe the English courts. Star Chamber is a high court of the king's counsel (not of the king), in cases involving the "state of the commonwealth" (not the king's laws or prerogative), made up of "good elements" (not of the king's appointees), and exercising the Censorian power for offenses less than capital (130–31; 85).

A reader has to wonder at this unmonarchical interpretation of the judicial side of English monarchy, and he must wonder especially at the un-English "Censorian." He will find the term used in Bacon's little *Treatise on Universal Justice*, the second appendix to his Latin account of civil science.[19] The *Treatise* distinguishes a Censorian power, which eases and tightens the criminal laws as needed, from a Praetorian power, which does the same for civil laws. In the *History*, that is, Bacon replaces the traditional names of courts royal, ecclesiastical, and of common law, and he is engaged in reconstructing more than names. The *Treatise on Universal Justice* suggests that Censorian and Praetorian powers should be in the hands of "many," not of "one," and requires for good laws a "good and moderate" governance. Upon occasion, it calls this a "republic" (aphorisms 38, 73). The target is church as well as king. In neither the *Treatise* nor the *History* does Bacon discuss laws of God or the ecclesiastical courts so powerful in Tudor England. In the *Treatise*, Bacon advises that statute law be separated from common law, which Bacon relegates eventually to the library shelves (61–63), and from start to finish he attacks custom, especially "obsolete" custom and "old fables," and praises reason and the adaptation of old law to present times.

Bacon's account of the third Parliament is more daring in importing Baconian policy into pretend legislation. The account begins by praising Henry as the "best lawgiver to this nation" since Edward, and ends with the explanation that "I" do what the best writers have not done: explain laws as "principal acts of peace" (147–48; 97). Bacon comes close to acknowledging the way instruction in law informs his history of laws; he moves partly by choosing "principal" laws and disdaining "vulgar," and mostly by explaining tendentiously Henry's "providence for the future," that is, his counsels (147, 243, cf. 240; 97, 161, cf. 159–60). Laws are interpreted as if instruments of peace, Baconian-style (i.e., means of common security). Consider his explanation of a law providing that farmhouses with competence of farmland be kept up forever. "Apparently, . . . if it be thoroughly considered," this law reflects "singular policy": a provision for middling men, between gentlemen and peasants, such that England will have "infinitely more soldiers of their native forces" than other nations (142–45; 93–95). This thorough consideration turns out to copy an argument in the *Essays* (29), right down to incorporating the same metaphor. It prescribes a variation on a trick of Machiavelli's, whereby princes are led, by the lure of empire, to arm as a native militia the populace who can then depose them. Bacon gives the trick his economic cast, whereby kings and nobles raise the industrious middle class that can then undermine them.

The various reinterpretations of laws complement Bacon's quiet revamping of lawmaking, a very quiet but more sweeping tendency toward subordinating kings to a representative parliament. Commentators have noticed the most conspicuous statements, although they have shied understandably from the radical implications. As Bacon is describing the highest English courts, he inserts an undeveloped qualification: "besides the high court of Parliament" (130; 85). Could Parliament be the "many" in whom final power criminal and civil should lie, according to the *Treatise on Universal Justice*? When Bacon remarks that "a supreme and absolute power cannot conclude itself" (241; 160), he startles commentators, who often cluck about Bacon's inexplicable blunder in attributing sovereign authority to Henry VII's supine Parliaments. Still, is such an error likely? Would a Bacon who served as the king's solicitor-general and Lord Chancellor, and as a leader of Parliament, err as to an explosive doctrine hardly heard in his time and absurd as a description of Henry's autocracy? Impossible. It is likely that Bacon shoots a dart, a formula that in the future can help produce the somewhat republican revolution that he wishes. Another passage has Henry seeking parliamentary authority to revive a nasty tax called a "benevolence," and this despite the fact, according to the records, that the writs for this benevolence were actually sent prior to the assembling of Parliament (176, n. 1; 116, n. 1). Eventually, Bacon has Henry submitting to the seventh Parliament such parts of his jealously guarded prerogative as matters of Star Chamber, the mint, wars, and martial discipline (356; 239).

Bacon's interpretations tend not only to exaggerate the authority of Parliament, but also to regularize it into an institution and to republicanize it into a representative body. The *History* is silent about what its chronology shows, which is that Parliament met erratically during Henry's twenty-four-year reign and met hardly at all once Henry established himself and his funding. There were seven Parliaments in the first twelve years of the reign and but one in the last twelve. Also, Bacon speaks always and distinctively of "Parliament," not of a great council preeminently of peers. He treats its members as "deputies" of the "people" (183; 120) or, in another significant but unhistorical formulation, "procurators of the commonwealth and representatives and fiduciaries of counties and boroughs" (60; 38). These accounts abstract from the facts, especially from the primacy of spiritual and temporal lords, and from the inferior role of the leading men of counties and towns, who were less members than subordinates.[20] Bacon thus insinuates a relation of representation and trust, a relation appropriate less to a council of estates and lords than to a republican legislature representing a rather homogeneous people.

As *History* proceeds, however, Bacon's intimations of a republicanized reign depart from his portrayal of the monarch. Few laws of which Bacon speaks appear during the last five of the eight Parliaments, and almost all such laws are mere instruments of the king and his revenue, wars, finance, exactions, and indictments. The sixth Parliament marks a turning point. While Henry excelled in good commonwealth laws, "he had in secret a design to make use of them as well for collecting of treasure as for correcting of manners" (240; 159). To "harrow the people," he accumulated them. Just before this passage, Bacon had remarked that Henry governed his subjects by his laws and his laws by his lawyers. He was describing the presence of king and queen at a feast, in the eleventh year of the reign, for the sergeants at law (a superior order of barristers). This "Prince" always countenanced "the professors of the law" (238; 158). Bacon notes in one sentence a second sergeants' feast eight years after, is silent as to royal attendance or favor, and inserts the reference after elaborating the streams of exactions enriching Henry and consolidating his dynasty (336; 225).

At the end of the reign and the *History*, the book dwells on the king's extraction of forfeitures under penal laws. It dwells especially on the manipulation of courts and laws through his instruments Dudley and Empson, who entrapped the rich in toils of law and then did their extorting. Bacon names names and estimates ransoms, and the descriptions are correspondingly memorable and make memorable the exploitations most galling to men of estate (327–29; 219–20). Bacon makes a special point of tying the oppressions to the monarchy. Empson and Dudley are pictured as birds of prey, but tools of Henry: wild hawks for themselves and "tame hawks for their master." There is a vivid conversation between Henry and the earl of Oxford as the king departed the earl's hospitality. Having noticed some liveried retainers (which were forbidden to nobles by law), the king says: "By my faith (my lord), I thank you for my good cheer, but I may not endure to have my laws broken in my sight. My attorney must speak with you," and with that the hospitable earl has to cough up fifteen thousand marks. The anecdote rests on Bacon's authority alone.[21]

At times, we can practically see Bacon using his own authority to reduce the king's. "I do remember to have seen long since a book of accompt (account) of Empson's, that had the King's hand almost to every leaf by way of signing." At other points, Bacon simply presents vivid images of the king's involvement. A written receipt for a pardon had an acknowledgment by "the King's own hand" as if signifying the king's satisfaction that the party had been satisfied. This tidbit, we are then assured, shows the "King's extreme diligence," or perhaps a certain "nearness, but yet with a kind of justness." With such praise of justice, who needs attacks on oppression?

Actually, Bacon never calls Henry's hunger for treasure a vice nor his ambition for power tyrannical, and while giving an appearance of disapproval, Bacon does not disapprove. He coolly explains the acquisition and the ambition as necessary. It is not that Henry was unjust in resisting the sharing of rule under law, in resisting, that is, political government. But he was shortsighted. While injustice proves to be not the point at issue in Bacon's account of the king's defects, farsightedness is. Republics may not be just, but republics and the appearance of justice are the way to make one's state endure in the future. But this is only after one has risen to state, and the main lesson of the *History* is that the winding stair for rising is first and foremost ruthless acquisition.

Thus it is that Bacon makes a point of defending Henry's avarice, and the point is its political fruits. "Avarice doth ever find in itself matter of ambition," for estate breeds a state of greatness (336; 225). In the concluding summary of Henry there occurs a model formulation (356–59; 239–41). It begins: Henry did "maintain and countenance his laws." It ends: he did maintain "state and majesty" as a device for obedience. The middle shows that Henry's regard for his subjects' security was caused by a secret desire for quantity and product. He ordered executions sparingly, "[b]ut the less blood he drew the more he took of treasure: and as some construed it, he was the more sparing in the one that he might be the more pressing in the other; for both would have been intolerable." Once in this long paragraph Bacon enters in the first person, and it is to defend Henry's avarice as necessary to his ambition: "whereunto I should add, that having every day occasion to take notice of the necessities and shifts for money of other great Princes abroad, it did the better by comparison set off to him the felicity of full coffers." Accordingly, Bacon praises the qualities that serve Henry's self and state, and the names of old virtues get the new, politic, and secretive Baconian meanings. Henry's "liberality was rather upon his own state and memory" than upon the deserts of others; he was of "high mind" and he "revered himself, and would reign indeed"; he was "wise," not admitting "any near or full approach either to his power or to his secrets."

Nevertheless, Henry was also unwise in his shortsightedness, and Bacon repeatedly tasks him for lack of foresight as to evils to come in the very long run. Henry did not think to introduce the civil institutions needed in order that his state endure.

Many of the Baconian corrections provide for such an enduring state. A law of the third Parliament stiffened the requirements for suits over landownership and thus quieted possessions; a second encouraged small farms, population growth, and military power; a third encouraged naval power. Others made criminal prosecutions easier, regularized and conserved the nation's money, and established a maximum price in a manner, Bacon interprets, that would stimulate clothiers to make what the customer can afford (141, 142; 92, 93). According to Bacon, the laws of this Parliament promote "happiness." He shows how public prosperity and private satisfaction alike can follow from security of property, a nation of power, and a state that protects person, property, and opportunities for gain and consumption. In short, peace and happiness is what follows from the regulations that also breed a great power, and thus, if one is ingenious, private happiness and public power may be made compatible. Good laws were the King's "retribution" for his treasure, as Bacon puts it, and in turn they served his treasure and power. The lessons are of the double profit, that is, popular satisfaction together with national resources, for the king, like the good merchant, can gain both on the export and the reimport. This is Bacon's version of Machiavelli's maxim that one leads by serving.

Yet Henry in fact was a king too imperious to be so civil and so ingenious. According to Bacon, he failed to satisfy the people, and they rebelled; he neglected channels for the nobles' advancement, and they rebelled; he failed to predict the death of a crucial ally at a crucial moment. In short, he failed to plan adequately in the Machiavellian sense, systematically for inevitable evils to come and especially for his own oblivion. Henry needed less kingship and better counsel, and Bacon's *History* is not only a chronicle of Henry's defect but also a counsel as to the remedy.

King and Counsellors

The *History* dwells noticeably on Henry's counsellors and most notably on the ingenuity of Archbishop John Morton and Bishop John Fox. "[I]n feeding the king's humour" these two "did rather temper it" (311; 208), unlike Empson and Dudley who but catered to it. Bacon particularly honors Fox, as "a wise man and one that could see through the present to the future" (275, cf. 317; 184, cf. 212), and his praise of the two bishops as farsighted goes beyond praise of particular counsels. While Henry himself gives only one of the seven set speeches quoted or paraphrased, Morton gives three. But we should notice the type of prominence. The praise for a politic *astuzia* abstracts from the holy offices of these ecclesiatics. In *Utopia*, More characteristically speaks of "the Cardinal" and introduces Morton as "the reverend prelate John Cardinal Morton, archbishop of Canterbury and also at that time Lord Chancellor of England." In the *History*, Bacon characteristically speaks of "Morton" or "the Chancellor" and rarely presents him as Lord Chancellor, archbishop, or cardinal. While More treats the divine office as the serious office, Bacon presents the bishops as shrewd politiques. "But whatsoever else was in the man," Bacon concludes a brief eulogy of Morton, "he deserveth a most happy memory, in that he was the principal means of joining the two Roses" (311; 208). Bacon neglects to mention that Fox, for example, loved Greek and Latin learning; upon his retirement, he reformed the clergy and founded a center of ancient learning, Corpus Christi College at Oxford.[22]

The technique is characteristic, for throughout the *History* Bacon interprets serious counsellors as Machiavellian and Christian counsellors as hypocritical. When Henry was failing in his attempt to obtain sainthood for Henry VI, "the general opinion was, that Pope Julius was too dear, and that the King would not come to his rates" (348, cf. 312–15, 139–40; 233, cf. 208–11, 91–92). For a similar reason Bacon takes care to bring out the bodily intricacies connected with consummation of holy matrimony (154–56, 320–21; 101–3, 214–15). In short, whatever may be the checks upon monarchy that the *History* encourages, Christian piety and Christian churchmen are not among them. Yet there is surely more to Bacon's reform of Christian counsel than the scoffing that is undoubtedly a key element, for in the *History*, one sees a number of churchmen who have been converted into sharp-eyed advisers in the world. While pious churchmen are worse than useless, Bacon seems to suggest, enlightened churchmen may be very useful, not least for channeling their pious brethren. A dart late in *History* intimates the plan: some preachers performed their "true duty," that is, they decried oppressions of the people by the king's creatures. Enlightened Christianity may be a channel for reformed Christianity and play its own part in the progress toward civil government.

Although Bacon's Henry appears a prince always calculating as to empire and state, Bacon never questions this preoccupation, and indeed he can be seen exaggerating it. Only grudgingly does he admit that Henry was actually quite devout and a patron of Christianity (312–16, 355;

208–12, 238), and he gives a cause that goes to undermine any support the example might provide for piety: Henry's devotions came upon him with anticipations of death. All the Henrician utterances that Bacon recounts and invents are free of serious Christian devotion. No mention of Christ or God leavens Henry's coldly brutal conversations with Charles of Castille and the earl of Oxford. It is true that in Henry's speech to the fourth Parliament, God is said to favor English arms and unity and Henry's sword—but only as a name in which to proceed (179–81; 118–19). Here and throughout there are at most but religious names shorn of sanctity. Henry's speech contains a cold scent of Christendom in what is in fact a coldly political argument, for he really justifies his request for a benevolence by alleging France's expansion, his challenge for the crown of France, and the force of England and her allies. Since Henry plans not the waging of war but the extorting of subsidies, even these words are a faithless fraud. In a nasty twist, Bacon says that only "the two bishops" (now so called), with a few others, knew of the lie.

This speech of Henry's is given beneath a "cloth of state," which happens to be just the formula used in *New Atlantis* to describe a canopy over the scientist-father from Salomon's House. Is the parallel mere happenstance? I suspect that the language symbolizes a state of opinion that should guide kings and scientists alike, although in different directions, and that while such an outlook seems to control the knowing scientist in imaginary Bensalem, it did not get through adequately to King Henry VII in real England. When Bacon allows that Henry was not superstitious "for those times," he allows that Henry was superstitious. Bacon's efforts at recasting the human outlook explain his reduction of Henry's kingship to Baconian statecraft, his reduction of religious men and ceremonies to civil instruments or hypocritical frauds, his celebration of Henry as a "wonder" and one of the "three magi" of his time (355, 364; 238, 244), and his description of the victory over Warbeck as an occasion when "every Saint did help" (287; 192). It also explains why, after the account of Warbeck's rebellion of the faithful, Bacon inserts an account, explicitly out of chronological order, of Henry's patronage of the explorer John Cabot's discoveries. Let kings be kept in worldly fear by wariness as to their neighbors, and be kept in worldly hope by a vision of real discoveries to come. Real fears and hopes will replace otherworldly fears and hopes, under the aegis of an enlightened state of mind.

Still, such enlightened counsel to a state-builder is likely to be talk without teeth. As soon as Henry secured himself, he discarded Morton and Fox in favor of Empson and Dudley and their more direct satisfactions of his desires. The great politics of a founding may require an enlightened despot, but "reason of state," a common formula in the *History*, requires that a civil state be laid on the foundation and on the despot as well.

Notes

1. Busch, *England under the Tudors.* Vol. 1: *King Henry VII* (1485–1509) (London: A. D. Innes & Co., 1895), 416–23; see F. Smith Fussner, *The Historical Revolution: English Historical Writing and Thought, 1580–1660* (London: Routledge & Kegan Paul, 1962); F. J. Levy, *Tudor Historical Thought* (San Merino, Calif.: Huntington Library, 1967).

2. Quoted in *Works* XI, 20–23; VI, 8–10.

3. *The Trials of Counsel: Francis Bacon in 1621* (Detroit: Wayne State University Press, 1976), 149–200.

4. *Trials of Counsel*, 169, 157, 67, 107, 119, 161, 186.

5. "Henry VII," in *The Great Tudors*, ed. Katharine Garvin (London: Eyre & Spottswood, 1956), 3, 4, 9–10.

6. *The History of the Reign of King Henry VII*, in *Works* XI, 147; VI, 97. Page references in the text will appear thus: (147; 97).

7. *Trials of Counsel*, 157, 162, 175, 187, 195. See Jerry Weinberger, "The Politics of Bacon's *History of Henry the Seventh*," for a refutation of a historicism that interprets the *History* in light of an evolving civic republicanism [*The Review of Politics* 52 (fall, 1990); 553–78].

8. *Trials of Counsel*, 201.

9. II, i–iii, ed. Wright; *Works* VI, 194–96; III, 337–38.

10. II, ii, 5, ed. Wright; *Works* VI, 194–96; III, 337–38.

11. II, ii, 8, ed. Wright; *Works* VI, 193; III, 336.

12. II, ii, 9, 10, ed. Wright; *Works* VI, 194–96; III, 337–38.

13. II, ii, 12, ed. Wright; *Works* VI, 197; III, 339.

14. II, ii, 13, ed. Wright; *Works* VI, 197; III, 340.

15. II, i, 2, 6, ed. Wright; *Works* VI, 183–84, 187–88; III, 325–30, 332–33.

16. II, iii, 1, 2, 3, ed. Wright; *Works* VI, 199–200; III, 340–42.

17. *Peace among the Willows*, 53, 54; see "The English Solomon: Francis Bacon on Henry VII," in *Social Research* 24 (winter, 1957); 450–67. See also Weinberger's "The Politics of Bacon's *History of Henry the Seventh*."

18. Ed. George M. Logan and Robert M. Adams (Cambridge: Cambridge University Press, 1989), 15–28.

19. *De Augmentis* VIII, in *Works* IX, 311–344; V, 88–110.

20. Albert Frederick Pollard, *The Evolution of Parliament* (London: Longmans, Green and Co., 1926), 12, 261–65, 431.

21. Busch, *England under the Tudors*, 421.

22. Alfred Frederick Pollard, "Fox, Richard," in *The Encyclopaedia Britannica*, 11th ed., 1910.

Chapter 9

The Great Power

Civil Politics

There are clear Baconian directions for making a state a civil state and, in particular, for making a growing nation-state. This chapter concentrates on the key direction, which is "Of the True Greatness of Kingdoms and Estates" (29). Essay 29 is long as the Baconian essays go, but it is extraordinarily compressed. Bacon has produced here a sort of ingenious literary explosive, one with many parts attached to a long fuse. It consists of a tough measure of political success—capacity for empire—and ten counsels to that end. It is meant to produce directly a key instrument for blowing apart the old order and establishing a new, new counsellors of state. Their efforts can undermine the kingdoms and estates and replace them with efficient civil institutions in which such counsellors, and their Baconian counsel, will have a great place. While state-builders, such as Henry VII, may not on their own initiative make a state civil, their enlightened counsellors can initiate such changes under the cover of reason of state. Essay 29 addresses itself to "counsellors and statesmen," but provides "an argument fit for great and mighty princes to have in their hand."

In the next chapter, we examine the more common and popular promises of the Baconian civil order, that is, the promises of economic prosperity, legal security, and participation in the cause of universal and humanitarian liberty. These are famous promises of progress, and they, with the most famous promise, of technological and scientific growth, dominate the appearance of Bacon's works.

In fact, the power politics so prominent in essay 29 might seem contrary to the benevolent humanitarianism of the methodological works, of the *New Atlantis*, and even of essays such as "Of Goodness and Goodness of Nature" (13) and "Of Regiment of Health" (30). It seems out of

183

place in the earnestly utilitarian *Essays* as a whole, which is solicitous of its readers' "business and bosoms" and contains no other thematic discussion of weapons, tactics, courage, soldiers, generals, or armies and navies. But while promises of prosperity, security, and humanity are of conspicuous importance, they are not the whole story of Bacon's civil politics. They are not the fundamental story. For some men's bosoms harbor "a natural malignancy," as Bacon also says in "Of Goodness and Goodness of Nature." Theirs is the desire to rise above and exploit other men, and their desire is the fundamental business of politics, "the fittest timber to make great politics of." Such seekers of domination seek a state of domination of their own, although Bacon will not necessarily provide such suitors all that they want, and such a state requires a continual war of acquisition. The making of a state is the theme of the *History of the Reign of King Henry VII*, and Henry's wars against rivals at home and abroad are omnipresent. He is a founder-conqueror with the ambition that makes fighting worthwhile and the rank that makes it less dangerous. The making of a state into a civil state is the theme of the *Essays*, and a civil war at home (at least by insinuation of a new state of things) is omnipresent; the rising elite is shown how to advance itself in advancing a civil state that can both expand itself and defend itself. While essay 29 may appeal to the ambitions of kings and estates, it moves toward superseding them with a popular nation-state, which is able to mobilize both the men of ability and the industry of the people and thus to wield great wealth, populations, armies, and navies.

This warlike mixture of public imperialism and private ambition is Machiavellian. Essay 29 is probably the most thoroughly Machiavellian of Baconian writings, although Machaivelli is not mentioned by name and his preoccupation with fighting is somewhat modified by commendations of economic growth, defensive war, and naval forces. While Bacon's civil teaching is more pacific, and designed to improve on Machiavelli's wolf-like republicanism, private security requires public security, and a state fit for national security must be fit for war. The comprehensive essay 29 sets forth the military forces and how to produce them, while the whole work, as well as the qualifications in essay 29 itself, modify Machiavelli's militarism in light of Bacon's new ways to expand and to mobilize.

Essays and the Civil State

At first glance, and even after more than one searching look, the political teachings of the *Essays* seem scattered and perhaps slight. Only seven of the fifty-eight essays are political in title, such as "Of Empire" (19), and another six or so titles might be thought ambiguously political, such as "Of Plantations" (33) and "Of Negotiating" (47). The remaining three-quarters promise discussions philosophic, religious, moral, and private. Among all the essays, nevertheless, "Of the True Greatness of Kingdoms and Estates" stands out, both initially and after consideration. It proclaims its greatness and truth, is longest, and has the longest title. It is also the first of two central essays, and these two alone have titles that refer to rule or rulers. Also, more than any other essay, its argument is both obviously important and completely orderly. The argument consists of an introduction on the task of expansion, ten counsels on how to do it, and a conclusion on what is gained. Compressed and compact despite its extent, essay 29 is a little masterpiece of realpolitik. It seems even a catechism containing the ten maxims of statecraft. Such a conceit, in which ten Baconian counsels replace ten commandments of dutiful righteousness before the Lord, may be fit for more than a simile.

> To conclude: no man can by care taking (as the Scripture saith) add a cubit to his stature, in this little model of a man's body; but in the great frame of kingdoms and commonwealths, it is in the power of princes or estates to add amplitude and greatness to their kingdoms; for by introducing such ordinances, constitutions, and customs, as we have now touched, they may sow greatness to their posterity and succession. But these things are commonly not observed, but left to take their chance.

The counsels of essay 29 are, in short, Bacon's formulas for constituting an imperial nation-state, and they are openly imperial and ruthless to an extent unique in the *Essays*. After the introductory paragraphs, which define true counsel as ability to amplify a state and true greatness of a state as aptitude to enlarge or command, there are the counsels themselves. The first five show how to produce a nation that can be mobilized, the last five, how to produce the attitudes and incentives for mobilizing. A state bent on greatness needs a militia or infantry of natives; taxation not burdensome or rather by consent; a middling and independent people not subordinated to gentlemen and nobles; a population expanding by easy naturalization and plantation of colonies; and a distribution of manly arts to natives and of delicate manufactures to strangers. These first prescriptions are republican, and four are manifestly derived from *The Prince* or *Discourses*. The last five counsels prescribe the attitudes leading to empire; four of these contain examples and phrases drawn from the *Discourses*. A nation should profess arms as its principal "honor, study, and occupation"; should have customs that provoke "just occasions (as may be pretended) of war"; should indulge in foreign wars for "exercise" and for a veteran army; should attend to naval power; and should glorify generals to reward conquests. Bacon's prescription for nation-building moves from mobilizing peoples for a nation in arms to mobilizing generals through promise of glories.

Essay 29 is the crucial civil part of the art of life which Bacon calls, in *De Augmentis,* "the new and unwonted art of making one's fortune." It is a formula for producing a power for the public man, the armor for "the statesman in armor" of which the essay's alternative title, in *De Augmentis,* speaks. The essay will benefit founders as well as statesmen, for it sets forth the "ordinances, constitutions, and customs" that make the founder's plan a governing force.

Bacon's attention to artificial but fundamental "constitutions" moves some way toward Locke's later constitutionalism, but only a small way. There is nothing of necessary and legally defined powers, government by consent, or fundamental law. Machiavellian channeling according to realistic maxims, not fixed public law, is more like Bacon's point. Admittedly, there is an un-Machiavellian attention to justice as well as law in the fourth counsel, which dwells upon the importance of protecting the rights of all, and Bacon's universalism of law and individual right foreshadows the liberal focus on rights, and on security of person and property, in particular. This is no slight part of Bacon's project. In the *Treatise on Justice,* discussed in our next chapter, Bacon generalizes private law by finding its "foundation" in private interests, and the work shows by its full title a design to spur a comprehensive reform of jurisprudence: *Example of a Treatise on Universal Justice or the Foundations of Equity, by Aphorisms: One Title of It.* Nevertheless, the basis of all this is somewhat closer to Machiavellian individualism and imperialism than to Lockean natural rights.

Counsellors as Framers and Administrators of Growth

From its start, essay 29 equivocates in ways that call for clarification, and the obvious equivocations lead to the most important clarifications. There is in the first sentences a conjunction of "counsellors and statesmen" that is replaced by "counsellors and governors," and the title's conjunction of kingdoms and estates is mingled with "state" and "estate." Bacon alludes, I suggest, to the two great novelties that had been established in the set of essays (19–28) that lead up to essay 29. Through counselling kings, counsellors may rise to govern, and these counsellors will introduce a new state of things that is favorable to rising men. The old advisers to kings, such as priests and nobles, are to be replaced by governors sub rosa, wise for their own estate or possession.

Earlier, in "Of Counsel" (20), Bacon had said that counsellors should attend to "business" (not the person of the king), should attend to "persons" (and not class, character, or "idea"), and should be open to petitions from those outside the government. They should prepare business by committees of "indifferent persons" and by "standing commissions" of no mean powers: "for trade, for treasure, for war, for suits, for some provinces. . . ." Such advice tends to subordinate kings to staff, to administrators, and to committees and commissions responsive to the people and to people's interests. It develops something at least of what came to be called the administrative state, one that ministers efficiently as it attends solicitously.[1] Such a state will replace traditional kingship and its circles of family, priests, and nobles.

In "Of Empire" (19), Bacon had reduced kingship to empire, rather than divinely or morally guided authority, and questioned the force of kings, who lack "some predominant desire that should marshal and put in order all the rest." Kings as kings have achieved their status, and hence they are erratic and unguided except by illusions. Bacon means to remove illusions, at least the illusion that kings might locate noble or divinely inspired advisers, and to rouse an incessant desire for a more secure fortune. Since men like more "profiting in small things than . . . standing at a stay in great," let princes not merely provide against dangers when near, but seek "solid and grounded courses to keep them aloof." The reliable mover of princes is magnified fear, and growing power can be their solid and progressive satisfaction. Fear thy neighbor, "Of Empire" suggests, and any growth in his power to annoy. Fear wives, children to a degree, powerful prelates, and armed men in a body and used to donatives, and worry about managing nobles and gentlemen for your "business." Amidst all this spreading of suspicions and apprehensions, the common people are more or less exempted, and favor is bestowed unequivocally on one class alone: merchants.

Essay 29 completes the transvaluation of civil values begun by the earlier attempts to undermine traditional kingdoms and counsellors. The target is partly the feudal monarchy of Bacon's time and the Christian theology that sustained it, but it is also more. The essay begins with the authority of Themistocles the Athenian, who "could make a small town a great city," but its focus is not the city, redolent of the Greek *polis* and of ancient political philosophy, and it eventually recommends a "nation" or "state" that can encompass cities and even nations. The great step is the new priority of power: one must make "the right valuation and true judgment" concerning the force of an estate. One must, that is, evaluate by forces, and true judgment is as to what produces a larger force. Seek a power apt to become great, "apt to enlarge or command" and to be "the foundations of great monarchies." The analogy is blasphemous: the kingdom of heaven that Scripture compares to a mustard seed apt to get up and spread. An empire spreads over the nations not by encouragement of virtue and justice, and not by submission to the Lord. The secret to overcoming chance is provision of one's own force and as much as possible.

Five Formulas for a Growing Nation

The first ordinance of essay 29 is simply Machiavellian: develop a warlike people, that is, a "militia of natives." This blunt counsel is advanced for any state, or any prince or state, or princes, or any estate or prince. Might the equivocations hint that the advice is universal and applies to any leader, to leaders of sects, for example, as well as of governments? However that may be, Bacon is emphatic on the need for change. Multitudes, riches, mercenaries—none are adequate where a "base and effeminate people" exists. Adequate for what? Two examples refer to the two military conquerors of the world, Alexander and Rome. The shock of such models is softened by citations from works of an ancient poet (Virgil) and an ancient sage (Solon), but Bacon misapplies his authorities in a manner that points to a more shocking lesson.

In the original pastoral, Virgil recounts a contest between poets competing for honor and offering lambs to a god and never mentions the lesson that Bacon alleges: that a wolf is unconcerned with sheep, whatever their number. Bacon substitutes the way of the wolf for the poet's concerns with literary pleasures and honors and the gods. A similar lesson is drawn from Solon's visit to Croesus's luxury (i.e., that one with better iron can take this gold), and in this case the example and the lesson are Machiavelli's. They supersede Solon's actual words (as Plutarch recounts them): only he is happy whose life ends fortunately and who lives in moderation.[2] The fruit of Bacon's indirection: one needs not only armed forces and armed conquest but also and chiefly the armed heart, that is, a wary opportunism freed from devotions to illusions such as virtue and reason, the gods, and the pleasures of poetry and philosophy. To take care for the people as a force, as soldiers for the great power, the first step is the conquest of your inclinations to look up to what seems high in them and above them. Do not overlay a people with taxes, or, rather, tax by consent. The novelty of this second ordinance is its calculated deference to popular freedom and property, and this novelty, too, comes out in the examples. England displays "in some degree" the benefit of taxes levied by "consent of the estate," and thus Bacon intimates, what he develops elsewhere (as in the *History*), that England's Parliament should be further democratized. Essay 29 says explicitly that taxation by consent is present "notably" in the low countries, which are called elsewhere "democracies" that "excel" in "their government" without need of a nobility and because of equality in the burdens ("Of Nobility" 14). "For where there is an equality, the consultations are more indifferent, and the payments and tributes more cheerful." But Bacon also alludes to the need for a democratizing more profound than a civil democratizing, a democratizing of the mind. He had begun discussion of the second precept by quoting the Old Testament, the context being Jacob's blessing on his sons that leads to one king of Israel, the people bowed even to slavery (Genesis 49:9–14). He ends with a political principle: "no people overcharged with tribute is fit for empire." In a relevant essay, Bacon writes that superstition erects "an absolute monarchy" in men's minds ("Of Superstition" 17).

The third ordinance cautions against another part of the old regime, nobles and gentlemen, and then prescribes a rather democratic farming economy that will produce free people and rough fighters. Bacon praises England for a stout and armed middling class (unlike a peasantry such as France's), but he never praises England for its various aristocratic classes. In fact, the praise is for a land policy that will destroy an aristocracy, since it fosters middling farms to breed a man not servile or needy, a man who works for himself and not by "hirelings"; for this innovation Bacon ironically and equivocally credits Henry VII ("wherein I have spoken largely in the history of his life"). Conversely, he praises the English aristocracy for its patronage of independent servants (i.e., of freemen). He then urges nobility and gentlemen alike to "splendor and magnificence and great retinues and hospitality," although the previous essay had counseled frugality for those who would wax rich ("Of Expense" 28). There is another dose of malicious policy here, which Bacon must have enjoyed. Let rising men save themselves into power, and aristocrats spend themselves out of it.

"Of Sedition" (15) had elaborated this plan for revolution by economic development, attacking the multiplying of "nobility and other degrees of quality," and extending the attack to scholars and an "overgrown clergy" and to idle funds as well as idle hands. "Above all things" good policy demands that moneys be not restricted to "few," else a rich state may starve or at least neglect profitable investments. Busy money and not leisured money is the key, since "money is like muck, not good except it be spread," and the hidden fruit of the new plantings will be new classes to undermine the old.

The fourth prescription: let the state be liberal in accepting strangers by naturalization or by colonization. While Bacon uses the models of pagan Rome and Christian Spain, he begins with a biblical analogy: the trunk of "Nebuchadnezzar's tree of monarchy" must be great enough. Nebuchadnezzar dreamed of a monarchy over all peoples, nations, and languages, but the Lord cast him down, that man would know that the Lord rules the kingdom of man and gives it to whom He will (Daniel 4:10–17). Bacon corrects the Lord. One can will a universal dominion for oneself, if one forgoes the exclusivity that accompanies a promised land for superior or godly people. The discussion turns to the model of Rome's empire, and from this universal empire of the world Bacon extracts two policies: liberal naturalization of strangers, including individuals, families, cities, and sometimes whole nations, and "Plantation of Colonies." Putting together these "Constitutions," as Bacon then calls them, "you" will say that "it was not the Romans that spread upon the World, but it was the World that spread upon the Romans." The message seems to be that the worldly Romans, not the Holy Romans, found "the sure way of greatness," although the phrasing might remind one of the eventual victory of the Holy Romans. The counsel, the model, and the equivocation remind one of Machiavelli, who discredited Sparta and elevated Rome realistically reinterpreted, with a view, that is, to real empires of the mind as well as of arms. Bacon follows the reinterpretation. Rome grew to the "greatest monarchy," essay 29 says, which may well be Augustus's rule of the world, but could refer to the biblical God, or at least to Christ's improvement on Jewish exclusivity.

Yet the "Constitutions" of expansion are not exactly Machiavelli's in their attention to justice and to economic colonies, and Bacon shows here two of his important improvements.

The secret of Rome's liberal naturalization is a right of citizenship (*ius Civitatis*), and, in un-Machiavellian fashion, Bacon sets forth six insistences on justice that amount, in effect, to rights to trade, intermarriage, and inheritance, as well as to suffrage and office. While I discuss Bacon's jurisprudence in the next chapter, I call attention here to his advocacy in such a context of a justice that is commercial, rather democratic and distinctly individualistic, and accordingly universal in its appeal to private needs. A new world of equal opportunity can appeal to whole peoples. In the same context, Bacon substitutes for "monarchy" the phrase "crown or state." We can see that Baconian justice, like the rest of Baconian policy, fosters a nation monarchical only in name if at all. To repeat, *New Atlantis* portrays a cosmopolitan nation with a king who is never seen and whose authority, called once "the crown," is shadowy, regulated by laws, and equated with the state. The nation of Bensalem contains Jews as well as Christians, and Persians, Chaldeans, and Arabians as well as Europeans, and has thus managed to dilute and subordinate old faiths and nationalities to a common faith in progress by invention. Essay 29 shows the economic and legal secrets of the civil side. It plans an empire that attracts immigrants and even nations by offering security, liberty, and opportunity, that grows in men and wealth, and that expands by immigration as well as production.

In another essay, "Of Plantations" (33), Bacon discusses the colonization that in essay 29 receives a bare mention. Unlike Machiavellian (and Roman) imperialism, Bacon's will be humane or at least appear humane. "I like" a colony where natives are not displanted, he says at the start, although he eventually tolerates displanting, preferably by enlightened persuasion. If "savages" are present, use them "justly and graciously," and win them by converting them to a "better condition than their own." The promise of opportunity may work with savages, too. Yet Bacon allows "sufficient guard," and while he discourages participation in tribal wars, he allows participation in the tribes' defensive wars. In short, he blends colonialism with the attractions of opportunity, while only indicating the irreducible harshness and the hard life inseparable from new colonies among savage peoples.

The secret of Baconian colonialism is economic ingenuity: empire through private gain. The *Essays* talks of "plantations" by private investors, not of public colonies, and "Of Plantations" is a do-it-yourselfer's guide for venture capitalists. Bacon speaks of "planting" men and women as well as plants and animals, for people may be regarded as a crop, a factor of production, and, in general, a force to be expanded for an empire over time as well as place. When "the plantation grows to strength, then it is time to plant with women as well as with men; that the plantation may spread into generations, and not be ever pierced from without."

What investors see as an instrument of gain, is a colony, and more than a civil colony, for it is also a beachhead of an enduring empire with a worldly cause that can replace the old faith. While the "sinfullest thing" is to neglect a colony, we are here told, this colony is stocked with the industrious and run by one with counsel, not stocked with the devout and run by those with revelation. The new-style colony may be more an outpost of empire for the new movement and the colonists of this new world, than an outpost of the old-style mother-country and the old-style original investors. Bacon encourages nobles and gentry to be the investors and governors; unlike the impatient merchant, he suggests, they are likely to settle in for a long-term investment. Here is a Baconian channel for old estates to join in making the new world. But the channel may not serve them well, since they are thus induced to help found a world without aristocrats, and they may lose control precisely if the colonies are enterprising and successful. At one point in "Of Plantations," Bacon calls the colony a "country." If these inferences are correct, an aristocracy is led to raise up antipathetic powers abroad, and to lose by investing abroad a portion of their riches at home, and generally to be the witting beneficiaries and unwitting instruments of a colonialism that contributes, in the long run, to their worldwide downfall.

Returning now to essay 29, we see that Bacon closes his discussion of colonies, easy naturalization, and cosmopolitan empire with a quick glance at Spain. Spain manages to hold a great empire, despite few natives and strict restriction of naturalization, by employing "all nations" among ordinary soldiers and high commands alike. Spain, one may say, mixes Christian exclusiveness with Christian comprehensiveness and can win much of a world by promising to save it. Yet Spain is short of natives. Perhaps Bacon alludes to its Christian inclinations to celibacy and exclusiveness and its monarchical tendency to oppression. His worldly and popular faith can avoid such defects, for it can produce growing populations at home and growing colonies abroad.

Bacon's fifth ordinance deals with the problem posed for a military disposition by a sophisticated economy. Leave "sedentary" arts and "delicate" manufactures to strangers, he counsels, while directing the bulk of "vulgar natives" toward rougher occupations, such as those of farmers, free servants, smiths, masons, and carpenters. Bacon replies in advance, as it were, to Rousseau's *Discourse on the Arts and Sciences*, which criticized the effects of enlightenment upon republican virtue and especially upon fighting virtue. Bacon acknowledges that the ancients solved this problem differently, for they staffed their manufactories with slaves. But slavery is abolished by "Christian law," and while Bacon acknowledges no other reservation in principle as to slavery, and undermines many other Christian laws, he does not propose to restore slavery. One might speculate that slavery is incompatible with Bacon's efforts to foster industriousness (the slave having little motive to work hard and the master little motive to work at all), to foster in all a sense of adversity and a hope for bettering one's condition, and to foster a universal cause that can appeal to peoples and nations everywhere. The Baconian remedy for the softness bred by factory labor is to relegate such work not to slaves but to immigrants.

The remedy is of capital importance, and yet, even setting aside the injustice, it is unsatisfying. The problem is not merely that the prophet of the arts and sciences subordinates them to national security and especially to a popular aptitude for fighting, but also that a military disposition is discussed without mention of courage. Bacon discusses only an habituation to heavy work. He seems to be aware of this, since he plays with nobler words, such as "strong and manly," but he applies the words to arts and not characters. Bacon would probably reply that he ignores imaginary courage, of which few are capable, and by rough occupations produces a reliable toughness for a popular army. Necessity drives the worker to courage enough.

But is the economic remedy adequate to the military problem? Bacon advocates both a refined means of production, in which technology lightens tasks, and extensive consumer goods, which soften tastes. Such an economy will make life progressively easier and people progressively softer, as Bacon is perfectly aware (if one judges by the servile and passive crowds amidst the luxurious consumption of Bensalem). Actually, precisely this difficulty is alluded to in the concluding essay ("Of Vicissitude of Things" 58). The context is the cycle of changes in a state, and Bacon says that in its youth, arms flourish; in middle age, learning; in its declining age, "mechanical arts and merchandise." Does a Baconian nation arise with a state-builder's discipline and arms, flourish with civil regulation and republican arms, and inevitably decline as consumption and the developed arts erode the popular disposition to endure hardship, industry, and battle? Is this a defect inherent in Bacon's growing nation, a defect whose inevitability Bacon himself indicates (albeit in a way that practically conceals the problem)? Does Bacon conceal the problem so as hardly to acknowledge that an enlightened nation's faith in continual progress is an illusion?

Five Formulas for Mobilizing a Nation for War

The last five precepts in essay 29 prescribe preoccupation with war, as many commentators correctly note, although with small qualifications not so commonly noted. Bacon defends the professing of war more than the fighting of it, praises fighting chiefly as a way of developing a veteran army whose reputation will bring conquests, praises an island or naval empire that can take as little or as much of war as it wishes, and praises triumphal celebrations only to ridicule and bury them in subsequent essays. While Bacon here encourages the military shield needed by any expansionist state, I conclude, he fundamentally advances more delicate arts of empire, especially economic and political arts that breed power almost automatically. One can avoid the risks of conquering empire if one can grow to it. Several essays on producing and acquiring wealth embellish the remarks on economics in essay 29; no essay on military topics elaborates its many remarks on war. While all politics is war, one wars more safely and surely by production of power than by conquering it.

"[A]bove all, for empire and greatness" a nation must devote itself to war. Precept five had advised building soldiers through the harsher arts and occupations; precept six, the second of the central precepts, subordinates all arts and occupations to the art of war and all nations to the great conquerors. Bacon praises Rome, Sparta, and successive empires down to the Turks and Spaniards of his day, and speaks of Rome and Turkey, who continued long in the "profession" of war, as having done "wonders" (just as in *History* he presents Henry's state-building as a "wonder" to surpass revealed wonders).[3] Essay 29 explicates a national aptitude for war, in place of the old faith, and puts Christian Spain to the new measure as well as Sparta, the ancient city admired by the ancient philosophers. To confirm the transformation of creeds and philosophies, Bacon here sprinkles in one reference to oracles and one to an invented (and blasphemous) proverb, and misuses a doctrine from *Nicomachean Ethics*.

The seventh means to greatness is "incident" to the sixth; Bacon expressly connects only these two. A state should have "laws or customs" that justify war, and this precept is related to the new and warlike faith advocated by precept six. For customs, the discussion soon substitutes "sect"; for just occasion, it substitutes "cause," and I infer that, given the "calamities" of war, people must be driven to it by some quasi-religious belief. Again the Turks and Romans are examples. The Turk propagates his law or sect, "a quarrel that he may always command," but about the Romans' cause, Bacon is coy, and he is also strangely silent here about a connected phenomenon, Spain's propagation of Roman Christianity. He simply proceeds to three prescriptions of his own. First, let nations pretending to greatness be sensible of wrongs, either upon "borderers, merchants, or politic ministers." The mention of merchants is distinctive. Is foreign trade the cause that will induce preparedness? Second, let nations aid confederates as did the Romans. One might infer that Bacon commends simply the cause of civil expansion, perhaps through mercantile expansion. Yet the third prescription portends more without prescribing more: Bacon cannot well justify wars anciently made for a party or for "tacit conformity of estate." The tone is negative, and yet the language is ambiguous and the ensuing examples are suggestive. Rome warred for the liberty of Greece; Athens and Sparta warred for democracy and oligarchy; "foreigners" war to liberate the subjects of others under pretense of "justice or protection." In short, Bacon indicates the need for a faith, hints at a faith civil and not religious, and intimates, perhaps, that the faith should promise justice and protection to merchants, politic men, liberty, peoples, and oligarchs. He hints finally that such promises are devices to win subjects. What does this all mean?

I suspect that these light steps indicate the international implications of the *Essays'* new creed of equal opportunity for making one's fortune. It will attract foreigners and persons acquisitive and ambitious, provide liberty and power in a way that appeals to both the poor and the rich, and promise universal security. Besides, as a creed (albeit an enlightened creed), it will appeal like the old creeds and sects.

The eighth precept focuses on a tough implication of the new imperialism: a warlike nation needs the occasional war. Actually, a reader might have expected more, after the talk of excuses for war and the examples of Spain, the Turks, and Rome. Bacon suggests merely that foreign war is the exercise that keeps a political body in health, or at least breeds a veteran army that makes for greatness. There is more than at first appears. For exercise is identified with warring on others, not with a fitness of body subordinate to fitness of soul, and Bacon indicates the radical implications by unobtrusively equating health with "happiness." This confirms both his equation of kingdoms and estates with a politic "body" and his decisive rejection of a connection between happiness and activity of soul. While true exercise requires a "just and honorable" war, the sequel shows that a foreign war (as opposed to a civil war) fits the bill. Dropping the old touchstone of happiness, Bacon eventually asserts that "without all question" being for the most part in arms makes for greatness, as if that were reason enough. The example is Spain, as if to suggest that success even in otherworldly warfare depends upon civil armaments, and war is simply one policy to raise a great power.

Although the discussion rejects limits of scruple, it advances limits of policy. Bacon's first celebration of war as true exercise is applied to "a kingdom or estate." Is it especially the old regimes that should plunge nobly (and heedlessly) into wars? The reason given is the danger of a "slothful peace," but that reason does not apply to states occupied with an industrious peace. Then qualifications show up—a state need be only "for the most part" in arms—and the argument drifts to the disadvantages of arming. A veteran army is a "chargeable business," which (only) "commonly" is a useful means. Bacon does not exactly recommend conquest: a veteran army gives "the law, or at least the reputation," among neighbor states, and Spain is the example again. Military power is to be husbanded, perhaps to shield internal development and the spread of reforming constitutions and beliefs.

The moderating of military expansion continues with the ninth precept, which proposes naval force and a British naval empire, in particular. The beginning is singularly abrupt and odd—to be master of the sea is an "abridgment of a monarchy"—and forces one to wonder whether a turn to sea forces fosters republicanism. There is evidence for such a speculation. The next sentence relies (through words of the respectable Cicero) on the authority of Themistocles, whose turn of Athens to the sea and naval strength also turned the city, because of the ensuing dependence on common oarsmen, toward democracy. Bacon then pumps up the case in a way that seems to reassure monarchs: navies fit "great rulers," for rule of the world has turned on naval battles. Pompey (last champion of the Roman aristocrats) might have tired out Caesar if he had kept to the sea; Actium gave Augustus victory over Antony; Lepanto gave Christendom (Italy and Spain) victory over the Turks. Sea power thus seems a tool for monarchs, even for great emperors. Still, to keep one's head amidst these enthusiastic reassurances, one needs to recall that monarchs or aspirants to great rule also lost in each of these battles.

One can then see Bacon retract his reassurances while turning to address new-style politicians: seafights are final only when "princes or states" have set up a decisive battle upon them. He goes on to supply a safer formulation that retreats from the charm of a great battle. Navies are useful because they enable one more easily to avoid a fight. He who commands the sea has great liberty to "take as much and as little of the war as he will," and in face of such certainties, land powers are often at a disadvantage. Bacon applies this cautious (and qualified) lesson "at this day, with us of Europe." Most European kingdoms are bounded by sea, and the wealth of "both Indies" is but accessory to command of the seas. One can infer, I think, that a shrewd empire of the seas can thus fence in France and Spain, while reaping the riches that have hitherto propped up Spain. We have been led to another part of Bacon's strategy for replacing old European regimes with great powers, in this instance with British naval power.

The tenth and final formula for warlike empire is crucial but incomplete: manage honor so as "to inflame all men's courages." While this counsel sets the problem of how to motivate, especially how to motivate leaders, it does not solve much of the problem. In offering a broad solution, it only prepares the particular incentives provided by other essays. This is the culminating counsel of essay 29, which moves from provision for a people stout and warlike, to the seasoning of a veteran army, to a power to move those who move the rest.

There is a twofold problem of "latter ages," the depreciation of worldly glory and the absorption of glory by monarchs. In Machiavellian fashion, Bacon appears to commend ancient ways, ways since superseded by a charitable and otherworldly devotion to Christ, and he praises trophies erected for victories, funeral eulogies and monuments for the fallen dead, personal crowns and garlands, the name of emperor (*imperator*, by which Roman soldiers saluted their victorious general), and, above all, the triumphs, the Roman parades to celebrate great victories. While the triumphs gave glory to the general, riches to the treasury, and donatives to the army, the "great kings" appropriated the name of emperor even in Rome. Bacon is working out the problem for incentives which is posed by monarchy or dictatorship; triumphs for generals may not "fit" monarchies. Yet the argument turns more sinuous. Triumphs were suitable for some Roman emperors and their sons—for such wars as they achieved in person. The Baconian prescription for managing generals by honors ends by showing how a warlike monarch can impropriate the great honors; he can manage generals by "some triumphal garments and ensigns."

The final formula for expanding a nation-state shows how its leaders can be used by an emperor and his house, and it concludes with a quotation from Scripture, as if to remind us that even the emperors of the later Roman empire were kings in divine garments, themselves generals to the king of kings and his son. The Scriptures' author saith limits to nature, in a passage Bacon quotes from Matthew 6:17; the Lord requires reliance on the Lord, according to a portion Bacon does not quote. The *Essays*' author promises amplitude to "kingdoms and commonwealths," if "princes or estates" follow the ordinances "we" have touched. It is Bacon's political science that promises mastery of political chance, and Bacon, as I believe this last precept to suggest, who triumphs by the victories of the leaders who will be his followers.

At the conclusion of his ten counsels, at the end of essay 29, Bacon indicates a place for "commonwealths" as well as states, and appeals to "estates" as well as princes. We may ask: what honors or incentives make estates of a kingdom become leading citizens of a commonwealth, that is, of a republican nation-state? Abstracting now from the rewards of the great imperialists, such as a Henry VII, a Julius Caesar, or an Augustus, what moves the leaders of the civil nation-state who will, in effect, be the followers of Bacon's plan? The answer is in the ten counsels, for it consists in the motives of their addressees, the new classes that Bacon fosters. Essay 29 shows the crucial leaders of the civil society to come. It begins by addressing politiques, counsellors of the ways of empire, and concludes by alluding to the author of the enlightened ways of empire. Their relation, the relation of politique to the author of the defining "ordinances, constitutions, and customs," contains the general formula for all useful relationships in the Baconian civil state.

Together, politique and politic philosopher establish "greatness," an expanding nation-state, as the aim of enlightened public policy. The ten precepts first aim to produce one people, a rather homogeneous body, each able to provide for himself and together assimilable into a unified force. They revise the contempt for the vulgar common to aristocrats, priests, and philosophers, depreciate nobility and gentry as unproductive, and disdain the contemplative outlook that priests and philosophers share. They encourage instead a representative assembly, free farmers, easy assimilation of additional people and peoples, and, in general, an entrepreneurial outlook and a general devotion to the arts of production.

The remaining precepts are all formulas for inducing militancy, that is, for mobilizing such a nation. Except for a veteran army and navy, and the generals, Bacon does not enumerate the classes that implement these last policies. How can a rather democratic people be so mobilized? The answer lies in economic and administrative classes that will lead but will not rule: merchants, entrepreneurs, investors, and financiers; experts, counselors, professionals, and judges. Elites will replace the old ruling estates. Elites in the modern sense are groupings of the successful, and those who rise to success are, unlike the the old fixed castes, educable as to their long-term interests in Bacon's worldly sense. While not exactly of the common people, they share common interests, often rise from common beginnings, and are expert at satisfying common needs and wants, which are private needs and wants. They can lead civilly and almost invisibly.

The civil way of motivating civil leaders is nicely symbolized in the literary dissolution, so to speak, of the Roman-style "triumphs" praised at the end of essay 29. In subsequent essays, as we have noted before, triumphs are treated as but "shows," little dramas "since princes will have such things" (37, 1, 19), and eventually as but private ostentation that is virtually invisible. While essay 37 is titled "Of Masques and Triumphs," triumphs go unmentioned, masques are reduced to shows, and where a show is needed, Bacon praises those of an "elegancy" that will "take the sense," not those of an honor that will take the soul. In "Of Building" (45), the discussion is of a "princely palace," which turns out to be a private mansion without public rooms, but with a great banquet room for "feasts and triumphs." Glory seeking in the civil state, I conclude, is to be decisively limited by the prominence of the power seeking and the profit seeking, and by a certain vanity of luxury. When ages grow to "civility and elegancy," according to "Of Gardens" (46), they seek refined and stately buildings. Even "great princes" of the usual sort may be distracted from rule, piety, and fortifications by planning a "royal," "prince-like," "princely"—garden.

To real counsellors, nevertheless, essay 29 shows the real triumph their enlightened endeavors might reap. Under the guise of contributing to the true greatness of kingdoms and estates, they can produce and control an empire and thus can have a great power, not merely a show. While Bacon manages acquisitiveness, he does not neglect ambition. It is the motive of those to whom the *Essays* is principally addressed and to whom essay 29 is certainly addressed. Bacon means to form enlightened founders and a certain enlightened governing elite.

He must then share the spoils, although his form of sharing proves to be a managing. Those "triumphing over all opposition or competition" arouse the most envy, according to "Of Envy" (9), and wise men therefore do "sacrifice to envy." They allow themselves to be overborne in little things, and in big things they bring on "the stage" others upon whom "to derive the envy." Henry VII had ministers such as Morton and Dudley "to take the envy." Bacon, the godlike planner of future states, grants future generals and princes their triumphs—and envy—and grants what we would call the upper-middle class leaders of a refined republic their conspicuous consumption—and envy. He will attract followers through promises of triumph and luxury, while nevertheless confining followers within the broadly homogeneous nations that sustain them and sustain his plans.

The *Essays'* last overtly political essay discusses another part of the new political elite—judges ("Of Judicature" 56). While I consider in the next chapter Bacon's reinterpretation of judging and of law, I note here that judges are to be a humane complement to the hard-nosed counsellors of greatness directed by essay 29. Counsellors may produce national power; judges can "make inequality equal" and protect person and property. The judge is like a doctor, regulating while providing directly for individual security. Bacon compared the counsellor at his most powerful with the ancient democratic statesman Themistocles; he compares the judge with an interpreter of God's laws and mercy. Judges prepare a sentence as God prepares his sentences; they "should imitate God, in whose seat they sit," giving "grace" to the modest, for their court is a "hallowed" place. By such remarks and by a multitude of Latinisms and scriptural authorities, Bacon would elevate judges as a new priesthood. More cautiously put, he prepares them to be revered instruments of humane policy, and thus to replace the old priestly estate and to replace also the old judicial instruments of royal power and biblical righteousness.

But judges will also serve the new state of things planned by the politic philosopher. "Lions under the throne," they may be, but lions nevertheless. While Bacon raises judges in the civil guise of interpreters of the law, he counsels them to become revisers of law in accord with "true policy." "For many times the things deduced to judgment may be *meum* and *tuum*, when the reason and consequence thereof may trench to point of estate." Enlightened as to the connection of the new justice to the new policy, judges can open the channels of industry, provide the protection that fosters widespread security and satisfaction, and promulgate as civil law and customary law Bacon's new constitutions and ordinances. In their ways of protecting a people, enlightened judges help produce and mobilize a great popular state.

Notes

1. Michael Oakeshott describes the "Cameralists" of the seventeenth and eighteenth centuries, mostly professors of public administration in German and Imperial universities, who aimed at organizing an "administrative machine." "It was to be composed of boards, commissions, organizations, agencies, bureaux, authorities, and research institutes; of ministers, counselors, directors, intendents, superintendents, accountants . . . , whose business it was to collect information, to draw up plans, to devise projects, to give managerial advice, and to implement the decisions of 'rulers.' " ["On the Character of a Modern European State," in *On Human Conduct* (Oxford: Clarendon Press, 1975), 300].

2. Plutarch, "Solon," 27, 28, in *Plutarch's Lives*, tr. Aubrey Stewart and George Long (London: George Bell and Sons, 1881), I, 154–56; Virgil, *Eclogues*, vii, 55; Machiavelli, *Discourses on Livy*, ii, 20.

3. *Works* XI, 355; VI, 238.

Chapter 10

The Politics of Hope

The military side of Baconian empire building, the side that more or less governs the decisive essay 29, is at its core derivative. It is a mixture in Machiavellian idiom of leaders bent on glory with peoples hoping for security. But Bacon improves on Machiavelli. He thought that civil states could rely more on hope and less on the fear in which Machiavelli specialized.

Machiavelli had his popular appeals to liberty and *patria*, but they were pointedly secondary to the management of force and of words about force. Even in the more republican *Discourses on Livy*, the force was less to be disguised than to be flaunted where needed, and the need was typical even if not continual. Ruthless leaders and ruthless peoples were needed at home as well as abroad and repeatedly as well as originally, and executive power meant foundings and refoundings by awe-inspiring ruthlessness, not least by spectacular executions. Although a Machiavellian prince should mix satisfaction with cruelty, and thus hope with fear, cruelty should take priority. "It is safer to be feared than loved," since men break the obligations of love "at every opportunity for their own utility, but fear is held by a dread of punishment that never forsakes you."[1]

While Bacon, too, thought that state building and state keeping depend on judicious use of terror, as his Henry VII showed in awing his subjects by killing Sir William Stanley and the dowager duchess of York, the Baconian additions are not to executive decisiveness but to management by incentives. Bacon specializes in "the politic and artificial nourishing of hopes, and carrying men from hopes to hopes" ("Of Seditions and Troubles" 15), even while building his hopes on the dark foundation of fear. Addressing his plans to the insecurities of life, Bacon, like Machiavelli, promises progress in the means of security, but he can promise much more. While his great instrument is the science that yields visions of new inventions (a topic of our final two chapters), there are also more civil means, which are touched in the comprehensive essay 29 but amplified elsewhere. This chapter samples the amplifications. It considers certain essays on the economics of growth, three important discussions of progressive law and protective judges, and the religion of humane liberty set forth in *Advertisement Touching a Holy War.*

The Economics of Progress

"Bacon is the acknowledged progenitor," wrote the late Michael Oakeshott, "of that understanding of the character of a modern European state in which it is recognized to be, and not merely to have, an 'economy'."[2] I suspect that Oakeshott is correct in this impressively original formulation, but one does not find much corroboration among the economists. Recent writings on economic history and doctrine contain few references to Bacon, and where acknowledgments exist they remind one of old monuments in a modern city, the distinctive features blurred and forgotten amidst change and the winds of time.

Occasionally an older text notes tributes from the first modern economists, such as Sir William Petty (1623–1685). Petty explicitly followed Bacon's *Advancement of Learning* in understanding the "Body Politic" as one should understand the "Body Natural," and this evidently meant that the political economist should focus on increase of power, people, and wealth, not on qualities or activities of soul or mind.[3] Now and then a contemporary author notes a connection between present doctrines and Baconian innovations. In his instructive examination of the doctrine of economic growth, for example, H. W. Arndt calls Bacon "well ahead of his time" because of his utilitarian vision, " 'the endowment of human life with new inventions and riches' as the real and ultimate goal of the sciences."[4] But Arndt shies away from exploring Baconian reasoning, as if it might seriously illuminate the premises underlying the doctrine of growth, and the cause of his reluctance is an all-too-common historicism. Resting on the authority of John Maynard Keynes, Arndt holds that the idea of progress obtained "a specifically economic facet" only after eighteenth-century advances in technology and accumulations of capital. Economic progress was the precondition for the idea of economic progress, for "even utopia must be conceivable." But this generic reduction of plans to events is particularly unconvincing as to Bacon, who conceived in the early seventeenth century a utopian Bensalem given over to progressive increase, not only in technology but also in general affluence and the means of production. And what of the *Essays,* which specifically ad-

Liberate acquisitiveness (handwritten margin note)

vocates both the priority of economic growth and the crucial means to growth, including manufacturing, the prominence of merchants, a work ethic, frugality for the sake of riches, liberated acquisitiveness, and—an art of economics?

There is a recent economist, the Austro-American Karl Pribram, who like Oakeshott finds the Baconian innovations crucial, and who indeed credits Bacon with the decisive formation of modern economic science (although he eventually muffles this arresting claim). Pribram quite consciously takes a larger view than most economic historians. Economic science has been cut off from its roots in general "methods of reasoning,"[5] and one should bridge the gap between histories of economic thought and histories of thought. Contrary to the usual view, economic science is no mere superstructure on economic development, according to Pribram, and indeed the reverse is true: it was new methods of reasoning that established the "capitalist institutions" that defined the modern economy. Modern thought is responsible for modern economic thought and modern economic practice, and Baconian thought is most responsible.

Pribram calls the first stage of economic science "Baconian and Cartesian Economics" and provides a catalog of Baconian innovations: the beginnings of scientific method, the elimination of "teleological characteristics" from social analysis, the connection of "civil society" with the "will of its individual members," and the presuppositions that each individual cares for himself, that management of private advantage is the way to public advantage, and that "utility" is the end of real knowing. The later and more systematically economic thinkers, including Petty and Locke (the apostle of the right to acquire property by labor and the author of essays on interest rates and money), are in fact children of this comprehensive beginning.[6]

Assumptions of Economic Science (handwritten margin note)

Apart from a few such atypical suggestions, Bacon's economic views are usually treated as unoriginal reflections of "mercantilism," that being understood as the school that more or less prevailed in England prior to Adam Smith's discovery of a real economic science. This is a very influential interpretation, and it may may go back to Smith himself. "Mercantilism" is an anachronism, used by neither Bacon nor his contemporaries, and it is frequently said to have been devised by Smith to distinguish one prior school of economists, who believed in the primacy of commerce, from the physiocrats who gave primacy to agriculture.[7] According to Smith, the mercantilists are nationalistic as well as mercantile; they encourage a nation to accumulate more "treasure" than its rivals and to slight domestic production, and they dwell on balance of trade and recommend excises, subsidies, and regulations to favor exports over imports.

Mercantilism (handwritten margin note)

Bacon vs Smith on economics (handwritten note)

Smith criticizes the preoccupation with money, superiority in trade, and pervasive controls, but he criticizes most the mercantilist's premise: nations come to think "their interest consists in beggaring all their neighbors." While commerce among nations ought be a "bond of union and friendship," the mercantilist school teaches a nation "to look with an invidious eye on the prosperity of all the nations with which it trades." The first of liberal economists finds the mercantilists unphilanthropic and unmoved, in particular, by "the most sacred rights of mankind."[8]

But is Bacon a mercantilist so defined? Smith's mercantilism lacks the gist of Bacon's economic plan: the focus of domestic policy on a society devoted to business and to growth by the most productive means, including manufacturing linked with scientific innovation. This sophisticated acquisitiveness, given priority and channeled toward national growth, is what we mean by an "economy" in the modern sense, or at least by a market economy. This is not to deny that Bacon would foster trade and merchants, but it is to insist that he principally encourages national development, liberates acquisitiveness, suggests a society of individuals in which "utility is their bond," subverts priorities such as justice, leisure, and religion, and fosters a work ethic, investment, technological advance, and experimental science. His is not even the usual type of mercantile class. Bacon means to produce the enlightened middle class with which we are familiar, that is, men and women much more systematically occupied with gain, work, and enterprise, and much more at home with scientific and technological advance, than might be expected from the usual merchants or from those simply of middling property. It is undeniably true that Bacon's policy is more restrictive than Smith's "system of natural liberty." But it is more important to see that essays such as "Of Riches" (34) systematically liberate acquisitiveness from moral and religious limits, and from the old political, social, and religious hierarchies.

It is true that Bacon also sets forth the outlook that Smith calls mercantilist, the view that each nation-state is to maximize its power and to subordinate private prosperity to national advantage, and that Bacon's economics is not limited by the natural rights that Smith derived from John Locke, Baron Montesquieu, and Jean-Jacques Rousseau. Bacon encourages imperial ambitions, whereas Smith's political economy directs the wealth of nations to "subsistence" and "public services" (including, of course, defense).[9] Nevertheless, Bacon, too, fosters a popular and rather humane economy, one that leads to increasing and widespread affluence and is to be protected by a quite republican state. His thoughts on wealth and production are part of a broad teaching that encompasses humanitarianism, and management by incentives, as well as the great power.

One may go further than saying that Bacon anticipates Smith. Bacon's economic planning seems more comprehensive than Smith's. Smith neglects somewhat the need for planning in even a free economy, because he supposes that manufacturing civilization follows from "progressive improvement," and this not from plans but from a developing division of labor that is the "natural course of things." Smith supposes that progressive civilization follows from a historical process, for he thinks that growth in population necessarily sets economic progress in motion.[10] But is the process necessary? Why should population growth cause ingenious economic provision, instead of, say, what Machiavelli observed: episodes of starvation and bursts of exploitative conquest and decimating war? The ingenious provisions had to be devised. Smith supposed that history grants what Bacon, Locke, Montesquieu, and their ilk saw as the need to plan: a transformation of attitudes and systems to elevate the acquisitive and the economic over the glory seeking and the military.

This very question, as to whether mercantilism is part of a broader reform of civilization, is controversial among its recent historians. There, too, the prevailing opinion is that the changes resulted from circumstance and evolution, not from a plan. The well-known economic historian E. Lipson, for example, explicitly denies the assertion of older historians, that a comprehensive policy underlay mercantilist policies, even if he has to acknowledge that a general "trend of thought" and "co-ordinated lines of policy" underlay the relation of imperial power with producer colonies.[11] While, indeed, "a cunning crept into trades," the technological revolution was a "continuous movement," according to Lipson, and not the product of an intentional instauration of useful arts and sciences.[12] But there are distinguished dissenters among the writers on mercantilism, and a very distinguished historian, Eli Hecksher, draws attention to the importance of Bacon's economic writings. According to Hecksher, mercantilism is part of a rarely discerned plan "for the total reconstruction of society, as well as the state and institutions," and he even used as epigraph for his immense history the analogy for the state supplied by essay 29: a mustard seed apt to get up and spread. Hecksher devotes an appendix to summarizing essay 29, and he is clearly astonished by its cold and forebidding ruthlessness. It "reminds of the most violent theories of power in our own century; . . . the commercial wars of two centuries were caused in part by such theories"; Bacon's is an "extreme and one-sided" outlook that elevates the military disposition even over the commercial.[13] Yet Hecksher, too, finally thinks that the Baconian plan for a new state follows from "the rise and consolidation of states," rather than from an aim to plan the rise and consolidation of states,[14] and even he skips most of the economic parts of the *Essays* and leaves obscure what they make clear: the connection between radical increase in commerce, industry, and technology, and the new political science of power. The key connections are the antimoral foundation in self-interest, which Bacon expounds in the essays "Of Expense" (28) and "Of Riches" (34), and the corresponding rational art for organizing society through mutual interests, which is exemplified in the essay "Of Usury" (41).

"Of Expense" and "Of Riches" free wealth-getting from religious and moral restraints and disdain, and then go on to invent a new and useful attitude combining calculating frugality with enterprising acquisitiveness. They attack especially the defense of leisure: the supposition that leisured activity, not economic work, accords with the best in human nature, and the deference to nature: the supposition that occupations that cultivate plants and animals are preferable to trade, lending, or manufacturing. After toying with such traditional scruples, Bacon teaches that shrewd gaining is all and that one gains most by most exploiting nature. The principle of the seditious new revelation he had summed up earlier, in the Latin and the language of the old: "And it cometh many times to pass that *materiam superabit opus,* that the carriage and work is worth more than the material—and enricheth a state more." He added, as illustration, that the much-praised low countries, whose "bond is utility," have "the best mines above ground in the world." Manufactories that work the material more are the way to add the most value ("Of Seditions and Troubles" 15, "Of Nobility" 14).

There is no doubt that "Of Riches" appears compressed and ironic and is one of the richest and funniest of Baconian essays. But its scoffing and argument commit deadly serious sedition against the attitudes that sustain the old regime, and it advances seriously new attitudes that fuel one's gaining and a nation's progress. The essay moves quickly from allusions to Christian and Aristotelian disdain for wealth-getting to exhibitions of how really to pile it up. Freeing the desire for gain is a big part of the sedition; Bacon's dance through respectable opinions, part of the humor. "Believe not them that seem to despise riches," he concludes; the argument confirms that the parsimony recommended by "Of Expense" (28) violates the precepts of liberality and charity. But whereas "Of Expense" is about gaining by small savings, "Of Riches" is chiefly about big gains and where to invest them. It mentions riches by good means and just labor, by improvement of the ground, by ordinary trades and vocations. But such ways are "slow." It dwells on the fast track: great holdings of cropland, mines, and animals, a little riches used to play markets and be "partner in the industries of younger men," resales, and usury. Investment in useful inventions or privileges may occasion "a wonderful overgrowth of riches," and the example is a colony in the New World—"as it was with the first sugar man in the Canaries."[15]

Precisely in this economic context, Bacon reveals a crucial point about his method or logic. If a man can play "the true logician, to have as well judgment as invention, he may do great matters especially if the times be fit." The art of invention is but an instrument; true logic is judicious as to what to invent and when. "Of Riches" proceeds to show the judicious way to invent real riches and even an empire of riches. Diversify one's efforts, and especially with a view to mixing gain with security. "Guard adventures with certainties." Bacon commends secure ways, such as monopolies, riches through service and office, and, more soberly now, investments. Yet risk must remain part of the formula; sometimes riches "must be set flying to bring in more." In short, the essay reconstitutes wealth as riches to produce more riches (i.e., as capital), counsels a mixture of great enterprises with security of one's stake, and, in effect, fertilizes the means of production. The essay's last words discourage large inheritances or magnificent and pious benefactions.

Note the suggestion of investing in technological enterprises. Bacon uses the incentive of private gain to foster the venture capital needed by his sophisticated new means of production. Some readers may wonder whether such comprehensive planning exists, but the inference is supported by the language of "logician," so redolent of Baconian science. There is plenty of other evidence. In the *New Atlantis*, the model civic leader is a Jewish merchant who both leads the stranger from Christian Europe to the scientific establishment and is selected by the state to entertain the great scientist. Bensalem breeds merchants who spread the gospel of enlightened science and whom an enlightened state patronizes accordingly. Among the scientists of Bensalem are "merchants of light" who travel incognito, secretly obtain European discoveries and inventions, and return to Bensalem with new "light of the growth of the world." The enlightened merchant complements the judicious scientist, who is also a broker between enlightened technique and the means of production.

What is native to future progress, however, is strange to Christian Europe. Prominent civil figures will perhaps be dissenting Christians, or Jews who incline to be more worldly, more attuned to gain, and more receptive to an anti-Christian outlook. Such considerations may help explain a number of notably obscure Baconian references to strangers, such as the supposition in essay 29 that "strangers" are to be welcomed for their skills at refined arts and delicate manufactures. The technologically skilled (and perhaps the financially skilled) are to be welcomed, however strange their piety or impiety. In *History*, Bacon had described enigmatically a law that encouraged employment of the "procedures of foreign commodities," brought in by "merchant strangers," upon "native commodities."[16] Such strangers provide not products but means of production: technology, or perhaps mere ingenuity, to replace or mix with craftsmanship.

In "Of Usury" (41), Bacon shows with remarkable directness how the new foundation in self-interest allows him to devise a systematic economic art for managing part of public affairs. Hecksher was startled by the innovations in this essay, especially by its weighing of lending at interest according to merely political-economic considerations.[17] Here Bacon dismisses quickly religious and moral scruples, lists the "discommodities" and "commodities" of taking interest in terms of satisfying consumers and providing incentives to merchants, and sets forth a policy that magnifies the advantages while minimizing the disadvantages. The seven disadvantages of interest all concern the effects of high interest on trade, prices, improvement, and estates—except the fourth, which condemns bringing the "treasure of a realm or state into few hands," for the usurer is "at certainties," while other enterprises are at uncertainties. Kings and oligarchies, and their bankers, will be undermined by the new economics (as we noted in chapter 3). The three advantages of interest are the advancing of trade (especially the greatest part, which is driven by young merchants), the prevention of bankruptcies caused by the cycles of trade, and a provision of the profit that induces lending. Bacon's general policy is a two-tier rate structure that will "grind the tooth" of lending, while still inducing the moneyed to lend to merchants. A low rate (say, 5 percent) for the public will ease borrowing, raise the price of land, and encourage investment; precisely the low rate will "encourage and edge" industrious and profitable improvements because many will "venture" rather than take low interest. A higher rate (8 percent) is permitted under license to fuel the merchants, who can in any event afford to pay more. Note that Bacon plans interest rates; he does not, like the liberal economists beginning with Locke, leave them to laws of supply and demand.

Bacon seems much aware of the power and novelty of his economic planning, and he takes trouble to make his readers aware. Near the essay's end, he compares his discussions with other men's "inventions" of such instruments as banks. That is, Bacon presents his economic counsels as themselves useful inventions. The arts or science of economics are the great economic invention, for they contain the crucial judgments as to the selection and production of other inventions. "Of Usury" is a model of the new systematic art, because it shows how to produce systems that blend the force of private acquisitiveness with the growth of public wealth and power. In so exchanging commodities and discommodities, Bacon becomes the authoritative merchant of light as to the growth of the world, the true logician who guides invention.

Law as Effectual Security

A similar promise, that private satisfaction may be mixed with an effectual state, governs Bacon's reform of law and judging. Some might wonder whether Bacon is not merely following the common law and jurisprudence of his time. His little *Treatise on Universal Justice*, for example, presents itself as instruction in interpreting the laws: it will be useful to lawyers, judges, and the various legal commentators and recorders for which it calls. But this modest view catches only part of the work's comprehensive intent. The *Treatise* concentrates less upon law than upon absence of law, as in obscure laws and cases omitted by the laws, and it goes beyond supplementing to correcting and refounding. It questions the existence of "obsolete" law and custom, for example, and would replace it by means of a "Digest" (which Bacon equates with a "new instauration of law" (59–64), by new "Praetorian or Censorian" courts of review (32–46), and by establishing judge-made law by means of the reports, or perhaps reconstructions, of court reporters and epitomes. In short, Bacon provides for various officials in the legal establishment an account of interpretation that moves toward an account of enlightened law making— "for the power of supplying, extending, and moderating laws, differs little from that of making them" (37).

This is a little treatise on private law and is best understood as a complement to Bacon's other discussions of the function of justice, judges, and law. We will review several of these discussions as a preface to the *Treatise*, and as a prefatory summary of Baconian jurisprudence. The most important are the relevant passages in essay 29 and the *History of King Henry VII*, which provide the big political context and which we can revisit cursorily, and the important thematic discussions in "Of Judicature" (56) and "Aphorisms on the greater Law of nations, or the fountains of Justice and Law." The "Aphorisms" go rather openly to the humane and republican foundations of Bacon's jurisprudence and were left unpublished probably for that reason, as Daniel R. Coquillette suggests in his instructive survey of Baconian legal theory.[18]

Bacon's jurisprudence, unlike his political economy, has been quite

widely appreciated for its originality and its influence. Coquillette, for example, goes beyond the much-quoted praise of the legal historian William
Holdsworth, that Bacon's was "the first critical, the first jurisprudential,
estimate of the English law."[19] Bacon was original not so much in providing a critical account of English law, although he did that, but in devising
the critical theory of law itself, which was a "universal" account of law
and not distinctively English. According to Coquillette, Bacon is responsible for "the first sustained analytical, secular, and inductive approach to
jurisprudence," an approach which for three centuries influenced
Hobbes, David Hume, Jeremy Bentham, and other leading figures in
modern jurisprudence. The new theory focused on process, rather than
justice, "how to," rather than "what for." Hence the Baconian recommendations that judges attend to gaps in the law and avert their eyes from
obsolete laws, and the recommendations for reliable reports of decisions,
digests of precedents, restatements of the law, and codification of laws.
But over the new procedures hovered a substantive and explosive redirection, Coquillette argues. The *Treatise* and the unpublished *Aphorisms*
were utterly different from "anything that had gone before in the English
tradition" because Bacon lays universal foundations in a "utilitarian reciprocity," and these foundations look to "security and order," not to "religion or morality." Laws are the "sinews and instruments" of "public
policy." While Bacon's thought is not specifically English, neither is it a
"natural law theory" of a traditional sort. It is "a universal science of lawmaking, focussed on method and utility, although assuming a charitable
intent." This seems to me a broadly correct picture. My purpose in the
remainder of this section is to clarify the fundamental spirit, which seems
to me a political spirit, that ties together Bacon's jurisprudential emphases
on universality, procedure, utility, and charity.

To begin with, the new jurisprudence is a subordinate part of Bacon's
civil science. The great essay 29 called its ten precepts the "ordinances,
constitutions, and customs" of "empire," and among its constitutions of
public life was a special prescription for private law, a prescription mixing
humanity with policy: "all states that are liberal of naturalization towards
strangers are fit for empire." Taking empire as the end, Bacon can find
necessity and thus universality in the legal means. This little section of
essay 29 descends into the universal language, even while Bacon distances
the reader from Roman laws of God or nature. It recommends an easy
grant of *jus civitatis*, which is to include *jus commercii, jus connubii, jus
hereditatis*, as well as *jus suffragii* and *jus honorum*. The point is not ecclesiastical righteousness but full citizenship, including civil rights and

rights to vote and to hold office, and all such justice is to be available not only to "singular persons alone, but likewise to whole families; yea to cities, and sometimes to nations." The discussion arrives at a universal justice, indeed, but as an instrument to attract to a growing empire—and even to inspire to wars of empire. Another precept directs a state to "laws and customs that give just occasions (as may be pretended)" for war and cites "the Turk" and "Rome" for proof.

In the *New Atlantis,* the king seems subordinate to law and custom and only appears in his name and seal, as we have noted before; he seems but a symbol of a regulated state constituted by the laws and customs of its founders. And, again, the *History of the Reign of King Henry VII* shows by instructive distortions how a certain rule of law and lawyers may promote a transition from monarchs and state-builders to a more civil and republican state: as the king "governed his subjects by his laws, so he governed his laws by his lawyers."[20] Parliament is called "supreme and absolute," and we are given memorable pictures of Chancellor Morton advising, and Parliament passing, "good and wholesome laws" for peace and empire. "Good commonwealths laws" are celebrated, and the king is called "the best lawgiver to this nation after King Edward the First."[21]

While essay 29 outlines public and private law, and the *History* inserts such a republican legalism into the tradition of English monarchy, "Of Judicature" breeds the suitable outlook in judges. Its discussion of legal matters is thematic, not partial, and in this it is like the *Aphorisms on the Greater Law of Nations* and the *Treatise of Universal Justice.* While the *Aphorisms* addresses quite openly the foundations of law and justice, and the *Treatise* addresses such matters circumspectly while showing practical applications, "Of Judicature" addresses the process of judging, that is, one vehicle of application. Very much like the *Treatise,* it revolutionizes under the guise of preserving.

"Of Judicature" moves from exhorting judges to obey law, at its start, to urging a humane interpretation of law that follows "true policy," at its end. There may be parallels with doctrines of the judicial function that were common at the time among ecclesiastical, common, and civil lawyers, but Bacon takes advantage of familiar views for his own purposes. The discussion revamps judicial self-understanding to make courts less protectors of the existing powers and more agents of sedition and of a new state of things. From being oracles of a justice divine, royal, and aristocratic, judges are to become enlightened instruments of humane and republican policy.

"Of Judicature" begins with a preliminary exhortation to law-abidingness, and then discusses the four persons or bodies to which the judge's office is related, that is, parties, advocates, clerks and ministers, the sovereign and estate. The discussion abounds with references to justice, office, and duty, unlike the Baconian accounts of great place and counsel in essays 11 and 20. Judges seem to be creatures of a duty above them, and this initial impression is given especially by the essay's beginning exhortation. Judges are merely to interpret law. Bacon even translates *jus* as law, and he insists upon judges of integrity who are "learned," "reverent," and advised. But these attributes, if considered, go beyond simple obedience. What is to be learned? Who is to advise? What and who are to be revered? Bacon eventually replaces the first insistence that judges are merely to interpret law by suggestions that judges are to ignore obsolete laws, such as those of too much "rigor" in penal matters. Upon reconsideration, the language makes one wonder whether Bacon might be aiming the initial counsels of law-abidingness at judges tempted by the Reformation, judges who would bend the law to institute the righteousness that their Bible requires. Judges, Bacon writes, should be unlike the Church of Rome, which under pretense of "exposition of Scripture doth not stick to add and alter."

This suspicion is strengthened when Bacon turns to define the judicial office. The discussion is strangely indirect, because Bacon does not proceed to define judicial duty. Instead, he arrives at a definition of office by considering the "parties" that the judge should satisfy and the "advocates" that he should attend to, and the consideration of parties and advocates is itself indirect in moving to focus on the "cause" and "counsel." An introductory statement of the topic "parties" is replaced by "causes or parties" and of the topic "advocates" by "advocates and counsel." What is going on?

Under the heading of "causes or parties," Bacon actually sets forth a judge's "principal duty": to suppress force and fraud, a duty soon rephrased as "the virtue of a judge"—"to make inequality equal." These innovative formulas seem equivocal, and emerge obscurely from a welter of familiar-sounding words and distinctions, but the distinctive tenor becomes clear enough in the precepts that follow. These counsel the judge to stand against parties of great power, rigorous penal laws, and obsolete laws, and to stand for mercy to individuals. By abstracting from a justice above, and turning the reader toward a different cause and counsel, Bacon brings him to a democratic or humane task. Level the hills and raise the valleys, especially when "violent prosecution," "power," or "great counsel," appears on one side. One thinks of great nobles or even of the king, a thought that recurs with the next precept. Beware of strained laws, especially penal laws that can bring a shower of snares. The words are similar to those Bacon used to chastise the minions of Henry VII.[22] The subsequent precepts allude to other oppressions and the unobtrusive ways of reform. Let old penal laws, or those whose "rigor" is "grown unfit for the present time," be "confined in the execution." Bacon inserts a progressive tincture. A reason is provided in *Treatise of Universal Justice*: thus may laws of righteousness and of monarchy be put to sleep. Let judges show "mercy" to the person, Bacon proceeds, even while casting a severe eye on the example. One should be benevolent to individuals, even as one is disciplined by the needs of policy.

The theme turns from humane policy to the judge's policy when the essay takes up "advocates and counsel." Judges should learn from arguments at the bar and not be like judges who rule in lordly fashion, perhaps on behalf of "noted favorites." The reason lies in politic counsels as to prudent appearances, not in exhortations to follow the truth. A judge should defer to able counsel out of concern for the appearance to clients, and he should punish negligent counsel out of concern for the appearance to the public. "Of Judicature" shows a judge how to maintain his place, what "Of Great Place" (11) had shown to politicians. It shows especially how to make a place by supporting a humane legal order that defers to judges, lawyers, and the public, and not to kings, ministers, and estates who pretend to higher deserts. The first sentence of the next paragraph drops "of justice" from the introductory topic "clerks and ministers of justice," and treats only the court as just and hallowed. Not justice but judging is supreme, because not justice but rising by satisfying, moves the judge. But by learning a humane but efficient policy that promises general satisfaction, the judges may in their own way obtain a suitable place. They may obtain the reverence of a merciful provider. Judges "should imitate God, in whose seat they sit; who represseth the presumptuous, and giveth grace to the modest."

While the ensuing discussion of "clerks and ministers" of the court is ostensibly about discouraging scandal, the particulars seem aimed at those old judges who have judged mankind according to divine law, that is, at ecclesiastical clerks and ministers. A court is a hallowed place, Bacon says, and he would get rid of sowers of suits, quarrels over jurisdictions, tricky persons who pervert courts, and fee-mongers. If one considers a little, this blandness seems pointed. The great jurisdictional quarrels of Bacon's time were between civil and ecclesiastical courts and between common law and royal courts. The principal royal courts were Star Chamber and the High Commission, and, during the reign of James I and the last portion of Elizabeth's reign as well, they usually sided with the ecclesiastics.[23] The ecclesiastical courts were notorious for their many fees. While Bacon merely alludes to such quarrels and scandals, he pursues in the rhetorical shadows an effectual policy. He offers to the civil side the authority of his renovated judicature, and by silence and irony he withdraws support from the ecclesiastical side. An illustration of the irony: a play on *amici curiae*, those *parasiti curiae*, who puff "a court up beyond her bounds, for their own scraps and advantage."

"Of Judicature" finally provides an explicit discussion of the relation between judging and policy, although under the heading of judicial duty as it concerns "the sovereign and the estate." Despite prose that turns even more elliptical, Bacon intimates both the place for judges in civil reform and the place of Bacon in setting the agenda of reform. We learn what and whom is finally to be revered.

The very complex paragraph begins with an act of dictation as to what judges ought "above all to remember": *salus populi suprema lex*. This is the supreme law, and it is Bacon who legislates it. It is not nature's law or God's law; these are, perhaps, the "oracles not well inspired" that we are told here to avoid. The people's welfare is the supreme law. This is the maxim that Hobbes adopted and that served as epigraph for John Locke's *Two Treatises of Government*.

Accordingly, "Of Judicature" interweaves judicial duties with "business of state," not matters of religion or justice. While judges are told to consult with kings and states, and kings and states with judges, consultations with priests, the Lord, or the wise go unmentioned. The discussion turns to matters of *meum* and *tuum* (to which Bacon has reduced matters of justice), which may involve points of "estate." As if on cue, Bacon introduces himself to give a reconstituted definition. "I call matter of estate, not only the parts of sovereignty, but whatsoever introduceth any great alteration or dangerous precedent; or concerneth manifestly any great portion of people." The judge is to serve a great portion of the people, and to help constrain the sovereign to serve such a popular state, and all this in accord with the redefinitions of public, state, and service that are part of a new and enlightened state of things. Let no man think, Bacon now orders, that just laws are antipathetic to "true policy." While judges are lions under the throne (in the Baconian metaphor now famous), they are lions. They are not to roar royally, for they are not to oppose any "point of sovereignty," and yet they are to bite civilly, to forward a "wise use and application of laws."

In short, judges are less instruments of law than instruments of Baconian civil wisdom in using and introducing law. They will help suppress the old forces and frauds that threaten peoples and help introduce the new state that helps them and elevates enlightened judges as well.

These themes appear more directly, although by no means simply directly, in the recently discovered manuscript called *Aphorisms on the greater Law of nations or the fountains of Justice and Law*. This little work provides an unusual insight into the "theoretical basis of Bacon's political philosophy," as Mark Neustadt has said.[24] Despite the indirection, we can see many controversial opinions elsewhere to be inferred only with greater difficulty, including a novel law of nations, a derivation of the fundamental law (*salus populi suprema lex*), and a remarkable popular republicanism.

The start of the *Aphorisms* rebuts the "fancies of philosophers" and the "subtleties of the lawyers," roughly as Bacon does at the start of his *Treatise on Universal Justice*.[25] But here he openly commends a "legislator" instead, tacitly assumes the mantle, and explicitly announces that he embarks "on a new and untrodden path." What is the new path? The first aphorism says that "in human society either law or force prevails." The last aphorism (20) concludes that "it is fitting to use laws to entice men to great deeds with money and rewards of riches." One can make a "flourishing commonwealth" (*florens republica*) by building on the "boundaries" commonly established "in the course of peacetime and daily use." Here is the broad direction of the path taken by the legislator of legislators. He will give a new priority to the common laws protecting property (matters of *meum* and *tuum*), and, thus, to new customs that will foster systematically the acquisitiveness that fuels a growing republic or commonwealth. Law and economics join hands in the politics of hope. And what will a customary reliance on "rewards of riches" do to the old religion?

The *Aphorisms* quietly directs lawyers away from not only religous law but also moral virtue, and thus from the supposition that society should look up to, and be governed by, those of virtue (3, 4). The work is divided into three parts by subtitles, and at the start of the second part (12–19), Bacon argues immediately that "necessity" requires that "the most just and inward cause of the power of the laws in various dominions" is "wholly" the "supreme power" (*imperio*, 12). The subtitle of this part is "About the authority and obligation of laws." The ultimate inner authority is somehow merely power. Bacon had prepared the way in the first part, which is "About the origin and vicissitudes of laws." "Public laws" alone "impart order or proportion to things, and correct the wicked dispositons of the spirit" (*habitus animi vitiosos*, 3). However "excellent" the qualities of someone who is admired, it is "power," not laws, that bring people together (4). It follows that the origin of law is need, not justice, or, rather, a banding together out of necessity. The real "ground and basis" of law, the *fundamentum et firmamentum*, is the danger of injury from force, and of public law, the danger of injury from public or associated force (3). But one must account for the banding as well as the necessity. This, too, results from force or power. "Public laws . . . flow from private laws," because laws without teeth are useless, and one bites from one's own appetite (3). As Bacon puts it, "law requires execution" and requires therefore an *imperio*, which, as the primacy of "private laws" implies, is always someone's *imperio*.

The sequel, which concludes this first part, discusses how banding together has been subject to the vicissitudes of human vanity and profit, foreign customs, and mixture of nations or religion (4–6). It closes by pondering the chances for success of improvements proposed by a "single spirit" (*spiritu*, 7), one "author or composer" of a "provident spirit" (now *animi*, 8). He himself (as well as the state) may be "a certain power above the laws" that can change the laws (12), and indeed Bacon seems here to be talking about founding a new state of mind, a "region" (1) of custom. But since all change in the laws of a "*republica*" is "innovation," one has to be cautious in changing law "too easily or often" (9), or at least one has to innovate in the guise of holding to custom, as Bacon says in an aphorism that begins by quoting Scripture and proceeds to define law as "the hedge of the *reipublicae*" (10). The first part concludes by suggesting that change is inevitable, since times change, and he who "holds fast to custom (*consuetudinem*), and retains the appearance of antiquity in the face of change," is in fact "embracing a novelty" (11).

The middle section (12–19) shows how to do it, that is, how to legislate innovations for the human region. One must mix force with enlightened channels for force. Mix the necessary power over men (the *imperio*, 12), with a teaching of what is necessary to make men obedient to "the universal order of human society" (18) and ultimately to make them willing to die for "the state" (19). What is necessary is a state that serves mankind effectually and can be known or even felt to serve. The "authority and obligation of law" in its Baconian sense is its power, its capacity, that is, to attract a following. That power depends on the system of public powers and private rewards that Bacon introduces as his public law and private law. But it depends also on propaganda, on propagating the new jurisprudence and slandering the old religion and the old moral teachings. Having established the superiority of a supreme human power to all law (12), the sequel attacks old arguments that states cannot be changed, as if human freedom must be subjected and obligated to an eternal or immortal law (13). The thralldoms attacked include "religion." Here we see Bacon the lawgiver as liberator by enlightenment, liberating man from thralldom to some divinity put over him, or rather from what Bacon nastily calls "man's cunning and subtlety" (13).

The remainder of the work constructs a democratic foundation for legal authority and obligation, a creed as to the final authority of mankind or peoples. This is a version, perhaps the seminal version, of the famous liberal argument that the title to government is popular consent.

This revolutionary creed is advanced by indirection and even by negations. At first, Bacon appears to back away from "the tribune's opinion taught by lovers of liberty," that "in all sorts of commonwealths the supreme power resides with the public" (13). But the same aphorism proceeds to concede the opinion, and then to agree with it, although with important qualifications. Bacon goes on to discuss whether "if a government abuses its power then, justly, the power should be returned to the giver," and while raising (once again) many doubts, he eventually (once again) agrees (16). The people may overturn their government when "the safety of the people" is confronted by "defects in government concerning the safety of the people." Bacon proceeds to abuse an old Roman example, involving no less than the decision to assassinate Caesar, to prove that "a most cruel and evil tyranny" is "worse than sedition"; he thereby contradicts an apparently more direct statement, in a context of accomodation to customs of the time, that "anarchy is more malicious than tyranny" because "the lusts of a multitude" are worse than that of a single person (10). I am asserting that Bacon reveals very cautiously a fiercely republican animus, and a republicanism not of the old patrician type.

Bacon follows his political revolution with a devious reassurance as to morality (17) and religion (18), which actually separates both from the business of the law. While his assertion that all "civil laws" are changeable is "not to be taken" to derogate from "the reckoning of good and evil," Bacon proceeds to deflate good and evil to fit his jurisprudence of necessity. He equates moral reckoning with the finding of "justice and equity," which he had earlier traced to utilitarian reciprocity. He can then make the distinction famous from liberal jurisprudence, that between legal obligation and moral obligation, for he has made avoidance of injury, and hence growth in security, the serious business of the individual. Moral duty is replaced by calculated civil duty, duty to the society that provides opportunity and the state that protects us. Bacon follows up the separation of legal obligation from the moral quality of the law by another, a cautious separation of legal order from a supposedly universal divine law. Laws may vary from place to place, we are told, and we also told that they apply to all foreigners, even to "kings" and "legates" (18).

We can now appreciate the significance of Bacon's prescription of a "law of nations" or peoples (*gentium*), as the definitive kind of law, and his prescription of the defining content of the law of laws and the most just of justices: "The safety of the people is most rightly said to be the supreme law." *Nam salus populi suprema lex rectissime dicitur* (18). Thus the enlightened legislator proclaims in order to provide for, and win, the peoples who will follow.

The crowning proclamation as to justice and law that Bacon actually published is the *Example of a Treatise on Universal Justice or the Foundations of Equity, by Aphorisms: One Title of It.*[26] But this little work with an earnest title consists of ninety-seven aphorisms, almost five times as many as in the *Aphorisms on the greater Law of nations*, and its outline is at least as hard to follow as that governing "Of Judicature" (56). Still, the *Treatise*'s position, as an appendix to the skimpy account of civil science in *De Augmentis*, suggests its importance. Also, the aphoristic form is that of Bacon's most telling teachings, and the partial provision of an "example" and "one title" cries for writers to follow, as indeed they did. The *Treatise* proceeds, if I am not wrong, though four stages. After founding justice on private wants, and urging correction of omissions and obscurity in law, it suggests a new Digest or "instauration" of law, and then exhorts legal commentators and writers to rely upon a leader.

A brief preface reminds one of the beginning and end of the essay "Of Judicature"; it intimates a need to surpass the righteous appeal of "the Apostle" or "Rome." This may help explain the ponderously scholastic title. The preface then quietly rejects as inadequate all previous writings on law. Philosophers, perhaps such as Plato in his *Laws*, made "fair" arguments that are not suited for "use"; lawyers, perhaps such as Sir John Fortescue in his *De Laudibus Legum Angliae*, followed laws of their country or of the pope. This argument is actually more pointed than its mate in the *Aphorisms*. Bacon seems to wish a law of universal efficacy like the pope's, which is not merely a pattern of fairness above the multiplicity of legal practice, and yet with an effect not spiritual but civil. The author should be a "statesman,"[27] who knows of civil society, public welfare, natural equity, custom, and forms of government. While the *Treatise* does not speak of a "legislator" or of Bacon's new path, as the *Aphorisms* did, the several topics to follow are quickly equated with natural equity and policy and then with the foundations of justice and public utility (*utilitatis publicae*).

Actually, Bacon includes only one "title" of the discussion he proposes, and that is certainty in law, not justice, equity, or public expediency. But the incompleteness is less than appears, as is typical of Bacon's many incomplete works. For certainty is the "Primary Dignity of Laws," and this writing is a "model" for that of other titles.[28] Certainty in law is thus given priority over justice in law. This proves to give primacy to effective law, that is, to efficacy in the prince or state. The *Treatise* defines legal certainty as obedience by the people and limitation of judges' discretion, that is, obedience by peoples and judges (8). The dance of opinions thus gives a Machiavellian primacy to efficacy in regulation, just as *Aphorisms* gave primacy to efficacy in establishing fundamental law, and it foreshadows what is to come. Although the *Treatise* encompasses ninety-seven aphorisms under eighteen headings, not one heading mentions equity or justice. The big and idealistic title is a fraud.

In effect, the *Treatise on Justice* opens in public the jurisprudential road subsequently cleared and widened with the crude machinery of Thomas Hobbes. Like Hobbes, Bacon derives "public right" from "private right" (2–3), and private right from a universal ground (*firmamentum*) in necessary private want (1). He arrives in turn at the need for the domination of magistrates, majesty, a political fabric—and fundamental law (3). Still, Bacon's secretive aphorisms differ in more than form from Hobbes's blunt legalism. They are useful for policy, but destructive of inherent right. While Bacon applies the Machiavellian priority of efficacy to law and justice, and differs from Machiavelli in setting forth justice, private law, and public law as useful policy, he differs from Hobbes (as well as Locke) in lacking doctrines of natural rights and natural public law. Because Hobbes supposes that justice is naturally necessary, he can deduce the structure of sovereign government as naturally necessary. For Bacon, law and governance remain a policy, albeit ultimately the policy of a leader who obtains obedience in part by promising security.

Treatise on Universal Justice, then, is far from a traditional application of the laws of God or nature. The terms natural law, law of reason, and natural right never appear, although some odor of them remains in Bacon's remarks on common law, until that too disappears. Eventually, the *Treatise* advises separating statute law from common law, instituting a new digest of statutes, and relegating common law to the library's dusty shelves (61–63). From start to finish Bacon attacks custom, especially "obsolete" custom (42, 57, 58, 60) and "old fables" (60, 86). He praises reason and the adaptation of law to present times. However universal Bacon's jurisprudence, it is devised by human reasoning as to public utility, and its universality results from its attention to common necessities. Bacon knows the "general dictates of reason" that run or should run through the different matters of law (82).

The *Treatise*, then, shows how to combine the lawyer's application of particular laws, with the philosopher's attention to the general, through a universal statesmanship that arrives at "the laws of laws" (6). It is another of Bacon's "how-to" guides, this one for the busy lawyer or judge. The work appears merely procedural. The problem is how to interpret the law, and the prescription is not a set of laws, but a set of laws for interpreting laws. The *Treatise* governs the mind of judges in their actual work and thus provides what "Of Judicature" had prescribed.

But the bite is fiercer than the insinuating speech, for here too there is a lion under the throne. The *Treatise* attends little to its ostensible topic of interpreting law through, say, the law's terms and the lawgiver's intent, and instead deals with two stated topics: interpretation of cases omitted by the law (10–51) and obscurity in laws (52–97). Judges or experts are to fill in what the law leaves out. The point is more obvious when one faces up to the three headings not preannounced in the introductory sections (9, 10) or elsewhere: sections on retrospective laws that conflict with prior laws, on new digests of laws, and on conflicts of judgments about laws (headings 7, 10, and 18, prior to sections 47, 65, and 94, respectively). These three involve choices between later and former laws, selection of a code of laws, and, in general, judgments as to laws. While discussing the last and architectonic topic, Bacon allows himself to appear in the first person singular (90, 91), before disappearing again behind the "prince or state" and the authoritative lectures against learned lecturers that he inserts into the formula of a digest.

The model treatise on law is then fundamentally a disguised political plan. The purpose of certainty is obedience to law by both peoples and judges, and there are signs that only a model from "good and moderate" times (22), perhaps a *republica* (73), will pass the test. The signs are confirmed by the most political sections. Bacon distinguishes the supreme power (*supremis potestatibus*) from king and council (*sanctoribus consiliis*), and follows with the naming of a popular assembly (*comitius*, the assembly of the Roman populace during the republic) as a proper body to repeal a law (58). Hidden in legal reform is a formula for republican reform, which occasionally breaks the surface. If accumulated laws have grown so voluminous and confused that it is expedient to "remodel them entirely," let this be regarded as "heroic work" and the authors be "justly and deservedly reckoned among legislators and reformers of laws"(59). Such "instaurations" are superior in times superior in learning (64), an allusion, one may well think, to a time shaped by Bacon's great instauration of a new learning. Bacon indicates the persons and works by whom his legal instauration can obtain influence most directly: officials such as court reporters and authorized commentators, books of laws and of legal definitions, and books of rules, of antiquities, of summaries of law, and of forms of pleading. The Baconian laws of laws will act on commentators and commentaries to come. These addressees appear in a major portion that was merely semiunannounced, "Of Modes of Expounding Laws and Removing Ambiguity" (72–97). It is while noting the importance of court reporters that Bacon says that "judgments are the anchors of law, and laws of a republic" (73).[29]

We turn for further light to a more detailed consideration of the *Treatise*'s particular counsels, which treat, in turn, of the four causes of uncertainty in laws. In discussing the first cause, cases not covered by extant law, Bacon first warns mysteriously against following custom and then counsels guidance by reason. One might guess that here, as elsewhere, he warns especially against filling gaps in human law with the revealed righteousness customary among Christian nations. The sequel suggests that guidance by reason means guidance by the "public good" (12) and then advises leniency while applying penal laws and rigor while enforcing laws affecting the state. Ease up on the enforcement of righteousness; make effectual the civil state. Bacon's counsel as to "examples" confirms the point. Be guided by examples from times "good and moderate" (22), not tyrannical, factious, or dissolute. Bacon shows no distaste for impious times. Earlier, he had subordinated morality and religion to the well-being of the commonwealth (4), and now he proceeds to attack examples drawn from custom, fables, and fragments. What of the examples of divine lawgivers? In effect, Bacon treats all examples as but decorations to be managed. "[L]et them be so employed as to turn the authority of the past to the use of the present" (3).

Bacon applies the lesson immediately, elaborating supreme courts civil and criminal under the Roman names Praetorian and Censorian, a procedure, we noted in chapter 8, that slides his readers away from the British courts of his time and toward reform. The courts he names are said to treat extraordinary cases not covered by law—and yet are soon said to shape law. It is here that Bacon makes his great admission: "[F]or the power of supplying, extending, and moderating laws, differs little from that of making them" (37). The highest judges are like a legislature, and such an extraordinary court, he now suggests, should be composed of "many" (38). Yet popular judgment is not the last word; a court punishing with injury or death should follow fixed laws, and a court dispensing from law should not be excessively lenient. The spirit of all this guidance of judges and the people comes out when Bacon considers finally retrospective laws, laws that punish as criminal what was not criminal when done. Use them warily, he concludes, but use them where politic: to strengthen, for example, security of properties and contracts (49). For the "principal inconvenience" in punishing without notice is merely that it creates "disturbance" (49).

If one puts two and two together, true policy for courts proves to be the policy of civil peace, which requires rather republican courts lax in enforcing piety and morality, rigorous in enforcing civil control, warily legal in inflicting injury and death, and warily rigorous in instituting protection of property and instruments of exchange.

The second cause of uncertainty is obscurity in law, and the Baconian prescriptions for this problem also promote progressive reform, but in the guise of codifying and rationalizing. "Excessive accumulation" of laws is the first cause of obscurity, for which Bacon proposes an obvious and radical cure and then a less obvious but more radical change of attitude. The cure is innovation by codification: a "new statute" that "repeals and cancels all former enactments, and substitutes an entirely new and uniform law" (54). This is illustrated by an Athenian example (from a democratic era), whereby every few years commissioners (*delegatiis*) propose reforms to be approved by the assembly (*comitiis*). Bacon shapes democratizing codifiers to come. Drop "worse titles" (56) and "statutes which are obsolete" (57), he advises, and meanwhile, before the comprehensive codifying, let the criminal courts decree against "obsolete laws and statutes." A broader change in attitude shows itself: revere laws only if up-to-date and—Bacon adds very quietly—not injurious (58). Loosening the custom and caution of traditional lawyers, Bacon converts them into progressive reformers. Some he induces to be thoughtful progressives, according to his thoughts on what is really injurious.

That the up-to-date is not injurious may be supposed if legal instaurations occur in enlightened times (64). Obscurity in laws is due not only to accumulation of laws but also to confusion in drawing laws, and this second cause leads Bacon to the problem of clear words. While words themselves occasion "noise and strife" (66), they are needed in order that laws may avoid the dangers of majestic brevity, particularly in "these times" (67). Bacon may allude to majestic but willful kings, but he also says that words are the instruments to persuade assemblies (*comitii*) and peoples. For clear laws one needs the aid of learning, we are now told, and Bacon is quick to supply the requisite learning: "Of the methods (*modi*) of expounding (*enucleandi*) law and removing ambiguities." This topic, while not exactly announced, is the positive correction for the third cause of obscurity, "negligent and ill-ordered methods of interpreting law," which was announced as a topic but does not appear (52). Here Bacon asserts himself in prescribing what learning to follow in drawing and interpreting. After commending published judgments by a distinguished reporter, he attacks reliance upon doctors of law and other writers, and he follows this slap at scholastics and common law authors with a commendation of auxiliary books as to "the science and practice" of law (79). In place of the old books pointing toward higher law, Bacon commends textbooks summarizing and systematizing the law. A student should be able to consult Institutes, which are to focus on private law, which Bacon equates in effect with the "higher parts" of the law (80). He also recommends commentaries on legal terms, surveys of rules that exhibit those "general dictates of reason" that ground systems of civil law (82), summaries of law by topic, and collections of forms of pleading. Bacon directs lawyers and legal authors to the primacy of the private, the realistic, and the definite.

The last section on obscurity of laws, "Of Answers and Opinions," suggests that a director is needed by those in doubt as to how to secure themselves (89). Judges are not the final authority, especially as to the "opinions" (*consultis*) that Bacon adds to the topic previously announced. Let judgments issue from judges, while judges' opinions on disputed matters come from "the prince or the state" (92, "*Principe aut Statu*," which Spedding translates "king or state"). While Bacon had previously intimated that judges' views guide the state (55), he here says the reverse, and the argument in context hints at the judge's subordination to an authoritative state of mind and its author. The education (93) and governing (95–97) of judges and judgment must themselves be suitably governed so as to put controversies to rest, as the education fostered by "antiquity" did not (93). The key to legal education is Bacon's new formula of universal justice or the fountain of equity: the business of the law is "peace" (96).

In short, this *Treatise on Universal Justice* sets forth the nucleus of a new state of legal learning and thus of law. It evinces a public foundation, peace, and peace of a certain type that channels private forces, especially the appetites for security and gain. This formula guides the surface provision for humane laws of protection, politic channels of social advantage, and the civil system that contributes to an effectual but rather representative state. The work provides a legal creed that includes new customs, new laws, new courts, new authorities for public assemblies and legal writers—and new authoritative opinions. Yet the form is fit for action: counsel for judges in power, but in the dark about the law that is supposed to guide them. Bacon's formula moves judges to become instruments of enlightened judging. They learn to interpret law according to true policy; legislators learn to remake law by reform and codification; writers learn to modernize by rewriting law and custom, and in all these Bacon's treatise on private law and justice thus complements the public ordinances of essay 29. It moves judges to provide the legal securities that are a solid popular appeal of the growing nation-state; it supplies, under cover of law, many policies that lead to the new state of things.

The Fighting Creed of Humanity

How the new civil promise can help supplant the reigning faith is the theme of one of Bacon's strangest works, *An Advertisement Touching a Holy War*.[30] If the interpretation that follows is correct, the *Advertisement* is intended to reconstitute Christianity into the militant worldly creed prescribed by essay 29, a creed for the improvement of the human condition everywhere. The work discusses the enlightened politics of sect building, thus supplementing Bacon's discussion in "Of Vicissitude of Things" (58), and it shows authoritatively the place of other writings, including the whole *Great Instauration*, in Bacon's project.

This is a difficult little dialogue. It has two apparently discordant parts, a revealing personal dedication and a dialogue on holy war that is distressingly incomplete. The dedication contains Bacon's most straightforward revelation of the purpose and portions of his whole teaching. The dialogue discusses whether a holy war is defensible, and it is anything but straightforward; there are six announced speakers, of whom five speak, and six announced speeches, of which one is given. The two parts prove to be connected, nevertheless. To put it simply, a reconstituted Christianity is a creed that assures the resurrection not of Christ but of Bacon.

The dedication begins with a religious theme, consolation in the face of calamity, but the consolation suggested is not Christian and not religious. By one's writings one might provide "banks or mounts of perpetuity, which will not break."[31] Therefore, Bacon says, he published a *Great Instauration* for the "general good" of man in his "very being," a work of law for his "general good" in "society," the *History of King Henry VII* to honor his country (not his king), and the *Essays* as a recreation to bring honor to himself. None of these works call on the "temple," however, and *Advertisement* is to supply this omission. It is, one would think, the authoritative Baconian work on religion, and it is in fact dedicated to a saintly bishop-counselor just deceased, Lancelot Andrewes. In the dedication, Bacon twice tells us that his dedications have a serious purpose, and this dedication, unlike other Baconian dedications, does not flatter its subject. Like the others, nevertheless, it commits sedition, for the authority of a dead Christian is used to subvert Christianity. Bacon hints that he himself plans on "rising again," but in another sort of life after death and by a project mixing matters religious with civil and matters contemplative with active. Andrewes was a great Anglican divine, one of those moderate Christians who followed in the footsteps of the judicious Richard Hooker. While in Bacon's dialogue a "moderate divine" is announced, he never speaks.[32]

The dialogue discusses not the sanctity of Christ but the aptitude of Christianity for empire over men. Such a topic undermines sanctity by measuring Christ's teachings against worldly standards, and the argument undermines sanctity more. A hot-headed military man, Martius, criticizes Christendom for the meanness of its enterprises: while churchmen busy humankind with rites and ceremonies, merchants make a path in the sea to the ends of the world. Commerce is the way to order the world. Martius has to confront the case of Christian Spain, whose enterprises have more than doubled the habitable world. The explanation discounts faith as a motive, for Spain expands from desire for "amplification and enlargement of riches and dominion."[33] A more subtle indictment accompanies Martius' reduction of Spain's motives: the natives that Spain conquered were often quite civilized. While the Turks have been worse oppressors, the courtier Pollio proceeds nastily to invite speculation on the similarities between barbarous Turkey and Christian Spain; he reminds us that the Turks acknowledge "God the Father, creator of Heaven and Earth, being the first person in the Trinity, although they deny the rest."[34]

The one set speech is an investigation of the lawfulness of holy war by Zebedaeus, "a Roman Catholic zealot."[35] With friends so described, who needs enemies? After listing degrees of religious war, however, the zealot as reformed by Bacon becomes distracted and would set aside "the cause of religion" in order to suppress the empire of the Turks. He cautions against letting Christ become an idol that destroys men, and he equates divine law with laws of nature and nations in such a way as to dismiss Aquinas' mixture, the great Scholastic version, of natural and divine law. Zebedaeus also corrects revealingly Aristotelian natural right, for he restates the right of the more worthy to rule into the right of the "civil or policed" nation to subdue a "heap of people" unable to govern. This justifies conquest by a "Cyrus or a Caesar that were no Christian."

Yet Bacon's reformed zealot does not defend wars for mere "personal tyranny," and he espouses the traditional-sounding view that war is justified when the law of nature and nations is violated. But this proves not to involve some absence of purity or the presence of sin or idolatry. To count such as violations "subverteth all government." It is where people are mere swarms and multitudes that fundamental law is breached, where, that is, a "nullity of their policy and government" exists. The example is pirates, who are enemies to "human society," and this example is followed by allusions to "rovers" and "petty kings," as if the difference between small kingdoms and pirate bands may not be great. Are great kings but great pirates? Zebedaeus approves here a war alluded to in essay 29, that of Rome against Philip of Macedon for the liberty of Greece. Are the new wars to be for human society and liberty and against great kings? There follows a description of the "Kingdom" of the Assassins. It sounds rather like a Christendom in which the devout are assigned by their lord and master to topple schismatic or atheistical rulers. Is the King of Kings the great target? There follows an indictment of Anabapists. It reminds of many variants of Reformation and of Christ's kingdom in general, in which Christ's subjects act according to the "spirit." A "civil and policed" nation may rightly war against all such, that is, against all Christian nations. The remarks that follow suggest that it may war also against nations that elevate women over men, slaves over free, sons over fathers, and that practice cannibalism. A vaguely humane universalism, which takes account of the predominant forces in humans and among them, is the standard to uphold. In view of the evil of cannibalism, Zebedaeus allows Spain's conquests—and then indicts cruelty and allows war against "foreign tyrants." Spain is fair game in the new world, too.

In the *Advertisement*, Bacon revises Christianity toward a universal creed of humanity that will excuse war against Christian kingdoms and especially against Christ's kingdom. His Zebedaeus abstracts from faith in Christ and dwells on charity, and while he promises to speak of "propagation of faith" in the "proper place," he never speaks of it. The promise is itself omitted from the Latin version of *Advertisement*. Beside the humanitarian creed of charity, brother, and neighbor, Christianity appears "schismatic," that is, meanly and narrowly warlike and unsocial, and beside the civil creed of prosperity and empire it seems cruel, hypocritical, and impractical. The true holy war will be an enlightened war against religion and against nature on behalf of liberty and the real progress of humanity.

Notes

1. Chapter 17, *The Prince*, tr. Harvey C. Mansfield, Jr. (Chicago: University of Chicago Press, 1985).

2. *On Human Conduct*, 287–88.

3. *The Economic Writings of Sir William Petty*, ed. Charles Henry Hull (Cam-

bridge: Cambridge University Press, 1899), 129; cf. lxiv n., lxiii; E. A. J. Johnson, *Predecessors of Adam Smith* (New York: Augustus M. Kelley, 1965; repr. of 1937 edition), 93, 96, 110.

4. *The Rise and Fall of Economic Growth* (Chicago and London: University of Chicago Press, 1978), 5 (Arndt's italics).

5. *A History of Economic Reasoning* (Baltimore and London: The Johns Hopkins University Press, 1983), 585–91.

6. *Economic Reasoning*, 59–65. Pribram, for all his originality in recurring to Baconian premises, pays a price for conceiving them very formally, as but "methods of reasoning," and discounting them as basically old stuff. He limits himself to a catalog of the meaty Baconian opinions as to self, society, and economy and supposes that Bacon's method is really the hypothetical method of nominalism (*Economic Reasoning*, 587 and *passim*). One might prefer Pribram's theory to his friend Schumpeter's, which had held the "new departure" of the Baconians just a continuation of Scholasticism [Joseph A. Schumpeter, *History of Economic Analysis* (New York: Oxford University Press, 1963), 124–25 and 115–16], but Pribram's "nominalism" slights the defining practical bent of Bacon's method, for which skepticism is merely a precondition, and blurs the novel priorities underlying his economics.

7. Leslie Lipson, *The Age of Mercantilism*, vol. III of *The Economic History of England*, 6th ed. (London: A. & C. Black, 1961), 1; Adam Smith, *An Inquiry into the Nature and Causes of the Wealth of Nations*, ed. Edwin Cannan (New York: The Modern Library, 1937), IV 1, 397–419.

8. *Wealth of Nations* IV, 1, 549, 460, 423, 483.

9. *Wealth of Nations* IV, "Introduction," 397, 488–89.

10. *Wealth of Nations* I, 1, 2, 11, 242–43; II, "Introduction"; III, 1 ("Of the Natural Progress of Opulence"), esp. 359. See Peter McNamara's doctoral dissertation, *Political Economy and Statesmanship: Adam Smith and Alexander Hamilton on the Foundation of the Commercial Republic* (Boston: Boston College, 1990).

11. Lipson, *The Age of Mercantilism*, 1, 154.

12. Lipson, *The Age of Mercantism*, 54.

13. Eli F. Hecksher, *Mercantilism*, 2 vols, rev. ed., tr. Mendel Shapiro (London and New York: Allen & Unwin and Macmillan, 1955), 362ff.

14. *Mercantilism*, 21.

15. In chapter 9, I discussed Bacon's advocacy of producer colonies, which exemplify thoroughly economic society. See "Of Plantations" (33).

16. *Works* XI, 134; cf. 124, 145.

17. Hecksher, *Mercantilism*, II, 288.

18. *Francis Bacon* (Stanford: Stanford University Press, 1992). The Aphorisms, in both the original Latin and in a translation by Mark S. Neustadt, is appended to Neustadt's doctoral dissertation, *The Making of the Instauration: Science, Politics, and Law in the Career of Francis Bacon* (Baltimore: The Johns Hopkins University Press, 1987).

19. Quoted in Coquillette's *Francis Bacon*, 15. Subsequent references are to 294, viii, 283, 286, 279, 290.

20. *Works* XI, 238; VI, 158.

21. *Works* XI, 238, 141; VI, 158, 92.

22. *History of Henry VII*, in *Works* XI, 327–29; VI, 219–20.

23. W. J. Jones, *The Elizabethan Court of Chancery* (Oxford: Clarendon Press, 1967), 328–38, 389, 393; H. R. Trevor-Roper, *Archbishop Laud, 1563–1645*, 2d. ed. (London: Macmillan, 1963), 271; G. R. Elton, *The Tudor Constitution* (Cambridge: Cambridge University Press, 1968), 219; R. G. Usher, *The Rise and Fall of the High Commission* (Oxford: Clarendon Press, 1913), 107–99.

24. *The Making of the Instauration*, 244. I use Neustadt's edition of the *Aphorisms* and follow for the most part his translation.

25. See *De Augmentis* VIII, iii; in *Works* V, 88; IX, 311.

26. *Works* IX, 310–42; V, 87–109.

27. *Works* IX, 311; V, 88.

28. *Works* IX, 314, 342; V, 90, 109.

29. *Works* IX, 342; V, 109. Spedding here translates *republica* as "state," which obscures the point.

30. Weinberger pointed out its importance. "On Bacon's *Advertisement Touching a Holy War*," in *Interpretation* 9, nos. 2 & 3 (September, 1981). See also Michael Kiernan, ed., *The Essayes or Counsels, Civill and Morall* (1985), 231.

31. *Works* XIII, 186; VII, 13.

32. *Works* XIII, 191, 184, 188; VII, 17, 14, 13.

33. *Works* XIII, 196–97; VII, 21.

34. *Works* XIII, 199; VII, 22–23.

35. *Works* XIII, 204–18; VII, 26–36.

Chapter 11

Visions and Powers:
The Comprehensive Politics of Progress

Visionary Politics

Modern life displays an eery mingling of fearsome powers with its visionary hopes. Every modern country contains at least a residue of rising expectations for security and affluence, and idealists envision the liberation of humanity from war, poverty, and disease, and from the rule of man over man and of man over woman. But beneath the special contemporary demands for security and autonomy one hears the steady hum of industrial might and sees immense forces, of which nuclear weaponry is merely the most spectacular. For three centuries now, nations, tribes, and cities of the world have been modernizing into organized nation-states wielding growing populations, immense wealth, and potent inventions, and mobilized by economic systems, methodical science, representative governments, and new kinds of dictatorships wielding total control. This strange mixture of the visionary and the forceful is typical. It has shown itself in the liberal and socialist versions of developed and developing societies, as well as in various dictatorships, and it persists, despite a percolating disillusionment among Western intellectuals and the disintegration of many Marxist regimes that marked the extremes of hope and domination.

What accounts for these singular mixtures of humane vision and *realpolitik* organization? And how might the promise of progress best be combined with the powers of control? This chapter examines the answers to such questions in the seminal vision of progressive society, Bacon's *New Atlantis* (1627).

The *New Atlantis* is a utopian fantasy in a special form, that of a short but crammed adventure story that culminates in science fiction. European travelers in the South Seas encounter unfavorable winds and the island of Bensalem, and they are charmed and then won by a provision for sickness and want that is both gently caring and utterly efficient. Bensalem manages to mix a compassionate welfare policy and magical inventions with unerring control by scientists and the state. The Europeans are provided sustenance, an allowance, and medical care; some are told of religious, civil, and scientific foundings; two are shown the arrangements of ritual; one, the narrator who is finally instructed to proclaim in Europe the news of Bensalem, is told briefly of the arrangements of marriage and in complicated detail of a dominant research institute. What begins as a tale of adversity at sea, and of a saving heaven on earth, ends with a great scientist's methodical listing of techniques for extracting useful formulas from nature. The story combines in microcosm an attractive vision to rouse human hopes and an earnest method to provide real powers for satisfying them.

Yet the literary form of *New Atlantis* hardly appears a vehicle of an important plan, and many readers treat the work as less than serious. It is only a story, begins abruptly and breaks off abruptly, and is "a work unfinished" and unperfected according to the subtitle and the last word. Moreover, it is brief, enigmatic, allusive, and mysterious, apart from the accounts of the scientific establishment and its founding. While the fiction seems too dense to be merely playful, the descriptions seem too enigmatic to be in earnest.

I shall argue that *New Atlantis*'s literary peculiarities are rhetorical devices that accord with its revelation of a vision. They magnify the insinuating features of progress (such as ease, public compassion, and humane medicines), and conceal the repulsive features (such as dangerous inventions, pervasive control, and the overthrow of European faith, morals, and monarchy). This form of magnification and concealment proves to be an intentional variation on the vision of a world to come. The *New Atlantis*, I shall try to show, is a variation on the Bible and is meant to replace both the worldly Old Testament and the more visionary and otherworldly New Testament. The work thus packages progress to appeal to peoples, and especially to ambitious adventurers and intellectual projectors, and only indicates its connection with more sober Baconian works for other and more sober leaders. Nevertheless, the *New Atlantis* exhibits the most ominous of Baconian political innovations: the relationship between the promise of progress by control of nature and the management of peoples by control of human nature.

In recent years, as scholars have become skeptical of the scientific project and not least of the methodical organization of man, they have begun to reconsider the special Baconian vision. Charles Whitney, for example, has discerned in Bacon's work an ominous call to conquer nature by mind, a vision of a "radical and uncompromising modernity" that only the old French philosophes adequately observed. But Whitney also thought that he saw a serene vision, a biblical or classical myth extolling the "marriage of mind and the universe."[1] The corrosive tendency of Baconianism is limited, he argued, because in society, politics, and religion, at least, Bacon sought only a traditional sort of reform. But there are difficulties in this account of dual visions. Morals and politics are objects of Baconian science, according to *De Augmentis* and *New Organon*, and thus not separable from its impetus to conquest. Also, there are profoundly shocking and untraditional doctrines beneath the traditional appearances of the *New Atlantis*, and that is the paradigmatic Baconian myth.

Earlier in this century, the so-called critical theorists Max Horkheimer and Theodor Adorno had dwelled on the mixture of myth and science in the Enlightenment and its "herald Bacon," but they had found a single devotion to domination where Whitney saw a duality.[2] The element of myth dominated that of science, according to Horkheimer and Adorno, and the Baconian vision of enlightenment, like all myths, is merely a primitive rationalization of domination. But is Bacon primitive, and is his myth making like all the rest? Horkheimer and Adorno may see something of Bacon's hardheadedness, but the insight is blurred by dogmatism. They rely on a general theory of myth and ignore Bacon's own theory, and they simply dismiss the un-Baconian claims in traditional poetry, philosophy, and religion, whose devotees often appear contemplative or worshipful and assert that harmonies and perfections are higher than the human urge to dominate. While Horkheimer and Adorno assert otherwise, they do not prove otherwise, and one is entitled to suspect that they follow someone else's proof, perhaps their theoretical forebear Nietzsche. They, like he, presuppose two reductionist premises: that philosophy, poetry, and religion can be reduced to myth making, and that myth making is an instrument of power seeking. These premises were first proved or asserted by Bacon and other early modern thinkers, and thus, in the decisive respect, Horkheimer and Adorno seem creatures of the innovations that they critique. They miss the distinctiveness of Bacon's politicization of divinations and reduction of visionary politics. Leaders can dominate through visions that promise security to followers.

That *New Atlantis* hints at more than it says, and that it hints at a "morally problematic" and politically ominous liberation of appetites, is a thesis that has been extensively and instructively discussed by Jerry

Weinberger.[3] Where my findings differ, it is chiefly because Weinberger supposes that Bacon only advances "immoral means for moral ends." He argues that the "highest human possibility" for Bacon is science, in the manner of Plato and Aristotle's devotion to philosophy, and only the Christian circumstances of the seventeenth century required that Baconian science, in order to be autonomous, mask itself as a charitable servant of mankind. In chapters 4, 5, and 6, I argued otherwise, and in chapter 12, I discuss further the primacy of power in Bacon's science. I am contending that Bacon links a progressive state of scientific advance with other modes of controlling peoples, such as the state-builder Henry VII and the civil state set forth in the *Essays*.

There is one student of Bacon, Michael Oakeshott, who especially illuminates the importance of the state in Bacon's thought, and touches on the propagandistic or semireligious elements, while nevertheless obscuring the plan for a dominating vision. It was Bacon who first formulated the "European State," according to Oakeshott, "a state as a corporate aggregate to exploit the resources of an estate." *New Atlantis* and other Baconian works contain a model of centralized planning and control that is "teleocratic," that is, is calculatedly oriented to human purpose and, in particular, to the purpose of production. Politics thus becomes a political economy of worker ants who are graded, regulated, and protected, and kept industrious and in harness for an end beyond themselves.[4] Profoundly antipathetic to all this, Oakeshott was led to provide the best formulation extant of the comprehensive control, including the mind control, required by the Baconian state.

The engagement of the "ruler" of a state, who is Chairman of a Board of Technocrats, is not only to determine the grand strategy of the enterprise and to direct its day-to-day conduct; it is also to preserve its integrity by inhibiting all beliefs and activities which might hinder its pursuit. He will direct research, control agriculture, industry, and trade, regulate prices, determine the balance between investment and consumption, assign their several tasks to the members of the corporation according to their talents, reward diligence, suppress idleness and waste, protect the estate for which he is responsible from the intrusion of over-curious strangers and from the depredations of invaders, enlarge it by colonial plantation, guard the secrets of the corporation and organize industrial espionage in order to take advantage of the achievements of other such corporations. He will align the education of his subjects to the needs of the corporate enterprise, propagate beliefs favorable to it, and suppress those which might hinder it. He will "settle" religion so that it shall not interfere with the business in hand and exclude extraneous activities, distracting entertainments, holidays which are not preparation for work, music and poetry which does not celebrate the purpose of the corporation.[5]

This organization of mind and men is all a tool of science, "to make nature yield what it has never yet yielded," and yet Oakeshott did not think the movement, however comprehensive and systematic, the result of planning. It was the fruit of a Christian "calling." According to Oakeshott (and such commentators on utopianism as the Manuels),[6] Bacon's project arises not from a new vision but from late medieval circumstances and possibilities; only later and vulgar followers of Bacon made mere "satisfaction of wants" the aim. But this is untrue to Bacon's economic writings, and both assertions are contrary to the plain tenor of the *New Atlantis*. There is a visible conversion of the Christian Europeans to the new world of progress—"we took ourselves now for free men, seeing there was no danger of our utter perdition"—and they converted because of the promise of sustenance from the state, as well as free medical care, novel inventions, affluence, and effectual organization. Oakeshott's clarity about the rational organization of the modern nation-state, in short, is limited by his failure to pursue its connections with early modern culture, with, that is, the philosophers' rational vision of a state of progress.

"A Work Unfinished"—But a Literary Work Completed?

A tradition of commentary on the *New Atlantis* denies that it contains any important parts of Bacon's politics, and this seems to begin with the original preface by William Rawley, Bacon's chaplain and secretary. According to Rawley, the story ends abruptly because Bacon, being distracted by the inquiries in natural history that were his principal concern, omitted what he had planned, a model of a "frame of laws, or of the best state or mould of a commonwealth."[7] If Rawley is correct, then *New Atlantis* is incomplete in an important respect. Is he correct?

There is some reason to doubt that the writing is seriously incomplete. While Bacon left unpublished many manuscripts, completed and incomplete, he thought this one complete enough to publish and then supervised before his death a translation into Latin. Also, the ending, while abrupt, certainly seems to fit. Our narrator has reviewed Bensalemite institutions, and no one suggests that he inquire further about Bensalemite politics; on the contrary, he is instructed to "publish" what he has heard of the Bensalemite scientific establishment "for the good of other nations." The *New Atlantis* is a model to be implemented, and one wonders whether it might be a "work unfinished" (as the subtitle calls it), or even a work to be "perfected" (as the last word puts it), only in this sense. Might the apparent incompleteness be a literary device? This possibility is suggested not only by the text but by a relevant parallel. The original account of Atlantis occurs in Plato's *Critias*, to which *New Atlantis* alludes, and the *Critias* is also formally incomplete. It ends without a promised speech of Zeus, which was to rectify the injustice and wars of the kings of Atlantis. Plato seems to shadow forth the unlikelihood of justice in human politics, and perhaps Bacon uses the same device for his different purpose. His utopia can conclude with an exhortation to worldwide scientific enlightenment because his plan is attuned to universal human needs.

However one might speculate as to what is absent, one can say with certainty that Rawley's thesis ignores much politics that is present. Less than a third of the *New Atlantis* is about the scientific establishment. We see the manner of conversion of Europeans to progressive civilization, many institutions of enlightened Christianity and Judaism and of a civil and scientific nation-state, and the laws of a nuclear family and of liberated mating. There are tantalizing glimpses of officials and governors, an enlightened priest, a variety of fathers, a Jewish merchant, the state, and a supervising scientist.

In its allusive way, *New Atlantis* may be Bacon's most comprehensive political work, for alone among the political writings it encompasses the organization of science and scientists and ranks science among human priorities and arrangements. It may even be Bacon's most comprehensive scientific work in the decisive respect, although not, of course, in many respects. I repeat Bacon's crucial remark: the "true logician" must have "judgment" as well as "invention." The context is the economic use of the logic of invention ("Of Riches" 34). *New Atlantis* contains the crucial judgments that guide scientists in choosing what to invent and thus, broadly, what to investigate. Its list of twenty-four "preparations and instruments" for research reveals more than the nearest rival, *New Organon*'s ranking of "prerogative instances,"[8] because it identifies the inventions that Bacon thinks most obviously useful or most likely to be popular. In short, *New Atlantis* seems to show not only the place of science in Bacon's politics, but also the place of politics and judgment in guiding Bacon's science. It thus shows comprehensively the essentials of the Baconian science of government. But Baconian science is fundamentally an art of invention. *New Atlantis* exhibits a variety of advanced social and political inventions, from the great commercial nation-states to the welfare state (more or less), consumerism, and indirect management by experts. There is reason to think that *New Atlantis* is the culminating picture of Bacon's crucial inventions (in politics as well as in technology)—developed, in operation, and in their crucial connections. It seems an image of the Baconian future of humanity, the culminating part or product of his science of production. I agree with this opinion, which has been impressively set forth by Weinberger.[9]

Nevertheless, we have somewhat overstated the case. For the *New Atlantis* is obviously enigmatic and short, and it is especially enigmatic and short on the topic of government in the obvious sense. We are shown officials, but we see very little of higher officials. We hear of a king, a state, and laws, but receive little direct light as to any of these. If the work is comprehensively political, why is there so little light, or such refracted light, as to political governance and the governors?

First, let us be properly wary. Perhaps we expect too much. Should Rawley have expected a "frame" of law and government? Would Bacon tell everything to his readers, or even to his secretary and chaplain? He tells us that he was one alone, who followed in no man's track, and for a long time while serving in government communicated his plan to no one.[10] And he is explicit that one must be inexplicit about government. The science of government is a thing secret and reserved, to be handled with reverence and even in silence.[11]

This secretive handling of matters of government is obvious in the *New Atlantis*, for it is not only tacit but also explicit and even a thematic policy of Bensalem. Bensalem's governors reserve certain discussions to certain audiences, while secreting them from others. All the Europeans are admitted to Strangers' House, to the big parade for the Father of Salomon's House, and to a public audience with the Father. Ten, not the "meaner sort" or those who were inclined to sightseeing, hear an account of Bensalem's religion and foundings, and two are bidden to the Feast of the Tirsan. One alone seeks out Joabin, who is of "great policy" and knowing in "laws and customs." One alone is given "private conference" to hear the Father of Salomon's House reveal the promise and powers of science. More to the point: the first of the two policies of Solamona, Bensalem's most revered founder, is hiding Bensalem from strangers; founding the new scientific establishment is the second.

One may then suppose that *New Atlantis*'s peculiar mixture of revelation and concealment, of political comprehensiveness in an extraordinary way mixed with political indefiniteness in many ordinary ways, is calculated to serve a function. I suggest that it is a rhetorical function. *New*

Atlantis is calculatedly visionary. It proclaims a science to save humanity at large, and, in effect, it proclaims the duty to found a scientific civilization. Precisely for the sake of such a cosmopolitan aim, it appeals above governments and above the most controversial political differences within nations and among nations. It abstracts from controversies over forms of rule. In a few essays, as we have noted, Bacon intimates a plan to substitute a new vision, of power by human prediction, for the old suprapolitical prophecies, of salvation by divine providence.[12] *New Atlantis* parades the scientific and economic improvement to come, while it veils the divisions and revolutions, in morals, politics, and religion, also to be undergone. But it also indicates what it veils, for those who need to know what they're getting into.

Conversion Poetry

Because *New Atlantis* has the literary form of a story or fable, and not that of a sober proposal, some call it a romance, a product of imagination removed from rational intent. This won't do, if only because rational intent is so visible in the twenty-four "preparations and instruments" and in the carefully orchestrated welcome and conversion of the Europeans. Also, Bacon has a very calculated and political interpretation of poetry, as well as of rhetoric, and this is at odds with the veil of sentiment that romanticism would throw over *New Atlantis.*

In both *Advancement* and *De Augmentis,* poetry is subordinated to rhetoric, and the art of rhetoric is transformed into the art of communicating one's plans.

These thematic discussions treat poetry as but a product of imagination separable from nature, that is, from the "laws of matter." It is not an imitation that singles out the way things are, in light of some intuition as to what they might be at their best, for in this science as in others, Bacon's critique of mind leads to the conclusion that there are no such intuitions and no such natural perfections. Instead, poetry expresses the mind's wish for something more than nature supplies: "some satisfaction to the mind," a "more ample greatness" and "more exact goodness" than really occasion the events of life.[13] Bacon thus tacitly rejects Aristotle's suggestion that poetry imitate nature and, in particular, that it convey the outlines and fate of virtue and vice. Bacon dismisses accordingly the customary divisions of poetry, even the old landmark between tragedy and comedy.[14] Like the other arts and sciences that he reforms, poetry is to invent a way for human satisfaction beyond what nature provides. This does not amount to the later elevation of poetry by romantics and idealists such as Rousseau, Burke, and Kant. They, too, may have separated poetry from intellectual intuition, but they found in refined feeling an approach to nature and the beautiful. According to Bacon, however, poetry is not an expression of sentimental satisfaction above real desire, but a rational management of invented illusion to help satisfy real desire. Poets do not divine an ideal or feel the sublime. They incline to "submit the shows of things to the desires of the mind."[15]

Bacon's apparently complicated classification of poetry reflects this simplifying spirit. While he divides poetry into narrative (history exaggerated), representative (of events as if present), and allusive or parabolic, he discusses only the last. Allusive poetry he calls "feigned history," and it is perhaps the basis of the others. If poetry is the devising of shows for one's own purposes, the invention is most obvious in the "parables" and "fables" that are the stock in trade of allusive poetry. Like history, Bacon says briefly but in Machiavelli's idiom, allusive poetry is an account of modes of rising. Like all poetry, it originates in primitive times, when the human understanding conceived dimly and sensibly. Poetry is to science as hieroglyphs are to words and parables to arguments. Yet "now and at all times" it remains useful, for parables and fables are universal instruments, "to convey any point of reason which was more sharp and subtle than the vulgar" could perceive or understand.[16]

Poetry is then a way by which the sharp make themselves understood to the dull, and in light of this difference, which Bacon presents here and elsewhere as permanent, the next step is predictable. Allusions and illusions can prevent understanding as well as cause it; they can veil as well as clarify. Bacon explicitly recommends such dual service "when the secrets and mysteries of religion, policy, or philosophy, are involved in fables or parables." While there are implications as to the origin of religious proverbs and mysteries, Bacon's principal concern seems with policy, that is, with allusions that serve "a special purpose or conceit." One is reminded that a mixture of allusion and policy governs many of Bacon's works. It governs most obviously *Wisdom of the Ancients*, which exemplifies Bacon's interpretation of poetry. Into old fables of the heathen gods, such as Prometheus, Bacon inserts his desacralizing and civil teaching that man must provide for himself. His authoritative account of poetry, in *De Augmentis*, closes with three of these fables, and the three convey indirectly Bacon's desacralizing division of sciences into natural, political, and moral. They illustrate the use of imaginative literature in enlightenment, especially the way that a new secularization and a new learning may be spread under cover of familiar old images.

New Atlantis is the supreme Baconian fable in the sense just sketched. It is a fable mixing transformed familiarity with veiled novelty. Bacon has found a way to meld his scientific project with the reinterpreted hopes of the religious, and *New Atlantis* is the calculated poetry that puts the fabulous in the service of worldly progress. It is a politic variation on the Old and New Testaments that begins with Christian Europeans lost in the wilderness of waters, ends with a revelation of the saving science and an exhortation to spread the word to the nations, and contains reinterpretations of Christ's promise of salvation, the covenant with Abraham and the commandments of Moses, King Solomon's wisdom, God's creation of the world in six days, and the Christian Platonism of Sir Thomas More. It rejects as "poetical and fabulous" the diagnosis of utopianism in Plato's *Critias*, but puts the criticism in the mouth of a Christian priest who nevertheless proclaims the "light" of the kingdom to be a research establishment, not a church. The common reader is to be converted by obvious appearances, as most Christian Europeans in the story are converted by the name and signs of Christ and by sights of progress that masquerade as acts of Christian charity. Others are transformed by ways more rational, as the narrator is converted by observation of politic rites and by arguments as to high policy and the real powers of a new science. Biblical themes of promised land and conversion to faith in the savior are reconstituted into a politic movement and a cosmopolitan faith in progress.

Poetry, as Bacon understands it, is rhetoric, and the special tenor of *New Atlantis* results from following Bacon's explicit formula for a future-oriented rhetoric. While poetry arises from the earth, from a natural urge to satisfy need, Baconian rhetoric is an artificial power of mind to provide satisfaction by mastery. We repeat the hard-nosed definition: rhetoric is "reason applied to imagination for the better moving of the will." Its task is to govern the affections by reason, and its means is a "confederacy between reason and imagination against the affections."[17] The most rational imagining is that of future satisfaction, for an image of the future builds on the passion to endure and can thus become a strong lever to discipline blind passion. Eloquence is to make "things remote seem apparent." Bacon had learned much from the worldly success of Christianity and even more than Machiavelli had learned. The *New Atlantis* is Bacon's poetic image of a new world of increasing satisfaction, and it transforms, while appropriating, the future-oriented promise of Christ. It reminds us of a promised land and messiah by the Hebrew connotations of "Bensalem" and Joabin, by various identifications of Bensalem with Savior, Lord, and Virgin, by the Europeans' identification of their welcome with salvation, and by countless other details. Yet the new land promises not milk and honey in heaven, but Gatorade and Nutra-Sweet on earth; not immortality, innocence, and union with God, but security, luxury, and power. The provider of future bliss is not providence but the state, a progressive science, and their founders.

Not Utopia But Real Progress

New Atlantis points ahead and to the general, not up and to the rare. Bensalem is a realizable project of improvement to be achieved widely or universally, not a perfect pattern realizable rarely or no place, and in this it differs sharply from traditional utopias and in particular from the utopias of the philosophic tradition begun by Socrates.[18] Those who treat *New Atlantis* as essentially Christian neglect the essential distinction between modern and ancient utopianism.[19] *New Atlantis* is explicit, if elliptical, in correcting both Thomas More's *Utopia* and its Platonic predecessors.

In the second of his orientation sessions for the Europeans, the Governor of Strangers' House offers an anthropology that expressly diverges from the myth of ancient Atlantis set forth in the *Timaeus* and *Critias*. He notes various features of the *Critias'* description, such as descendants of a god; a magnificent temple, palace, city and hill; and a land rich with navigable rivers. He also adds and omits. He adds a reference to "degrees of ascent whereby men climb up" to the royal city: a "ladder to heaven." He omits many things, notably the land's natural abundance and its rule by ten kings. The addition epitomizes Bacon's criticism. Plato had thought to divine the true and just in light of which men and cities are judged. Bacon thinks divinations but artificial light, imaginings like all suppositions of divinity. The omissions may be understood similarly. Bacon's civil politics will not rely on nature, philosopher-kings, or royal approximations.

Plato's *Timaeus* had begun with a summary of the *Republic's* regime, and the Atlantis there pictured seems only a dim approximation of something better. Socrates had asked to see the best regime in motion, and we are shown two rather barbaric cities connected by war, Atlantis and Athens (which had defeated an invasion by Atlantis). In neither of the descriptions provided by the *Critias* is there rule of philosophers or communism of family and property. War appears the motion likely in cities, and the best city seems inept and perhaps impossible in such circumstances. Athens is presented as a republic of farmers, austere to the point of drabness and ruled Sparta-like by a mixture of temple and barracks;

Atlantis is magnificent but barbaric, ordered by absolute kings who are, in turn, ordered by "the god in them." Eventually the god weakens, the kings' desire for gain (*pleonexia*) comes to dominate, and a corrupted Atlantis embarks on war and empire. This suggests that the preeminent movement in politics is unjust, except perhaps under extraordinary political order. But the extraordinary order of Atlantis is in practice to be wished for rather than expected, if I read the signs aright, for all is impossibly geometrical, beneficent by nature, divinely provided. In short, justice, one type of correct ordering by speech, seems to be incongruous with the politics of even an Atlantis. In the *Timaeus*, Plato gives a further account of the war between Athens and Atlantis, an account that concludes with destruction of both cities by earthquake and flood, and then turns to stories of the world's creation, of elements and matter, and of the making of man's soul and body. The incongruity of speech with politics is connected with an incongruity of speech with body in motion. Perhaps that is the reason why even this physics appears in a tale.

In *New Atlantis*, Bacon dismisses Plato's myth of Atlantis as "poetical and fabulous" and sets forth both a physics able to deal with powerful natural motions and a rhetoric able to deal with human motions. The crucial dealing is the organizing of human motions. The Baconian innovations appear in an anthropology or history of man which is notably Machiavellian or of a realpolitik character. The world of old Atlantis was no bed of roses and certainly no Garden of Eden, but rather a world of imperial nation-states fit to trade and war. Atlantis is the continent of America as peopled with separate empires engaged in various imperial campaigns. That old system of empires can be resurrected from its fall; the true fall is not from grace but from a great "civil or policed" power (in the words of the *Advertisement Touching a Holy War*). Bacon cautiously links such a fall in the West to a succession of political-religious empires ending with Christian Spain. While disdaining a virtue above politics, Bacon offers a reliable policy to make a great power, a power secure against human malice and natural disasters alike. Plato had talked of old virtue in a story passed on by old men from an Egyptian priest. Bacon images forth new improvements attested by science and promoted by adventurers. He writes not a leisurely dialogue provoking reflection, but a taut narrative of real progress that will spread a new creed of action.

A striking allusion to More's *Utopia* shows that *New Atlantis* departs from More's rather Christian morality as well as from Socratic diffidence about politics. Among the Utopians, there was a notable mating arrangement that allowed those contemplating marriage to examine one another's naked body for defects.[20] Bacon's Bensalemites, however, fear that a refusal after such intimate knowledge will produce "scorn." They have a "more civil way," in which a friend of each views the other bathing. To avoid offending pride, one might think, they offend modesty, for they remove such exhibitions from those in love and likely to marry. More had insisted on reserving sexual matters for the privacy of the family. Bacon revises this. How severely is apparent when one notes that More put this risky little exercise under public tutelage, and not of friends but of a respectable and honored matron and a trustworthy man. The Bensalemites provide no such guards. Weinberger wondered about the desires aroused in these friends, their fidelity in reporting defects, and the gossip, comparisons, and suggestions that will be spread.

In More's *Utopia*, these mutual examinations are one part of a policy to promote faithful and lifelong marriage. The Utopians punish premarital intercourse by proscribing marriage forever, punish a first offense of adultery with severe slavery and a second offense with death, and make divorce very difficult (the approval of their Senate is required). Every such stricture is absent from Bensalem. One may infer that the aims of strict monogamy and of sex within marriage are absent also. Having more than one wife simultaneously is forbidden, but nothing else. We are fobbed off with a show of restriction, except for some indirect, minor, and long-term financial inducements to follow parental advice. Bensalem does require that a (whole!) month pass between first meeting and marriage, and that children of those who marry despite parental prohibition be somewhat limited in their capacity to inherit. There are no prohibitions of premarital sex, unnatural acts, adultery, divorce, or multiple remarriage. The spirit of the law encourages early marriage to "vent" desire; "marriage is ordained a remedy for unlawful concupiscence, and natural concupiscence serveth as a spur to marriage." This revealing formulation is silent as to unnatural concupiscence, and one might infer that unnatural desire is only unlawful desire. In short, Bensalem practices sexual liberation under a show of respectable restraint, with some mild channeling through parents and by long-run financial calculations. The channeling toward marriage is not for reasons of morality but for reason of state: thus the king obtains the growth in population and the family discipline that is highlighted in the Feast of the Tirsan.

All in all, it would be a mistake to maintain that Bensalemite arrangements are severe and promote virtue. Nor can one conclude that Bacon would regret the liberation that he authorizes, for Bacon presents Bensalem's more civil way as decisively superior to the sexual morals of Christian Europe. In fact, it may be that sexual liberation is another way to win peoples to the new faith. *New Atlantis* seductively advances the new possibilities with a quick tale of naked bodies, and *Essays* authorizes the same in its own way by amoral and immoral discussions of family, marriage, and love (7, 8, 10). Bacon even presents the new ways as more moral than the European ways, and the presentation is impassioned. While the *New Atlantis* generally abstracts from fierceness, it exhibits one fierce act: Joabin's bitter indictment of European sexual morals as hypocritical and ineffective. The disguised little lesson in the new easy morals is ushered in by a long and memorable indictment of Christian and aristocratic austerity. All the indignation, hyperbole, and nudity may distract the reader from the fact that Joabin never answers the narrator's fundamental question: do the Bensalemites keep marriage well? We can see, I think, an extraordinarily clever mode of liberating Europeans from Christian morals and from morality itself. Joabin concludes by expressly repudiating More's *Utopia*.

Progressive Visions and Civil Policies

It is possible to suppose *New Atlantis* a completed picture, and neither a romantic vaporing nor a traditional utopia, and still to deny that it comprehends Bacon's definitive political views. Such is the interesting argument of Howard White.[21] White distinguishes works provisional in the Baconian corpus from works definitive, and calls the works about practical politics but provisional. The political prescriptions in the *Essays*, for example, may take us to the new world of progress, but they are not part of it, according to White, while the definitive *New Atlantis* is indefinite as to morals and politics. White holds that the *Essays* sets forth the political arrangements of a monarchical, imperial, warlike, and Anglican Britain, and these are to be only temporary; Bacon "would be the last to call the *Essays* definitive."[22] On the other hand, the *New Atlantis* is enigmatic because Bacon denied the possibility of "imagining the best political order before great progress had been made in conquering nature." Definitive arrangements are not spelled out, White explains, because they depend on scientific knowing and shaping of the passions, an endeavor that Bacon thought barely begun. Until the development of scientific psychology, "the passions are not yet stabilized"; the "hierarchy and historical stability of the passions" could not be known.[23]

But this argument proves too much as to what White calls definitive, and it neglects the definitive character of much that he calls provisional. Bensalem is not without various definite political provisions, as to mating, governing, and a scientific hierarchy, and it is clear enough about such aims as health, conservation of bodies, and prolongation of life. White himself describes a "definitive" Baconian morality that aims at prolongation of life, the highest function of applied science, and *New Atlantis* clearly supposes the future importance of sexual desire and desires for fame and wealth. "For upon every invention of value, we erect a statue to the inventor, and give him a liberal and honorable reward." Besides, many arrangements in such works as *Essays* and *History* are definitive; they are complementary to Bensalemite institutions, not contradictory of them. While White alleges contradictions between *Essays* and *New Atlantis*, these seem to result from doubtful readings of the *Essays*. Its politics are not principally monarchical, but republican, its religion is far from Anglican, and its society is not decisively warlike and fierce.[24] The *Essays* chiefly promotes an economic and utilitarian society and an administrative and popular state, and these are the infrastructure and regulation for technological progress and a nation-state that grows to empire.

In short, the growing Baconian nation-state is more than a vehicle that travels to scientific civilization. It is a mobile home. A transformed Britain will protect and incubate the new civilization, but it will also sustain it, and Britain will not be alone. While in essay 58 Bacon indicates the inevitable softening and decline of every commercial empire, in essay 33 he hints obliquely that colonies once "plantations" may become "countries." Britain's colonies may become no longer subject to old Britain, but new countries with their own new orders.

Perhaps one can understand thus the title of *New Atlantis*. In the story, Atlantis is the continent of the Americas on which have existed various particular empires (such as Coya, now Peru, and Tyrambel, now Mexico). Bacon implies that his teaching can reach to a new continent or world such as America, from which adventurers, perhaps in new colonies and countries comparatively free of old traditions, proceed further in their conversion to enlightenment. Various civil empires will be carriers of one modern empire over the mind. *New Atlantis* seems to imply one comprehensive state of mind, one new world or scientific civilization, but not one world country, and that, I have suggested in chapter 3, is also Bacon's proposal in the conclusion of the *Essays*, "Of Vicissitude of Things" (58).

The Progressive Vision as an Exaggeration of Future Security

The genuine difficulties in understanding the *New Atlantis* result from precisely its focus, that is, its vision of a realizable new state of security for which humanity can hope. For, I shall argue, the vision is exaggerated.

The work exaggerates the goods to come, and it conceals the evils that Bacon knows will also come. It is an image of future bliss, but an image purposefully distorted, and the purpose is rhetorical or rather political (in Bacon's effectual sense): to mobilize the young and daring and thus to help bring the new order into realization. The story promises health, enduring life, affluence, security, power over nature, and employment for the able and inventive. It conceals what more sober works such as *Essays* better reveal: the continuance of disease and death; an unrelenting attack on faith and morals and on the old regime; new techniques and forces for manipulating and forcing; and a society of worker ants comprehensively controlled by the state.

With a small amount of digging, it is not hard to see that the old consolations of religion are hardly more than a shell or image. Bensalem's attractions may seem old as well as new, familiarly religious as well as engagingly satisfying, but they recast the promise of life everlasting into plans for amelioration on earth. The Christian Europeans "think themselves between life and death" as Jonah was who fled the Lord, seek "grace in the eyes of this people," are healed by Bensalem, call the prospect of remaining in Bensalem "a picture of our salvation in heaven," and devote themselves to their governor-priest in words reminding of the promised land and the savior. Their acceptance by the state assured, they think themselves "free men, seeing there was no danger of our perdition," and go on to live "most joyfully." *New Atlantis*'s first section thus images forth the progressive liberation of Christian Europe from Christianity, I suspect, and the insinuation of a promise of earthly ease in its stead. "Happy," recite the Bensalemites in the only rites not for strangers that we are shown, "are the people of Bensalem." Thus grace and graciousness attend compassionate officials, and humanity, proffered with parentlike care, replaces the mercy of a heavenly father. *New Atlantis*, to which the conclusion of essay 13 seems to allude, applies the passage's formula: an image of humanity is the cash value of Christian charity.

The only priest we see ministers not to Bensalemites but to Christian strangers. His office is separated from his priesthood. In this sense, his church is separated from his state, and accordingly he is called governor, not reverend or father. One official is described as reverend, but merely because of his impressively luxurious dress, and the scientist of Salomon's House is consistently called Father. Other than he, Joabin the Jewish merchant is the most prominent citizen, and Bacon's versions of Solomon and Joab evince the biblical revisionism that Weinberger has clarified.[25] Bensalem is not decisively Christian, and it is not certainly not decisively Jewish. It is anti-Christian and anti-Jewish, albeit in a devious way designed to conciliate and transform the Christian nations and to assimilate and elevate the Jews. Even the revelation of Christ to Bensalem was authenticated by Bensalem's scientists; science is the authority for judging of divine grace. Salomon's House is prior to Christian revelation in both dignity and origin, and the priest himself calls it the light, eye, and lantern of the kingdom. Did the scientists manipulate as well as confirm? One sign that the revelation was genuine was an apparently miraculous pillar of light. We are eventually told of the scientists' ability to represent "all manner of reflexions, refractions, and multiplications of visual beams of objects," and to represent also all manner of "false apparitions, impostures, and illusions." However that may be, the Bensalemite revelation of Christ is odd on its face. Salvation is assured merely by promulgation of revelation; neither faith in the Savior, nor His grace, is required. We see Bensalemites hanging on the procession of the Father of Salomon's House, not on that of a priest or bishop endowed with divine powers. Sin and the wages of sin seem forgotten. The governor-priest of Strangers' House is a very tolerant and undogmatic fellow, secure in his faith that Bensalem is the unknown knower and that Salomon's House is the knowing eye.

The only comprehensive rite we are shown is the family Festival of the Tirsan. A potpourri of trifling luxury and movement distracts from the distinctive absence of even a semblance of Christian sacraments or aristocratic primogeniture. Twice the Tirsan prays, both times in private. While an official rewards him and his children for producing children, no priest appears to regulate morals or faith, the natural father gives the blessing, and the state pays for the feast. These rites conclude not by pointing to heaven or hell, but with music, dancing, and other pleasures here and now. First described as natural, pious, and reverend, the feast is next characterized by the narrator as natural and finally by Joabin, wise in Bensalem's policies and customs, as an "excellent institution." It is a human construction. The feast serves the king's artificial policy of increasing his subjects (and of regulating them) and not the Lord's divine command to spread His word and righteousness.

The subjection of religion may be by direct control as well as by indirect management, although we receive only hints as to the controllers. At one point, the governor-priest waxes enthusiastic and didactic about Bensalem's salvation from infidelity, through the "apostolical and miraculous evangelism of St. Bartholomew." A messenger interrupts him when he pauses. When he returns, the topic is the marvel of Bensalem as unknown knower, and our governor-priest smiles at the suggestion that Bensalem benefits from supernatural spirits. Does someone listen and direct from behind the scenes? We may conclude that Bensalem's softened Christianity is but a show of the familiar for those to whom enlightenment is yet strange. The Bensalemite audience for the miracle had sat as if in a "theater"; the parade of the Father of Salomon's House is a "shew" not Christian; the scientist's authentication of the miracle is after looking and contemplating, not after the experimenting extolled in *New Atlantis*'s last section. While the *New Atlantis*'s undermining of the old faith has been well described,[26] its magnifications of the new has not. But there are many signs that exaggerated novelty is an important secret of the fable's visionary appeal.

The Europeans are charmed by the promise of health and prolonged life, but they hear nothing of incurable disease and of death. The story parades health officials, medicinal fruit, spacious hospitals, effective pills, "water of paradise" for "prolongation of life," healing pools, recovery of the sick. Immortality, however, is not promised and, despite 1,900 years of science, is certainly not assured. That the sick might die goes unmentioned, and yet it is perhaps very quietly intimated. While seventeen of the Christian Europeans are in "sick cells," only ten "chambers" are provided for those who recover. No death is mentioned, no Bensalemite suffering in pain, no cemetery; yet there are novices and apprentices in the research establishment because the succession of scientists will "fail." No infirmity is said to accompany the Tirsan's old age; yet he is old. While the promise of prolonging life is paraded, in short, Bacon hides the grim old enemy whom we work to conquer and who will conquer us. He also hides the grim new possibilities for injury and death that come with our new power. New poisons, genetic changes in animals as well as plants, and new weapons—such threats from progress are buried within long lists of scientific preparations and instruments.

Similarly, we are plied with a promise of pleasant affluence, but any system of painful industry and production is kept well behind the scenes. The strangers find themselves supported by the state, offered rich and smooth foods and drinks, viewing colors and textures and materials richer and finer than Europe's. The account dwells on amplitude, variety, and luxuriousness, rather than appropriateness, simplicity, and beauty of form. It certainly does not dwell on how all this is grown, manufactured, or paid for, and we are provided no account of the economy or of the daily life of the people outside Salomon's House.

Again, there are hints. Strangers' House can provide for strangers because it has provided for itself: it has "laid up revenue" for thirty-seven years. It has certainly saved. Has it also invested? Is some sort of prudent provision for one's future a characteristic feature of the Bensalemites? We get the barest indications of the prominence of the economic in ordinary life. Joabin, the most prominent nonscientist, is a merchant. Bensalem retains a great commercial fleet just for trading among islands under its authority. A more subtle sign is the distribution of participants in the scientist's parade. They include no military men, no popular crowd, no aristocrats, but fifty foppish attendants, two religious men, and the officers and principals of the "companies" or guilds of the city. The economic groups alone follow the scientist; the others precede him. This, taken with the prominence of the merchant Joabin, might suggest that a progressive commercial and industrious infrastructure is to follow the rise of the new science, even if wise practitioners of enlightened ways continue to set forth a face reminiscent of traditional ways. Only in the *Essays* does Bacon develop this economic complement to technological advance: the work ethic, independent smallholders, an industrious middle class, and the prominence of those who rise by work, frugality, trade, investing, and finance.

Finally, there is the pervasive and exaggerated order in Bensalem—with hardly a sign of who and what, apart from the scientists and their establishment, wields such power over all.

The order is a pointed order, an order of pervasive security. Bensalem's arrangements combine humane concern with efficient provision, in a combination that might remind one of the best aspirations of the welfare state. Even where force is displayed it appears humane; the glove is velvet, or rather ultrasuede. While Bensalemites at first forbid the Europeans' ship to land, they are armed with batons alone, warn with signs, and display no cries or fierceness. From first boarder to great scientist, their officials seem solicitous as to the visitors' needs and wants, and the people at large are similar: all are free to welcome strangers and do so. They are "civil."

Bensalemites are civil in welcoming strangers, rather than wondering at them, and in avoiding scorn of one another, rather than directly judging one another. Strangers' House was furnished "civilly," as if conveniently or perhaps comfortably. Civil ways, it seems, provide for human needs, avoid offending the self-regard of others, and are convenient for the purpose and policy at hand. The visitors, after being cautioned against the eyes and spies of Bensalem, resolve to conduct themselves soberly and civilly. Civil ways go easily with orderly ways, and, indeed, the Bensalemites are orderly to a degree extraordinary, absurd, even sinister. The people are found "standing in a row," in "better battle-array" than an army, "as if they had been placed." Here exaggeration stands out. What could Bacon be suggesting by such extravagant portrayals of civil order? Are the people drugged or perhaps psychologically conditioned? Is a new orderliness possible in progressive times? Do the civil satisfactions of progressive civilization make consent or consensus easy? The last is certainly visible, both in the Europeans' conversion and the Bensalemites' peculiar order. Bensalem is free from traditional religious and political strife, and it is possessed of a pervasive faith that unifies leaders, people, and the old sects. No struggles between Rome and reform appear, nor any theological disputations or persecutions. Jew as well as Christian believes Bensalem his own. No clashes are shown between people and leaders, rich and poor, king and nobles. Officials, state, king, governor, father, and Father of Salomon's House are unhesitatingly obeyed. Every official performs his function, and with a loyalty immune to bribes or tips. Indeed, everyone does what he is ordered, whether at command of conservator of health or messenger from a higher power. Nor do officials dispute among themselves. While a variety of functionaries and institutions command, the commands complement and enforce one another. The people are orderly and the officials ordered, even by subtle gradations as to function and the color, texture, and shape of their clothes. All this order is the more remarkable since the relation of king, city, nation, state, and scientist is not clarified. The order that orders, the security for security, is hidden.

Again, a harsh side is indicated, even if not exhibited. Bensalem contains a state of government that controls by managing and by forcing, as well as by benefiting, although it more or less conceals the managing, and conceals more the forcing.

The significant illustration of management is the defense of Bensalem against the Coyans by the civil founder Altabin. Knowing his strength and theirs, he "handled the matter" so as to "compel them to render themselves without striking stroke"—and then freed them humanely. The image is provocative but dark. It may signify much, not least the way a science of control can handle the human matter by channeling its strongest motions, its private and bodily motions, toward a humane liberation. Or, to use the formula of Solamona, the founder of Bensalem's secrecy and science, Bensalem blends humanity with policy.

Humane promises lead the Bensalemites to willing and rather juvenile subjection, and that is the secret of easy government. Bensalemites at large are like docile children. Their social landscape is dotted with fathers and houses, symbols of the "parent-like care" that is the technique of conversion and of hidden government. They can be so civil because they are not full of pride or righteousness; the civil society in *New Atlantis* is built upon Bacon's critique of truth, goodness, honor, and nobility (as in essays 1, 13, 14, and 55). A great lord remains at a distance from the visitors' ship, not out of "greatness," but because of a regulation providing against infection. This lord is free of the pride of priest or aristocrat, warrior or philosopher, and obeys an official whose order is concerned for the lord's health. This is utilitarian reciprocity in practice, the intermixing of public duties with private services, and it is typical, for leaders as well as followers are more content with their roles, with serving and being served.

But less mutual methods of management are also indicated. Subordinates seem manipulated. While the great official keeps his distance for his health, a lesser officer had already boarded without any show of distrust. Generally, Bensalemites are for the use of the king, or of whatever it is that governs. The father of the family gets the opposite of a contemporary family-planning award. If he lives to see alive thirty persons derivative from his body and above the age of three, he receives a royal scroll addressed to friend and creditor; "for the king is debtor to no man, except for propagation of his subjects." While leaders are to serve, they serve for their own advancement, and thus the line between serving and manipulating disappears. The Father of Salomon's House, to take the leading example, is described not as being humane but only as appearing humane. He "had an aspect as if he pitied men." The great parade, the first public appearance in years by a great scientist, is a "shew," according to our cool narrator. In mixing humanity with policy, then, the most knowing Bensalemites probably give priority to policy.

While *New Atlantis* does not even hint at the brutal recipe that benevolence is an image to be managed by malice (*Essays*, 13), many readers have been disturbed by the shadowy pervasiveness of uncanny controls. There are signs of a power that verges on the sinister.[27] Management gives way to coercion as soon as the Bensalemites depart from their channels. The priest is interrupted by a messenger just after he waxes evangelical, and is called away; we are later told of devices for transmitting sounds in pipes and lines. The Tirsan's orders and decrees are enforced by the state if they are not obeyed by family members; the whole family festival is paid for by the state and planned in accord with the governor. Even when governing is indirect, from behind the scenes, it is nevertheless all-seeing and efficacious. The crucial illustration is the one event, the conversion of the Europeans, that we more or less see from beginning to end. There occurs an exact and insistent orchestration, from initial but humane rebuff through various stages of winsome attractions and coy prohibitions. Satisfactions to attract, controls to force, shows to bamboozle—all solicit reverence for the new state of things.

There is one explicit illustration of comprehensive political planning in *New Atlantis*, King Solamona's refounding of Bensalem 1,900 years before the travellers' arrival. Solamona had sought to ensure perpetuity for his kingdom by new "fundamental laws." In the little *Treatise on Universal Justice or the Foundations of Equity*, Bacon suggests that for laws to win certain obedience, they should mix efficacy with satisfaction.[28] That foundation guides what we see of Solamona's refounding. While the Governor of Stranger's House reserves some particulars as to Solamona's work, he promises that what he does tell will "give you satisfaction." He reveals the fundamental mixture within a manmade providence that can provide increasing satisfaction.

The Europeans began by asking how Bensalem could know of Europe's "state and business," while itself remaining unknown. After smiling at the supposition of a divine and fearful cause for this unknown knowing, the enlightened priest gives the real cause: worldly powers and ingenious policy. Long ago Bensalem engaged in extensive trade and navigation with other nations, but this commerce decayed as the trading partners declined. In response, Solamona instituted laws of secrecy that cut off Bensalem's own trade and communication abroad. Bacon tacitly links knowing with gaining, and this link, which shows how science has been tailored to policy, becomes thematic when the priest elaborates a singular exception to the prohibition on travel.

Teams of scientists are dispatched ("designed") to reside abroad with concealed identity, there to search other countries' affairs and state. They seek especially "the sciences, arts, manufactures, and inventions of all the world." Bacon calls this "Light, God's Light," in a way that vaguely recalls the philosophic travellers authorized by the Nocturnal Council of Plato's *Laws*. But Bacon's hidden emissaries seek "light of the growth of the world." Thus our priest-governor varnishes the new with the traditional: this light is not of the Lord's revealing, nor of nature, but of the arts of human production. One might mention another little sign. In our priest-governor's account of religion, he calls Salomon's House the eye of the kingdom; in the subsequent account of Solamona's political refounding, he calls it the lantern of the kingdom. Those who are politic will know that the real light in Bensalem is artificial, and that its emissaries are dealers in scientific and technological development. The term "trade" varnishes the fact. For the emissaries abroad do not trade development for development, but money for development, and their work is really industrial and scientific espionage: buying things and rewarding persons, as the governor puts it. By adding copies of others' discoveries to the systematic pursuit of their own, Bensalem can outstrip the others. The teacher of this lesson was Machiavelli: perpetuity in a state comes from increasing its relative power. The Bensalemites trade not knowledge for knowledge, nor power for power, but money for the knowledge that is power.

From the governor's speech we glimpse a power not elsewhere discussed in *New Atlantis*, the imperial nation-state. The governor presents it as without need of founding, although in need of defense, and thus abstracts from the civil changes that will be needed. But profound changes are intimated. Bensalem looks back to two hero-kings, Altabin as well as Solamona. Altabin was wise and a warrior who defended the old island trading empire of Bensalem against Coya, and our governor presents an anthropology of great trading empires, as if they had always existed. Yet he also shows that natural disasters overtook them, and that men became primitive and bare and were without "letters, arts, and civility." In Europe, too, he notes decline. Foundings are needed, and in Europe and elsewhere one must found the civil state as well as the scientific establishment. The two complement one another, and this is the most obvious political connection between the *Essays* and the *New Atlantis*. The true greatness of a great power is ability to grow, essay 29 tells us, and true knowledge is the faculty for growth of power. The visionary *New Atlantis* attends thematically to those powers that promise peoples an easier life; to that extent only are political matters discussed. The work abstracts from the domination of a new state of government and dwells upon a new and scientific state of mind. It also dwells upon the attractions of the new state of mind and masks its domination.

A Vision of Science

The promise of *New Atlantis* culminates in a vision of human power limited only by possibility, a science that will enlarge "the bounds of Human Empire, to the effecting of all things possible." The visionary side of Bacon's politics, no less than the civil side, culminates in the pursuit of empire. But unlike the realm of the cold, cold state, this empire radiates light and benevolence. Still, the darkest of dark shadows are here.

We are presented with scientists who seem respectful of God, truthful about nature, and benefactors of man. The Father of Salomon's House appears as a religious figure revered by the crowd. He blesses the multitude of strangers, blesses the narrator as his son, and obtains a kneeling obeisance that no other Bensalemite—not the priest—obtains. This is a strange Christianity. The priest for his part reveres the scientist in place of bishop, pope, and perhaps even the Lord.

The pseudo-religious aura surrounding scientific men and instruments is a sign. Science only appears to teach of God's works. It really produces works that master the nature that God (or something) provides. Science aims at "human empire," the "effecting of all things possible," rather than looking up to things good or holy, and it aims more than it looks or contemplates. The human horizon is redefined in accord with our purpose and powers. For example, Bacon calls deep places for underground experiments the "Lower Region," high places for experimentation, the "Upper Region," and mentions hermits twice, once as useful objects of study while resident in caves, again as useful observers while perched on heights. The peculiarities of divine madness or devotion are replaced by a disciplined devotion to useful causes, and the hermits turn methodical or white-coated and are told what to observe. Bacon turns the hope for "water of paradise" to a chemical compound and away from holy water.[29]

The scientists promise to reveal any natural work or thing "pure as it is." But does the new science inquire of things as they are? Is truth its aim? Bacon is more explicit elsewhere. The collection of experimental data is less of "nature free and at large," and "much more of nature under constraint and vexed; that is to say, when by art and the hand of man she is forced out of her natural state, and squeezed and moulded."[30] His science aims to find the special forces or "secret motions" involved in changing nature, and this promise of mastery extends to human nature.

These conclusions are actually on the face of every one of the twenty-four means of production that are the "riches" of Salomon's House. We are promised invention of living plants and animals without reliance on seeds or natural generation, of new "kinds" differing from the "vulgar" (the chief scientist abstains from the words "species" and "natural"), of ways to prolong life by replacing parts that seem perished and by resuscitating some that seem dead. So far can the new method make things "by art greater much than their nature." Such particulars are in perfect accord with Bacon's general determination to "stake all on the victory of art over nature" in order to win the "empire of man over things." Obey nature we must, but only in order to command her.[31] In *New Atlantis*, we see that such powers extend to human nature and human things, to finding "what may be wrought upon the body of man" and to imitating and constructing his movements. They extend also to what may be wrought on him in more subtle ways: to finding "deceits of the senses."[32] Do they extend to the mind?

The list of research instruments moves from powers drawn from nature as obvious to us, to more artful powers that exploit nature's secret and fundamental motions. There seem to be five levels: (1) artificial imitations of natural depths, heights, fluids, weathers, and bodies; (2) transformation of natural living things to the point of inventing new species (a power set forth in the central paragraph of the work); (3) powers for making useful compounds, such as foods, drinks, and medicines, out of new simples or natural simples; (4) powers to affect the appearance of things to man—to produce things seen, touched bodily or by magnetism, heard, smelled, and tasted; (5) fundamental powers that can be used to produce and transform compounds in general—new heats, motions, mathematical instruments, and deceits of the senses.[33]

While listing all these new powers, the Father promises benevolent uses, such as prolonging life, curing disease, inventing nutritional and medicinal aids. But he also indicates much less attractive uses and consequences. Virtue is mentioned only as a bodily force or motion, such as magnetism. Poisons are mentioned quickly and ambiguously, followed by powers to dwarf and make barren. The new powers to produce motions promise chiefly production of new weapons: more, faster, stronger, and more violent projectiles; new explosives and machines of war; new fires; planes and submarines.

But there are more profound implications. The last power listed is that to deceive the senses. One wonders about the possible effects of this (consider the conversion of the Bensalemites through the image of a pillar of light), and then one wonders further: what of powers to deceive the thoughts? The Father then summarizes: the powers we have listed, my son, are "the riches of Salomon's House." Does Bacon thus hint at an answer to the question we have asked and that he seems to solicit? Are not these solid powers of mastery in fact deceptions of the mind, that is, promises of satisfaction that cannot fully satisfy, but which, like the pillar of light, can serve as baits whereby the purveyors of science can win people to a new faith?

After remarking on the power to deceive the senses, our Father of science immediately insists that scientists are forbidden to show nature "adorned or swelling, but only pure as it is." We seem on the right track in our suspicions, despite the appearance of a reassurance, for precisely this assurance is a deception of the mind. To repeat, every one of the twenty-four powers is an invented power to use or master natural processes, not merely or chiefly to show a natural process as it is. Also, the scientists in the story do not show all of their findings (whether true to nature or not), or all of themselves. They hide their nationality abroad, for example, and at home they conceal inventions and experiences, which they "think fit to keep secret." In addition, they simulate as well as dissimulate, our Father presenting himself in a "shew" to induce reverence and showing an "aspect" of benevolence that in itself is merely a seeming. Nor are such semblances exceptional. A power to "deceive any man's taste" may produce new sweets and wines, and a power to produce refined stuffs may result in a carpet "like the Persian, but far finer." These are the kind of artificial and substitute appearances that enticed the story's Europeans and have enticed consumers ever since.

The powers of science can win for scientists reverence and wealth from people at large because they provide the causes of luxury, pleasure, and security. The secret of the scientists' power is the science's power, and the visible power of science culminates in a secret power, a power for some men over the minds of men generally. This is the power thematically afforded by the moral and civil sciences, especially the secretive sciences not included in *New Atlantis*'s methodical list, but applied in the whole story. These, too, are studies of secret motions, and especially of the most secret art of dominating others by managing one's own motion to dominate. This most secret Baconian formula of power is set forth, as we have noted before, in what might seem a place very out of the way, in an account of the science of nature. But the place fits, for Bacon's science of nature is an art of mastery, and Bacon there gives the secret of dominating men through an art of dominating nature and their nature. This formula is the core of both the civil art of obtaining followers and of the technological method of conquering nature. Actually, the distinction between technology and civil arts breaks down, for the empire of mankind over nature is also the empire of Bacon over mankind: "In civil actions he is far the greater and deeper politician that can make other men the instruments of his ends and desires and yet never acquaint them with his purpose (as they shall do what he wills and yet not know that they are doing it), than he that imparts his meaning to those he employs."[34]

The Power of the State

Any such grave explanation of Bacon's civil and natural science must fit somehow the surface messages of his works. One can certainly say that the *New Atlantis*, his culminating picture of politics and science in action, appears secretive as to who or what is in charge. The mystery of *New Atlantis* culminates in the mystery of who governs. As to the government of science, at least, there may seem no mystery. Scientists decide what inventions are to be distributed to the public and communicated to the state. Yet who or what decides to institute a science of invention? There was a political founding of science, by King Solamona. But how did he become a king, and why did he seek the perpetuity of his nation? Political questions emerge. Might Salomon's House be the equivalent for Solamona of the statue that seems to be much of the scientist's reward?

As to political government in the ordinary sense, the mystery is famous. While Bensalem is occasionally called a kingdom, and a king is mentioned, neither a royal person nor a royal action is shown. The only two active kings mentioned, Altabin the defender and Solamona the refounder, are from very long ago, 3,000 and 1,900 years, respectively. The closest thing we see to a royal act is a king's charter with a seal of the "king's image," and it is granted as "of course, and of right." We have already wondered whether kingly power is not chiefly kingly image, as in constitutional monarchy, and have noted, as other evidence, that islands nearby are governed by the "crown and laws of this state."[35]

Let us begin by reviewing the obvious. The governing we see is done by officials. An "officer" is the first Bensalemite to visit the strangers' ship; the lord who instructs them at a distance is ordered about by a health official; the persons governing are called governors. Bensalem seems controlled, as White says, by a bureaucracy. Priests are subordinate and ordered about, and aristocrats are not to be seen, although the show of luxurious pageantry disguises the absence of both. No aristocrats appear in the parade (unless the fifty fops are Bacon's gibe), and horses, their traditional mount and plaything, are expressly excluded "to save the tumult and the trouble." Family arrangements and mating arrangements are studiedly anti-aristocratic. Bensalem is not an old regime of estates. In *New Atlantis*, the term "estate" is always used for the condition or whole of the nation. Bensalem is often called a country and a nation, and its inhabitants are repeatedly called "the people," in a way that does not discriminate among estates in the traditional sense.

How should we reconcile the obvious authority of officialdom with the rather classless makeup of the people? To begin with, the people of Bensalem, while never seen governing, show a certain self-government. Admittedly, we are told of a king and never of assemblies, political votes, or parties, and the common people we see are preternaturally passive, orderly, and ordered like an army. Yet their appearances also show them controlling themselves. We are shown Bensalemites only in a family festival, and at a public welcome and a parade, and told of their reception of Christianity and of their mating arrangements. In each case, there is self-government, albeit as managed more or less by laws and by experts behind the scenes. Visible self-government is mixed with less-visible managers. *New Atlantis* thus indicates, I suspect, a largely self-regulating civil society under a regulating state. This has governmental implications. We see one choice of ruler, the selection of our narrator for private conference with the Father of Salomon's House. He is elected, subsequent to a managed nomination. After showing his own initiative and supreriority, and being singled out by Joabin to convey an invitation from the establishment, he is "chosen by my fellows," without exclusion of any of the meaner sort. Even *New Atlantis* may hint at the regulated republicanism to be seen in the civil works. Yet it indicates chiefly the pervasive power that institutes and enforces Bensalem's regulations: "the state."

The first official we see had a salary "sufficient of the state;" the state and not the king defrays the Europeans' expenses; the crown and laws are of this state. The greatest mystery of *New Atlantis*, the mystery of the invisible controller, is illuminated through this hidden state. All wonders, Bacon suggests, can be reduced to "causes" or "secret motions," and the secret motion of *New Atlantis*'s state is the key to Bacon's secretive civil science.

The word "state" occurs twenty-two times in *New Atlantis* (if one includes the three occurrences of "estate"), and I can distinguish four different but connected meanings. Eight uses connote an active government. An institution of men pays, gives license, defrays, hears demands, offers and receives only partial revelation of scientific discoveries. Six uses (including two of "estate") connote an established condition of living and progressing. Nothing is more worth knowing than "the state of that happy land," the "happy and flourishing estate wherein this land then was," the "true state of Salomon's House," the "good estate" of the family. I include under this head two ambiguous uses: "our state and business," because the strangers do not thus clearly refer to government, and "affairs and state," because equated with the condition of the arts and sciences. Six uses imply a condition of reverence, five times by odd references to a canopy or throne connoting status. The Father's arrival is "in state." Over the Tirsan's chair is a "state" curiously wrought and mentioned thrice in one paragraph, and the Father of Salomon's House has a "rich cloth of state" over his head and is seated in a room "without any degrees to the state" (any steps to the chair of state, as Gough and Weinberger explain). Finally, two uses refer to Bensalem as a comprehensive whole, not limited to government or condition of life. The governor of Strangers' House refers to islands under this state and to a fear that returning strangers will reveal this estate.

New Atlantis's state is, first, the government that operates efficiently behind the scenes (the first three uses of "state" and the last refer to this). The government is not a ruler or rulers, however, so much as an institution fixed by fundamental law. The present king seems but the crown, and the only active kings mentioned, from millennia past, are a general who defended the nation by ingenious policy and a founder who gave it perpetuity by fundamental laws. The obvious and public institution founded was the house of humane science; the less obvious institutions, the new civil society; the most secretive institution, the new government. The secretive state of officialdom is able to force by arms when its insinuating offers do not suffice. In short, Bacon's politics incline toward an impersonal administration with a humane face: toward an efficient ministering to human desires and necessities. While *New Atlantis* exhibits especially the humane face, the secret operations of government are explained by Bacon's separate accounts of founding a state, as in *History of King Henry VII*, of civil government, as in the *Essays*, and of fundamental law, in the *Aphorisms on the greater Law of nations* and the *Treatise on Universal Justice*.

Second, like other Baconian institutions, government is part of a broader establishment, a new condition of life and prosperity that we may call a society or perhaps a civilization. Progress in health, wealth, security, and power is the visible sign and attraction. New institutions of religion, family, sexual pairing, commerce, and science are more secret causes. *New Atlantis* focuses on the true state of a natural science. The new scientists will themselves have civil power, for, as instructed by Bacon's judgment, they will minister to obvious human needs and earn a reverence hitherto reserved for holy men. While *New Atlantis* focuses on the scientists, it also indicates a new prominence for other apparently nonpolitical classes, especially the merchant who defers to the scientific establishment and has a politic understanding of it and his place in the civil whole, and the Jews, who will be freed from both Christian obloquy and their fierce old parochialism. As Weinberger emphasized, praise of scientists is surpassed by praise of Joabin, "a wise man, and learned, and of great policy, and excellently seen in the laws and customs of that nation."[36] An enlightened commercial class, businessmen as we call them, sustains the economy that complements technology and supports the scientific establishment and the governance that regulate the whole system.

Third, there is a comprehensive state of mind above the new elite of officialdom and of independent businessmen, scientists, and private citizens. The top scientist, for example, sits under a cloth of state; the Tirsan sits alone "under the state." For fathers of science, fathers of families, and politic merchants, enlightened authority follows upon the new outlook. Progressive countries are governed by progressive civilization, of which the secret cause is a new plan for progress. The true state of Salomon's House, for example, was instituted by the mind of Solamona. Again, who planned for Solamona?

New Atlantis explicitly draws attention to the feminine form of Solamona. In essay 15, "Of Seditions and Troubles," Bacon discusses a feminine form of sedition, slanders, as opposed to tumult. We might speak of revolutionary ideas, as opposed to open rebellion. "Seditious envies" can cause "the best actions of a state, and the most plausible, and which ought to give greatest contentment," to be "taken in ill sense, and traduced." This expresses rather well the critical or negative aim of New Atlantis. The old regime's promises of salvation, nobility, and majesty seem impractical and pretentious beside the new mixture, of worldly visions with realistic powers, that Bacon advances in their stead. The secret cause of Solamona's plan is the mind of Bacon. He is the one alone who is under no state, and conceals something from every state, but who has secured enduring life through his estate, the living state of mind he instituted.

Notes

1. *Francis Bacon and Modernity* (New Haven and London: Yale University Press, 1986), 199, 11, 15, 16, 196–203.
2. *Dialectic of Enlightenment*, tr. John Cumming (New York: Continuum, 1982), Introduction and chapter 1, esp. 3, 42).
3. "Science and Rule in Bacon's Utopia: An Introduction to the Reading of the *New Atlantis*," *American Political Science Review*, 30 (no. 3) (September 1976), 872, 884, and passim; Introduction, in Bacon, *The Great Instauration and New Atlantis* (Arlington Heights, Ill.: AHM Publishing, 1980), vii–xxix.
4. *On Human Conduct* (Oxford: Clarendon Press, 1975), 287–300.
5. *On Human Conduct*, 289.
6. Frank E. Manuel and Fritzie P. Manuel, *Utopian Thought in the Western World* (Cambridge, Mass.: The Belknap Press of Harvard University Press, 1979), 244, 248, 258, 260.
7. *New Atlantis*, ed. Alfred Bradley Gough (Oxford: Clarendon Press, 1924), xi.
8. *N O* II, 10–52, in *Works* VIII, 178–350; IV, 126–248.

9. "Science and Rule," 867–69.

10. *N O* I, 113, in *Works*, VIII, 145; IV, 102.

11. See chapter 7 in this volume, and *Advancement of Learning* II, xxiii, 47, ed. Wright; *Works* VI, 377–78; III, 473–74; *De Augmentis* VIII, i, iii, in *Works* IX, 233, 297–99; V, 32, 78–79.

12. 35 end, 42, 13 end, and 58.

13. *Advancement of Learning* II, iv, 2, ed. Wright; *Works* VI, 203; III, 343.

14. *De Augmentis* II, xiii, in *Works* VIII, 440; IV, 276.

15. *Advancement of Learning* II, iv, 3, ed. Wright; *Works* VI, 203; III, 343–44.

16. *Advancement of Learning* II, iv, 3, ed. Wright; *Works* VI, 204; III, 344.

17. *Advancement of Learning* II, xviii, 2, 4, ed. Wright; *Works* VI, 297; III, 409.

18. See Robert P. Adam, "The Social Responsibilities of Science in Utopia, *New Atlantis* and After," *Journal of the History of Ideas*, 10 (1949), 374–98, esp. 382, 384, 390; Howard White, *Peace among the Willows* (The Hague: Nijhoff, 1968), 1–13, 97; Eva Brann, "An Exquisite Platform: Utopia," *Interpretation*, 3 (no. 1) (1972), 1–26.

19. Manuel and Manuel, *Utopian Thought in the Western World*, 243–60.

20. *Utopia*, tr. Peter Marshall (New York: Washington Square Books, 1963), 89–90.

21. *Peace among the Willows*; "Francis Bacon," in *History of Political Philosophy*, ed. Leo Strauss and Joseph Cropsey (Chicago: University of Chicago Press, 1987), 366–85.

22. *Peace among the Willows*, 230–31, 243, 245.

23. *Peace among the Willows*, 196, 198; "Francis Bacon," 371.

24. See chapters 2–5, 9, and 10 of this volume.

25. "Science and Rule," 876–80.

26. See especially Paterson, "On the Role of Christianity in the Political Philosophy of Francis Bacon," 419–22.

27. Consider Weinberger's Introduction to *The Great Instauration and New Atlantis*, xxv–xxix.

28. Aphorisms 2, 8, 13, in *De Augmentis* VIII, iii, in *Works* IX, 312, 314, 315; V, 88, 90, 91.

29. References are to paragraphs 21, 32, 25.

30. *Great Instauration* ("Plan"), in *Works* VIII, 48; IV, 29.

31. *N O*, I, 117, 129, 130; cf. 114, 116, in *Works* VIII, 146–63, IV, 103–15. These aphorisms are in the culminating and most candid section of Book I (115–30), addressed to the most ambitious readers (cf. 129).

32. Paragraphs 44, 19–32.

33. Paragraphs 21–28, 29–33, 34–37, 38–41, and 42–44.

34. *De Augmentis* III, iv, in *Works* VIII, 511; IV, 364.

35. Paragraphs 15, 16.

36. "Science and Rule," 881.

Chapter 12

The Foundation of the Project

Danger and Disillusion

What once seemed visionary promise and beneficent power has come to look very different in this late twentieth century. The bomb, world wars, revolutionary terror, and distinctively modern totalitarianism are not the only causes of doubt—for these might be thought abuses of power—but there is now also a worldwide movement of "postmodernism" that would liberate humanity from the modern vision itself. The plan for progress is indicted as the worst of powers, as a constructed domination over authentic human spontaneity. Precisely technological thinking involves the "extreme danger" to man, according to Martin Heidegger, the spiritual stepfather of postmodernism.[1] But such an animus fails to take political care for the peoples established under modern civilization, and it is a question whether only technological thinking (even in Heidegger's profound sense) is the foundation of the problem. In Bacon's understanding, at least, the aim of the new "art of interpreting nature" was "the kingdom of man" over nature, but that aim depended on a foundation in an amoral and power-seeking self. A certain moral or anti-moral philosophy was at the foundation of his technological thinking. This concluding chapter first considers some contemporary diagnoses of the modern project and then reconsiders the Baconian diagnosis. The attempt at a science of power, and the starting point in a self driven to dominate, were problematic from the start.

"The road we have taken for granted," said the biologist Loren Eiseley, is now filled with "shadowy menace,"[2] and the words capture a foreboding now widespread. Eiseley's awe before Bacon's genius had been shaken by nuclear weapons and mass communications, but one has also to consider a more obvious political menace in the Baconian plan. Bacon had eulogized Severus and Augustus, and he urged upon dictators who fol-

lowed in such footsteps a ruthlessness and an image making resolutely
unscrupulous even compared to the originals, because systematically cyn-
ical as to moral restraint and as to goodness in general.[3] His model was a
more resolute Caesar with a new science. There are disturbing fore-
shadowings of the distinctly modern dictators, of a Hitler with propaganda and a mechanized Wehrmacht and of a Stalin with propaganda and
thermonuclear weapons. It is true that Bacon urged humane benevolence
and would restrict politics to protecting universal interests, but it is also
true that his humanitarianism was ultimately a policy for domination by a
leader and his cause, and that a type of brainwashing and exploitation
were involved in his management of men by their interests. The science
of power serves most those bent on power and encourages a radical exploitation of man as well as nature.

The problems that attend modern science are nevertheless separable
from the special problem of tyrants and conquerors, if only because the
means of manipulation and destruction are available for peoples, intellectuals, and oligarchies. One wonders, as Eiseley wondered, whether the
harnessing of the atom does not make the new science's power for death
overshadow its power for life. However grateful we have to be for the
cures, the prosperity, and the ease bestowed by scientific research and
modern management, the capacity to destroy humanity is an innovation
that accuses the whole movement to innovation. Defenders of Baconian
science rightly remind us of the overarching project to benefit humanity.
But does the benefit outweigh the harm? Two hundred years ago, Jonathan Swift described kings newly oppressive, because they were armed by
science, and peoples newly disoriented, degraded, and subservient, because of moral confusions and bizarre hopes for newfangled solutions. A
hundred years ago, Mark Twain, who no more than Swift was a friend of
mere reaction, pictured the cold destructiveness of idealistic Yankees
armed with machine guns and electric weapons. The poison gas, mechanized arms, and massed nations and resources of a first world war sobered
a broad spectrum of progressives, two decades before a second showed
how weaponry, mobilization, and terror might be multiplied exponen-
tially.

Yet it is a question whether even the new dangers from mass tyranny
and mass destruction are the chief modern dangers or even the most distinctive ones. They are not unlike floods, storms, epidemics, and earth-
quakes, which were once presumed the inevitable menaces of a shadowy
fate. It is a modern irony that the project to master fate has led to artificial
powers more ready, more destructive, and more attended with signs of
evil because more in our power. But it is also true that humanitarian
hopes for the relief of suffering often lead to exaggerated expectations of

peace, as well as exaggerated revulsion at the horror of war and the special horror of modern war. It may be that such expectations rely on strange hopes for the mastery of human nature (of "aggression," in this case), expectations that founders of the modern project fostered, but did not much share.

What of the moral and political disorientations less urgent than the dangers of the technological powers, but more serious, in many circumstances, for the soul? In Swift's parody of scientific civilization in *Gulliver's Travels*, the leading inhabitants of the mathematical-physical flying island have one eye aimed at the stars and another at the earth; they have to be reminded to listen and speak to a human. They disdain conversation and wisdom not mathematical or musical, and their wives, much as the female leads in any of a thousand contemporary films and novels, leave them for low-class ignoramuses who at least show some eroticism and spirit. Swift saw that preoccupation with progress engenders a comprehensive confusion in outlook, and his graceful if biting satire has become a twentieth-century industry. The theme is all about in indictments of the work ethic, the lonely crowd, specialists without heart and voluptuaries without vision, middle-class softness, consumer society and conformity, the joyless quest for joy, the culture of narcissism, the secular society, and liberation for nothingness. "Precisely if the bombs do not go off," Heidegger contended, there are more insidious menaces, especially the systematic organization that socializes, and the manipulative busy-ness and thoughtlessness of everyday life. Even if progress should ease unequivocally the conditions of life, it may be bad for life.

While this message is now broadcast wholesale, it has been a theme or the theme of every serious modern philosopher since Jean-Jacques Rousseau. Kant attacked the preoccupation with self-interest; Marx attacked acquisitive industrialism and the mean oligarchic entrepreneurs; Nietzsche and Heidegger attacked scientific rationality, mass man, and the bureaucratic and managerial state. The struggle became more bitter as the vision of equal rights and humanitarian policies, which Rousseau and Kant continued to defend and Marx somewhat to presuppose, itself came under attack. Great nineteenth-century empires of managed freedom and solid progress found themselves in desperate twentieth-century struggles against virulent enemies also theoretically inspired. While the fascists and the Marxists may have been defeated, this stage of the modern war of ideas is far from concluded. However the culture wars may work out in various countries and times, it is clear now that the philosophic attempt to restrict the human horizon to "real interests" has provoked philosophic revulsions almost without limit, and with a zeal to liberate mankind from any restrictions that reason might set.

But it would be cruel to punish whole peoples for a tradition that has fallen upon them, and it is fanatically cruel to punish irrationally and without limit. Statesmen who are not fanatics can distinguish well enough between difficulties in some modern theories, and the good and bad things (many not involved with theories) in this or that modern country. Vast peoples and cultivated classes alike find in the industrialized democracies their homes, freedoms, and prosperity, and much of their work, morality, and faith. Hope for the future is there a crucial faith, equal opportunity a needful condition and a principle of right, work and the fruits of labor an everyday occupation and discipline, economic and political systems the government. Also, these popular republics have had the benefit of great waves of reform. Locke's liberalism provided for representative government, popular spiritedness, and the natural rights of man; Rousseau insisted upon democratic justice, democratic citizenship, and a self at peace with itself; Kant's progressive liberalism gave priority to world peace and the moral dignity of persons; Burkean conservatism, to upholding character, church, and hierarchy. Still, sustaining even the renovated versions of the modern nation-state has not been easy, and the future may be harder, what with the revolt of much of the intellectual class that once devised, guided, and reformed. Practical statesmen will have to persevere despite self-described navigators often in mutiny and using an old compass much disdained.

Such a litany of commonplaces skirts powerful objections and will seem avuncular. But better a sympathetic uncle than a resentful stepson, at least when many are tempted to dismiss indiscriminately the accomplishments of modern times and to advance a sweeping irrationalism that could in its enthusiasm legitimate a Hitler as a triumph of the will. Disillusion now extends to the root. A large class of intellectuals is proud to be liberated, and to be liberated is to be alienated from modern civilization despite its almost worldwide triumph in the liberal democratic form. The alienation is not least from sobriety and prudence, since, under the guidance of Nietzsche, some intellectuals perceive practical reasonableness as indistinguishable from contemptible utilitarianism. Individualism, representation, and progress are equated with a disciplinary prison; technology and science, with alienation of our very being. Attacking the Age of Reason, such thinkers attack reason. Precisely *logos*, understood by unmodern philosophers not as just a tool but as the defining light, is called the prime oppressor. But can an attack on reason by reason even be stated coherently?

One wonders whether this attack on the core reaches the core, and, in particular, whether the liberating prescription is not infected by the special prescriptive rationalism that it would attack and to which it is accustomed. The counterculture of deconstruction often looks like a mirror-image of its enemy, a Baconian-style construction of civilization. It shares the first and preconstructive step, critical thinking. Only after Bacon condemned human opinions wholesale, as but a welter of prejudices, was he free to substitute wholesale a masterful method on a foundation of fear. While liberated postmodernists would deconstruct the enlightened and security-oriented constructions, they too disdain everyday opinions as but foundationless values or prejudices. They disdain especially the decisive distinction without which everyday life is unthinkable and impossible, that between good and bad. They are then constitutionally unfitted for the first requirement of postmodern prudence in a modern world, a thoughtful discrimination between better and worse versions of modern societies. Nor is the acid of critical skepticism the only inconsistent residue. In this late twentieth century, the call for liberation is commonly in the name of "autonomy," which cannot but remind of the "self" and, in general, of the singular individualism at the core of Baconian progress. Thinkers in our time are understandably troubled and doubting, but some are irrationally radical in their activism because they are not radical enough in their thinking.

The Problem of the Foundation

There is little doubt that Bacon's philosophy is of the sort now attacked as foundationalism; it probably originates the methodical empiricism that is the chief target.[4] At first, this reader like many readers had been most impressed with the versatility of Bacon's extraordinary genius. Bacon manages a variety of literary forms, and he revises and invents arts and sciences from chemistry, meteorology, and biology, to communications, the art of rising, and political economy. Yet the many sides prove to issue from a single beginning. It is not that all Baconian writings say the same thing, but that what each says seems calculated and disciplined with a view to the same basis, namely, skepticism of ordinary knowing combined with a plan for progress by controlled knowing. A distinctive unity differentiates the plethora of Baconian works from the many dialogues of Plato or the plays of Shakespeare. The unity of Bacon's works is calculated according to plan. Nothing by Shakespeare or Plato, or by Aristotle, for that matter, corresponds to the six-part "Plan" that explains Bacon's systematic arrangement of his *Great Instauration*, that is, his institution of the mind of man over the universe. At the very start of the *Instauration*, the "Proemium" gives the unifying spirit. "The entire fabric of human reason" hitherto employed in the "inquisition of nature" is ill-constructed, "like some magnificent structure without any foundation." There has been an initial and age-old error, a reliance on natural consciousness and especially on the "false powers of the mind." The mind is misled from the start because the senses are misleading from the start. Words have been derived from "notions," and "the primary notions of things," which the mind imbibes from the senses, are "false, confused, and overhastily abstracted." But the radical defect hitherto need not occasion despair, and it is even a reason for better hopes from new ways. We are "to try the whole thing anew upon a better plan, and to commence a total reconstruction of sciences, arts, and all human knowledge, raised upon the proper foundations."[5] This is the Baconian revelation. A clean sweep of learning, and even of intellect itself, can clear the ground for immense and progressive constructions on a solid foundation. What might seem a precursor to brainwashing, and to totalitarian mind control, is according to Bacon an ingenious method of concentrating effort on the real human necessities.

In light of present-day controversies, one should reiterate that this mixture of skepticism and resolution is, in Bacon's opinion, a radical break with all past thinking and especially with the tradition of philosophy. The old philosophers had "whirled" about in endless disputes with no "issue" or "result," and this not least because they were bewitched by notions from the senses and mind. A science that reasons thus about nature is like a kingdom or state, in Bacon's wonderful simile, that directs its affairs not "by letters and reports from ambassadors and trustworthy messengers, but by the gossip of the streets."[6] An examination of various opinions by conversational dialectic may be "the most ordinary method" of inquiry, according to Bacon, and it is even a very "simple and inartificial" method. But it is worthless. Precisely the ordinary and apparently natural mode of inquiry has "no foundation at all, but rests only upon opinions and is carried about with them."[7] To be useful, the natural consciousness, like nature in general as it has chanced to congregate, must be conquered and managed.

The problem is not solely with dialectical philosophy, but also with the old-style empirical investigations that are somehow oriented by the appearances of things. However "accurate" a work such as Aristotle's history of animals, for example, it is merely "composed for its own sake," contains "variety of natural species only, and not experiments of the mechanical arts," and in general fails to take advantage of "the vexations of art" in getting at the "secret workings" of things.[8]

The difficulty is not chiefly in the orientation by appearances, then, but in the lack of an orientation by human power. Bacon also attacks the pre-Socratic and materialist philosophers, whose attention to bodies and parts, beneath the surface of things as they appear to man, he is inclined to praise. At least the old corpuscularists removed God and mind, intelligible species and final causes, from an account of the structure of things.[9] But while Democritus, Empedocles, and the others may have attended to the right thing, they did so only in part and in the wrong way. It sometimes seems as if Bacon's praise of the pre-Socratics is but a tactic for putting down Aristotle and Plato.[10] Be that as it may, he concludes that the atomists, for example, are for the most part "so busied with particles" that they hardly attend "to the structure," wherein lies "abundance and excellence of power," and, while attending to "the material principles of things," they are negligent as to "principles of motion, wherein lies all vigour of operation."[11] Even if the old materalists attended to bodies and sensation, they, too, tended to inquire as to the "first principles of things and the highest generalities," whereas "utility and the means of working result entirely from things intermediate." They were too philosophic, one might say. They arrived at the atom by intellectually dissecting nature in a way not much different from Aristotle's arrival by abstraction at matter as pure potentiality—"things which, even if true, can do but little for the welfare of mankind."[12] In adopting uncritically notions such as "atom" and "elements," indeed, they were perhaps less self-critical than the dialectician Socrates, who spent his time examining opinions. Talking of being philosophers, they no less than the Socratics were really sophists and founders of sects.[13]

In short, Bacon does not return to the empiricism or natural philosophy of the pre-Socratics or of Aristotle. He is not an atomist, or an empiricist, but an experimentalist, and he does not return to induction, but turns to a "new form" of induction. His "greatest change" is this move from experience, or the old induction, which concludes "at hazard" from sensations, to experimentation, which is experience controlled by method as to object and question.[14] The pre-Socratics and the Socratics alike neglected the true question of natural science, which is, as Bacon says while discussing Democritus, the "practical question." It is the question "whether all things may be made out of all things."[15]

Out of concern for utility, it seems, Bacon abandons altogether philosophy as both the Socratics and the pre-Socratics meant it, that is, as a

quest for the most comprehensive truth, or for knowledge of the fundamentals of the whole.

This conclusion has always been disputable because of Bacon's equivocations, and it could appear that his science remains devoted to the "superiority of theory to practice," or at least that it continues the old devotion to contemplation in a modified form that focuses not on species
but on "a regular pattern of the corpuscles."[16] Bacon can be found to
declare very conspicuously that truth is the "sovereign good of human
nature," and that "contemplation of things as they are" is "in itself more
worthy than all the fruit of invention."[17]

But such statements are contrary to the general tenor of Bacon's discussions. They are also very few in comparison to the many massive dec-
larations that what is at stake is "no mere felicity of speculation," but the
"real business and fortunes of the human race, and all power of operation"; that "I am principally in pursuit of works and the active department of the sciences"; and that "the true and lawful goal of the sciences
is none other than this: that human life be endowed with new discoveries
and powers."[18]

Also, when one examines the traditional-sounding celebrations of contemplation, they are conspicuously incongruous in style (looking like little
catechisms), and they are at odds with the positions being staked out. The
eulogy of truth occurs amidst an argument that men love the lie, "flickering candle-lights," more than the truth. Those like Lucretius who profess love of truth are actually ambitious for a security above the dangers
of life; such philosophers really seek to make a name and found a sect.[19]
The eulogy of contemplation is a tiny aftermath of Bacon's famous portrayal of the new science as a means to the greatest of names. Since the
art whereby "all things else may be discovered with ease" can "establish
and extend the power of the human race itself over the universe," its
founder can acquire the most imperial and lasting of honors.[20] In context,
then, the effusive little professions of an old faith look suspiciously like
reassurances for the gullible.[21] Both passages praise "light" as a likeness
of truth or contemplation, although the light that Bacon's works finally
commend is the "lantern" of experimentation made by man for his purposes, not the natural light that shows things as they appear to man. Besides, Bacon elsewhere corrects the old philosophers' self-understanding
of themselves as philosophers. Talking of love of truth, they were really
moved by "vain-glory"; talking of philosophy. they were really the sophists that they would disdain.[22] The vaunted Aristotelian logic of inquiry
was really only a mode of overcoming "an opponent in argument."[23]

This is not to deny that Bacon's is a modified form of knowing, but it is to assert that the decisive modifications are determined by an end that is productive, rather than contemplative. The object of knowledge indeed involves patterns and corpuscles, the "latent structure" of things (as Bacon calls it), but it involves principally laws of action and forces, the "latent process" that produces effects in things.[24] This principal effect or object is the secret of the superiority of the new logic to the old, "the effect of the one being to overcome an opponent in argument, of the other to command nature in action." In short, Bacon certainly sought real knowledge of what nature is, not mere techniques of production, but he held such knowledge and all serious knowledge as instrumental to the victory of art over nature—and not as an object for its own sake. There is a famous formula. "Now the empire of man over things depends wholly on the arts and sciences. For we cannot command nature except by obeying her."[25] We look at nature not out of wonder but out of necessity, and we obey what we must in order to command what we can. Knowledge is useful, and real knowledge is necessary for real mastery. "For though it be true that I am principally in pursuit of works and the active department of the sciences, yet I wait for harvest-time, and do not attempt to mow the moss or to reap the green corn. For I well know that axioms once rightly discovered will carry whole troops of works along with them, and produce them, not here and there one, but in clusters."[26]

In a crucial part of the *New Organon*, Bacon actually shows how his science is deduced from "foundations which have relation to practice." A section of nine aphorisms introduces the definitive Book II, and its topic is eventually described as the "scope of doctrines" (*doctrinae scopo*, II, 10). The fourth aphorism, defining the object of knowledge, is singularly free of equivocation. While the roads to "human power and human knowledge" lie close and are nearly the same, nevertheless, because of the "habit of dwelling on abstractions," it is safer to begin and raise the sciences from those foundations which have relation to practice, and to let the active part itself be as the seal which prints and determines the contemplative counterpart." The practical end determines the type of knowledge sought. It determines, in particular, the quest for laws, what Bacon elsewhere calls "laws of action" or "rules of operation." For when one considers "if a man wanted to generate and superinduce any nature upon a given body, what kind of rule or direction or guidance he would most wish for," it is a direction "*certain, free, and disposing or leading to action*" (Bacon's emphasis). We may be resigned as to knowing fundamentals, but we must be resolute as to formulas of production. Antonio Pérez-Ramos catches the relation: Bacon insists that "the true aim of science is absolute certainty in operation, whilst emphasizing the provisional character of theory."[27] There is no doubt that Bacon is devising new forms of induction and of theory-building, the new logic of which he was so proud. But the new logic is for useful knowledge, and the use shapes the logic. Bacon is not imposing utilitarian ends upon some neutral instrument, and he is not simply accepting some practical or productive philosophy from the past. He is innovating as to experimentation, analysis, and generalization, but these obtain their imprint from the end of power, from the end of "human empire" or the "kingdom of man" that he repeatedly calls decisive.[28] The chief methodological innovations are an orientation by our questions rather than by the way nature presents itself; by questions as to the causes of production ("whereby" rather than "wherefrom"); by the kind of answers obtained from the arts; by "analysis" of parts rather than consideration of wholes; by torturing or forcing nature rather than experiencing or contemplating it; by "subtlety" or latent process and structure; by the "passions" or motions of matter more than by particles as such; by "axioms" that will systematically generalize causes; by "intermediate" axioms especially; and by a progression to more general and powerful laws. The new scientist is to try nature in a new court, in short, for the purpose of extracting knowledge useful to his state. Actually, the proper analogy for the laboratory is less a court of justice than a unit of a vast army. Bacon's famous language is not of equity in knowing the truth about nature, but of the "conquest of nature" for the relief of man's estate.

To summarize, Bacon's science is not principally contemplative of nature, for it begins by considering nature as material for human power. It is more like a productive art than traditional philosophy or science, and in the *New Organon*, Bacon calls it an art, "the art of interpreting nature."[29] It will give power over nature by discovering and managing the powers in nature. While the new science continues to presume that philosophy is possible, or at least that knowledge is possible, it is so far from the old philosophy that Bacon refuses even to argue on the old ground. He will not abide "a tribunal which is itself on its trial," since he questions all that "premature human reasoning which anticipates inquiry, and is abstracted from the facts" rashly and too soon. Let his method be judged by its own measure, that is, by its "results," for his way is not an opinion to be held but a "work to be done."[30]

But how true is a science that is oriented more to power than truth, that is more art than science? A theoretical difficulty arises with the turn by theorists to "foundations which have relation to practice."

If the art of interpretation seeks what in nature serves our purposes, does it show nature as it is, or merely aspects as they affect our purposes? Does it even show us that a "nature" is present? Is its purposive interpretation merely a construction of utilitarian meanings, and merely systematically misleading for being methodical?

This difficulty has been well known at least since Nietzsche and is well known within the precincts of science itself. According to the physicist Werner Heisenberg, in *Physics and Philosophy*, "the ground" of modern physics has in the twentieth century come to seem arbitrary, that is, reflective of the scientists' "subjectivity" of method and especially of their judgment as to what will count as "results." "What we observe is not nature in itself but nature exposed to our method of questioning."[31] Heisenberg traced the problem to the founders of the new physics in the seventeenth century (he does not mention Bacon). They focused, he said, not on a fundamental substance, as had the ancient materialists, but on the "dynamic problem." They supposed that the world consisted of things in space and time; things consisted of matter; matter can produce and be acted upon by forces; events follow from the interplay of matter and forces. Such formulations made up the classical concepts, according to Heisenberg, and they accompanied a change from a contemplative to a pragmatic attitude toward nature. "One was not so much interested in nature as it is; one rather asked what one could do with it." Each science was pictured as "a crusade of conquest into the material world." But the consequence of a searchlight so focused is a very narrow illumination, and physics in particular looks at "a very limited part of reality," a small portion of the universe.[32] Yet the classical physicists believed that the new method would lead to the decisive truth about nature, not merely to useful tactics and strategies. Bacon supposed the same, despite his foundation of science in practice and his description of science as "art." The new method was a path to knowledge as well as to power, he presumed, and the knowledge gained by methodical investigation of powers will reach the processes fundamental to nature.

But this assumption leads to another difficulty: methodical knowing proves to presuppose the pre-methodical knowledge that it disowned. "Simples," "particles," "latent processes," and "latent structures" are not merely working hypotheses, since they define what to look for. Also, they are assumed as true in Bacon's initial dismissal of other accounts of nature (such as Aristotle's suggestion of natural species or forms), and, above all, in his dismissal of the natural senses and understanding themselves. Prior to experimentation and prior to epistemology, Bacon assumes that he knows that species are imaginary, that natural senses miss the "subtlety" that alone is real nature, and that "intellect" fixes on notions that are really imaginary abstractions. If this is true, then the argument for experimentation relies on pre-experimental notions. But such notions are the "anticipations of mind" that Bacon decried as misleading abstractions and imaginings. At the foundation of Baconian skepticism is dogmatism. Underlying the critical thinking that underlies his method is an assumption that nature is composed of bodies and forces. If this difficulty is real, one must consider in nonexperimental ways the adequacy of Baconian experimentalism and of its assumptions as to nature.[33]

The Problem of the Self

For the Baconian science of nature, these difficulties come to a head with the science of human nature, especially the sciences moral and civil. There is little doubt that Bacon extends the reign of his new science or art to such topics, for he says so, and *De Augmentis* contains such sciences. Progress requires that "natural philosophy" be applied to particular sciences, including "what might one more wonder at, moral and political philosophy, and the logical sciences"; else they will not be "profound" and will glide along "the surface" of things.[34] Many Baconian works revamp ethical and political science in just such a spirit. "Nature in men" is said to be an underlying force that can be mastered by being channeled, and this outlook on human nature leads to arts of domination quite different from the Socratics' orientation by natural ends or at least by opinions as to the good.[35] It is true that Bacon can be found to say that "the received philosophy, or others like it," may deal with discourse and the "business of life," and one could infer from such remarks that he confines his new science to nature while leaving moral and political science to ancient political philosophy.[36] Yet these reassurances seem to be rhetorical smoke. In the prefatory distinction of his philosophy from the received philosophy, for example, only Bacon's own way is said to deal with "invention"—the other is mere "cultivation" and called "anticipations of the Mind." The context is again that of allaying heart burnings of those devoted to the ancients, and the reservation of some place for ancient learning is distinctly equivocal. The formulation leaves room for "other" philosophy "like" the received opinions in attending to human business, room that the *New Atlantis*, *Essays*, and other such civil and literary works manage to occupy.

What then is the foundational relation between Bacon's science of nature and his account of human ends? "Our steps must be guided by a clue, and the whole way from the very first perception of the senses laid out upon a sure plan."[37] Bacon may be famous for method and vast plans, but there is a "clue" at the bottom of it all. The clue has to do with the human purpose of power and progress. In the *Essays*, the practical work *par excellence*, Bacon tells us that the "true logician" has "as well judgment as invention,"[38] and that not only inventions, but also studies in general, are merely useful instruments. "Simple men" may "admire" studies, but "wise men use them; for they teach not their own use; but that is a wisdom without them and above them, won by observation."[39] What then is the crucial wisdom as to "use" that guides all studies, but is from observation?

The crucial observation is of one's revulsion from death, or at least of one's desire for continuing; "immortality or continuance" is that "whereunto man's nature doth most aspire."[40] The key observation as to what is useful is the feeling of a passion, not an observation through the senses or an inkling of the intellect. It is actually a mix of feelings or passions, as we contended in chapter 4. The elemental human motion mixes a fundamental concern for "endur(ing)" or "long-lasting," of which the essay on health policy speaks in significant tones ("there is a wisdom in this beyond the rules of physic," 30), with a spirited revulsion from death and in general from our situation of adversity, of which the essays on anger, adversity, and revenge speak (4, 5, 57). Perhaps all human beings are moved by fear, but those of wit and will are moved also by "spirit," that is, by a passion for revenge against those who consign them to oblivion and by an anger against their fate.

The wise plan can satisfy both the many and the few. Bacon's is the wise plan. Given a certain possibility of "electing" one's customs and dispositions, and thus superinducing "natures" on one's body and on those of others to follow, one can make a name and thus an afterlife through benefiting others. One can make a state that provides peoples with security here and now and the ambitious few with an enduring name for themselves. This then is the "observation" and the "wisdom" at the foundation of Bacon's manifold projects and plans.

There are difficulties in Bacon's account of nature, and they boil down in his account of human nature to these: what Bacon calls the basic observation is a dogmatically pruned observation, and what he presents as a passion prior to the "abstractions" of perception and mind is dependent upon them. These paradoxes infect the paradoxical doctrine of the "self." Bacon maintains that the self is bent on "continuance" or "enduring," mere life pruned of human qualities, but he also assumes that life involves the qualities of being an individual and a human individual. The life of the self is thus central, since all is for its sake, but it is by itself idiosyncratic to the point of hollow, and it proves to depend on qualities outside itself. It strives like all human selves to overcome its own vulnerability, but it tends toward the merely individual with no definite shape or form. The seeds of the strange modern tensions between objectivity and subjectivity, and of the paradoxical doctrines of autonomy, self-making, self-expression, and self-overcoming, are there from the start.[41] We turn to defend these assertions.

Is the primary Baconian "observation" a real observation, as Bacon must maintain, or is it an artifical reduction pruned according to theory? While anyone may feel within himself the powerful presence of fear, anger, or revenge, he may also discern opinions about what is fair and good, and feel inclinations to, say, friendship and to what is beautiful. That not all feel the same things is true but irrelevant, for not all feel fear, anger, and revenge as most powerful, and universal feelings are not necessarily the measure of what is good and true. Actually, the two classes of things (feelings and inclinations or opinions) are not separable, because a decent person feels shame, if out of fear he fails to do what is right, whereas a nasty person does not. Nor are opinions and inclinations without power in themselves. According to Bacon's own account, ambitious princes of the order of Julius Caesar pursued friendship at cost to their own projects ("Of Friendship" 27). But Bacon treats friendship as illusion and denies it any moral force, despite the feeling and force that a Caesar might observe.

The reason for Baconian reductionism is at first glance his understanding of nature. "Of Friendship," for example, explicitly reduces friendship to the "ordinary course of nature." The attraction of friends is like that of "bodies" in general, where "union strengtheneth and cherisheth any natural action." The example is characteristic, for Bacon reduces feelings of the good, the true, and the beautiful to illusions which are not real or natural. But that means that a theory of nature controls Bacon's decisive observations; it controls what was supposed to control it.

At the bottom of Baconian reductionism, however, is finally a skepticism as to the naturalness of human ends, or of what is opined to be good. Critique of morality seems to be the first step in pruning what one might observe into what, according to Bacon, is really to be observed. "So that we are much beholden to Machiavel and others, that write what men do, and not what they ought to do."[42] Bacon's primary observation of human feeling is not primarily an observation, because it is shaped by the moral skepticism of Machiavelli.

It is not as easy as one might think to follow such critical thinking.

Apart from what Bacon arbitrarily dismisses, there is a problem with the primary feeling that he claims to observe. The account depends on notions that his theory would exclude. The difficulty is in part that which Rousseau diagnosed in the foundation of Hobbes's thought. While Hobbes sought to found his political structure on a passion, a fear of death, he used notions of "death" and apprehensions as to the future that are inextricable from speech and reasoning. Apprehensions as to death involve more than mere passion or animal instinct, although simple revulsion from pain or danger may not.[43] But the difficulty in the Baconian foundation is more far-reaching. To begin with, a mere passion cannot be as such a "foundation" for any political teaching, since an "is" cannot give birth to an "ought" (in the formulation of Hume); mere facts, in the sense of forces, cannot justify a conclusion as to "values" (in the formulation of Nietzsche). But all such objections still do not reach the root, because they suppose that human nature can be understood as merely forces.

The gravest difficulty is a reliance on notions of human quality that Bacon's critical epistemology would exclude. It excludes "abstractions," the impressions of wholes given by senses and mind, but Bacon's account of "enduring" presumes that it is *human* enduring for which humans long. Anything endures in a vague sense, if only as a residue; a once living body, when dead, remains as earth, air, chemicals, or whatever. But this is not what Bacon, or we, think to be immortality or even "continuance." If Bacon had not thought of death as death *qua* human being, he need not have worried about our continuance. While he (and we) think of a human being as a living whole, it is just such "abstractions" or "wholes," such primary notions of species, that Bacon counts as "improperly and over-hastily abstracted from things, vague, not sufficiently definite."[44] His thinking cannot do without such intuitions, but his critical thinking cannot permit them.[45]

These difficulties result in a "self" that is at once all-important and ephemeral. While nature in men is but a force blind and insecure,[46] the self is the invented capacity that alone enables one to overcome natural adversity. The key conquest of human nature is of the natural human consciousness, that is, of the senses and especially of the mind's eye, for the most misleading of human illusions is of an intellect loving the good, the true, and the beautiful. Men are bewitched by love for what they think they divine, and thus, by nature, they neglect themselves and especially their necessities.[47] So Bacon reduces truth to an instrument, love to sexual passion, nobility to a hypocritical elite, goodness to a tool of the strong, magnanimity to rising to great place, divinity to illusory wishing for a provider, friendship to witchery, and, above all, intellect to ingenuity or invention.[48] The conquest of natural consciousness in the *Essays* culminates in the key invention, a power able to obtain great acquisitions and especially to acquire great places. That power is the opportunistic self, and the greatest of great places that it can acquire is a life free of adversity and, in particular, a life free of death to the greatest extent possible. While natural death comes because "the matter is in a perpetual flux, and never at a stay,"[49] the artful self can invent monuments that will overcome the vicissitude of nature (or almost overcome it). The Baconian arts of life and state culminate in "deliveries of the self" that will keep one's name alive. By conquering men's minds, one provides by art what a niggardly nature does not provide.

But how can a life only in name be a real life, if names are "mere" words as Bacon portrays them? In the world away from these strange reductions, ambitious men seek honors, the most ambitious seek to live on in a splendid glory, and honorable men are solicitous of reputation. "Take my good name, and you take my life," is an understandable sentiment in an honorable man. But Bacon discredits names as nothing in themselves. They are tools of desire, and not badges of honor, and the continuation of one's tools is not the continuation of one's life. We come around to the same point. The Baconian conquest of death can stand only by importing a stature for reputation that the Baconian critique denies. Hobbes was more consistent if less believable, reducing glory to vainglory and confining the aims of politics to preservation of bodily motion.

The Baconian self seems both hard and soft, ruthless and superficial, and the opposites are incompatible. It is a ruthless power, concentrated upon making its fortune and thus producing a world of security, and it is superficial in its activity, always looking to a future life that is a life only in name. Perhaps any life lived for honor partakes of some emptiness and superficiality, for it depends on others' judgments, rather than one's own, and it also looks beyond honor, men often seeking honor to assure themselves of their quality.[50] But the difficulty in Bacon's account is more profound than the contradictions of a public life, for it arises from a theory. The Baconian individual seeks to preserve not a good name but his purely individual name. The "self" has nothing human to look up to (for the higher is but illusory), has nothing human to look down to (for the nature within is an inhuman force), and nothing more than a hollow image to look forward to. Life is the resolute quest for an ersatz life.

Remove the old veils and the tacit but imported premises, and one can discern the gray shades of contemporary nihilism. Does a pursuit of power without limit deconstruct what delimits human being and therefore what defines a life worth living?

No doubt such terms as "the self" can be used reasonably—they are used all the time—and can be accounted for truly. But a sound account would have to attend to what is caught in the many-layered fabric of our speech and, since language however natural is hardly unequivocal, especially in observant and intelligent opinions. If we listen, and try to tune out the pervasive static left by modern theories, we rarely hear the term "self" as a substantive noun, as "a self" or "the self." It is always or almost always part of a conjunctive expression, such as "myself," "herself," "himself," or "itself." These expressions qualify subjectivity. "I" am a human being or rather a particular one, a man rather than a woman, and a slim and handsome devil rather than a slob gone to seed. What is implied seems obvious. An individual is not a free ego, but an ego that almost inevitably thinks itself to be an example of a certain kind of being or animal. Another sign: "myself" is often used wryly and knowingly to allude to foibles, that is, to one's particular and sometimes peculiar bent. Some can smile at themselves, because they think about themselves more knowingly. But such urbanity tacitly acknowledges a character free from oddities, and thus an intuitive awareness, if one often beclouded, of the virtues that befit a human being. If these remarks are true, they suggest that Bacon's "self" replaces something more obvious, the notion of the individual as an example of the human kind and as inevitably of a certain level or quality of being.

In short, Bacon had to borrow from precritical and prescientific human awareness, moral and intellectual, in order to destroy the authority of morality and ordinary knowing. Intellect, soul, justice, the noble, beauty, friendship, and even life, become but reconstituted shadows, artificial and calculated representations and powers of the self. But the new constructions cannot be extricated from the new criticism. The things that Bacon's theory alleged to be real, such as "bodies in motion," "power," and the self itself, are in his formulations reducible to but artificial and invented abstractions. The conquest of nature may afflict man's environment, but the most serious effects are on man. However fruitful of human power and the security of human bodies, the project of progress leads toward an emptiness for human being.

What seems in contemporary philosophy a crisis of nihilism has its origin in the foundation of modern philosophy. It is then a limited crisis. There remain now as ever paths to serious lives, to delights that befit human nobility, to statesmanlike judgment, to free republics, and to philosophy and poetry as they once were. This is not to forget the obvious benefits from Bacon's extraordinary genius. The spirit of progress has roused peoples to immense feats of industry, ambition, learning, and freedom, to widespread self-reliance, and to deeds of great humanity and generosity. Private and public empires are raised, popular governments succeed in huge nation-states, millions or billions of men seek the freedom to improve their fortunes and the prosperity to lead decent lives. These achievements should have the respect and protection they deserve. However great they are, however much they ought to be defended and renovated by the Roosevelts, Churchills, DeGaulles, and Adenauers to come, it is not by Baconian terms that the justice and the grandeur can be measured.

Notes

1. *The Question Concerning Technology and Other Essays*, tr. William Lovitt (New York: Harper Colophon Books, 1977), 26–35.
2. *Francis Bacon and the Modern Dilemma* (Freeport, N.Y.: Books for Libraries Press, 1970), 65.
3. See chapters 5 and 6 in this volume.
4. "Before Bacon," according to Richard H. Kennington, "no modern philosopher advocated the necessity for, or himself composed, a treatise on a universal method for seeking truth in the sciences. After the *New Organon* of 1620, treatises on method are produced, although often left incomplete or unpublished, by Descartes, Hobbes, Spinoza, Locke, and Leibniz, all well-known readers of Bacon" ["Bacon's Critique of Ancient Philosophy in *New Organon I*," in D. Dahlstrom, ed., *Nature and Scientific Method* (Washington, D.C.: Catholic University of America Press, 1991), 236].
5. *Works* VIII, 17–18; IV, 7–8.
6. *New Organon* I, 98, in *Works* VIII, 133–34; IV, 94.
7. *N O* I, 82, in *Works* VIII, 114; IV, 80.
8. *N O* I, 98, in *Works* VIII, 134; IV, 94–95.
9. *De Augmentis* III, iv, tr. in *Works* VIII, 509–10; IV, 363–64.
10. This is a tactic of the *Essays*; see chapter 5 in this volume.
11. *N O* I, 57, 104, in *Works* VIII, 85–86, 138; IV, 60, 97.
12. *N O* I, 66, in *Works* VIII, 97; IV, 68.
13. *N O* I, 66, in *Works* VIII, 94–97; IV, 66–68.
14. *Great Instauration* ("Plan"), in *Works* VIII, 42; IV, 25.
15. *Thoughts on the Nature of Things*, in *Works* X, 291; V, 422–23. Bacon parades before us the aptly named Hero, "a mechanical man," to correct an assertion by "Democritus, who was a distinguished philosopher" (*Works* X, 290; V, 421). If well directed by such a hero of the useful arts, nevertheless, a search for ultimate "seeds or atoms" may be "most useful of all." A methodized atomism—an exper-

imentally based atomic physics—might lead to "all the secrets of nature's work-shop" and lead to that general law of dynamic action that is "the supreme rule of act and power and the true moderator of hopes and works."

16. See Jerry Weinberger, *Science, Faith and Politics: Francis Bacon and the Utopian Roots of the Modern Age* (Ithaca, N.Y.: Cornell University Press, 1985), 176; Kennington, "Bacon's Critique of Ancient Philosophy in *New Organon I.*"

17. "Of Truth," the first of the *Essays*; aphorism 129 in *New Organon*, I.

18. *Great Instauration* ("Plan"), in *Works* VIII, 48, 53; IV, 29, 32; *N O* I, 81, in *Works* VIII, 113; IV, 79.

19. See the discussion of essay 1, "Of Truth," in chapter 4.

20. *N O* I, 129, in *Works* VIII, 162; IV, 114–15.

21. At the start of the *New Organon*, Bacon gives signs of wishing, for the "allaying of contradictions and heart-burnings, that the honour and reverence due to the ancients remains untouched and undiminished; while I may carry out my designs and at the same time reap the fruit of my modesty" ("Preface," in *Works* VIII, 62; IV, 41). In chapter 2 of this volume, I discuss Bacon's art of masking the new in the familiar.

22. "Socrates, Aristotle, Galen, were men full of ostentation" (*Essays*, 54; cf. 44). See *New Organon* I, 66, and chapter 5 of this volume (on the *Essays'* attack on ancient political philosophy). See Timothy Paterson, "The Secular Control of Scientific Power in the Political Philosophy of Francis Bacon," *Polity*, 21 (no. 3) (Spring 1989), 457–80.

23. *Great Instauration* ("Plan"), in *Works* VIII, 41; IV, 24.

24. Baconian knowledge has been called "maker's knowledge" in a serious study by Antonio Pérez-Ramos, who remarks that "the appraisal of truth *qua* utility which Bacon's idea of science suggests is not external to science itself, as though coming from a separate set of values, such as religion or a specific political project." *Francis Bacon's Idea of Science and the Maker's Knowledge Tradition* (Oxford: Clarendon Press, 1988), 291. While Baconian science is not a neutral instrument, it is a suitable instrument, I think, for his political project, that is, his determination to increase human power.

25. *N O* I, 129, in *Works* VIII, 162–63; IV, 114.

26. *Great Instauration* ("Plan"), in *Works* VIII, 48; IV, 29.

27. *Francis Bacon's Idea of Science*, 291.

28. Pérez-Ramos suggests the influence of an "idea-type," the maker's knowl-edge tradition, that has been "deployed in philosophical discourse" throughout the ages. But the pre-Baconians he sketches either have to do with "theology, craftsmanship, and mathematics," not philosophy, or are what he calls "Christian skeptics." The philosophers whom he mentions, Descartes, Mersenne, Gassendi, Hobbes, Vico, and so forth, have been influenced by Machiavelli and Bacon. In short, Pérez-Ramos does not show a serious natural philosopher prior to Bacon who is of the tradition alleged to be prior to Bacon [*Francis Bacon's Idea of Science*, 48–62].

29. The last aphorism of the *New Organon's* Book II slips easily from "philos-ophy" to "science" to "art." This is similar to the movement from "wisdom" to "art" to "policy" in an important essay on civil subjects ("Of Simulation and

Dissimulation" 6) discussed in chapter 2 of this volume. Note Bacon's successive retitlings of the *New Organon*, from an initial mention of "the Truer Exercise of the Intellect," through a mention of "true directions concerning the interpretation of nature," to omission of any reference to truth and, instead, a final equation, by an "or," of "the Interpretation of Nature" with "The Kingdom of Man" (Spedding inserts "and" where the Latin has *sive*). *Works* VIII, 55, 57, 67, 167; IV, 35, 37, 47, 119.

30. *Great Instauration* ("Preface," end) in *Works* VIII, 37; IV, 21; cf. *N O* I, 61, in *Works* VIII, 89; IV, 62.

31. *Physics and Philosophy* (New York: Harper Torchbooks, 1962), 58. Judgments similar to this are now common: "the thinking of our science proves itself only in action, in the successful experiment. To experiment means to exert power upon nature. The possession of power is then the ultimate proof of the correctness of scientific thought" [C. F. V. Weizsacker, *The World View of Physics* (Chicago: University of Chicago Press, 1952), 199]. "It has become clearer than ever before that knowledge and power belong together. We have to give up forming concepts about objects which cannot become the objects of a subject, at least in principle. Pragmatic science has the view of nature that is fitting for a technical age" [Weizsacker, *The History of Nature* (Chicago: University of Chicago Press, 1949), 71]. These references were supplied by Thomas Hickman.

32. *Physics and Philosophy*, 52, 197.

33. Heisenberg had been led toward other kinds of natural science by discoveries, through experimental science itself, of other kinds of nature. Waves and fields prove to have effects not reducible to motion of particles, and discrete jumps or decreases ("quanta") in radiation, despite a uniformly varying application of energy, showed that particles do not vary uniformly with motion or force. Such findings, together with theories of relativity and quantum mechanics, led Heisenberg to challenge the adequacy of the old physics in everything from its concepts of matter, effect, prediction, and objective knowledge, to its laws of conservation of matter, of action and reaction, and of gravitation. While he continued to stand by modern physics in certain areas, the areas are limited because the old materialism does not account for the stability of certain atoms, certain peculiarities of heat, electricity, and magnetism, and especially the features that distinguish human life: the function of organs and the phenomena of affection, soul, and mind. Heisenberg found the whole language of physics to be an artificial "idealization," which often conceives of reality as merely a "mathematical structure," and he cautioned against the skepticism as to common speech that arises from the scientific movement (and is, of course, a Baconian prescription). He would turn away from artificial method and return to "natural language," which possesses an "immediate connection with reality" and can speak of life and mind and, in general, of what belongs to different levels of things. (*Physics and Philosophy*, 58, 80ff., 88–89, 99, 103–7, 197, 200, 202). Consider also Leon Kass's *Toward a More Natural Science* (New York: The Free Press, 1985).

34. *N O* I, 80, in *Works* VIII, 112; IV, 79; cf. *N O* I, 127, in *Works* VIII, 159; IV, 112.

35. "Of Nature in Men" (*Essays*, 38). The two sentences just stated in the text summarize the arguments in chapters 3–6 of this volume.

36. Kennington, "Bacon's Critique," 249.

37. *Great Instauration* ("Preface"), in *Works* VIII, 32; IV, 18.

38. "Of Riches" 34.

39. "Of Studies" 50.

40. *Advancement of Learning* I, viii, 6, ed. Wright; *Works* VI, 168; III, 318.

41. According to Charles Taylor, the modern understanding of the self "is much richer in moral sources than its condemners allow," although this richness is rendered invisible by "the impoverished philosophical language of its most zealous defenders" [*Sources of the Self, The Making of the Modern Identity* (Cambridge, Mass.: Harvard University Press, 1989), x–xi]. I am arguing that impoverishment begins at the beginning and even so presumes upon riches that it denies. Taylor is instructive in showing how "so many goods" have been read "out of our official story"; he does not prove that premodern thinkers such as Augustine contributed a spiritual and moral outlook to modern individualism.

42. *Advancement of Learning* II, xxi, 9, ed. Wright; *Works* VI, 327; III, 430. See, in general, chapter 3 of this volume.

43. *Discourse on the Origin and Foundations of Inequality among Men*, ed. Roger B. Masters (New York: St. Martin's Press, 1964), 102, 96.

44. *Great Instauration* ("Plan"), in *Works* VIII, 41; IV, 24.

45. Leo Strauss, "An Epilogue," in *Essays on the Scientific Study of Politics*, ed. Herbert J. Storing (New York: Holt, Rinehart and Winston, 1962), 315–16.

46. See chapters 4 and 5 of this volume. In an account of "Locke's Punctual Self," Taylor discusses the growing modern ideal "of a human agent who is able to remake himself by methodical and disciplined action" [*Sources of the Self*, 159; cf. 159–176].

47. *Essays* 40, 10, and the discussions in chapters 2, 4, and 5 of this volume.

48. In Book I of *New Organon*, in a subsection of eight aphorisms on human nature (45–52), five of the eight begin with the word *intellectus* and then explain away its alleged activities as really imaginings. Things intellectual are inventions of ingenuity (*ingeniam*), Bacon implies, as if a restless inventiveness seeks some satisfaction for its endless longings and hence produces suppositions such as a natural order and final causes. Hence, all unmethodical science is merely "science as one would." As Bacon proceeds through the whole section on idols, he seems to replace intellect, which in Aristotle's account both grasps and calculates, with mind (*mens*), which invents and calculates quantitative relations (*N O* I, 45). To liberate us for a free play of ingenuity in invention and policy, one must first be "resolute" in sweeping away all common notions (*N O* I, 97), including the notion of intellect. Or, in another formulation in the "Plan" of the *Great Instauration*, to provide efficiently for "a line and race of inventions that may in some degree subdue and overcome the necessities and miseries of humanity," one must begin by laying "it down once for all as a fixed and established maxim, that the intellect is not qualified to judge except by means of induction and induction in its legitimate form" [*Works* VIII, 44–45; see also 17–18, 31–32, 41–49; IV, 26–27 and 7–8,

17–18, 24–30]. According to Karl Popper, Baconian method was the same as Aristotelian induction, and both equivalent to Socratic dialectic; all appealed to the "authority of intellect" [*Conjectures and Refutations: The Growth of Scientific Knowledge* (New York: Harper Torchbook Edition, 1968), 7, 12, 15, 17].

    49. "Of Vicissitude of Things" (58).

    50. Aristotle, *Nicomachean Ethics*, 1095b, 22–30.

Appendix 1

Civil Image of Julius Caesar

Julius Caesar had from the beginning a fortune full of exercise: which turned to his advantage: for it took away his pride and braced his sinews. A mind he had, in desires and affections turbulent, but in judgment and intellect very serene; as appears by the ease with which he delivered himself both in action and speech. For no man decided quicker, or spoke clearer: there was nothing embarrassed, nothing involved about him. But in will and appetite he was one who never rested in what he had got, but ever pressed forward to things beyond. And yet he was not hurried from one action to another by a humour of weariness, but made the transitions at the just periods: for he always brought his actions to the most perfect closes. And therefore he that after winning so many victories and making himself so secure did not despise the relics of civil war in Spain, but went in person to put an end to them; as soon as ever that last civil war was concluded and peace established everywhere, immediately set about an expedition against the Parthians. Greatness of mind he undoubtedly had in a very high degree; yet such as aspired more after personal aggrandisement than merit towards the public. For he referred everything to himself, and was himself the true and perfect centre of all his own actions: which was the cause of his singular and almost perpetual felicity. For he allowed neither country, nor religion, nor services, nor kindred, nor friendships, to be any hindrance or bridle to his purposes. Neither was he much bent upon perpetuity; as one who neither established the state of affairs, nor founded or erected anything remarkable either in the way of building or institution; but as it were referred all things to himself. So also he confined his thoughts within the circle of his own times. Only his

---

The four appendixes reprint the "Images" of Julius and Augustus (*Works* XII, 27–44; VI, 335–47). Translations are by William Rawley, Bacon's chaplain, except that I have translated "Civil Image" in the titles (where Rawley put "Character").

name he wished to make famous; because he thought he had himself some interest in that. And assuredly in his private wishes he cared more for power than reputation. For he sought reputation and fame not for themselves, but as instruments of power. By natural impulse therefore, not by any moral guiding, he aspired to the supreme authority; and aspired rather to possess it than to be thought worthy of it: a thing which gave him favour with the people, who had no dignity of their own; but with the nobles and great persons, who wished also to preserve their own dignity, procured him the reputation of covetousness and boldness. Wherein assuredly they were not far from the truth: for he was by nature extremely bold, and never showed any bashfulness except when he assumed it on purpose. And yet for all that, this boldness was so fashioned as neither to impeach him of rashness, nor to make him intolerable, nor to bring his nature into suspicion: but was thought to proceed from a simplicity of manners, and confidence, and the nobility of his birth. And the same held good in all things else, that he was taken to be by no means cunning or wily, but frank and veracious. And though he was in fact a consummate master of simulation and dissimulation, and made up entirely of arts, insomuch that nothing was left to his nature except what art had approved, nevertheless there appeared in him nothing of artifice, nothing of dissimulation; and it was thought that his nature and disposition had full play and that he did but follow the bent of them. Yet for the smaller and meaner artifices and precautions, to which men unskilled in affairs and depending not on their own strength but on help from without, are driven for the support of their authority, he was not at all beholden to these; as being a man exceedingly expert in all human actions, and who managed all business of any consequence for himself, not by others. How to extinguish envy he knew excellently well; and thought it an object worth purchasing even by the sacrifice of dignity; and being in quest of real power, he was content during the whole course of his life to decline and put by all the empty show and pomp and circumstance of it: until at last, whether satiated with power or corrupted by flattery, he aspired likewise to the external emblems thereof, the name of king and the crown; which turned to his destruction. The sovereignty was the mark he aimed at even from his youth; the example of Sylla, the relationship of Marius, the emulation of Pompey, the corruptions and perturbation of the times, readily suggesting it to him. But he made himself a way to the sovereignty in a strange order; first by means of a power popular and seditious, afterwards by a power military and imperatorial. For at first he had to break the force and authority of the senate; during the maintenance of which no man could find a passage to immoderate and extraordinary commands. And after that, he had to overthrow the power of Crassus and Pompey, which could not be done except by arms. And therefore (as a most skilful carpenter of his own fortune) he raised the first structure by means of largesses, corruption of the courts of justice, revival of the memory of Caius Marius and his party (most of the senators and nobles being of the Syllan faction), agrarian laws, putting in of seditious tribunes, secret favouring of the madnesses of Catiline and his conspirators, banishment of Cicero, upon whose cause the authority of the senate turned, and a number of the like arts; but most of all by the conjunction of Crassus and Pompey first with one another and then with himself, which completed it. Which part of his design being accomplished, he immediately addressed himself to the other; obtaining the proconsulship of Gaul for five years, and then again for another five years; and so making himself powerful in arms, legions, and a warlike and opulent province, in a position to threaten Italy. For he saw well that as soon as he had strengthened himself with arms and military power, neither Crassus nor Pompey would be a match for him; seeing that the one trusted to his wealth and the other to his fame and reputation; the one waxed old in years, the other in authority; neither had sound and vigorous safeguards to rest upon. All which things fell out to him according to his desire: the rather because he had the several senators and magistrates, and indeed all persons who had any power, so obliged and bound himself by private benefits, that there was no danger of any combination being formed to oppose his designs, before he should openly invade the commonwealth. Which though he had always intended to do, and at last did, yet he did not put off his mask; but so carried himself that, what with the reasonableness of his demands, what with the pretence of a desire of peace, what with the moderate use of his successes, he turned the envy on the other party, and made it seem that he was driven for his own safety into a necessary war. The hollowness of which pretence was clearly proved, when the civil wars being ended, and he being in possession of the sovereign power, and all the rivals that could cause him any anxiety being removed out of the way, yet he never once thought of restoring the commonwealth, no, nor cared to make so much as a pretence of doing it. Which plainly shows that the desire and purpose of obtaining the sovereignty had always been in him, and at last came out. For he did not merely seize an occasion that offered itself; himself made and shaped the occasions. It was in the business of war that his ability was most conspicuous; and so great it was, that he could not only lead an army but make one. For he was not more skillful in conducting actions than in the management of men's minds: and that not by any ordinary kind of discipline, that inured them to obey commands, or awakened a sense of shame, or enforced by severity; but one that inspired a wonderful ardour and alacrity, and won the battle almost before it began: and endeared him to the soldiery more than was good for a free commonwealth. Versed as he was moreover in every kind of war, and uniting civil arts with military, no accident took him so unexpectedly but he had a remedy prepared for it; nothing fell out so cross, but he drew some advantage from it. For his own person he had a due respect: as one that would sit in his tent during great battles, and manage everything by messages. From which he derived a double advantage; first that he went seldomer into danger, and secondly that if ever the fortune of the day were going against him, his own presence was as good as a fresh reinforcement to restore the battle. And in his warlike arrangements and enterprises he did not conduct things merely according to precedent, but would invent with consummate judgment new devices framed to the occasion. In his friendships he was constant enough, and singularly kind and indulgent. And yet he made choice of such friends that it was easy to see that he meant their friendship to be an instrument and not an impediment. And since his aim both by nature and principle was not to be eminent among great men, but to command among followers, he chose for his friends men that were of mean condition, but industrious and active, to whom he might be all in all. Hence the saying "Let me die, so Caesar live," and the like. With nobles and equals he made friendships according to his occasions; but he admitted no man to intimacy except such whose hopes rested entirely in himself. In letters and learning he was moderately well accomplished, but it was that kind of learning which was of use in the business of life. For he was well versed in history, and had wonderful knowledge of the weight and point of words; and because he attributed much to his felicity, he affected to be learned in the stars. Eloquence he had also, natural and pure. To pleasures he was naturally inclined, and indulged freely in them; which in his early times served the purpose of simulation; for no one feared any danger from such a disposition. But he so governed his pleasures, that they were no hindrance to his interest and main business, and his mind was rather invigorated than made languid by them. At the table he was sober, in his lusts not particular, in public entertainments gay and magnificent. Such being the man, the same thing was his destruction at last which in the beginning was his advancement, I mean the desire of popularity. For there is nothing so popular as the forgiveness of enemies: and this it was which, whether it were virtue or art, cost him his life.

Appendix 2

Imago Civilis Julii Caesaris

Julius Cæsar a principio fortuna exercita usus est, quod ei in bonum vertit; hoc enim illi fastum detraxit, nervos intendit. Animus ei inerat studio et affectu turbidus, judicio et intellectu admodum serenus: hocque indicat facilis illa sui explicatio, tum in rebus gerendis, tum in sermone. Nemo enim aut celerius decernebat aut magis perspicue loquebatur: nil impeditum, nil involutum quis notaret. Voluntate autem et appetitu is erat, qui nunquam partis acquiescebat, sed ad ulteriora semper tendebat: ita tamen ut non immaturo fastidio, sed legitimis spatiis, transitus actionum gubernaret: semper enim perfectissimas clausulas actionibus imponebat. Itaque ille, qui post tot victorias et tantam partam securitatem, reliquias belli civilis in Hispania non contempsit, sed præsens subegit, post extremum illud demum bellum civile confectum et omnia undique pacata, expeditionem in Parthos continuo moliebatur. Erat proculdubio summa animi magnitudine, sed ea, quæ magis amplitudinem propriam quam merita in commune spiraret. Prorsus enim omnia ad se referebat, atque ipse sibi erat fidissimum omnium actionum suarum centrum: quod maximam ei et perpetuam fere felicitatem peperit. Non enim patria, non religio, non officia, non nceessitudines, non amicitiæ, destinata ejus remorabantur, vel in ordinem redigebant. Nec magnopere versus in æternitatem erat; ut qui nec statum rerum stabiliret, nec quicquam egregium, vel mole vel instituto, fundaret vel conderet; sed veluti ad se cuncta retulit. Sic etiam ad sua tempora cogitationum fines recepit. Nominis tantum celebritate frui voluit, quod etiam sua id nonnihil interesse putaret. Ac in propriis certe votis, magis potentiæ quam dignitati studebat; dignitatem enim et famam non propter se, sed ut instrumenta potentiæ, colebat. Itaque veluti naturali impetu, non morata aliqua disciplina ductus, rerum potiri volebat; iisque magis uti quam dignus videri: quod ei apud populum, cui nulla inerat dignitas, gratiosum erat; apud nobiles et proceres, qui et suam dignitatem retinere volebant, id obtinuit nomen, ut cupidus

287

et audax videretur. Neque multum sane a vero aberrarunt, cum natura audacissimus esset, nec verecundiam unquam, nisi ex composito, indueret. Atque nihilo secius ita ista efficta erat audacia, ut eum nec temeritatis argueret, nec fastidio homines enecaret, nec naturam ejus suspectam faceret; sed ex morum simplicitate quadam et fiducia, ac nobilitate generis, ortum habuisse putaretur. Atque in cæteris quoque rebus omnibus id obtinuit, ut minime calidus aut veterator haberetur, sed apertus et verax. Cumque summus simulationis et dissimulationis artifex esset, totusque ex artibus compositus, ut ni hil naturæ suæ reliquumesset, nisi quod ars probavisset; tamen nil artificii, nil affectationis appareret, sed natura et ingenio suo frui, eaque sequi existimaretur. Neque tamen minoribus et vilioribus artificiis et cautelis omnino obnoxius erat, quibus homines rerum imperititi et qui non propriis viribus sed alienis facultatibus subnixi, ad auctoritatem suam tuendam uti necesse habent; utpote qui omnium actionum humanarum peritissimus esset, atque cuncta paulo majora ipse per se, non per alios, transigeret. Invidiam autem extinguere optime norat; idque vel dignitatis jactura consequi, non alienum a rationibus suis duxit; veramque potentiam amplexus, omnem illam inanem speciem et tumidum apparatum potentiæ æquo animo per totum fere vitæ cursum declinavit et transmisit: donec tandem, sive satiatus potentia sive adulationibus corruptus, etiam insignia potentiæ, nomen regium et diadema, concupivit; quod in pernicem ejus vertit. Regnare autem jam usque a juventute meditatus est; idque ei exemplum Syllæ, affinitas Marii, æmulatio Pompeii, corruptelæ et perturbatio temporum, facile suggerebant. Viam autem sibi ad regnum miro ordine sternebat: primum per potentiam popularem et seditiosam, deinde per potentiam militarem et imperatoriam. Nam initio sibi erant frangendæ senatus opes et auctoritas, qua salva nemini ad immodica et extraordinaria imperia aditus erat. Tum demum evertenda erat Crassi et Pompeii potentia, quod nisi armis fieri non poterat. Itaque (ut faber fortunæ suæ peritissimus) primam structuram per largitiones, per judiciorum corruptelas, per renovationem memoriæ C. Marii et partium ejus (cum plerique senatorum et nobilium e Syllana factione essent), per leges agrarias, per seditiosos tribunos quos immitebat, per Catilinæ et conjuratorum insanias quibus occulto favebat, per exilium Ciceronis, in cujus causa senatus auctoritas vertebatur, ac complures hujusmodi artes, attollebat et evehebat: sed maxime omnium per Crassi et Pompeii et inter se et secum conjunctionem absolvebat. Qua parte absoluta, ad alteram continuo partem accingebatur, factus Proconsul Galliarum in quinquennium, rursusque in alterum quinquennium, atque armis, legionibus, et bellicosa et opulenta provincia potens, et Italiæ imminens. Neque enim eum latebat, postquam se armis et militari potentia firmasset, nec

Crassum nec Pompeium sibi parem futurum; cum alter auctoritate senesceret; neuter veris et vigentibus præsidiis niteretur. Quæ omnia ei ex voto cessere; præsertim cum ipse singulos senatores et magistratus, et denique omnes qui aliquid poterant, ita privatis beneficiis devinctos et obstrictos haberet, ut securus esset de aliqua conspiratione vel consensu adversus suos conatus ineundis, antequam aperte rempublicam invaderet. Quod cum et semper destinasset, et aliquando tandem faceret, tamen personam suam non deponebat; sed ita se gerebat, ut æquitate postulatorum, et simulatione pacis, et successibus suis moderandis, invidiam in adversas partes torqueret; seque incolmitatis suæ gratia ad bellum necessarium coactum præ se ferret. Cujus simulationis vanitas manifesto deprehensa est, postquam confectis bellis civilibus regiam potestatem adeptus, omnibusque æmulis qui aliquam ei solicitudinem injicere possent e medio sublatis, tamen de reddenda republica ne semel quidem cogitavit, neque hoc saltem fingere aut prætexere dignaretur. Quod liquido declarat, cupiditatem et propositum regni adipiscendi ei et semper fuisse, et ad extremum patuisse. Neque enim occasionem aliquam arripuit, sed ipse occasiones excitavit et efformavit. In bellicis autem rebus maxime ejus virtus enituit, quæ tantum valuit, ut exercitum non tantum duceret, sed et effingeret. Neque enim major ei scientia affuit in rebus gerendis, quam in animis tractandis: neque id vulgari aliqua disciplina, quæ obsequium assuefaceret ad mandata, aut pudorem incuteret, aut severitatem usurparet; sed quæ miris modis ardorem et alactiatem adderet, et victoriam fere præriperet; quæque militem erga ipsum plus conciliaret quam liberæ reipublicæ conducebat. Cum autem in omni genere belli versatus esset, cumque artes civiles cum bellicis conjungeret, nil tam improvisum ei accidebat, ad quod remedium paratum non haberet; et nil tam adversum, ex quo non utilitatem aliquam derivaret. Personæ autem suæ debitas partes attribuit; ut qui sedens in prætorio in magnis præliis omnia per nuntios administraret. Ex quo duplicem fructum capiebat; ut et in discrimen rarius se committeret, atque ut cum res inclinare coepissent, prælium per ipsius præsentiam, veluti nova auxilia, instauraretur. In omni autem apparatu et conatu bellico, non tantum ad exempla res gerebat, sed nova et accomodata summa ratione comminiscebatur. Amicitias satis constanter et singulari cum beneficentia et indulgentia coluit. Amicorum tamen hujusmodi delectum fecit, ut facile appareret, eum id quærere, ut instrumenti, non impedimenti, loco amicitia eorum esset. Cum autem et natura et instituto ferretur ad hoc, ut non eminens inter magnos, sed imperans inter obsequentes esset, amicos sibi adjunxit humiles sed industrios, quibus ipse omnia esset. Hinc illud, "Ita vivente Cæsare moriar;" et cætera id genus. Nobilium autem et æqualium suorum amicitias ex usu suo asciscebat: ex intimis autem neminem fere admittebat, nisi qui ex se omnia speraret. Quin et literis et doctrina mediocriter excultus fuit, sed ea quæ ad civilem usum aliquid conferret. Nam et in historia versatus erat, et verborum pondera et acumina mire callebat; et cum multa felicitati suæ tribueret, peritus astrorum videri voluit. Eloquentia autem ei nativa et pura erat. In voluptates propensus ac effusus erat, quod ei apud initia sua loco simulationis erat; nemo enim periculum ab hujusmodi ingenio metuebat. Voluptates autem suas ita moderabatur, ut nihil utilitati aut negotiorum summæ officerent, et animo potius vigorem quam languorem tribuerent. In mensa sobrius, circa libidines incuriosus, in ludis lætus et magnificus. Talis cum esset, id ad extremum ei exitio fuit, quod ad principia sua incremento fuerat; id est, studium popularitatis. Nil enim tam populare est quam ignoscere inimicis: qua sive virtute sive arte ille periit.

Appendix 3

Civil Image of Augustus Caesar

Augustus Caesar was endued, if ever man was, with a greatness of mind, calm, serene, and well-ordered: witness the exceeding great actions which he conducted in his early youth. For men of impetuous and unsettled dispositions commonly pass their youth in various errors; and it is not till middle age that they show what they are. But those whose nature is composed and placid may flourish even in their first years. And whereas the gifts of the mind, like those of the body, are contained and completed in three things—health, beauty, and strength—he was certainly in strength of mind inferior to his uncle Julius, but in beauty and health of mind superior. For Julius being of a restless and unsettled disposition, though for the compassing of his ends he made his arrangements with consummate judgment, yet had not his ends themselves arranged in any good order; but was carried on and on with an impulse that knew no bounds, aiming at things beyond the reach of mortality. Whereas Augustus, as a man sober and mindful of his mortal condition, seems to have had his ends likewise laid out from the first in admirable order and truly weighed. For first he made it his aim to be at the head of affairs: then to become the position and be esteemed worthy of it; next he considered it fit for him, as a man, to enjoy the height of fortune: and lastly, he thought to apply himself to some real work, and so transmit to the next ages the impression of the image and the effects of the virtue of his government. In the first period of his life therefore he made Power his object; in the middle period, Dignity; in his declining years, Pleasures: and in his old age, Memory and Posterity.

Appendix 4

Imago Civilis Augusti Caesaris

Augusto Caesari, si cui mortalium, magnitudo animi inerat inturbida, serena, et ordinata: idque indicant res illae omnium maximae, quas ab ineunte adolescentia gessit. Nam qui ingenio commotiores sunt, ii fere adolescentias per varios errores transigunt, ac sub mediam aetatem demum se ostendunt: quibus autem natura est composita et placida, ii prima etiam aetate florere possunt. Atque cum animi dotes, sicut et bona corporis, sanitate quadam, pulchritudine, et viribus contineantur et absolvantur, fuit certe avunculo Julio viribus animi impar, pulchritudine et sanitate superior. Ille enim inquietus et incompositus (ut sunt fere ii qui comitiali morbo tentantur) se ad fines suos nihilominus summa ratione expediebat; sed ipsos fines minime ordinaverat, sed impetu infinito, et ultra mortale appetens, ferebatur ad ulteriora. Hic autem sobrius, et mortalitatis memor, etiam fines suos ordine admirabili descriptos et libratos habuisse visus est. Primum enim, rerum potiri volebat; deinde id assequi, ut dignus eo fastigio existimaretur; dein etiam, frui summa fortuna humanum esse ducebat; ad extremum, addere se rebus, et imaginem et virtutem sui principatus seculis post se futuris imprimere et inferre meditabatur. Itaque prima aetate Potentiae, media Dignitati, vergente Voluptatibus, senectute Memoriae Posteritati serviebat.

Index

Index to Discussions of *Essays or Counsels, Civil and Moral*

About the Author

Robert Faulkner teaches political science at Boston College. He has also taught at Princeton University and, as visiting professor, at Dartmouth and Wellesley colleges. He became interested in political philosophy as an undergraduate at Dartmouth, was a Marshall Scholar at Oxford University, and obtained his doctorate at the University of Chicago. He has held fellowships from the Ford, Mellon, Earhart, and Bradley foundations and the National Endowment for the Humanities. Faulkner is also the author of *The Jurisprudence of John Marshall* (1968) and *Richard Hooker and the Politics of a Christian England* (1981), as well as various articles on topics of moral and political philosophy and of American politics. He is co-author of a collection of essays on the founding and preserving of American democracy, also to be published by Rowman and Littlefield.